FELLOWS PARK, WALSALL
CENTRE STAND
WALLOWS LANE TURNSTILE ENTRANCE
BLOCK F ROW D SEAT 86 PRICE £3.50
WALSALL - 4 MAY 1985
THE JOHN PLAYER LEAGUE
PROGRAMME SCORECARD
Yorkshire v Glamorgan
at Hull June 21st 1981
20p
HULL CITY
SCOTTISH FOOTBALL ASSOC
SCOTLAND
THE SCOTTISH FOOTBALL ASSOCIATION
The Rous Cup
SCOTLAND v ENGLAND
PHIL McINTYRE
THE CRAMPS
plus Support
at THE CITY HALL
on SUNDAY
30th MARCH
at 7-30 p.m.
£5-00
MAIN FLOOR
Row — K
TIM (THE NEW POSEY MANAGER AT THE DOOR) IS HOLDING A PARTY ON
FRIDAY 26th JULY 1985
9.00 1.30 a.m.
GET SMART - GO CRAZY
£1 ADMISSION WITH THIS TICKET
Management Reserve The Right To Refuse Admission
Signature
Signature of Guest
SPIDERS
CLUB
CLEVELAND ST. HULL
HULL
LEEDS UTD. v HULL CITY
Guest
NN 172
PADD CENTRE STAND
Leeds Utd.
ELLAND ROAD
LEEDS LS11 0ES
TICKET AND MATCH INFORMATION
Brighton & Hove Albion FC
West Stand Extension
SPECIAL MATCH
OPPONENTS, DATE & KICK OFF TIME AS AVERTISED
Row Q
CONGRATULATIONS!
YOU HAVE JUST MET
Hull City
Hull City Football Club
NatWest Trophy
QUARTER-FINAL
YORKSHIRE v SUSSEX
at HEADINGLEY
WEDNESDAY, 30th JULY
10.30 a.m.
HULL CITY A.F.C. plc
Boothferry Park, Hull HU4 6EU
DIVISION TWO
SUNDAY 22nd FEBRUARY 1987
Kick-Off 12.00 noon
HULL CITY v. LEEDS UNITED
R. M. Linney
SECRETARY
(Plan of Ground Overleaf)
GROUND
ENTRANCE NORTH ROAD
HOME SUPPORTER
ADULT £3.00
№ 0279
WIGAN ATHLETIC
V HULL CITY
CENTRE STAND
CANON LEAGUE
DIVISION III
SEASON 1984/85
WIGAN ATHLETIC
V HULL CITY
KICK OFF 3.00PM
CENTRE STAND
CANON LEAGUE - DIVISION TWO
VISITORS STAND SEAT
BRADFORD CITY
VISITORS STAND
ENTRY TO GROUND MUST BE MADE THROUGH TURNSTILE
9
YOU MAY OCCUPY ANY SEAT IN THE STAND NUMBERED
HULL CITY A.F.C
THE MINORITY
UP NORTH WE DONT SLASH
WE JUST PUNCH
HULL CITY A.F.C. plc
Boothferry Park, Hull HU4 6EU
DIVISION TWO
THURS. 26th DECEMBER 1985
Kick-Off 3.00 p.m.
HULL CITY v. GRIMSBY TOWN
ADULT £3.50
CHILD/OC £2.00
R. M. Linney
SOUTH STAND SEAT
ENTRY NORTH ROAD BOOTHFERRY PARK
YOU MAY SIT IN ANY SEAT EXCEPT THOSE MARKED 'RESERVED'
HULL CITY A.F.C.
BOOTHFERRY PARK, HULL
SEASON 1985-86
GROUND (EXCEPT
ADULT
748
NOT TRANSFERABLE
Watford
THE F.A.
WATFORD V HULL
SAT 09 JAN 1988
KICK OFF 15:00
EAST STAND
BLOCK A ROW L SEAT 15
MATCH PROGRAMME INCLUDED ON
HULL K.R.
at the BOULEVARD, HULL
Sunday, 3rd January, 1988
(or any alternate date)
Kick off 3.00 p.m.
Ground Only
Adult £3.00
Inc. V.A.T.
TO BE RETAINED
BURNDEN STAND
CANON LEAGUE DIVISION
HULL CITY
8 SEP 84 K/O 3.00
RESERVED SEAT (INCL. VAT) ADULT
£ 3.65
Secretary
HALIFAX TOWN AFC
v HULL CITY
1st Round 1st Leg Milk Cup
NEW DELPHI CLUB
MEMBERSHIP CARD
1989
Name
Member's No.

Also available at all good book stores

9781785316470

9781785313929

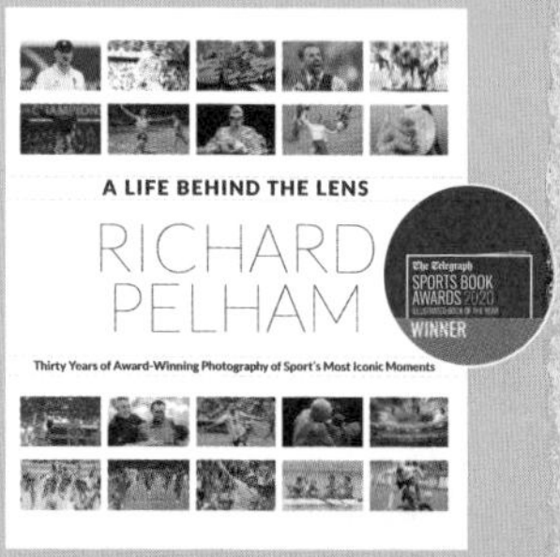

9781785315466

9781785317576

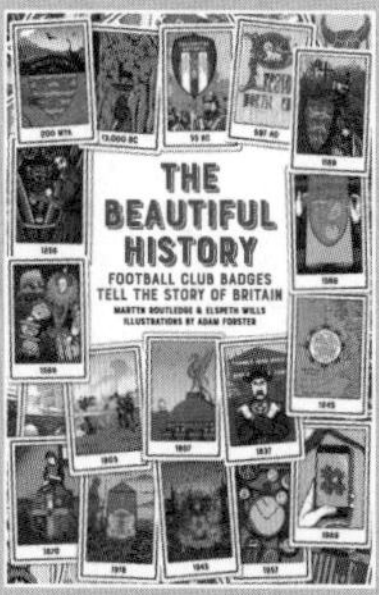

9781785317927

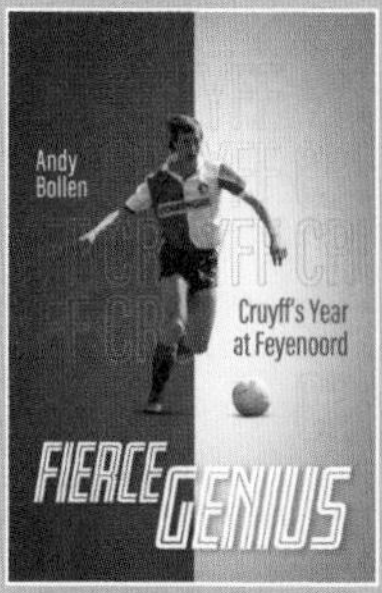

9781785318245

9781785318450

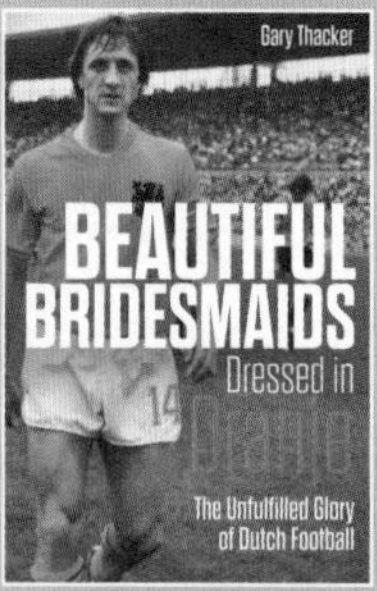

9781785318467

9781785318399

NOT ALL TICKET

FROM WITHERNSEA HIGH TO BOOTHFERRY PARK HALT

RICHARD LUSMORE

Foreword by Brian Horton

pitch

First published by Pitch Publishing, 2022

Pitch Publishing
A2 Yeoman Gate
Yeoman Way
Worthing
Sussex
BN13 3QZ
www.pitchpublishing.co.uk
info@pitchpublishing.co.uk

A CIP catalogue record is available for this book
from the British Library.

ISBN 978 1 80150 059 3

Typesetting and origination by Pitch Publishing

Printed and bound in India by Replika Press Pvt. Ltd.

Contents

This book is dedicated to various people…

My numerous work colleagues, who at one time or other over the past 30 years have remarked that my talents are perhaps not best served by a career in the civil service or the oil and gas industry. I'm assuming they meant it as a compliment.

The mates I've made in the years since the period in which *Not All-Ticket* is set, most of whom were too young to feature in the tales contained herein but have probably heard many of them countless times since. Foremost among these is Finchy, another friend taken from us far too soon and whose exhortations to 'gerrem down in print, Slush' were always a timely source of encouragement.

Derek Maxwell, the man who unwittingly set the ball rolling when allowing me to tag along with him and his sons to Boothferry Park on a warm September afternoon in 1975.

My wife Alison and daughters Emma and Katie, for whom the past five or six years (it must seem a lot longer to them) have consisted largely of waiting for 'Grumpy' to finish his book. Well, it's finished now. I do hope the wait was worth it!

Acknowledgements

I BEGAN this book in the hope of having it published to coincide with Hull's year as the UK City of Culture in 2017. To kick things off – and to gauge opinions – I shared the first few chapters with local author Nick Quantrill and my friend from schooldays, Gary Hook, a companion for many of the tales recounted here and also my go-to Hull City 'anorak'. That was in 2014. Seven years on, Hull's time in the national spotlight has been and gone. It is therefore testament to both men's patience that they have remained sounding boards for me all along the way. I am similarly indebted to Matthew Rudd for his excellent knowledge of the subject matter along with his meticulous proof-reading and handy tips, as I am for the help received from Andrew Vaughan, whose wonderful *Faded Lois Dreams* (along with Andrew-Henry Bowie's *Two Miles To Tynecastle*) not only provided inspiration for *Not All-Ticket* but also convinced me that somebody somewhere might find it worth reading.

In these social media-dominated days, my thanks also to the 'Tiger Twitterati', in particular Gary 'Jonah' Jones for whom I have the utmost respect, not least for his uncanny ability to grab me a newspaper cutting within minutes of my request! I am similarly grateful to Pete Dixon's 'Boothferry Park Memories' Facebook group, many of whom were only too willing to allow my use of their pictures (with special mention to 'Sue Cr' for the initial access to some great HDM originals). I am also indebted to James Richardson, whose brilliant 'TigerTube' library of videos acted as another rich seam of source material.

This was never intended to be a definitive account of events, but instead a personal insight into what I consider to be an overlooked era in Hull City history. Wherever possible, I've backed this up with contemporary accounts, most of which have come from various managers' programme notes. I'd like to thank Joe Clutterbrook and Hull City for their kind permission in allowing me to use these. Similarly, the detailed description of events, as written by the likes of Simon Redfern, David Lamont and David Bond (among others) for the *Hull Daily Mail* have also helped immensely in joining the dots.

There have been many excellent additions to the Hull City 'library' in fairly recent times, with Richard Gardham's tome *The Decade* in particular providing a veritable treasure trove of first-hand accounts from some of those involved. As such I am extremely grateful to him for granting me extensive use of the quotes he so diligently gathered. A nod goes towards another esteemed author of Hull City publications, Nicholas Turner, for his help is accessing many of the other photographs I've used, along with Greg Whitaker and Ian Bunton for their readiness to offer general support in bringing things to fruition.

The musical content of the book would not have been what it is without the contributions of Kari Brown and Tony Menzies, whose knowledge of the early years at The Welly filled a big void in the story. I have also leant heavily on the memories of Ian Mowforth, which were first put into print in one of the fanzines I co-edited 'back in the day'. They also provide an excellent illustration of the Hull scene at the time. My thanks go to Lee Hartley and others from among the

Hull rockin' crowd for providing memories that will live with me forever; Andy Roe for access to his extensive collection of photos that captured Spiders Nightclub in all its pomp and, indeed, the 'Spiderlings' and Adelphi gig-goers whose simple presence brought so much joy at a precious time in my life.

Obviously, I owe a huge debt of gratitude to those whose feats inspired me to write this book, foremost among them the players, management and staff of Hull City Association Football Club between 1982 and 1988. Ideally this book would be in lieu of being able to thank each and every one of them individually. Sadly, during the time it has taken me to bring *Not All-Ticket* to fruition, we have said goodbye to, among others, Les Mutrie, Pete Skipper and only recently, Chris Chilton, Colin Appleton and Mike Smith. If nothing else, I hope that the tales I recount herein will ensure that the magnitude of what they and their fellow Tigers achieved can be appreciated by those of a younger generation in the same way as it was/is by those of us fortunate enough to see it at first hand.

I reserve my main thanks for those who shared the same trip as me and whose company and presence helped make it all the more enjoyable. Many could probably merit their own chapter (or book!) given the amount of colourful anecdotes they undoubtedly also have. Prominent among them are my schoolmates Gary, Carmo and Darren, who, despite lack of mentions are present throughout the story and remain among my closest friends to this day (not forgetting Jonesy who would often complete our Saturday night quintet). Then there's City supporters' 'cult hero' Simon Gray, whose 'door-to-door' away match coach service helped cement the bond between our young group and our football club. Among his list of fellow passengers are names that still prompt a smile nearly 40 years later. Firstly, there are the 'out of towners' from those early days, the lads who would often have the bus well-filled by the time we'd commuted along the A1033 to Hull's Baker Street departure point: Big Al H (RIP), Dave I (RIP), 'Brush' Brown, Bogey, Doug P, Col M, Swell & Stivvy, Rico, Budgie, Waitesy (RIP) & the Keyingham crew, Tash & Wardie, Steve C (RIP), Tony D, Locky, Ginge, Slick, John B & Nibsy, Scam & Timmy Grubb; Crow, Mark P & Scott Mc ('39th hardest') and the Goodison brothers. Hopping aboard in the city centre were a host of proper characters, including 'super fan' Trev Pearce (who probably still holds the record for consecutive City matches seen live), the 'City/Spiders legend' that is Pozzy, brothers Sned & 'In-Town' Brown, Metzy, Maysey, Stocksy, Glen, Col 'Theakstons', 'Rabid Ray' and the Yorkshire 'Mad Dogs', Wally, Dave S, Paul J, Mike T, Charlie P, Parky, the Bean twins, 'Orville', 'Oggy', Rich M, 'Beige', Beverley duo Gary S & Tom B, and the group we knew collectively as the 'Bransholme boys': Jenner, Big Andy S, Dave H, Trog, Col F and 'Big Gil & Lil Gil'. Heading westward out of town we'd pick up the Brough contingent, including Jubby, Derek J, Bruce, Binny and Swat. And then our last regular pick-up came near Goole, where 'Carlton Paul' & his 'Hairy Biker' sidekick would join us and the real story-telling could begin. Of course, no away day acknowledgement would be complete without a nod in the direction of the C&G bus drivers, those men constantly urged to 'Get yer reet foot doon on gas pedal!' Anyone who ever boarded a coach driven by the likes of 'Jock', 'Awd' John, Barry, Fred, Ken or 'Grumpy' George will appreciate just how much these genuine characters contributed (often unwittingly) to the day's enjoyment.

Apologies to anyone who might have also reasonably expected to be named but isn't – your omission is due to no other reason than my absent-mindedness, poor memory and of course the fact that sometimes names were never known; just a nod and a knowing look being enough to mark someone out as a fellow member of the 'Tiger Nation'. The journey we undertook together is one I will cherish to my final days. For those of you who embarked on it with me, I hope you gain the same amount of pleasure reading these stories as I have had writing them. I can only apologise for any factual inaccuracies or misrepresentation of individuals herein, none of which was intentional.

Finally, I am hugely indebted to Brian Horton for his support, as I am to all at Pitch Publishing, along with their help, their professionalism and, in particular, their belief that *Not All-Ticket* is a story worthy of being shared with others.

Richard Lusmore

July 2021

Foreword by Brian Horton

I AM delighted to contribute the Foreword to this account of what Richard rightly describes as a dramatic and largely forgotten period in Hull City's history. It's a club I have great affinity to having enjoyed two spells there, first as player-manager and director between 1984 and 1988 (the first time such a role had been combined in the Football League), then as assistant to Phil Brown from 2007 to 2011.

Although left disappointed on both occasions by the manner in which things ended, I have many happy memories from my time in the city. Many people will be familiar with the Tigers' achievements during my second stint there, in particular reaching the top flight of English football for the first time in the club's history after a memorable day at Wembley. However, perhaps fewer people will know just how close we came to doing the same thing during my time as manager back in 1985/86. Had we enjoyed the same run of form just a year later, it would have clinched Hull City a place in the inaugural promotion play-offs and as we have seen on many occasions, once in there anything can happen.

Hull was my first managerial job, after a playing career with Port Vale, Brighton and Luton. I'd been recommended to Hull chairman Don Robinson by the likes of Jack Charlton, Emlyn Hughes, Malcolm Allison and David Pleat, which was fantastic in terms of endorsement. After the briefest of meetings, Don told me the job was mine if I wanted it. I weighed up my other options, which included extending my playing days in the top flight with Luton, albeit in more of a bit-part role, or becoming player-coach to new manager Tommy Docherty at my boyhood team, Wolverhampton Wanderers. In the end I chose the option that I felt was right for me at the time and one that I hoped would secure my future in the game. Despite a drop in salary, I accepted Don's offer to become player-manager at Hull City and I joined my new team on a summer tour to Florida.

After a spell in the doldrums, following relegation to the Fourth Division and then becoming the first Football League club to go into receivership, the Tigers had bounced back superbly. The previous season had seen them come within an ace of claiming back-to-back promotions. My immediate task was to finish the job that Colin Appleton had started and I did that at the first time of asking. After achieving the same at Brighton and Luton as a player, it completed a hat-trick of promotions in my first full season at a club. Making this latest one all the more special was that it was clinched at my old stomping ground, Walsall – the club that had released me as a 17-year-old – and my parents were there to see it too.

If there was any disappointment in that first season it was perhaps that we should have finished higher than third. I always felt we were good enough to win the title. The following season would see us have a real go at promotion to the First Division for what would have been the first time in the club's history. We grew into the season and claimed some big scalps along the way, including Leeds United, which I know delighted our supporters. A disappointing April eventually dashed any hopes of promotion but we still achieved a final placing of sixth, the third-highest position in the club's history. To achieve that in our first season back in the Second Division – and finish above all our local rivals – was an achievement that I still feel didn't really get the recognition it deserved.

The following season we struggled, largely due to unbelievable bad luck with injuries but in 1987/88 we began like a train and by Christmas we were second in the league, playing some wonderful football. We took some big scalps – Aston Villa, Manchester City and a double over Leeds – and there was again real belief that we could have a tilt at promotion. We didn't lose a league game at home until the February but then things went awry. Beating Leeds at home in early January proved to be my last win as manager. The ensuing poor run of form not only scuppered any hopes of going up but also cost me my job. Although I'd had a feeling that something was afoot, it was still a shock when Don told me he was sacking me.

Despite the way things ended, I look back fondly at my time at Boothferry Park. As well as Don, I worked with some wonderful people: Chris Chilton, Dennis Booth (my best mate in football), Tom Wilson and Jeff Radcliffe. I also inherited a good side with players who were already regarded as heroes by the supporters for what they'd achieved from adversity; among them the likes of Garreth Roberts (a great captain), Tony Norman, Steve McClaren, Peter Skipper and 'Big' Billy Whitehurst. As well as improving the squad during my time in charge, bringing in players of the quality of Frankie Bunn, Alex Dyer, Richard Jobson and Garry Parker, I'd also like to think I built on what was already a very good youth policy nurtured by Dave King and Freddie Cowell. Thanks to accepting Don's offer to become a director, following promotion from the Third Division, I also learnt a lot of things about the business side of football, which was reflected in some shrewd dealings in the transfer market. My first spell at Hull therefore proved a real education.

To be able to revisit these times in Richard's book will bring back many happy memories, not least of the atmosphere created at Boothferry Park during the halcyon days of promotion and those games against the 'big boys' back in the Second Division. It also serves as a reminder of how quickly fortunes can change in football as well as shining a light on what was a real sporting city, with both Hull and Hull Kingston Rovers competing for the major honours in rugby league at the time. It's obvious from what he's written that Richard is proud of his local area. As my twins Matthew and Lucy were both born in Beverley, I too share that sense of attachment and, with it, a feeling of personal pride in the fact that what we achieved at Hull City helped bring a bit of cheer to people during difficult times. To be able to then taste success again with the Tigers 20 years on was another huge privilege.

Enjoy the read.

Brian Horton
July 2021

Prologue:
Hull, Hell and Happiness

Wembley Stadium: Saturday, 24 May 2008

At 5.01pm, referee Alan Wiley blows the full-time whistle and 40,000 fans bedecked in black-and-amber roar their approval. Hull City have reached the top flight of English football for the first time in their 104-year history. Dean Windass, local hero and scorer of the game's only goal, comes tearing out of the dugout and slides to his knees in joyous celebration at the City end. All around me, grown men and women are jumping up and down, hugging complete strangers and generally behaving in a manner that would be deemed unbecoming in almost any other circumstances. Meanwhile, supporters listening to BBC Radio Humberside are assured by match commentator Burnsy that 'it's alright to cry'. And I do.

* * *

For those unfamiliar with the story of Hull City Association Football Club, it is one that for the main part would struggle to set pulses racing. Certainly prior to *that* day at Wembley, they remained anonymous as far as most football pundits were concerned. Indeed, until the Tigers secured their place in 'the greatest league in the world', success in any tangible form had been hard to come by.

The pre-war years were particularly barren, with the notable exception of the 1909/10 season when Ambrose Langley's team was denied promotion to the old First Division by 0.29 of a goal. In 1930 the Tigers reached the FA Cup semi-finals, losing controversially to Arsenal after a replay but it's the immediate post-war years that City fans tend to point to as the club's first 'golden era'. Under the stewardship of the great Horatio 'Raich' Carter, City won the Third Division North title in 1948/49, playing in front of magnificent crowds at their new Boothferry Park home. A club record attendance of 55,019 watched that season's FA Cup quarter-final in which visitors Manchester United progressed thanks to the game's only goal.

The mid-1960s was the next era recalled fondly by supporters, in particular 1965/66 when Cliff Britton's team clinched the Third Division championship and also enjoyed a wonderful run in the FA Cup. The Tigers took glamorous Chelsea to a sixth-round replay thanks to two late Ken Wagstaff goals at Stamford Bridge. The following Thursday over 45,000 fans descended on Boothferry Park to see the London side end hopes of a first semi-final appearance for 36 years. Five years later, Terry Neill's Hull would again reach the quarter-finals only to surrender a two-goal lead in defeat at home to Stoke. Combined with a tilt at promotion to the top flight, it signalled the last of the good times as the club fell into a period of decline. Hull City AFC reverted to the role of 'sleeping giant'.

In his 2016 book *Moving the Goalposts: A Yorkshire Tragedy*, Anthony Clavane says that Hull 'became a byword for soccer underachievement, notorious for being the biggest city in Europe never to have hosted top-flight football'. Indeed, at the time I began my regular attendance at matches, the city's football club was considered as being below not only both Hull rugby league teams in the sporting pecking order but – for a fleeting period – even the local speedway outfit (with whom I also formed an allegiance, albeit a brief one). Struggling to garner so much as passing interest among the populace, the Tigers rarely roared. Exposure on the telly was hardly forthcoming, even via the regional highlights programme. Typically, when the club did make the headlines it was for all the wrong reasons. On 25 February 1982 Hull City AFC became the first Football League club to call in the official receiver. There was a distinct possibility that it could disappear forever.

Instead, the revival that followed brought with it a period of hitherto unprecedented success. Two promotions, separated in between by a heartbreaking near miss, were followed by a genuine flirtation with elevation to the First Division for the first time. It's a quite remarkable chapter in the Tigers' history, yet one that has been all too easily overlooked in the wake of Wembley. For those for whom 'big games' have become the norm over the past decade or so, the events of the 1980s disappeared with the demolition of Boothferry Park, to be filed alongside the club's previous fleeting glimpses of glory in a folder marked 'Ancient History'. City's post-receivership renaissance remained a story that required revisiting. Hopefully this book will go some way towards addressing that.

Helping my memories of the era is the fact that this was my coming-of-age period, a time when for nine months of the year the fortunes of 11 men in amber and black dictated my mood in a way nothing else could (for the other three, I relied on 11 men in flannels sporting a White Rose). Supporting City during the 1980s remains my most enjoyable period of an association with the club that began in September 1975 and now spans five decades. Like all relationships we've had our ups and downs, our fall-outs and, indeed, the occasional bust-up. But even at times of estrangement, my love for the club remains a deeply held one, rendered so by those formative years. While those experiencing the same journey in recent times have seen the club dining at the game's top table, playing in front of sell-out crowds at a brand-new stadium and testing themselves against some of the finest players in the world, the Tigers I first fell in love with were a very different beast. The 'underachievement' referred to by Clavane was exemplified by relegation to the Football League basement and the very real threat of closure. Had you predicted to any of us travelling on a Simon Gray 'out-of-towners' coach back then that the club we supported would one day play in the FA Cup Final and the Europa League, we'd have guessed you'd been at the Clan Dew favoured by one of our more flamboyant passengers! Even the prediction of becoming 'the first team to play on the moon' (to be explained later in the book) seemed less fanciful. We'd have happily taken 14th place in the old Second Division.[1]

Football during the 1980s is also largely remembered as being a sport that was in desperate need of rescue. Although Dominic Sandbrook (quoting Lincoln Allison) describes it as 'the supreme expression of the "identity, the loyalty and solidarity" of countless working-class communities', by the 1980s it was in a 'wretched condition'. It certainly wasn't the glitzy, family-friendly affair it is portrayed as nowadays, watched by big crowds in modern all-seater stadia. By the end of the decade the beautiful game had been turned ugly by hooliganism and terminally scarred by tragedies such as Valley Parade, Heysel and Hillsborough. Attending games was a risky business, with a surrounding air of menace that is, thankfully, largely absent now. Saturday brought the prospect

---

1 Later often referred to by fans as City's 'accustomed position'

of something beyond the football, even in the unlikeliest of places. It was a time to keep your wits about you. Pre-match in Hull I soon learned which pubs to avoid and even which route to take to the ground. For away trips, it soon became second nature to check the day's fixture list in advance to ascertain which – if any – rival supporters might be encountered along the motorway.[2]

It wasn't just rival hooligans that helped ensure away games were an unpleasant experience. Although Sandbrook was writing about the previous decade when describing football stadia, most of his observations still held true. Particularly for away supporters, grounds often offered the coldest of welcomes, 'grim, dilapidated places' complete with peeling paint, rusting stands and 'the terraces stained with urine, rainwater and even the blood of those supporters caught up in the game's growing culture of violence'. This lack of comfort was matched by food outlets and toilet facilities that were often unfit for purpose, along with a local constabulary that had little time for niceties with away supporters. The argument that football supporters in the 1980s were treated as second-class citizens was a particularly strong one. As the author Pete Davies told the *Vincerà* podcast in 2020, they were 'utterly uncared for and utterly uncatered for'. How different it all sounds to what awaits travelling fans in the 21st century. Regardless of all this the matchday experience was one that my mates and I came to live for. Clichéd it may be but following Hull City home and away really did become my religion, with Boothferry Park the regular place of worship.[3]

2 Sandbrook, Dominic, *Who Dares Wins – Britain, 1979–1982* (London: Allen Lane, 2019) pp.212–213; George MacDonald Fraser's cowardly Victorian-era anti-hero

3 Sandbrook, Dominic, *State of Emergency – The Way We Were: Britain 1970-1974* (London: Allen Lane, 2010) p.557; *Vincerà! The Story of Italia 90* podcast, Episode 4: Quarantine

Similar to its football club, the city of Kingston upon Hull (to give it the title bestowed upon it by King Edward I in 1299) has largely been overlooked for much of its history and, when national attention did come its way it usually wasn't via a good news story. In 2013 Andrew Dixon, director of the city's successful UK City of Culture bid said, 'Hull suffers from negative perceptions going back 400 years.' He may well have been referring to John Taylor's 1609 *Thieves Litany*, which listed Hull (along with Hell and Halifax) as a place to avoid at all costs on account of the Gibbet Laws.

Hull Gaol was reputed to be one of the most feared places in the north of England and the city suffered by association. Indeed, throughout its history, Hull has copped more than its fair share of flak, quite literally in the Second World War when it became the most bombed British city outside London. Before the slum clearances of the 1960s, Hull had more terraced houses than any other city in the country, many of which lacked running hot water or an inside toilet. In 2003 it was named the country's 'Crappest Town' in a magazine called *Idler*.

Along with the collapse of its two main industries – fishing and the commercial docks – Hull consistently ranked near the bottom of every indicator when it came to socio-economic wealth: property prices, wages, employment and education. Similarly, the only time it was highly placed in statistical tables was for those involving teenage pregnancies, obesity, crime rates and the claiming of benefits. No wonder then that Charlie English dubbed it 'Britain's poorest city' in a 2014 article for *The Guardian*. Two years later, in another piece for the same paper Rowan Moore described 'the hard knocks' that have blighted Hull, among them the 'misguided attempts to experiment with council housing construction' and the poor choices of redevelopment. Moore blamed those responsible for succumbing to the 'modern municipal belief that shopping centres are the answer to urban decline'. For his part English added, 'Because of its isolation, Hull has had little sympathy. The common reaction from outside the city is scorn.'[4]

All this should have changed some five years on from *that* day at Wembley when Kingston upon Hull beat Leicester, Dundee and Swansea Bay to the title of UK City of Culture 2017. In announcing the award on 20 November 2013, Maria Miller MP, Secretary of State for Culture, Media and Sport, described it as 'brilliant news for Hull and everyone involved in the bid there'. She expressed hope that the city 'will make the most of all that being UK City of Culture can bring', while Hull City Council leader Stephen Brady said the award was 'a real game-changer'. In Hull Truck Theatre, where those involved with the bid gathered to hear the announcement, there were 'cheers, tears, and even a conga' when Miller confirmed the decision. 'No one in the city has any idea what she said next,' said Hull Truck artistic director Mark Babych who added, 'I feel 20 feet tall.' He wasn't alone.[5]

Hull made the most of its year in the limelight. The city was chosen to host events as diverse as the Turner Prize, the BBC Proms, the Royal Ballet and Radio 1's Big Weekend. Each proved a success. The 'Made in Hull' light show that launched proceedings proved a huge visitor attraction, as perhaps more surprisingly did a 75-metre-long wind turbine rotor blade that was displayed in Queen Victoria Square. It wasn't just a city centre thing either. The estates got in on the

---

4 https://www.theguardian.com/cities/2014/sep/11/-sp-to-hull-and-back-the-rebirth-of-britains-poorest-city, *The Guardian*, 11 September 2014; https://www.theguardian.com/culture/2016/feb/14/hull-uk-city-of-culture-2017-rowan-moore, *The Guardian*, 14 February 2016

5 Trinder, Richard, https://www.yorkshiretimes.co.uk/article/Hull-Is-City-Of-Culture, *Yorkshire Times*, 20 November 2013; https://www.bbc.co.uk/news/uk-england-humber-25014341, BBC News, 20 November 2013

act, with Black Grape playing a gig in front of a frozen food store on Bransholme in north Hull and Badly Drawn Boy appearing at the Freedom Centre on Preston Road to the east of the city. The idea of Hull 'culture' was extending beyond the stereotypical pattie butty and chip spice.

In fairness, long before being awarded its culture title the city already boasted an impressive range of live music and arts festivals, as well as offering an eclectic mix of nighttime attractions, from traditional live music venues to a thriving café culture. Hull is also home to an award-winning local radio station and a burgeoning industry in crime writing, via the works of David Mark and Nick Quantrill among others. The national award simply gave such things the chance to shine, as well as providing City fans with a chant with which to serenade visiting supporters: 'You're only here for the culture.'

It's not just culturally that Hull boasts a new confidence. The city is now established as the focal point of the so-called 'Energy Estuary' with aims to become 'the renewable capital of the UK' (the blade that was put on public display came from the huge Siemens development that has revitalised part of the old docks). The city centre continues to be transformed by multimillion-pound redevelopment. This has already yielded one of the country's biggest visitor attractions in The Deep and, at time of writing, includes plans for a proposed ocean-going cruise terminal and the £1.5bn Lagoon Hull waterfront project. Those in charge are determined to live up to their rebrand. For those familiar with the Hull portrayed in this book it's not before time.

Along with giving Hull a platform to help make it 'a prime visitor destination', Brady hoped that the City of Culture award would also transform perceptions. The immediate reaction of one of their beaten rivals suggested there's still some way to go. Swansea council leader David Phillips was quoted as saying, 'The residents of Hull had to have something to look forward to.' It was obvious that the city's standing among those too lazy to visit had improved little; even among fellow northerners who should know better. While Phil Redmond, Liverpudlian TV writer and chair of the independent expert advisory panel supported the argument that the city was 'coming out of the shadows', England cricket hero Andrew 'Freddie' Flintoff declared he thought the award 'an April Fool's joke'. It was indicative of the low esteem in which the city was held by those failing to look beyond the rusting trawlers and abandoned docks.[6]

Such sneering attitudes were especially prevalent during the 1980s. As with many industrial cities of the north, Hull was rarely home to good news. A city whose fortune was built on the back of its close proximity to the sea had been hit hard by the loss of fishing grounds in the wake of the Cod Wars of the 1970s. Then the deepest recession for half a century took its toll. Unemployment figures soared and social unrest simmered on the streets. Hull typified the desolate nature of much of Britain's post-industrial and inner-city landscape. It was one of countless places for which The Specials' smash hit 'Ghost Town' could have been written. In 2009 Nik Townend, founder member of 1970s Hull ska band The Akrylykz, painted a gloomy picture when looking back: 'All in all, at that time Hull had the air of a depressed post-industrial city in decline, but unlike many other British cities struggling to recover from the trauma of the war and post-war hardships it didn't seem to be receiving any treatment for its depression. London, Liverpool, Birmingham, Manchester and Sheffield had ... been reinvigorated by the swinging '60s and the hard-rocking and punky '70s. Hull, by comparison, was catatonic

6 https://www.bbc.co.uk/news/entertainment-arts-25008856, 20 November 2013

and barely bothering to breathe … a dull, depressed, comatose, bomb site with docks full of rusting hulks of forgotten fishing fleets, and the kids of unemployed dockers and trawlermen drinking to excess in the pop discos and working men's clubs before throwing up their guts in the streets after bloody brawls.'[7]

Along with Clavane and Townend, Vince Groak comes up with a similar image in *Last One Out*, his excellent account of the 1980 all-Hull Rugby League Challenge Cup Final. But despite such descriptions – and notwithstanding the fact that I'm not from the city (having been born in the 'leafy shires' of the East Riding) – I quickly came to love the place. Moreover, I would also come to defend it with the same sort of defiance that has been a Hullensian trait since the city Governor said no to Charles I at the start of the English Civil War! Even if to do so was often a thankless task. Much of Groak's grim depiction of things in the run-up to that momentous day out at Wembley still applied for the period that my story covers. The Hull of the 1980s had nothing like the sort of selling points that the City of Culture has. But who cared? It may well have been considered a shithole. But it was *our* shithole. Even for those of us from outside the city boundary.

Although 'county people' were and are often depicted as being aloof when dealing with our city-dwelling neighbours, it didn't prevent us from visiting Hull on a regular basis. As Charlie English (a resident of county town Beverley) writes, we went there to work and 'spend money … to shop; watch films at the ABC and the Cecil; go to exotic Italian or Indian restaurants; pass a few hours at the bowling alley'. For my part, spending was largely restricted to Sydney Scarborough Records, Spiders and the Adelphi. Along with my mates, I also

7 marcoonthebass.blogspot.com/2009/01/exclusive-interview-with-nik-akrylyk.html, 5 January 2009

chose Boothferry Park rather than the bowling alley to pass a few hours on a weekend, and as for those 'exotic' restaurants, I rarely ventured beyond Yankee Burger, Bun in the Oven or Bob Carver's – although I did 'fine dine' at The Gainsboro fish restaurant once in a while! Nonetheless, Hull gave me my 'Bright Lights, Big City' calling and despite the image portrayed it was one I revelled in.

A big part of this 'calling' came courtesy of the pubs, clubs and fashion outlets. Although Townend says that what 'very little night life [there was] in the city ... tended to be uninteresting and mainstream', there were several notable exceptions and as we shall see, in Spiders Hull had a real jewel in the crown. Similarly, while Everything But The Girl singer Tracey Thorn bemoaned the fact that Hull was 'forever left off the tour circuit' and lacked live venues that boasted 'any rock glamour', I'd like to think my book paints a different picture, with the Welly, Dingwalls (fleetingly) and the Tower all capable of attracting the latest music press faves. Then there was the Adelphi, the 'shabby chic' Victorian-era terraced property on De Grey Street taken on by the legendary Paul Jackson in 1984. It soon became 'the musical capital of Hull', renowned for hosting some of the biggest up-and-coming names in the business along with the cream of the local crop. During the period I capture here, the Housemartins fell into both categories and became the flagship of a vibrant Hull scene. Sadly, despite *The Tube's* 1983 special and plenty of exposure on Radio 1 many of the city's other hopefuls fell by the wayside, failing to justify the optimism of 'London 0 Hull 4'.[8]

However, even if what Jools Holland termed the 'Humber Sound' failed to emulate 'Merseybeat' or 'Madchester', there's

---

8 Clavane, Anthony, *Moving the Goalposts – A Yorkshire Tragedy* (London: Riverrun, 2017) pp.12–13; The title of the Housemartins' debut LP

definite evidence that the region helped forge a collective identity, with many bands leaning heavily on their hometown for influences and ideas. In his *Melody Maker* review of Nyam Nyam's 1984 LP *Hope of Heaven*, Colin Irwin describes how 'Hull [played] its part in their grimly vivid sounds', '[Vocalist Paul] Trynka talks rather poetically of the big Victorian houses, cheap accommodation, military history and the pervading atmosphere of violence which shaped his songs. "It was a geographical cul-de-sac and felt very isolated," he reflects.'[9]

Sadly, the city also proved a musical cul-de-sac for most young hopefuls with Hull never deemed 'trendy' in the same way as many of its northern counterparts. Therefore it was perhaps fitting that when the first homegrown band made a big splash nationally, they did so while wearing 'two cardigans and a tank top'. As the UK found out in 2017, Hull doesn't do pretentious, never has done. As such the city forms the perfect backdrop for a story of an unfashionable young man following an unfashionable football team in what in many ways were unfashionable times.[10]

9 Irwin, Colin for *Melody Maker* (1985), reproduced on https://nyamnyamhopeofheaven.wordpress.com/2012/11/28/buried-treasure/comment-page-1/

10 Wagg, Michael, https://www.theguardian.com/music/2012/jan/26/old-music-housemartins-sheep, *The Guardian*, 26 January 2012

1

'And We Play all The Way'

Withernsea High School: September 1977

I want to say Hull City. I really do. Hull City, a club steeped in history going back as far as 1904. The club of Carter, Bly, Wagstaff, Chilton and Ian McKechnie's oranges; Third Division champions in the year of my birth and a team who'd recently come close to reaching the 'Promised Land'. Their Boothferry Park home was considered one of the finest grounds outside the top flight, unique in having its own railway halt and six free-standing floodlight pylons. Despite being 20-odd miles away (as opposed to Grimsby Town just across the Humber) the Tigers of Hull are my local team. They are also the only team I'd actually been to see live, which ensured I qualified as a supporter as opposed to merely a fan. And trumping all these claims to fame for a football-mad schoolboy, Hull City was the only club name whose letters you couldn't colour in. So, Hull City it was then. And then the doubts set in. You see, for all the above, City had never been more than a 'sleeping giant'. Recently they hadn't just been asleep but almost comatose. Let's face it, in most people's eyes City were shit.[11]

---

11 Having been seen buying an orange after training one day, it soon became a pre-match routine at City home games for McKechnie to be pelted with oranges by the home fans! (Source: *Sunday Post*, 12 July 2013)

'And what's your name?' the teacher asked the lad sat in front of me. He was called Alex but we all knew him as 'Pom'.

'Who do you support, Alex?'

'Hull City, sir.'

You could almost taste the mixture of pity and ridicule. While some shook their heads in disbelief, the majority reacted as if 'Pom' had just cracked the funniest joke ever. Ever! Even the girls laughed. I didn't. I panicked. Then it was my turn. Come on, don't be a wimp. Just say it.

'And what about you, Richard, who do you support?'

'Leeds United, sir.'

Cue cheers and boos in equal measure. It was my Judas Iscariot moment.

It was also my first of seven years spent studying at Withernsea High School. Our classroom was the subject of the teacher's simple familiarisation procedure: favourite football team for the boys, favourite pop group for the girls. Given the era it wasn't surprising that the most popular lads answers were Liverpool, Leeds and 'Man U' (aged 11, you didn't waste energy saying Manchester United). In those formative weeks your answer to this type of question went a long way towards ingratiating yourself. There was nothing worse than being ridiculed, hence my answer. In my defence I wasn't being wholly untruthful. It pains me to admit it now but back then it was Leeds's results I usually looked for first. As did seemingly half the country; well, half my science class anyway. And in a trait I always thought was only peculiar to Hull and surrounding area, whichever big team you named as your favourite, it was taken as read that your 'second team' was Hull City. Not that this made me feel any better.

My journey to this point had begun in Withernsea Hospital. Originally a prestigious three-storey hotel built in 1855, its change of use allowed patients to take advantage of the clean fresh sea air as part of their recovery. I was born there on Sunday, 13 March 1966 and despite the fact that the number one song at the time was 'The Sun Ain't Gonna Shine Anymore', I'm fairly sure Mum, Dad and (even) my older brother felt reasonably pleased about my arrival. Home was (and still is) a few miles south of Withernsea in the coastal village of Easington. Situated towards the south-eastern tip of the plain of Holderness, it is bordered by the North Sea on one side and the Humber Estuary on the other, with the only road through eventually taking you down to the barren beauty of the Spurn peninsula. In 1965, a writer in the *Holderness Gazette* described Easington as the place 'where you find the real Yorkshire philosophy and humour'. Who am I to disagree?[12]

During my younger years the village population of around 600 was enough to sustain three pubs and three shops, although one of the former and each of the latter have since disappeared. There was a purpose-built youth club, a church hall and a Royal British Legion hut, which were used for a variety of community events. On the cliff edge was a caravan site, which attracted many visitors from Hull and the West Riding. The latter gained the nickname 'Comforts' on account of having only 'come for t'week'. The clubhouse there provided *Hi-De-Hi*-style entertainment and was frequented by many locals. Among them were Mum, who liked to go dancing, and Dad, who liked to watch from the bar.

According to hearsay, it was only the apparent intransigence of local farmers that prevented Easington from becoming the destination for the Hull to Holderness railway in 1854. As a result, its arrival transformed Withernsea – at the time a smaller village – into a bustling holiday destination for

12 *Holderness Gazette*, 12 April 1965

Victorian workers and their families. The Beeching Report and subsequent closure of the line in 1964 signalled the beginning of the end for the town. Conversely it was a line coming from the opposite direction that would eventually put Easington on the map. In September 1965 gas was discovered in the North Sea, 40-odd miles off the East Yorkshire coast. In July 1966, drilling of the production wells began in BP's West Sole Field and in March the following year the first gas was piped ashore to the brand-new Easington Terminal. By the turn of the millennium, a fifth of the country's gas was coming ashore in the village.

* * *

Prior to the mid-1960s, Leeds United Football Club had also barely brokered national attention. Largely ignored even in their own city, they would become perhaps the most reviled team in English football. And yet theirs was a real rags-to-riches story of the sort that would normally have fans of the game swooning. When Don Revie was appointed manager in 1961, football was the poor relation in a 'parochial oval-ball town' that boasted five rugby league teams. United were struggling at the wrong end of the Second Division and in dire straits financially. Revie changed that. Promotion to the top flight in 1964 was just the start. Between 1965 and 1974 Leeds never finished outside the top four in the First Division. They were twice league champions, twice Inter-City Fairs Cup winners and they lifted both the FA Cup and the League Cup. Along with these successes was an unenviable record of second places; during the same period Leeds were runners-up in the league five times, losing finalists in the FA Cup three times, runners-up in the Fairs Cup once, and also beaten narrowly by AC Milan in the European Cup Winners' Cup Final.

Despite this impressive pedigree they failed to win over their detractors. As Anthony Clavane writes: 'Revie's Leeds' were seen as 'just another brutalist blot on this soulless, '70s landscape' and 'an ugly monument to a deeply regretted decade'. Their reputation for gamesmanship and brutality earned them the label 'Dirty Leeds' to which another, 'Damned United', was added some 40 years later. Led by a manager seen as a dour, controlling patriarch, Leeds were a 'real bastard of a team' who have remained unloved and 'unforgiven' ever since. Clavane termed their style 'ultra-professionalism'; According to Alwyn W. Turner, Brian Clough was a tad less complimentary. He called them 'the dirtiest and most cynical team in the country'.[13]

6 May 1972
FA Cup Final: Arsenal 0 Leeds United 1

The fact that they were derided nationally didn't matter to me and many other youngsters in the East Riding. We didn't care about what others thought. Leeds United were Yorkshire's 'big club' and what's more, they were successful. When you were young, that was all that mattered. My childhood affinity to the club took root on Christmas Day 1970 when I received two football kits. One, from Auntie Monica and Uncle Ted, was Hull City's combination of plain amber shirt, black shorts and amber socks. The other was the minimalist all-white number of the club from Elland Road, brought to me by, well, Father Christmas of course. Both strips were very stylish in their simplicity but what set the latter apart was the badge depicting a blue owl sat on a perch. Had both kits been bought only a year later, I like to think I'd have plumped for the cool

13 Clavane, Anthony, *Promised Land* (London: Yellow Jersey Press, 2011) p.115; Turner, Alwyn M., *Crisis? What Crisis? Britain in the 1970s* (London: Aurum Press, 2008) p.99

tiger's head that City had added to the centre of their jerseys. As it was, I went with the owl. It wouldn't be the only time my sporting affinity was determined by a piece of kit geekery.

If that kit was the first kiss, consummation of my relationship with the club came two years later. FA Cup Final day saw Leeds lining up to face holders Arsenal in front of a full Wembley and millions more watching on the box. Among them was the Lusmore family of 10 Turmarr Villas; or at least two of them. Dad wasn't watching. He never was a lover of the 'Beautiful Game', instead preferring the crack of leather on willow. Although not born in the Broad Acres, Yorkshire maternal roots and a virtual lifetime spent in the county helped reinforce his White Rose credentials and ensured that mealtimes in our house were a case of 'love Geoff Boycott and eat your greens'. Dad's interest in football extended little further than a Littlewoods pools round he had in the village. If pushed for a team to which he felt any allegiance, he opted for Stoke City (for reasons known only to himself). He later developed a soft spot for Grimsby Town, which was far easier to explain – it was purely to annoy me.

My older brother was also absent. Chances are he was probably round our nan's. He used to spend most weekends there. She liked the company after Grandad's death a year or so earlier. Like Dad, my brother also had no real love of football, though he purported to support Everton whenever asked. Mum was the only other real football fan in our household, which wasn't surprising given her background. Along with several of her sisters she'd grown up supporting three of her four brothers who played regularly for local village teams. As such, she also encouraged my interest in the sport and was there on the touchline to watch me play at both junior and senior level, something she continued right up until her untimely death in 1989. And it was Mum who was there in front of our black-and-white telly that May afternoon in 1972.

The entertainment began long before the three o'clock kick-off. It's hard now to appreciate just how big an event the FA Cup Final was in the days before Murdoch's money transformed our national sport. For years, it was the one game that everybody wanted to watch and could watch for free; and its outcome often went a long way to shaping childhood allegiances. Cup final day began mid-morning, with both BBC1 and ITV offering celebrity-filled schedules in a tussle for ratings. 'Auntie' tended to be the preferred choice in the Lusmore home and it was Frank Bough rather than Dickie Davies who would have welcomed me to Wembley.

Alongside Bough and legendary commentator David Coleman, reporters were posted to both teams' 'lucky' hotels from where they would accompany them en route to their 'lucky' dressing rooms. This particular year, the Beeb also had a special feature on 100 years of the FA Cup, along with the annual Goal of the Season result. But the real highlight was *It's a Cup Final Knockout!*, featuring supporters of both clubs in a 'special contest'. Among them were radio DJ Pete Murray for the Gunners and Ronnie Hilton, whose status as a 'Hull White' would in time come to be regarded by me as the lowest of the low. Mum would have joined me in time for Tommy Steele and the Band of the Royal Marines School of Music leading the crowd in the singing of 'Abide with Me'. The traditional FA Cup Final hymn was her favourite (it has since become mine too) and she liked to sing along (unlike many of those inside the stadium it seemed). There followed the national anthem, introduction of the dignitaries and teams and, finally, the game – over five hours after that initial welcome to Wembley. Unfortunately for the neutrals, the 1972 final proved anything but a classic, as Nick Hornby recounts in *Fever Pitch*: 'The game itself was as dismal as all other Arsenal-Leeds games had been: the two teams had developed something of a history, and their meetings were usually violent and low-scoring … What made it worse was that it was the Centenary [FA] Cup Final; I am sure if the top brass at the FA had a free hand in choosing who the two finalists would be, Arsenal and Leeds would have come pretty low down on their list.'[14]

Early in the second half came the pivotal moment, the one goal that would eventually separate the two teams. 'An example of the Leeds one-two,' as described by Coleman in that inimitable style of his, volume and tempo increasing perfectly with the move. 'Number seven, Lorimer; Mick Jones out on the right, number nine; trying to take McNab on the outside, he's round the back; CLARKE – ONE-NIL!' I cheered. So did Mum. Mum also supported Leeds United *and* Hull City.

* * *

As was our wont back then, when not catching our heroes on the telly we would be impersonating them on the school field, complete with jumpers for goalposts. I was always Eddie Gray, the jinking left-winger (I'd have actually preferred to be Peter Lorimer but I fell well short of possessing 'the hardest shot in football', especially with my right peg). Such games were a feature of many long summer nights of my youth. If not the old school field, it was the strip of grass adjoining the youth club until 'Yogi' Day's propensity for putting the windows through put paid to that option. As long as we had enough for three-a-side or 'Attack and Defence', it was game on. We were all football-crazy, football-mad.

---

14 Hornby, Nick, *Fever Pitch* (London: Victor Gollancz, 1992) p.65

My aspirations of playing for the school team lasted for one miserable trial. I'd incurred the displeasure of the PE teacher for having the temerity to take a throw-in while playing in my favoured Eddie Gray position. 'What are you doing, Lusmore? *Full-backs* take the throw-ins!' boomed Mr Beale. I answered him back and my card was numbered. Thus my experience of the Association rules was restricted to the village. Easington Boys team had been formed by Uncle Frank while I was still at primary. Our opposition usually came from the various local cub scout troops. We weren't very good and had a penchant for scoring first (often straight from kick-off) before going on to lose by a considerable margin. For a short time things improved when a man named Neil with rumoured past links to Aston Villa took us for some 'proper' coaching sessions. His efforts paid off: we still lost but at least we kept our opponents to single figures.

A few years later we joined the newly formed Holderness & District Boys Under-14s League. Not that our fortunes improved much and we finished second-bottom out of eight in our first season. That 'qualified' us for the Doris Cobb Shield, a sort of losers' cup for the bottom four in which we reached the final. We beat Keyingham 7-4 in the semi. I played up front and scored four – and I took throw-ins, *so there* Mr Beale! Sadly we lost the final and, more disappointingly, I played poorly. I think I shed tears at the final whistle, though this may have had more to do with the fact that my performance blew my chances of winning the affections of a girl I'd had my eye on for some time. She opted instead for our right-winger who, despite the defeat, had played a blinder. The bastard.

* * *

Playing for a losing team could still be enjoyable; unlike supporting a winning one when for once they didn't win, and especially when they were most expected to. Just a year on from beating the Arse, Leeds succumbed to one of the biggest cup final shocks in history when losing to Second Division Sunderland. I might have cried that afternoon too. Two years on the tears flowed again when they became the second English team to appear in the European Cup Final, only to lose to German champions Bayern Munich in Paris. It was a defeat steeped in controversy and was accompanied by crowd trouble that led to Leeds being banned from European competition.

At least I wasn't subjected to such violent scenes first-hand, thanks largely to Dad's lack of interest in going anywhere near a live match. The only games I was allowed to attend were those played at the village sports field on a Saturday afternoon. So I became a regular supporter of Easington United. Like the boys' team, United played on a field situated around the back of the White Horse pub. The ground is known as Low Farm, which was quite appropriate given that the pitch doubled up as grazing pasture for the farmer's livestock. Thus individual skills were often displayed on grass festooned with cowpats and sheep droppings. The animals were no respecters of the dollops of sawdust that were supposed to mark the pitch perimeter. With the livestock cleared and play commenced, we'd stand perched on two wooden boards propped up against the tin changing room at Low Farm to form a type of terrace. By kick-off there could be up to 20 of us. A proper little firm! With the team at that time sporting a stylish replica of the Netherlands World Cup strip, we all adopted Hull City scarves to signal our support. My mate Rob went one better; his mum made him a stunning black satin scarf adorned with the word 'EASINGTON' in orange felt. We all wanted one.

For the next two to three years I could be found on our Farm Kop cheering on the team we regarded as the 'Pride of

Holderness' – despite the fact they were struggling around the lower divisions of the East Riding County Football League. Some of us were lucky enough to get to travel with the team to away games and became familiar with other far-flung rustic football outposts; from Howden to Holme-on-Spalding Moor, Market Weighton to Molescroft. I enjoyed everything about these trips, from the grown-up conversation (much of which I laughed along with even if I didn't understand it) to the post-match ritual of quietly listening to James Alexander Gordon reading the classified results on Radio 2. I loved my Saturdays, me.

Given Dad's disinterest I relied on the telly for my earliest experiences of watching professional football. This also went a long way to shaping allegiances. The *Match of the Day* cameras rarely ventured out as far as East Yorkshire but those Leeds stars with the sock tags and named tracksuits were regularly featured. Similarly, after we lost Anglia TV's *Match of the Week* in 1974 (following Yorkshire's acquisition of the Belmont transmitter) we received *Football Special* where, with Keith Macklin usually to be found describing the action, Leeds became all too easy to identify with. The famous Admiral shirt with the 'smiley' badge was many lads' choice of kit for school 'games' lessons and, to be fair, there weren't many City ones among the others.

* * *

So I'd said Leeds. Now I had to live with the consequences, one of which was the situation that developed with the two lads sitting either side of me in class – 'Olly', and his pint-sized sidekick 'Molly'. The former was on a mission to be crowned undisputed first year middleweight champion, a feat he sought to achieve by popping all the reputed hard kids from the other primary schools (including my mate Rob who I'd foolishly touted as Easington's main contender). I'd already annoyed them by refusing to swap places with their mutual friend 'Tyse'. This would not only have been in flagrant breach of the classroom alphabetic seating policy but would've put me next to Spencer. Nobody wanted to sit next to Spencer back then. So I stayed put, much to their chagrin. Announcing my support for Leeds only antagonised them further. Olly and Molly were 'Man U' fans and back then that rivalry was regarded as big on *both* sides of the Pennines. My card was well and truly marked. It's fair to say that during those first few months at high school, I had plenty of time to wish I'd said Hull City after all.

2

Earning My Stripes

Boothferry Park: Saturday, 20 September 1975

Walking up North Road, my excitement mounts with every step that brings me nearer the stadium. On the concourse the overriding smell of cigarette smoke is the first thing to hit me, along with what Arthur Hopcraft masterfully termed the 'rancid' air of 'beer and onions and belching and worse'. It's brilliant. On taking my seat I stare in wonder at what's before me. For someone used to watching his football in black-and-white, this is technicolor majesty. The bright blue sky combines beautifully with the lush green pitch below, separated in between by a Boothferry Park in all its four-sided glory. It is an aesthetically pleasing venue. Directly opposite is the North Stand, not too dissimilar in style to the one I'm sitting in. It's complemented by the Best Stand to my left, with the shallow Well terracing running along in front and the East or Railway Stand to my right, which in later years I will come to know and love as the Kempton.

Although by no means full, the colours sported by most people in the ground add to the kaleidoscopic effect, completing a wonderful canvas. Directly below me is the hub of the home support, the so-called 'bootboys' of the Bunkers Hill Choir. I stand up and crane my neck to get a good look at them. Their footwear from which their name originates is complemented by multiple scarves worn in various combinations: round the neck, on the wrists and in some cases through the belt lapels of their skinner jeans. There are so many types of scarf, from the basic black-and-amber bar version and its more modern companion with the additional white bit added, to the named scarf on which the words 'HULL CITY AFC' are book-ended by two fearsome-looking tiger heads. Then there's the real fashion accessory of the 1970s, the satin or silk scarf. Wonderful. Everywhere I look it's a sea of black-and-amber.

* * *

In 1975, Britain entered a 'double-dip' recession as the economy contracted for the second and third quarters of the year, leaving over a million people unemployed. To add to the gloom, the IRA were mounting more and more atrocities on the mainland, Peter Sutcliffe (the Yorkshire Ripper) carried out the second of 23 known vicious attacks on women and in Hull residents lived in fear of another of Britain's most prolific serial killers, 'Daft Peter' Dinsdale. Not that many outside the area would have noticed. Hull was an ignored part of an unloved county (Humberside having come into creation, perhaps aptly, on April Fool's Day 1974). Its downtrodden inhabitants were in need of something more than a proposed bridge that never looked like being finished and a new purpose-built shopping centre that many of them couldn't afford to use. Instead, they watched the TV news of British and Icelandic vessels clashing in the third Cod War, one that would have far-reaching ramifications for the industry and their city.[15]

Sport offered little by way of distraction. By the mid-1970s the Tigers were a tough sell to a kid used to watching winning teams on the telly. Crowds at Boothferry Park had

15 The Humber Bridge and the Prospect Centre on Paragon Street (on the site of the old Hull Royal Infirmary)

dropped to around the 5,000 mark. From being 'the Third Division side with the Second Division outlook and the First Division ground', City were on their way to being just a Third Division side with what one disgruntled supporter memorably termed a 'tatty, fish town image'. Terry Neill's flirtation with promotion to the top flight looked unlikely to be repeated any time soon. Instead, nervous glances were being cast in the opposite direction. Ridicule had replaced potential as the favoured choice of word association. City had become a club quietly ignored save for the downbeat tone of Elliot Oppel's weekly observations on Radio Humberside. The Tigers were in no way burning bright.[16]

The pervading gloom wasn't just confined to Hull City AFC. Both of the city's rugby league clubs had found themselves in the bottom tier following the reintroduction of two divisions and despite Rovers gaining promotion in 1975 neither club was pulling in the punters. Vince Groak highlights a weekend that March in which Hull's three professional clubs failed to muster 10,000 supporters between them. Just 5,248 watched City against Cardiff but even this figure eclipsed the combined rugby attendance. A crowd of 3,380 watched Rovers play Doncaster, while the 983 who turned up to welcome bottom club Huyton to The Boulevard constituted Hull FC's lowest-ever attendance. Desperate times indeed.[17]

Those who did attend matches weren't always there for the sport. Football hooliganism competed for headline space with the nation's other woes. The start of the 1975/76 season left papers like the *Daily Mail* and *Daily Mirror* (which had

16 Tordoff, Shaun, *City Psychos: From the Monte Carlo Mob to the Silver Cod Squad'* (London: Milo, 2002) p.11; Groak, Vince, *Last One Out ... When Hull Invaded Wembley* (Leeds: Scratching Shed, 2017) p.5

17 Groak, Vince, *Last One Out ... When Hull Invaded Wembley* (Leeds: Scratching Shed, 2017) p.12. The Hull FC attendance figure has been quoted elsewhere as 976 and even 721

previously run a 'Thugs' League') spoilt for choice. There were 14 stabbings and over 80 arrests at Wolves versus newly promoted Manchester United. Trouble also accompanied the games at Leicester, Nottingham Forest and along Southend seafront where Sheffield United fans ran amok. On the last Saturday in August, Chelsea fans rioted at Luton, Liverpool supporters smashed up a football special on the way back from Leicester and the Red Army ran riot at Stoke. Who in their right mind wanted to go to a football match?

* * *

Being of simple country stock, I'd not really experienced the depressing image of Hull portrayed in the media. It was somewhere I'd only ever visited for family shopping trips, the annual pantomime and hospital appointments (of which there were a few). The thought of heading there for a football match and without either of my parents was a fanciful one. But in September 1975 that's what I did. What's more, neither Mum nor Dad seemed to mind. In later years I'd resent the fact that Dad didn't seem to regret missing out on accompanying his son to his first match. There was no 'tell me all about it when you get home'. Nothing. My first City game went almost unnoticed – a bit like the club itself.

Hull City's summer had been tinged with sadness due to the death of chairman Harold Needler. 'Big Aitch' was revered as 'the father of Boothferry Park'. His legacy was everywhere around the ground he built in 1946 with grandiose plans to eventually hold 80,000 supporters. It was in the train that ran from Paragon Station to Boothferry Park Halt (instigated in 1951). It was in the six floodlight pylons that dominated the skyline on our approach to the ground (invested in 1963). It was in the South Stand, the superb cantilever structure built on what was once the open terracing of Bunkers Hill. And as we climbed the steps up to this stand, it was also behind us in the shape of the superb gymnasium the players used for training, another of the improvements instigated in order to try and secure top-flight football for the first time. Sadly, Needler didn't live to see his club reach their goal. Instead, the years after his death would see the Tigers heading in the opposite direction, accompanied by dwindling crowds rattling around a decaying stadium, muttering how 'Harold Needler will be turning in his grave'. And I was there the day it all began to go wrong.

20 September 1975
Football League Second Division:
Hull City 1 Fulham 2

Boothferry Park: South Stand seats; no ticket or programme

In a year in which the Conservative Party elected a female leader (later to become the country's first female prime minister), *Fawlty Towers*, *The Good Life* and, er, *Jim'll Fix It* debuted on our TV screens and the Sex Pistols played their first live show, my maiden appearance at Boothferry Park comes some way further down the list of 1975 'firsts'. But it was one that would be seen as pivotal to my later direction in life. The home team I went to see that late summer afternoon had actually made a solid start in their attempt to 'do it for Harold' and win promotion. They came into the Fulham game on the back of a 2-1 away win at Brian Clough's Nottingham Forest, their fourth victory in six outings. Their three previous home matches had yielded a 100 per cent return. Fulham were the previous season's FA Cup finalists and the prospect of seeing a side that included World Cup-winning captain Bobby Moore and fellow ex-England star Alan Mullery attracted 3,000 extra fans through the gate. Among them were my chaperone Derek and his sons Tom and Jim, at whose joint invitation I was making my Hull City debut.

The emergence of the teams added to the spectacle. After years of wearing plain amber shirts, the Tigers were resplendent in their stylish new Europa Sports shirts of broad black-and-amber stripes with white trim, paired for the first time with white shorts and socks. The roar that greeted them befitted a team in form. John Kaye's starting 11 was a blend of youth and experience: Jeff Wealands, Frank Banks, Roger de Vries, Chris Galvin, Stuart Croft, Dave Roberts, Vince Grimes, Malcolm Lord, Alf Wood, Peter Fletcher and Roy Greenwood. The substitute was club captain Jimmy McGill, whose personal underachievement was to be indicative of the team as a whole. Sadly there was no place for the legendary Ken Wagstaff; his final season in City colours was beset by injury and would end prematurely two months later. Fulham sported their traditional Umbro combination of white shirts, black shorts and socks that they'd worn at Wembley. Among their number was the aforementioned Moore. Derek told us all we were privileged to be seeing the maestro in action. Sadly, I was too young to appreciate this fact at the time.

There were 8,471 spectators in attendance. It looked and sounded like many more. Perhaps this was because of our close proximity to the 'choir', gathered at the top of Bunkers between exits B and C directly behind the goal. Watching their hands rise in rhythmic clapping was fantastic, as was deciphering the content of some of their chants. Not many were appropriate for my young ears but that made them all the more memorable. I giggled as the visitors from London were variously told, 'You're gonna get your fucking 'eads kicked in,' 'you're going home like Sandy Richardson' and 'you're going home in a Yorkshire ambulance'. As the game neared its end, the visitors were promised another treat, to the tune of 'Tom Hark', 'At 20 to five, you're going to die.' However, the best song I heard was 'Mrs Hall's Sausage Rolls'. Said to have originated among followers of the oval-ball game across town at Hull Kingston Rovers, it hailed Mrs Hall's culinary offerings as the greatest because 'they're made from the milk from her tits', which prompted them to 'fall to bits'. It was all very educational for a wide-eyed nine-year-old.[18]

The tale of milky tits aside, most of the stuff heard simply reflected this as the era of football aggro. Given that we were safely ensconced among the home support this shouldn't have bothered us. Except – confession time again – we were supposed to be Londoners for the day. Derek hailed from Putney and was an avid Fulham fan. As such, his sons said we were supporting their dad's local team rather than ours. Talk about awkward! But I wasn't going to blow my first chance to see City – even if it meant having to be a young Tommy Trinder for the day. Another skeleton to place in my cupboard!

Given our supposed allegiances, Derek hadn't thought through his choice of seats, which as previously described were literally within spitting distance of the most partisan home supporters. So when our chaperone sprang up to hail what looked a certain Fulham goal, only to be thwarted by a brilliant Wealands save, we were suddenly very exposed. Seemingly every bloke around us turned to focus on a very embarrassed Fulham fan and his three young companions. For an Eighth Army veteran Derek looked somewhat unnerved. Rommel's Afrika Korps were one thing, the local Sledmere Fusiliers quite another. Thankfully for our sakes, he restrained himself when two Viv Busby goals (I believe) turned the game on its head after Grimes had given City the lead.[19]

18 Sandy Richardson was a character in long-running ITV soap *Crossroads* and was confined to a wheelchair following a traffic accident

19 The Sledmere Fusiliers was one of several names attached to City's 'bootboys' of the period, the name originating from Sledmere Grove, a street that ran behind the South Stand end of Boothferry Park

Aside from that Wealands save, City's goal is the only action I can recall with anything approaching clarity. It was scored at our end. A free kick about 25 yards out saw the ball played sideways to Grimes who smashed it into the top corner. I half-cheered, inviting Derek's disapproval in the process. Years later, I obtained a black-and-white photograph showing the immediate aftermath, in which Chris Galvin can be seen virtually on the goal line dancing gleefully in celebration. In the background the famous Hull Savings Bank clock on the North Stand is showing 3.15pm. It marks the first significant milestone of my life as a City supporter. An hour and a quarter later marked another one – my first City defeat. Many more would follow. When the final whistle blew, Bunkers quickly emptied as City's 'bootboys' streamed across the south-east corner intent on atoning for their team's shortcomings. By the time they got there the Fulham contingent were already aboard the train waiting to take them home. I watched wide-eyed and must confess I found it quite exciting. Good job. It was a scene I'd become all too familiar with over the next decade.

Fulham's win lifted them up to third behind Sunderland and pacesetters Notts County but they would eventually miss out on promotion. City remained seventh and wouldn't win for another seven games. They finished the season in what I would later come to know as their accustomed mid-table position. By then Wagstaff had retired, Roy Greenwood had joined Sunderland in a big-money move and skipper Jimmy McGill had departed for Halifax Town. Far from honouring the memory of 'Big Aitch', the Tigers were at the top of a slippery slope that would culminate in relegation to the Football League basement by the end of the decade.

* * *

Two years elapsed before I doubled my City match tally. It was 1977, the year I turned Judas in class. The summer saw the Queen's Silver Jubilee celebrations. The Sex Pistols sang 'God Save the Queen', while 'The King' popped his clogs in Memphis, news that I recall cast a real shadow over our Sunday school trip to Bridlington. The first *Star Wars* was released, *Starsky & Hutch* rivalled *Match of the Day* as the must-watch TV programme of Saturday nights and Hutch himself topped the UK pop charts. The cool wore sneakers, drove around in a Ford Gran Torino and sang about a 'Silver Lady'. The uncool wore a school uniform and supported Hull City. Or so it appeared as autumn arrived and John Kaye departed, sacked after a home defeat by Mansfield; 'Bloody Rubbish Mansfield' as I would come to know them.

Dad was again nowhere to be seen as I accompanied my cousin John and his young sons Craig and Karl to Boothferry to see another London side, Charlton Athletic. On a damp grey November afternoon the ground resembled the sort of backdrops to be found on the weekly Spot the Ball coupons that Dad collected. The visitors would ensure the sort of grey, joyless afternoon that City fans had come to expect. New boss Bobby Collins had suffered just one defeat in eight matches, a run that included a dream start courtesy of a 2-0 home win over leaders Spurs, with Alan Warboys bagging his first two goals since his £25,000 move from Fulham. But the honeymoon period was over. Collins's public criticism of the players following a 4-1 win over Cardiff backfired and City wouldn't be victorious again for the next nine matches. Charlton was the second of these. Despite the arrival of Billy Bremner amid much fanfare from Leeds the previous season, City's status as the longest-serving club in the Second Division was coming to an end.

We took the train from Paragon Station and stood on Bunkers Hill – both firsts for me – and in a crowd of just 5,699 there was enough space even for this pipsqueak to see everything that was happening. I might have been better emulating young Karl who spent the whole game running up and down the terracing, largely oblivious to what was going on in front of him. The basic facts of the game are as follows. Only Wealands, Roberts and Grimes remained of the team I'd seen two years earlier. Les Berry fired the visitors ahead after just three minutes and Mike Flanagan (one half of the Addicks' prolific strike partnership with Derek Hales) confirmed the win just 12 minutes from time. At the other end, the Tigers' vaunted strike duo of Bannister and Warboys neither smashed nor grabbed in a 2-0 loss, although I seem to recall that City had three goals disallowed and I went home convinced the ref had 'robbed us'. There must have been an abundance of poor refs that season as the Tigers were relegated to the Third Division, ending a 12-year stay in the second tier. Collins was gone before this was confirmed. He was sacked in March after just four months in charge, thus becoming the shortest-reigning manager in the club's history. The job of waking the sleeping giant was proving difficult.

My drawn-out indoctrination to the Tiger Nation continued the following September. It ranked alongside seeing *Star Wars* at the Dorchester cinema as my highlight of 1978; that and a World Cup in which I'd revelled in the long-distance shooting of Arie Haan, marvelled at Archie Gemmill's goal in Mendoza and moaned at the 'cheating' hosts. Closer to home Nottingham Forest, that struggling Second Division team beaten by City the week before my first Boothferry Park visit, were about to play European Cup football having been crowned First Division champions for the first time in their history. Their conquerors that day in 1975 didn't have such lofty ambitions for the upcoming campaign but hopes of a swift return to the Second Division were boosted by a fine start.

12 September 1978
Football League Third Division:
Hull City 4 Walsall 1

Boothferry Park: South Stand seats; no ticket or programme

The summer of 1978 was a busy one at Boothferry. New manager Ken Houghton brought in three new players for his first full season in charge: John Farley, Micky Horswill and a certain Keith Edwards, bought for £60,000 from Sheffield United. 'Hull's new "Goal-Machine"' was the moniker *Shoot!* magazine bestowed upon him and the 21-year-old Teessider did his best to live up to it. Opening his account in the 3-1 win at Tranmere, a hat-trick against leaders Chester soon endeared Edwards to the supporters as City got up among the early pacesetters. When Walsall arrived on a balmy September evening, the top three beckoned. My mate Clarkey said his dad would take us. On a school night too! Having seen City score just once prior to the game, I was spoilt rotten as the Saddlers were swept aside. Edwards capped things off with a goal that ranks as the best I ever saw at Boothferry Park. Had it been netted nowadays it would go viral on YouTube. Instead we must settle for the scorer's description in his autobiography: 'I picked the ball up in our own half and just went on and on, even dribbling past one bloke twice when he kept catching me up. When I got to the edge of the box I simply passed the ball into [the] net. It was one of my best ever goals, everyone raved about it and even though I say it myself, it was a super effort.'[20]

---

20 *Shoot!* (9 September 1978); Edwards, Keith (with Pack, Andy), *Edwards … One-Nil!: The Keith Edwards Story* (Vertical Editions, 2014) p.95

Talking to David Bond some years later, Edwards described the goal as his 'favourite at Boothferry Park' but added that he still doesn't know what he was doing in his own half in the first place! David Goodman said the striker's 'brilliant display' made him a 'hero in the making'. Edwards's return of 24 league goals in his first season was the best by a City striker since the 1960s. Among the survivors of the team that had gone down the previous summer, Bannister and Lord also scored on a wonderful night. But it was the newly crowned 'King Edwards' who stole the show.[21]

Sitting in the South Stand again, it was my first night match experience and Boothferry Park, bathed in floodlights, looked magnificent. A Bolton fan once told me he used to regard the stadium as 'the Wembley of the north'. On an evening such as this it was easy to see why. City's players were also pleasing on the eye, not only in their performance but in another kit that met with this budding young geek's approval; those striped shirts now being matched with black shorts and amber socks. The win took them up to third and I was buzzing at school the next day, even working out a way of getting to Saturday's home game against Chesterfield. City were going up, of that I was certain. Cue my first experience of the character-building condition known today as #TypicalCity. I didn't get to the Chesterfield game (a 1-1 draw) nor did I go against Oxford a few weeks later – let down at the last minute after another mate's promise of a lift with his dad didn't materialise. At least he was let down too; City lost 1-0. In fact I didn't get to see the Tigers again that season.

I didn't miss much. The Oxford reverse was the second of three straight defeats and it was another nine games before the Tigers won again. Ironically, it came in #TypicalCity fashion

21 Goodman, David, *Look Back in Amber* (Manchester: Parrs Wood Press, 2005) p.51

thanks to what the *Sunday Mirror* termed a 'Hull smash-and-grab' four-goal rout of leaders Watford, in which Warboys and Bannister finally linked again to good effect. As for Edwards, he proved the one shining light in otherwise depressing times.

29 November 1978
Friendly: England 1 Czechoslovakia 0
Wembley Stadium: South Terrace; ticket £5;
Programme 30p

Having cut my teeth at City, my next live football experience took me to a whole new level. It was one that saw a crowd of 92,500 attracted to the Empire Stadium, Wembley. Yes, *the* Wembley. The original one with the Twin Towers, not the rebuilt version I attended with City 30 years later. Not only was going to see an England match another boost to my credibility ratings but for a very lucky band of second-years and fifth-formers from Withernsea High, it also provided the bonus of a day out of the classroom.

Born in the year of England's greatest triumph, my emotional addiction to the national team's fortunes began as a six-year-old on a Saturday night in April 1972. It was one of the rare occasions that Dad sat down with us to watch football. Together we saw a West Germany team end England's 20-year-long unbeaten record at Wembley. Several football historians have cited that rainy night as the real moment in which the fortunes of the two countries diverged in opposite directions. West Germany went on to win the Euros and the 1974 World Cup; eight years would elapse before England even qualified again for a major competition.

By November 1978 things were at least looking up. Although coming too late to salvage World Cup qualification, Ron Greenwood had overseen a run of just one defeat in 11 matches and was well on the way to restoring a reputation sullied somewhat under predecessor Don Revie. Hungary were thumped 4-1 in May in what Gary Jordan terms Greenwood's 'best moment in international management', and the Home Internationals were sealed by victory at Hampden, with Steve Coppell's goal spoiling Ally's Army's World Cup leaving party. The Manchester United winger was also on target in my first England match but he wouldn't grab the headlines. Instead they went to one of the players involved in the build-up, Viv Anderson. Nottingham Forest's 22-year-old right-back made history by becoming the first black player to represent England in a full international. Already the first black player to have a League Cup winner's medal and the first to appear in an English championship-winning side, his senior international call-up came complete with a telegram of congratulations from the Queen.[22]

The friendly against the reigning European champions was the last scheduled international of the year. I was really excited and somewhat in awe of what lay ahead. I'd borrowed an England scarf from a schoolmate and felt like 'the dog's bollocks' as few others on the bus had one. That scarf would be much needed when taking up our seats on a bitterly cold night. A light dusting of snow covered the pitch and somehow added to the sheer size of the place, although some wag in our group maintained, 'It's not much bigger than Boothferry Park!' I was bursting with pride when the Central Band of the RAF struck up with 'Land of Hope and Glory'. His Grace the Duke of Marlborough, honorary vice-president of the FA, was then introduced to the teams and the anthems were played. This was big time; football at 'The Home of Football'. Unfortunately, memories of the match itself have been lost amid the overall experience. I've since heard players

---

22 Jordan, Gary, *Out of the Shadows: The Story of the 1982 England World Cup Team* (Worthing: Pitch Publishing, 2017) p.58

describe their first Wembley cup final as being something of a blur. This was my equivalent and completely passed me by. In the days immediately after the game I read and re-read the programme from cover to cover in an attempt to bring my experience back into focus. The more I read the more I became convinced of two things. Firstly, that Ron's boys were a shoo-in for the 1980 Euros; secondly, that Antonín Panenka's moustache had to be fake. I was wrong on both counts.

Anderson's debut was part of an 'experimental' England line-up. Peter Shilton replaced first choice Ray Clemence in goal, while Phil Thompson partnered Dave Watson at centre-half. A 4-2-4 formation had Tony Currie and Ray Wilkins in the middle and the width provided by Coppell and Peter Barnes. Up front, skipper Kevin Keegan was partnered by Anderson's Forest team-mate Tony Woodcock. Jordan describes the game as a bit of an anticlimax, with England thankful to 'the tracksuit bottom-clad' Shilton on numerous occasions. Czech skipper Zdeněk Nehoda was 'a marauding threat' but England had their own bright spot in the performance of Anderson. It was from one of his 'trademark surging runs' that the winner came in the 69th minute, Coppell bundling home from close range after the keeper and a defender had made a hash of dealing with Currie's cross. Over 90,000 people stood to celebrate, including me. It was the first time I'd ever cheered any goal scored by a Manchester United player and it was enough to secure a scrappy win, England's fifth in ten full internationals between the countries.

The final whistle didn't quite signal the end of the night's excitement. The inter-club rivalry that would often simmer beneath the surface at England games reared its head at a motorway service station on the way home, courtesy of an altercation between some of our fifth-formers and similarly aged fans of 'Bloody Rubbish Mansfield'. Insults were traded and blows briefly exchanged on the tarmac. I remained seated on the coach and felt no need to get involved. Not that I'd have been much use in any case.

* * *

So, aged 13, I'd seen England's only World Cup-winning captain in action in Hull, a full England international match against the reigning European champions at the national stadium *and* Leeds United's greatest-ever skipper playing for Hull City. The next chapter in my football education took me to Ewood Park, home to one of the oldest clubs in England. There I watched Blackburn Rovers host Sheffield United in a Second Division relegation battle, courtesy of another 'jolly' with Clarkey and his Blackburn-born dad, a lifelong fan of the Rovers. We watched a 2-0 home win from the Riverside Stand, a result that did little other than to drag the Blades down with their hosts. Although enjoyable, the trip to one of football's founding fathers wasn't enough to sway either Clarkey or me from the paths we'd already set out upon. On our return to God's Country, Clarkey reverted to Liverpool and I went back to supporting Hull City – and Leeds United!

3

Boulevard of Broken Dreams

The Boulevard: Wednesday, 2 May 1979

We've just piled out of our minibus and our youth leader Barney is handing out our tickets. Within minutes I'm stood in the ground alongside the rest of the Easington contingent. Many of those around me have been drawn in by the unmistakeable odour of Castrol R and the 'collective rhythmic roar of 500cc, methanol-burning engines thrumming with each twist of the throttle' that make 'the ground shudder with a combination of anticipation and protest'. Supplemented by the smell of fried onions, the sound of dozens of air horns and the prospect of seeing 'Jelly Man' in full flow, it proves a heady cocktail; but not as heady as the thrill of a chance encounter with the girl reputed to be the 'best kisser' in Holderness.[23]

* * *

Of all the ill-fated romantic pursuits that tended to occupy far too many thoughts during my school days (and beyond) perhaps none was as fanciful as my speedway attraction in the summer of '79. Thankfully, it was one I kept to myself. Well, until now that is.

---

23 Burford, Brian *Kelly Moran: A Hell of a Life* (Stroud: History Press, 2014) p.11

How the lovely 'BK' (for that is how she must be known) gained her unofficial title wasn't something I ever found out. Nor did I happen to know anyone on the adjudication panel and I certainly didn't have a hand in it myself! She was a few years older than me and drop-dead gorgeous with looks straight out of *Charlie's Angels* and a figure fit for Legs And Co. I used to see her regularly around school and 'down town' in Muggys at lunchtimes. She was often there with her boyfriend. He was a local hard case who'd already left school and came complete with peacock haircut, turned-up jeans and ox-blood Docs, all topped off with a City shirt (I bet nobody ever laughed at his choice of team). In contrast I was a 13-year-old weakling, clad head-to-toe in regulation school uniform and I didn't even have a pair of Docs (Mum bought me Major Domos instead). What's more, I was prone to going red at the merest hint of a girl saying hello. I wasn't an obvious object of anyone's affections. BK was. She was proper schoolboy crush material, even if, as in my case, it was never likely to be requited. But I'm a Piscean and we aren't known as 'the dreamiest men alive' for nothing. I dreamed a lot that summer, even if most of them were dashed amid the strains of Roxy Music's 'Dance Away'. Bryan knew the score when it came to affairs of the heart.[24]

In the overactive imagination of a love-struck teenager who watched far too much kelt on the telly, there was one place where I felt I might just attract this luscious young lady's attention. That was The Boulevard – hardly the most romantic of venues I think you'll agree but somewhere that held mutual attraction for us both. For in 1979 Wednesday night was speedway night at Hull FC's rugby league ground.

---

24 'Muggys' was slang for the local amusement arcades; Major Domo boots were seen as a rip-off of the famous Doc Martens (Doc's) although some people regarded them as longer-wearing despite being cheaper

BK was a speedway fan. I was a BK fan. So when Easington Youth Club began running trips to every home meeting, I booked on. Easington was big on speedway at the time, having two of the team's stars residing in the village. This was something I hoped to use to my advantage. The fact I didn't actually know either of the young Yanks in question was immaterial; Wednesday nights had suddenly become more exciting. Instead of three blokes trailing the great Ivan Mauger for four laps of the circuit, I was on my own chase to impress BK about my imagined American acquaintances. The fact that it coincided with the most memorable season in the history of Hull Vikings proved a happy coincidence.

* * *

Hull's fragmented history with speedway has been diligently chronicled by Roger Hulbert. It began in 1930 when 'dirt track' meetings were held at the old White City circuit 'situated in Anlaby Road and Calvert Lane, roughly a mile to the west of The Boulevard'. Team racing there was first reported on Saturday, 12 July 1930 when a Hull side took on Leicester in a challenge match. The sport moved east of the city in 1948 when the former aerodrome at Hedon became home to new National League Division Three outfit, Hull Angels. Around 6,000 spectators saw the official opening and a special road/rail terminus (Hedon Halt) was built to ferry fans from the city. But midway through their second season dwindling crowds, loss of revenue and rumoured noise complaints forced the Angels to disband and their licence passed to Swindon Robins. Concerns over noise also thwarted initial plans to introduce speedway to The Boulevard in 1966, but five years later Hull's third incarnation of the sport finally surfaced via a purpose-built track laid around the perimeter of the rugby pitch. Once again concerns were raised, as remembered by promoter Ian Thomas. The Boulevard's location meant that 'along with Exeter it was situated in the most populated area of any track in the United Kingdom' and there was also an issue with the track itself. Esteemed sports journalist Dick Bott described it as 'so narrow that even the mice went round in single file'. Indeed, it only met the minimum required width of 25 feet thanks to the wily Thomas using his own tape measure – 'with the first foot cut off' – at the official inspection.[25]

Hulbert says 'some people wanted to retain the Angels nickname' but with feeling being that speedway's family image wouldn't be best served by a name that sounded like Hells Angels, Hull Vikings came into being – although only after a vote organised by the local paper, which resulted in the name 'Kestrels' being totally ignored. The Vikings spent a decade at The Boulevard, during which time they became major contenders. Having benefited from Coatbridge Tigers' decision to drop down a level, the ambitious Thomas bought the Scottish club's Division One licence for 1974. As part of the deal, Vikings acquired the services of Bobby Beaton who would remain with them until the club's demise. Although the team finished second-bottom that first season in the top flight, they were well-backed with a record crowd of 7,500 attending the inaugural Yorkshire TV Trophy meeting in August.[26]

The arrival of world champion Barry Briggs MBE inspired Vikings to the Inter-Divisional Knockout Cup and the Yorkshire Cup in 1976. His inability to commit for the following year prompted a return to mediocrity but in January 1978 Hull again came up trumps when recruiting another

---

25 *Hull Vikings 2020 Souvenir Programme* (Issue 1) p.4; Burford, Brian, *Kelly Moran: A Hell of a Life* (Stroud: History Press, 2014) p.16

26 Hulbert, Roger, *Hull Speedway 1930–1981* (Stroud: Tempus, 2004) p.36

Kiwi, Ivan Mauger, for a then-world record fee. The capture of the reigning world champion and a man later to be voted the greatest speedway rider of the 20th century was seen as a massive coup. In the *Hull Daily Mail* of 3 January, speedway correspondent Richard Tingle described it as 'the most sensational transfer deal in their seven-year history'. 'Despite tremendous opposition', Hull co-promoters Ian Thomas and Bryan Larner 'paid out a world record £12,000 fee to West Country track Exeter Falcons to sign reigning world champion Ivan Mauger'. Mauger announced the move himself in a press conference at the Piccadilly Hotel in Manchester. He had signed a three-year deal, one that Tingle wrote would see him 'remain the highest-paid rider of all time in the British League' during his stay in Hull. In John Chaplin's book about the five-time world champion, Sky TV speedway commentator Nigel Pearson remembers the news 'as though it was yesterday' and writes, 'I was in the back of my dad's car listening to BBC Radio Humberside when the breaking news was reported, "Hull Vikings have signed world champion Ivan Mauger." I couldn't believe it, Dad couldn't believe it – and Mum, who was also in the car, was wondering what all the fuss was about.'[27]

Tingle said negotiations had been 'shrouded in secrecy', with Exeter desperate to keep him and both Birmingham and Cradley Heath keen to secure his services. Along with his five world titles (equalling Ove Fundin's record and including an unprecedented hat-trick between 1969 and 1971) and triple wins in the long-track format too, Mauger had also brought major honours to every club he'd raced for. Most recently he'd transformed unfashionable Exeter into British League champions. Thomas told the *Hull Daily Mail*, 'He's just what

27 Chaplin, John, *Ivan Mauger: The Man Behind the Myth* (Stroud: History Press, 2012) p.105

Hull speedway needed, because we have remained a mid-table team for too long and now it is our turn to taste some glory.'

The start of the 1978 season saw a crowd of 'over 6,000' witness Mauger's perfect debut and the first of numerous 15-point maximums. The fans continued to flock. Team-mate Graham Drury later referred to the 'colossal' crowds attracted by Mauger's arrival at the Vikings and with Hull FC struggling, speedway was soon the bigger draw at the ground.

Hulbert describes the city as 'buzzing that summer of 1978' with the speedway club 'making all the headlines'. This was a boom period for the sport in Britain. Brian Burford describes the standard in the 1970s and '80s as 'very high indeed' with 'so much talent around'. And because of Mauger's arrival, some of that talent was soon to be found in Hull. Burford says Moran came to Hull Vikings predominantly because 'it was a chance to ride with Ivan Mauger'. The young Californian was followed across to England by future world champion Bruce Penhall who joined Cradley Heath, prompting an 'onslaught of American talent into Europe'. Bobby Schwartz (Cradley Heath), Ron Preston (Poole), Steve Columbo (Birmingham) and Tommy Morley (Sheffield) would all follow in 1979. Meanwhile Joe Owen, regarded as one of Britain's brightest prospects, who'd only been at Hull for a year and wanted to leave due to his dislike of the track, changed his mind on news of the arrival of the world champion: 'I'd have been well gone if they hadn't signed him.'[28]

Despite the anticipation, Mauger's first season as skipper didn't yield that elusive first title. Vikings finished third behind Coventry Bees and Belle Vue Aces in the British League. Still, this easily constituted their best season and in addition they won the Yorkshire Cup for a second time. The general feeling

---

28 Burford, Brian, *Kelly Moran: A Hell of a Life* (History Press, 2014) p.14

was that injuries to Owen and Moran had scuppered their title hopes. Owen, a former National League Riders Champion and European Under-21 Championship runner-up, had adapted slowly to life in the higher league on joining from sister track Newcastle Diamonds. However, according to Hulbert he'd been 'showing sparkling form' when suffering a 'near-fatal' crash in the second half of the home league win over Hackney on 28 June. The young rider sustained 'multiple injuries, including a punctured lung, a broken arm and a broken nose'. Hulbert says he 'was very close to losing his life and his condition was critical for some days'. Two months later, Vikings lost their other hot young starlet. Aged 17 on arrival in March, Moran was only allowed to race due to Thomas exploiting a loophole in the age regulations, with Pete Rovazzini agreeing to be his legal guardian. Belying his age, he soon acquired the nickname 'Jelly Man' on account of his astounding cornering technique, which saw him literally hanging off his bike. Moran also had a knack of spectacular dashes from the back to win races, which made him an instant hit with the fans. Unfortunately, just as he was 'beginning to turn in some big scores', he too sustained a horrific crash in Heat 8 of an Inter-League Knockout Cup tie, away at Hackney on 25 August. Moran was 'taken to hospital with a broken arm and leg, hip, shoulder and back injuries and a fractured pelvis. He was to have several weeks in traction as part of the recovery process.'[29]

Given these two huge setbacks, a third-place finish in the league was very creditable. Vikings had shown they were not just a one-man team. And in their young Yank especially, the club had a potential star in the making. As Hulbert writes, 'Mauger led by example, maintaining an average of just under ten, but even he would concede that Kelly Moran was

29 Hulbert, Roger, *Hull Speedway 1930–1981* (Stroud: Tempus, 2004) p.95

Mr Excitement at The Boulevard in his debut season.' His popularity was helped by what Burford called 'a cheeky grin and a wild glint in his eye'. The youngster certainly became an instant hit in our village, where his antics became legendary. His move to Easington from Beverley in 1979 was due to the 'distractions' created by his rising popularity. As Owen recalled of his team-mate in Burford's biography, 'The first year he came over he was only a kid then. He was quite a handful, a bloody handful. He used to drink a lot, which was a shame really because he had a lot of talent that he wasted.'[30]

* * *

With Moran and Owen both fit again, hopes were high for 1979. The team was largely unchanged, with the exception of Dennis Sigalos as replacement for Phil Kynman (who'd joined Berwick Bandits). The 19-year-old Californian soon became the second hot young Yank to be found residing in Easington. Meanwhile, a sponsorship deal with Bridlington-based Satra Motors, importers of Lada cars, led to claims that Hull was the first fully sponsored team in the British League. Convinced that this would be *the* year, crowds flocked to The Boulevard, among them a regular minibus-load from Easington Youth Club. Once inside the ground, our vantage point was the Airlie Street End terracing, which ran in a curve behind the rugby posts. A bend was chosen due to it being in prime position for the spills, which – let's face it – was why most people stood there. That said, it brought its hazards too – choose the wrong time to partake of refreshment and you had yourself the local delicacy that was the 'Boulevard gritburger'!

So there I was – a boy with absolutely no interest in any form of wheels whatsoever – about to witness at first-hand the

30 Burford, Brian, *Kelly Moran: A Hell of a Life* (Stroud: History Press, 2014) p.21

most dramatic of seasons. I even looked the part thanks to Phil lending me his blue-and-white Everton scarf. That scarf and me would get to see some of the most thrilling speedway the city has ever hosted, with the record books showing that it all came down to one of the most famous showdowns in the sport's history, at Coventry's Brandon Stadium on Saturday, 13 October.

However, there was many a twist and turn in the tale before then. The tone was set in the first few weeks. A Mauger-less thumping defeat away at Eastbourne Eagles first time out was seen as a blip and from the moment reigning champions Coventry were dispatched 51-27 in the opening home fixture, Hull Lada Vikings were established as the only side capable of preventing a second successive title for 'Great Dane' Ole Olsen's team. In particular, returns of 11 and eight points from the returning Moran and Owen suggested that both riders were fully recovered from injury. Back-to-back defeats in the Northern Trophy were inconsequential, and a loss at Mauger's former track Exeter was offset by a hard-earned home win over Wolverhampton in which the Vikings captain equalled his own track record of 70.4 seconds.

2 May 1979
Speedway World Championship and Grand Prix

The Boulevard: Airlie Street End Terrace; no ticket; programme 20p

The arrival of May brought a break from team racing as Hull staged a qualifying round of the World Championship and Grand Prix. It is one of only two meetings for which I still have the original *Super Speedway '79* programmes (an ill-judged clear-out some years back left me with only five issues to show for three years' attendance). In their notes for the Sunday Mirror World Championship and Berger Grand Prix,

Larner and Thomas describe the merged competition as 'the greatest of all speedway double bills', in which 'all the world's top riders have a say'. Although none of the sport's biggest names were on show in Hull (with the exception of Mauger) there was still a fine cast, with the out-of-town riders headed by the 'Aussie flyer' and five-time World Championship finalist Billy Sanders. American Steve Gresham, Dane Alf Busk, Norwegian Tormod Langli and Jan Andersson of Sweden strengthened the overseas contingent. A decent list of British riders included Halifax skipper Ian Cartwright and the presence of four Hull riders (Beaton, Owen, Moran and Mauger) ensured plenty of local interest. All in all it had the makings of an exciting night.

Larner and Thomas also explained how the event worked with regards to qualification for the showpiece final in Katowice in September. This was 'for the benefit of any newcomers to speedway this season' (i.e. me). Despite this I still didn't really have a grasp of what was going on! Suffice to say the 16 riders were set to take part in 20 heats, with only the nine British entrants having their points count towards World Championship qualifying whereas all the competitors were chasing Grand Prix points. Confused?

Anyway, to the delight of the crowd the home riders enjoyed a successful evening, all scoring well. Not that any of them got near to Mauger who cruised to victory, complete with a maximum points haul and a new track record of 70.2 seconds. It was the latest stage en route to a sixth World Championship title. He was undoubtedly the best in the world – and for the time being he was *ours*.

* * *

The quiet surroundings of Easington to which Kelly Moran (and later Dennis Sigalos too) relocated was seen as a safer option than the lively market town in which he'd been residing. Some of Moran's exploits in Beverley became legendary, such as the time Ian Thomas had to call out the local fire brigade to help extricate his rider from the retractable bed in his flat, which had sprung back into its wall space after a 'high' Moran had jumped on it off the sideboard. On another occasion the Hull co-manager had to bail him out of police custody twice in the same night.

Even when not partying, Moran could get himself into trouble. His lack of knowledge of England's road network and in particular its roundabouts led to hilarious stories of him getting lost on the way to meetings, with Burford reporting how during a trip to Newcastle he somehow found himself in Liverpool!

Moran's new abode in Easington was a spacious house just off the main road into the village, which had extensive grounds and out-sheds where he could store his bikes. Owner Veronica Chapman had answered a request from her friend, the Vikings' secretary Lesley Sharp, for a family to look after a young rider. Moran and Sigalos soon became local celebrities. Veronica had never been to speedway before but like many locals she now caught the bug. She remembers how Moran in particular 'fitted in well with village life, everybody liked him and anybody would help him out – he was well loved'. For his part, Burford recalls that Moran used the distinctive black-and-white lighthouse at nearby Spurn Point as inspiration for a quip about his new home: 'It's pretty bleak after California but it does bring a regular spot of light into my life!'

The young Americans soon became heroes to many of the local youngsters and speedway was suddenly *the* sport to be interested in. Wednesday nights would see a large exodus of villagers all bound for The Boulevard with many locals trying to use their Stateside guests' place of residence to their advantage.

Terry Keyworth was one such beneficiary, telling me how Moran would get him and his mate into home meetings for free as his 'mechanics'. 'One night,' he remembers, 'Kelly came a cropper and his bike ended up careering over the fence. It looked fairly serious. We said, that's it, we won't see him for a while.' However, by the time the pair got back to the village pub, 'There was Kelly on his third pint of mixed! We couldn't believe it.'

Being converted to pints of 'mixed' (half bitter, half mild) was just one example of how the move to Easington had done little to curtail the rider's thirst for partying. Many have tales of his stay in the village; other stories are recounted by Burford. His unorthodox use of transport is a recurring theme: coming back from away meetings asleep in the Chapmans' car boot; making the quarter-mile trip to the White Horse pub on Veronica's seven-year-old daughter's bike and coming back from there on the bonnet of Sigalos's Lada; or running his own sponsored Lada into the ground (and ditch) while taking on buses along the winding rural roads. After acquiring a caravan on the nearby clifftop site, Moran actually missed a Vikings home meeting due to, er, 'entertaining'. As Veronica put it, 'There was always a party going on where Kelly was.' Similar to many hell-raising sportsmen, his activities rarely appeared to affect his performances. As the season progressed his scores improved and two weeks after the Grand Prix he achieved a first British League 'maximum' in the Inter-League Four-Team Tournament at The Boulevard. I was there to see it.

16 May 1979
Speedway Inter-League Four-Team Tournament

The Boulevard: Airlie Street End Terrace; no ticket; programme 20p

The four-team format was very popular, involving clubs from both the British and National Leagues. Eight teams progressed from group stages to the semi-finals and final staged at a 48-heat, all-day meeting at Sheffield's Owlerton track in June. The Vikings' qualifying group included league rivals Halifax Dukes and Sheffield Tigers, along with Newcastle Diamonds from the National League. The Dukes were billed as Hull's 'old rivals from The Shay' and were seen as the ones to beat. They'd already done the double over the Vikings in the Northern Trophy and they counted among their number the 'World Championship/Grand Prix sensation' Kenny Carter, soon to become the sport's pantomime villain.

I recall Halifax always bringing a decent following to Hull, which often led to a cracking atmosphere. But this was a night for the Boulevard faithful with 12 of the 13 races won by a Hull rider. In fact it was Heat 12, when Bobby Beaton was beaten by Michael Lohmann, before the hosts tasted their first defeat. The Vikings were off to a flyer. They were then relegated to third place as Sheffield won the second leg at Halifax, although their 22 points kept them in first place overall. But when they then finished third on a rain-affected track at Owlerton, their overall lead was down to just three points.

The final Four-Team Trophy qualifier at Newcastle's Brough Park saw Owen top score with 11 points in a comfortable win that sealed Vikings' place in the Sheffield showpiece 13 days later, while wins over Birmingham, Halifax and Reading kept them in the thick of the league title race. The Four-Team Trophy final came the day after the World Pairs final at Vojens, meaning several big names were absent and offsetting Hull's loss of Mauger and Moran to injuries. Bobby Beaton starred in the tight semi-final win before Exeter, Cradley Heath and Hackney were dispatched in a rain-affected final, with Beaton and Sigalos both scoring maximums. It was only the Vikings' second national cup win, following 1976's Inter-Divisional Knockout Cup success. However, given subsequent events, it would provide scant consolation for a season that promised so much.

* * *

On the league front, just prior to start of the Four-Team Tournament, Vikings were at last able to field a full-strength side. In a sign of things to come they dismantled King's Lynn Stars 56-22 at The Boulevard. In between the Four-Team's second and third legs, a brief return to league action saw Exeter beaten at home despite Falcons' Scott Autrey equalling Mauger's track record in a win over the home skipper. In the next home league fixture, Belle Vue skipper Peter Collins repeated Autrey's feat of beating Mauger in Heat 1 and in doing so set a new track record of 70 seconds flat. Again it proved immaterial as Vikings won 42-36. By May the various knockout cup competitions were also in full swing. Two days after their home leg win in the Four-Team Tournament, Vikings travelled to the Blantyre Greyhound Stadium where they brushed National League Glasgow Tigers aside in the Inter-League competition. Sheffield Tigers were then beaten in the 18-heat British League Knockout Cup, thanks to an unprecedented 11 5-1 wins in the record second leg 81-25 result.

On conclusion of the Four-Team qualifiers, a superb win at Birmingham and a comprehensive defeat of Hackney further reinforced the Vikings' league title credentials. A rare defeat at Ipswich was followed by the hugely popular Yorkshire TV Trophy event. Ivan Mauger became the first man to win the trophy twice and also became 'the first man under 70 seconds at The Boulevard, recording 69.8 seconds in Heat 8 and then equalling the new best time four heats later'. All of which was lost on me despite my being there! Kelly Moran recorded a maximum as Eastbourne were beaten 50-28 before Vikings faced title rivals Coventry in the British League Knockout Cup quarter-finals. In a superb meeting, the Bees held a 12-point lead at the end of the first leg. Deprived of Mitch Shirra and Alan Molyneux for the return the visitors' advantage never looked enough. Indeed, it took Vikings only five heats to pull back the deficit and from then on a place in the semi-finals was assured. Bobby Beaton's win over Ole Olsen was the highlight of a 75-34 victory.

Vikings took their stunning form into the league, although not before Mauger's late arrival and engine failure for both Moran and Owen contributed to a narrow defeat at Reading Racers. On the back of the cup win over Coventry, Belle Vue were demolished 49-29 on their own track and bottom club Leicester Lions were taken apart in a 60-18 rout at The Boulevard. The following night brought a trip to Wimbledon and a meeting that many Vikings fans – and some riders – would come to regard as decisive in the eventual destination of the title. Burford writes, 'For all of Ian Thomas's brilliance with the rule book, he didn't manage to galvanise the rest of the team with the collective responsibility that was required to bring trophies to Hull. Wimbledon had been flying high near the top of the league, so when the Vikings visited Plough Lane for a match on 26 July, the last thing they needed was to take them on while understrength. As the start time approached, Hull took to the track missing Frank Auffret, Bobby Beaton and Graham Drury, who had failed to arrive, and they lost the fixture by five points.'[31]

Hulbert agrees: 'There was no doubt that two points were thrown away at Wimbledon.' The decisive five points came in a race in which Hull could only field Moran after reserve

31 Burford, Brian, *Kelly Moran: A Hell of a Life* (Stroud: History Press, 2014) p.90

Sigalos had run out of rides. When Moran fell, the Dons recorded the required clean sweep. Years later, there is still a bad taste about what went on. In John Chaplin's book each of the riders involved explains his absence, with Drury's being due to his involvement in a fatal traffic accident on the M1. As for Beaton and Auffret, neither man emerges with much credit, given the quotes attributed to them. According to Beaton, 'I don't think we wanted to go. Wimbledon wasn't one of our favourite tracks.' Auffret is somewhat vaguer, 'There were reasons which would probably upset Ivan, so best kept private … as far as the outside world were concerned, Bobby and I were travelling together and broke down on the M1.' To compound matters, a narrow defeat at Cradley Heathens completed a costly three days in the title race.[32]

Wins over Ipswich and Swindon helped repair some of the damage and going into the last third of the season the Vikings trailed Coventry by six points with four meetings in hand. The return to form in the league was carried over into the Inter-League Knockout Cup where, with Poole's Ron Preston standing in for the absent Mauger, Vikings edged past Eastbourne. Victory in the return against Wimbledon maintained the title push until fate intervened once again. Joe Owen broke down on the way to Swindon and although replacement Sigalos racked up 'a magnificent 15-point maximum, Vikings were held to a draw, and the feeling was of another point tossed away'. The August Bank Holiday began with a 62-16 mauling of Poole Pirates in the first of a double header but victory in the return two nights later was denied when the referee found a faulty silencer on Mauger's machine. A four-point win thus became a draw. It was another costly slip.[33]

---

32 Chaplin, John, *Ivan Mauger: The Man Behind the Myth* (Stroud: History Press, 2012) p.61

33 Hulbert, Roger, *Hull Speedway 1930–1981* (Stroud: Tempus, 2004) p.104

There was celebration in the air when Halifax arrived at The Boulevard on 5 September, three nights after the World Championship Final in Katowice. Not only had Ivan Mauger claimed a record sixth title but Kelly Moran, in his first World Championships, finished fourth. Ian Thomas was determined to celebrate the fact. Believing that Hull Vikings were looked upon by the rest of the sport as 'a team from a backstreet town' he was delighted to see them parade the newly crowned champion and 'the world number four who was the hottest prospect in the sport'. Two open-top Rolls-Royce cars were hired to parade the stars before the supporters and both Mauger and Moran were presented with 72-piece gold cutlery sets (worth in the region of £700) 'as a permanent reminder of their achievement and what it meant to the club and its management'. Ironically both men then proceeded to have nights they'd rather forget. Mechanical gremlins plagued Mauger, while Moran – possibly still the worse for wear after his partying in Poland – had to be locked in the changing room after falling off his bike in both his rides! Thankfully, Joe Owen's maximum ensured a 43-34 win as Vikings closed in on the championship. The following night Moran was back, playing his part in a convincing 20-point winning margin at Sheffield and the Tigers were beaten 57-21 in the return the following Wednesday. Vikings were just two points behind Coventry with two fixtures in hand.[34]

The season was reaching its climax with Hull still in the hunt for four trophies to add to their Four-Team success. The Yorkshire Cup was duly logged courtesy of a win over Halifax that went almost unnoticed. Progress in the British League Knockout Cup was maintained when they overturned a 12-point first-leg deficit to beat Exeter in the semi-final. Their

---

34 Burford, Brian, *Kelly Moran: A Hell of a Life* (Stroud: History Press, 2014) p.88

opponents would be Cradley Heath who in the meantime ended Hull's interest in the Inter-Divisional Knockout Cup with a 50-27 semi-final win over a weakened Vikings at Dudley Wood. In the league things couldn't have been tighter. A narrow defeat at Kings Lynn was offset by a similarly nail-biting win at Leicester. Cradley Heath's slim hopes of pipping both Hull and Coventry to the title were ended by defeat at The Boulevard, meaning the Vikings' fate would be sealed by the outcome of three away fixtures. A 'slightly flattering' 45-33 victory at Hackney was backed up by a record 52-26 success at Wolverhampton. Hull Lada Vikings needed just a draw from their trip to Coventry to be crowned British League champions.

A reported paying attendance of 26,500 packed the Brandon Stadium for the winner-takes-all decider. Crucially, not only did the Bees have home advantage, they also didn't have to face Kelly Moran who had suffered a broken collarbone in what Hulbert called 'a meaningless second half-race' the previous week. With Alan Molyneux absent for the Bees, Vikings couldn't promote Tom Owen. When replacement Graeme Stapleton was then stretchered off after Heat 2, it proved too much of a handicap to overcome. According to Hulbert only Mauger and Beaton looked likely race winners for the Vikings and although only two points separated the teams after Heat 7, 'It always looked like Coventry had something in reserve.' The match was lost 42-36. Defeat hit Mauger badly. Ian Thomas recalled, 'Everything was flying in all directions; helmets, steel shoes, race jackets.' Joe Owen describes just how livid the skipper was: 'It was worse because Olsen was Coventry's top man and it was just like rubbing salt in the wound. Ivan came steaming in, he didn't even have a shower that night, took his leathers off, threw them in the bag, put his clothes on and went. He was so mad. If someone had said something he would have torn a strip out of us all. It was lost before Coventry and he knew that. We weren't going to win at Coventry.'[35]

A few days later, in his column for *Speedway Star*, Mauger wrote, 'I'm convinced that had Kelly Moran been fit to ride the Lada Vikings would today be champions.' But he knew the title hadn't been lost at the Brandon. His opinion – like many others – was that the pivotal moment had come at Wimbledon back in July. Nonetheless, the record books show that defeat at Coventry consigned the Vikings to finishing as runners-up, as well as giving the sport the finale the season deserved. A massive contingent had travelled down from Hull, with Easington having filled its own coach. Speedway forum contributor 'Robbo28' recalls 'organising the fleet of coaches' from Hull, while another described the crowd at the Brandon as 'packed like sardines on the terraces'. Ironically, despite it being the biggest occasion in my fledgling speedway-attending career, I sat it out in favour of watching Easington United lose a league cup tie away at Beverley side Longcroft Vets. Yes, really.

The league hangover extended into the Knockout Cup Final first leg two days later. With Moran still injured and Graham Drury crashing out in the opening heat, the Vikings did well to restrict their hosts to a 16-point advantage. The second leg was then controversially abandoned due to the rain-affected track with the Heathens having extended their aggregate lead by another four points. The new date was set for Halloween. Moran bravely returned and contributed eight points as Vikings fought back from a poor start to lead by eight after Heat 11. It didn't last and the Heathens bounced back to take the match 58-50 and the final 120-96. A season of such excitement and one

35 Same as [34] p.90; Not only was Ole Olsen a main rival of Mauger's but in 1976 the 'Great Dane' (then at Wolverhampton) had refused to join Hull having been allocated to them by the Rider Control Committee. He joined Coventry instead. From that moment on he became a villain in the eyes of Vikings supporters.

that had promised so much had ended in bitterly disappointing fashion. I was at The Boulevard to see this one, though perhaps not surprisingly, I remember little about it.

* * *

The summer of 1979 constituted a peak that would never be reached again. Not only for the Vikings who never again came as close to title success at The Boulevard but also for me whose continued attendance over the next two years was more a force of habit than something I actually looked forward to. It just wasn't the same. For a start my infatuation with BK had passed, having merely proved the first of many such fanciful chases at school, which in turn prepared me nicely for the countless knock-backs to follow at Spiders. And secondly, the Vikings were no longer a big draw; in fact the next two years were very forgettable.

One of the few standout nights was Kelly Moran's return to Hull, which saw him in the red and yellow of Birmingham Brummies. It followed something of an acrimonious split from the Vikings, recounted in some detail by both Burford and Hulbert. The Brummies had also had some difficulties in their acquisition of the 'hottest prospect in the sport' and when Moran again rode out under the Boulevard floodlights, it was for a battle between two teams at the wrong end of the division. He was expected to do well on a track he was so familiar with. Instead, his return proved something of a damp squib. Hulbert writes how the home fans 'went wild when John Cook beat the former Vikings favourite in Heat 11'. Moran won just one race all night and his team were thumped 51-27. It was the last time I got to see our former local celebrity in action.[36]

---

36 Hulbert, Roger, *Hull Speedway 1930–1981* (Stroud: Tempus, 2004) p.112

By this time the youth club had stopped running its weekly trips, so I was travelling to speedway with two local brothers Shaun and Chris in a suitably decorated Lada. Vikings' lack of success can probably be gauged by the fact that the night's high spot was usually the stop-off at Marfleet chippy on the way home! The racing remained little more than an entertaining distraction to my midweek sojourn. After two mid-table finishes in 1980 and 1981, the sun finally set on speedway's time at The Boulevard. The last programme in my collection records the visit of eventual champions Cradley Heath in July 1981 for a meeting I watched from the Threepenny Stand. The Vikings at least ended the season on a high with success in the Yorkshire Cup, although even this proved pyrrhic – there was no actual presentation as nobody knew where the trophy was! If that was mildly amusing, no one was laughing when landlords Hull FC terminated the speedway licence at the season's end. They cited breaches of contract, something the Vikings' owners vigorously denied. Rumours were rife that the rugby club no longer needed speedway and wanted them out. They got their way and the city of Hull's latest speedway chapter closed.

* * *

There was one last hurrah for Hull Vikings. In 1995 the club resurfaced across the city at Craven Park, where they raced on a strip laid between the rugby pitch and the greyhound track. Although again competing at Elite League level in 1999, it was in the Premier League where they enjoyed most success, including an unprecedented treble of league title, Knockout Cup and the Craven Shield in 2004. A year later, financial difficulties again forced the club to close its doors. I never felt an urge to go during this latest renaissance as it could never replicate those teenage Boulevard nights. The Easington connection had long gone as had the girl with the perfect pucker and even Marfleet fish shop was reportedly no longer the fryer it once was.

The saddest thing about writing this chapter is that it's clear to me now just how little I actually took in at the time, beyond the general thrill and slight rebelliousness of being out with my mates in town on a school night. As such I never truly appreciated the drama that unravelled in front of my eyes every Wednesday, particularly during that year the Vikings 'lost the league'. More than this, I never grasped what a privilege it was to have been at The Boulevard in 1979. I didn't realise it back then but I had been in the presence of greatness with two of the world's best riders in action together on my doorstep. That combination of Mauger's total professionalism and Moran's often gung-ho brilliance was irresistible and was one I really should have savoured. I bet many of you there at the time did. Sadly, both are no longer with us. The six-time world champion died in April 2018, following a long battle with Alzheimer's and dementia. Moran passed away in 2010 at the age of 49, having finally succumbed to complications of emphysema. His last message from his hospital bed, delivered with typical good humour, ended, 'Don't smoke and don't drink!'

It's a line that will bring a smile to many a resident of Easington.

4

Rugby Town/Football City

Boothferry Park Halt: Saturday, 17 November 1979

We're on the shuttle train about to head back to Paragon Station after seeing City beaten by a Barnsley side that looks set for bigger and better things. The crowded carriage is not the place to be if you're a bloke with three black-and-amber-bedecked youngsters in tow. There aren't many friendly faces around. Although only 13, I can feel cousin John's discomfort as the vast majority of those around us – sporting red-and-white favours and NCB Donkey Jackets – make our short journey into what seems like a long, tortuous experience. I wince as John takes plenty of flak. The inference is that 'watchin' that sharte' is no way to bring up kids. 'Rahnd 'ere, thar should stick to rugbeh.' On the evidence of what I've just watched, it's hard to disagree.

* * *

Between 1978 and 1981, speedway wasn't the only sport vying with a fading football club for the attention – and money – of the Hull public. There was the rugby league 'revival' too. Although both Hull clubs boasted seniority in age over the Tigers, it could be argued that prior to this the oval-ball game's place in the pecking order had always been somewhat overstated. In his book charting what he sees as the fall from grace of 'Old Yorkshire' as a sporting county, Anthony

Clavane's opening chapter uses Hull FC as the yardstick by which the city's sporting rise and fall can be gauged. He labels Hull as 'the plucky, underdog, oval ball city' and describes how in the years following the Second World War, its 'revival was highlighted by [Johnny] Whiteley's black-and-whites'. Moreover, he states that 'football was still seen as the interloper' long after City had been formed and that the Tigers were not only 'in the shadow of both rugby league clubs' but for much of the 20th century they had struggled to 'make inroads into the city's sporting psyche'.[37] I'm not having that.

While there is definitely an argument to suggest that Hull FC (and cross-city rivals Hull KR) enjoyed more success on the field, support-wise it was City who usually held sway. For all their later success, the Airlie Birds never bettered their record attendance of 28,798 set back in 1936 and rugby attendances came nowhere near the figures wooed to Boothferry Park by Raich Carter's Tigers or the team of Waggy and Chillo. Indeed, there is an argument to be made that rugby league moved from Saturday afternoons due to its inability to compete with crowds for football. Even City's fall from grace during the mid-1970s didn't initially see a surge in popularity for Hull or Rovers. Despite their dwindling crowds, the Tigers remained the best-supported show in town. But all that was set to change.

17 November 1979
Football League Third Division:
Hull City 0 Barnsley 2

Boothferry Park: Bunkers Hill Terrace; no ticket; programme 20p

In 1978/79, Hull Kingston Rovers were crowned rugby league's First Division champions and Hull FC created a

37 Clavane, Anthony, *Moving the Goalposts – A Yorkshire Tragedy* (London: Riverrun 2017) pp.17–46

record by winning all 26 matches en route to the Second Division title. Crowds at both Craven Park and, particularly, The Boulevard rose accordingly. The Airlie Birds were soon flying in front of five-figure gates with the Robins hovering not far below. It was the start of a period of unparalleled success for both clubs, one that would lead to use of the term 'rugby town' to describe Hull whenever sport was discussed. Never more so than on one particular day in May 1980 – but I'll get to that later.

The Tigers also had reason to cheer at the end of the 1978/79 campaign. Unlike prime minister 'Sunny Jim' Callaghan, Ken Houghton's side emerged unscathed from a 'Winter of Discontent' and prospered in the spring. A run of 11 games without defeat – their best in a decade – staved off fears of relegation and secured a final placing of eighth. It would stand up well against what was to follow. Despite a summer of cautious optimism – fuelled by more talk of ground redevelopment and an influx of new players, including then-record signing Mick Tait for £150,000 – the Tigers were already embroiled in another struggle against the drop by the time of my next visit to Boothferry Park. My chaperone was again my cousin John, sidelined by injury for Easington's match at Gilberdyke that same day and therefore opting instead to take his sons and nephew to see City. It proved to be another character-building exercise.

This game constitutes the start of my Hull City programme collection, although it's a slightly spoilt one given the adornment of some fake players' 'autographs' as well as incorrect scores on the centre pages. I blame Karl, aged seven. The cover photo was taken at the opening home game against Colchester and showed City in their new 'mash-up' kit, comprising the Europa Sports shirts of recent years (a replica of which would be in the young Richard's Christmas stocking) with Adidas shorts and socks. Yes, I know, even back then I needed to get out more.

The Tykes were on a roll under the management of Allan Clarke, or 'Billy Casper in a suit' as Clavane dubs him. The hero of Leeds's 1972 FA Cup Final victory had 'transformed Oakwell'. Promoted from the Fourth Division at the first attempt, Barnsley would be in the Second Division within another year. By contrast the Tigers were experiencing what Ken Houghton labelled an 'unfortunate sticky period' of no win in six games. In his programme notes, he said his players had 'responded exceptionally well' to the previous week's 3-0 loss at Reading, adding, 'They know what I require from them.' He described that week's 'practice match' as having been 'a joy to watch'. The real match that followed certainly wasn't. A much-changed City side got off to the worst possible start when future Republic of Ireland manager Mick McCarthy headed home Graham Pugh's corner in the very first minute. Houghton later called it 'a real kick in the teeth'. He then described the 'hoodoo' that 'struck again' at the start of the second half when Ronnie Glavin's right-wing cross was spectacularly headed into his own net by the unfortunate Derek Hood. Having witnessed it from his usual seat in the Best Stand, my mate Gary still maintains that it's the best own goal he's ever seen at Boothferry. I can't even remember it, which perhaps tells you how traumatic that post-match train ride must've been![38]

Houghton felt the result was harsh on City, highlighting how busy Barnsley keeper Peter Springett (brother of England international Ron) had been in comparison to City's Eddie Blackburn (rated by many City fans as one of best understudy

38 Clavane, Anthony, *Moving the Goalposts – A Yorkshire Tragedy* (London: Riverrun 2016) pp.153–157; Match programme (Hull City v Barnsley, 17 November 1979)

goalkeepers in the league). None of this will have been of concern to a sizeable away following, which helped comprise Boothferry Park's fourth-highest gate of the season, 8,327. They went home happy but not before several of them had enjoyed a good chortle at our expense.

* * *

A fortnight later, following a disappointing FA Cup replay exit at the hands of Carlisle, fewer than 4,000 spectators saw Dave Hawker's goal earn City a home point against Wimbledon. The 'unfortunate sticky period' now extended to eight games. It eventually stretched to 15, the club's worst run of results in 44 years and one that cost Houghton his job following a shocking 7-2 defeat at Brentford. Replacement Mike Smith arrived in December on the back of having led Wales to the European Championship quarter-finals. His first game saw City stuffed 5-1 at Portsmouth.

Sweeping changes in personnel followed and the new boss improved the Tigers' home form enough to give them a chance of survival. A win over fellow strugglers Southend in the penultimate game on 3 May 1980 would save City at the expense of their opponents. In the event it was Keith Edwards's 19th league goal of the season that settled a very tense occasion in the Tigers' favour. The *Hull Daily Mail* described the 'amazing scenes' at the final whistle. 'Hundreds of young fans raced to the directors' box cheering and waving scarves and banners,' wrote the newspaper, and when Mike Smith and his players reappeared, 'they were greeted with ecstatic applause' from the majority of the 3,297 crowd. Despite being bolstered by the handout of free tickets to local schools, it was barely a tenth of the number that had been in the same ground 14 years earlier to see the same result against the same opponents help City clinch the Third Division title. Yet the *Hull Daily Mail*'s David Bond described the attendance as 'amazing in itself'. In future years, to have been a City supporter at Boothferry that day became a badge of honour to be worn with pride. The reason why could be found 200 miles to the south.

3 May 1980
Rugby League Challenge Cup Final:
Hull KR 10 Hull FC 5

Wembley Stadium: Upper West Terrace; ticket £2.50 (lost); programme 60p

My attendance at the 1980 Challenge Cup Final is up there with that childhood support of Dirty Leeds as the largest skeleton in my sporting cupboard. Not so much on account of forsaking the Tigers in their hour of need – I was barely averaging one City game a season as it was – but more for my chosen allegiance at Wembley. Although ostensibly travelling as a rugby league tourist, I chose black-and-white over red-and-white.

My reasons were twofold. Firstly, and rather naively, I believed that the Airlie Birds' close proximity to Boothferry Park made them the obvious choice for any City fan. Secondly, my brother adopted Rovers for the day, which meant I simply had to do the opposite! As someone who for the past 30 years has been a regular follower of the Robins, the guilt of being at their finest hour but unable to savour the result is another stick with which to beat myself.

Prior to Wembley, my experience of 'rrrrrragby leeeega' had been confined to the telly and the distinctive tones of Eddie Waring. For five decades the voice of the sport, Waring was part of a golden stable of BBC sports commentators of the era. Clavane isn't wrong when he says he was 'better known than any football, let alone rugby league, presenter is today'. Phrases such as 'up and under', 'he's goin' for an early bath' and my personal favourite, 'I don't know whether that's his head or the ball but we'll soon know if he gets up' helped illuminate what often looked to me like glorified mud wrestling. Waring added colour where previously there had been only *This Sporting Life* greyscale.

Not everyone shared this view. As Clavane observes, Waring's 'jocular persona … tended to wind up over earnest northern fundamentalists'. He was resented by many rugby league followers who accused him of turning their game into 'music hall comedy'. It was an image not helped by his other appearances on prime-time telly, either as the co-host of *It's a Knockout!* or as the subject of one of Mike Yarwood's Saturday night impersonations. A petition of 12,000 signatures implored the BBC to replace him. The Beeb stood firm. And so when – for the first time in the competition's history – both Hull clubs made it to Wembley for the biggest date in the rugby league calendar, Eddie Waring was at the microphone. However, this time I wouldn't need him to tell me what was going on.[39]

* * *

Hull Kingston Rovers were in search of their first Challenge Cup. Their previous three finals had ended in defeat, including their only other Wembley trip – a 13-5 loss at the hands of Widnes in 1964. Having clinched their third league championship the previous season, they had finished a disappointing seventh this time round. I knew little of this at the time, nor was I aware of the injury concerns over influential second-row 'forrad' Phil Lowe. But like most local

39 *This Sporting Life* (1963) film, based on David Storey's 1960 novel set against the backdrop of rugby league; Clavane, Anthony, *Moving the Goalposts – A Yorkshire Tragedy* (London: Riverrun 2017) pp.20–21

kids, I'd heard of Roger Millward and Clive Sullivan. By the end of the Challenge Cup Final, I'd be familiar with a certain Steve Hubbard as well.

Hull FC's appearance at Wembley was the culmination of a meteoric rise for a club relegated at the end of the 1977/78 season. They had stormed back, winning all their league games and rattling up 702 points in the process, 243 more than runners-up Hunslet. The 1980 final was their ninth, three of which had come beneath the Twin Towers where they were yet to win. In fact their overall record in the showpiece occasion was an unenviable one; their only previous success having come in 1914 when a try by Jack Harrison, later to win a posthumous VC at Oppy Wood in the First World War, helped beat Wakefield 6-0 at Halifax.

The common consensus was that FC were favourites. They had finished above their rivals in the league and had accounted for them in the final of the BBC Floodlit Trophy (though Rovers had enjoyed the better of things in the league meetings including a win at Craven Park just prior to Wembley). Hull also boasted ace goal-kicker Sammy Lloyd. In the promotion season Lloyd had been successful with 172 kicks, making him the top points scorer in both divisions. His overall tally for the season was an amazing 369, a figure that included a drop goal and ten tries. He also became the first player to score more than 1,000 points in the First Division and had kicked Hull to their semi-final win over Widnes. A large 'Sammy's Golden Boot' banner left no doubt as to whom most Hull fans saw as their prized asset at Wembley.

Interest in the game had been at fever pitch ever since FC had beaten the Chemics at Swinton to ensure an all-Hull final (Rovers having cruised past Halifax the previous weekend). The May Day holiday was suddenly etched large in most calendars on Humberside and it appeared that everybody wanted tickets. Dad managed to procure three. The next few weeks saw banter levels ratcheted up among pupils at Withernsea High. Despite our location as far to the east of the River Hull as is possible, black-and-white was the predominant combination in the run-up to Wembley. Connoisseurs of the game could claim this was due to the fact that Hull FC had started life east of the river, while Kingston Amateurs (Rovers' forerunners) were formed by a group of boilermakers in the Hessle Road area of west Hull. But I doubt many of my fellow pupils were aware of this. I wasn't. Instead the predominance of FC favours was because most people perceived them to be the more 'glamorous' club.

I had mates in both camps although my closest were Rovers fans. Gary and Darren were regulars at Craven Park and Darren's dad was the Robins' assistant coach. They tolerated people like me suddenly developing a new-found interest in the sport and even getting tickets for the final. But I could sense their resentment when it came to any pretence of being a supporter. Little wonder then that when I turned up at school on the eve of the big game with a brand-new black-and-white scarf bought for the occasion, they weren't best pleased. Mild irritation turned to outright animosity. 'You don't even like rugby!' 'How many games you been to?' 'Who's your favourite player?' 'Name 'em, go on, name any of 'em.' I couldn't. Well, apart from Sammy Lloyd. And 'Knocker' Norton. I was guilty as charged. I was as plastic as plastic could be. My only defence was that I wasn't alone in jumping on this particular bandwagon. Today it would be called 'Whataboutery' of the highest order.

Having dozens like me prompted a change of mood at school as the game got nearer. As the number of new scarves on both sides increased, break times began to see charges across the playing fields involving 'fans' of both clubs.

These gatherings weren't always good-natured; blood was occasionally spilt and detentions were served. Such was the 'cup fever' that it was almost impossible not to come down on one side or the other. I've not seen anything like it before or since and I'm not sure the city of Hull and surrounding area ever will again. There appeared to be very few disinterested observers, even among the girls. The only group of lads who remained steadfast in the face of such hysteria was the small but hardy band of Tigers followers who began to appear as endangered as the animal they represented.

* * *

Similar to football's premier knockout competition, the Rugby League Challenge Cup Final is no longer the centrepiece of the season, now playing second fiddle to Super League's Grand Final. But back then 'Wembley Weekend' was the highlight of the sporting *and* social calendar for rugby league supporters across the north. Almost half the crowd inside Wembley would have bought tickets well in advance of the date. Vince Groak states that 'each year, up to 6,000 travelled down from Hull no matter who was playing'. The Spread Eagle pub in Withernsea was typical of many establishments whose annual trip had many unfortunate souls on the waiting list, just hoping for a vacancy to emerge between the sounding of the final hooter at one final and the teams lining up for the next.[40]

Perhaps not surprisingly, the 1980 final sold out in record time. An estimated 60,000 fans – almost a quarter of Hull's population – created a unique exodus. Clavane writes, 'The whole city, it appeared, had migrated en masse to London, briefly taking possession of a self-regarding capital believed, by its transient occupiers, to be living off the honest toil of the

40 Groak, Vince, *Last One Out … When Hull Invaded Wembley* (Leeds: Scratching Shed, 2017) p.136

downtrodden north.' Twelve 'special' trains ran from Paragon Station on the Saturday, along with three on the Friday and eight charter trains. The number of coaches must have run into the hundreds. Dad booked us on to one of the numerous ones organised by local man Simon Gray, who at that time was a complete stranger to me but whose choice of carrier – Easington's Connor & Graham Ltd – meant door-to-door service. With no affiliation to either team, Simon's coaches contained a mixture of Hull and Rovers fans, as indeed did many making their way to Wembley that day. There we were, a family with divided 'loyalties' (I use the word lightly) on a coach full of families with divided loyalties driving along a motorway full of cars, vans and coaches that also included families with divided loyalties. The atmosphere all the way down was fantastic, there was a real sense of anticipation and both sets of supporters seemed convinced that victory would be theirs.[41]

Inside the stadium, although we were in the end nominally reserved for Rovers supporters, it soon became apparent that there were plenty of black-and-white favours to be found too. But as Clavane writes, if looked at from above the stadium, Wembley 'would have resembled a giant comfort blanket of red, black-and-white'. Prior to the game the crowd were 'entertained' by *It Ain't Half Hot Mum*'s Windsor Davies and Melvyn Hayes who led the community singing, backed by the Band of the Welsh Guards and culminating in 'Abide with Me'. For those like Mum watching back at home, BBC broadcast *Grandstand* live from Wembley. Just before kick-off, Frank Bough handed over to that man Waring who, according to Clavane, provided 'a suitably wistful commentary' as the teams came out on to the hallowed turf, 'Lamenting the passing of a once great

41 Clavane, Anthony, *Moving the Goalposts – A Yorkshire Tragedy* (London: Riverrun 2017) pp.19–20

maritime port, he invoked the "sailing ships of days gone by" and compared the teams walking out of the Wembley tunnel to "two ships coming into the port of Hull".'[42]

Having Phil and me line up on opposite sides of the divide left Dad in something of a quandary: which son should he upset? His decision was made after just seven minutes when Brian Lockwood's set-piece pass sent Hubbard racing in from 40 yards for what proved to be the game's decisive try. As the move unfolded, a very attractive young lady began to climb all over Dad in increasing anticipation. Not one to look a gift horse in the mouth, he grabbed hold of his new-found acquaintance and they reached the climactic moment together. I'd rarely seen such a big smile on his face, certainly not at any sporting event. I later noted that he failed to mention that bit to Mum when she asked if we'd all had a good time.

Hubbard missed the conversion but added a couple of penalties as Rovers established a 7-0 lead in a scrappy game that saw both sides adopt an aggressive approach. Millward copped a high shot from Ronnie Wileman that broke his jaw – the third such injury he'd suffered in a year. Tim Wilby went over for Hull but, crucially, Lloyd missed the kick. Millward dropped a goal and Rovers led 8-3 at the break. Lloyd kicked FC back into range at 8-5 on 51 minutes but despite relentless pressure, they failed to add to their tally. Sammy's boot proved anything but golden, converting just once in five attempts. At the other end Hubbard landed nine points on the day, his final penalty five minutes from time confirming a 10-5 win. Despite his injury, Millward managed a beaming smile as the Queen Mother presented him with the trophy. 'That has obviously got to be the highlight of my 25 years with Rovers,'

---

42 Same as [41]

he said later, 'not only the game but also all the camaraderie of the rival sets of fans.'

At the final hooter, I felt no need to cry and I remained detached from the contrasting emotions on display all around me. When a disconsolate Hull fan thrust his flag in my direction, saying, 'Take that and ram it up Sammy Lloyd's arse,' I acquiesced to the first part of his request, thinking how it would provide a fine souvenir of my day out. Similarly, on the way home I was far more concerned with other people's personal experiences than determining just where 'my' team had gone wrong on the day. It was almost as if defeat didn't matter – which in truth it didn't. Rovers had just beaten their biggest rivals on the biggest stage in front of the biggest TV audience, yet I really couldn't give a toss. I was a day-tripper gatecrashing the diehards' biggest day. I'm certain I wasn't the only one. I was young. I would learn.

I've since read accounts of the magnificent reception afforded Hull FC and in particular Sammy Lloyd on their return to The Boulevard the following day. I've often wondered whether my 'flag man' was there, singing his praises of the big man. I wasn't. My rugby league days were over for now. But while my choice of team that day still rankles, being at Wembley gradually became easier to accept. Any guilt about City would be more than atoned for over time. As the prospect of another all-Hull Wembley final becomes ever more remote, that day in May 1980 really does feel like a once-in-a-lifetime occasion.

* * *

Wembley ushered in a new era of success for both rugby clubs. Following their win, Rovers lifted the Premiership Trophy in 1981 (again beating Hull in the final) and were crowned league champions in 1984 and 1985, the first of which was combined with the Premiership in a historic 'double'. Further success came via the John Player Trophy, Yorkshire Cup and the BBC Floodlit Trophy. For their part Hull FC completed a 1982 double of their own, winning the Challenge Cup and the John Player Trophy. They were crowned champions in 1983 and also won a hat-trick of Yorkshire Cups between 1983 and 1985. Such success fostered a brooding resentment among some City supporters that lasts to this day.

It wasn't just the silverware accrued by the two clubs but also the arrogance displayed by some of their followers, particularly fans of City's west Hull neighbours. Gary Clark describes how Hull FC fans were invited to the Brentford game at Boothferry Park in April 1980 as part of an official Wembley 'send-off', 'A couple of hundred turned up, stood together in the North Stand and supported Brentford!' Over the next few years I found very few City fans with a good word to say about rugby league in general and Hull FC in particular. And every time such comments were aired, my mate Gary would give me one of those knowing looks that highlighted the previous error of my ways. Thankfully, I was still young enough to put things right. Consigning rugby league to the bin (for now), I was determined to throw myself fully behind City.[43]

28 July 1980
Anglo-Scottish Cup Group One:
Hull City 1 Grimsby Town 0

Boothferry Park: West Stand; no ticket; programme 30p

If you're going to make a new start then do so at the beginning. And so, with the cricket season in full swing (the previous day I'd been at The Circle to watch Yorkshire) I accompanied

43 Clark, Gary, *From Boothferry to Wembley* (Hull: Riverhead, 2008) p.34

Gary and his dad to Boothferry Park for the first pre-season fixture. For the first time I sat in the Best Stand. George Kerr's resurgent Grimsby were the visitors in the Anglo-Scottish Cup, one of those long-lost competitions devised to 'spice up' pre-season. Although Brian Clough credited success in the 1977 tournament as giving his players a taste for glory, most top-flight English clubs treated it with thinly disguised disdain. It's last hurrah came in 1980, meaning it had outlasted its predecessor – the Texaco Cup – by just a year.

City and Grimsby were in a group with Sheffield United and eventual winners Chesterfield. Eight Second Division clubs, seven from the Third Division and Bury from the bottom tier comprised the English entry, with the four group winners going through to meet the winners of the four Scottish quarter-finals over two legs. With the likes of Rangers, Hearts and Kilmarnock among the Scottish clubs involved, there was a potential for some proper giantkillings. It was this that ensured the game at least carried some semblance of importance. Pictured on the front of a 20-page match programme, manager Mike Smith, chairman Bob Chapman, commercial manager Gordon Dimbleby and club secretary Mac Stone all wore broad smiles and oozed optimism. Smith had released 16 players and brought in five, a figure that included Nick Deacy, Dale Roberts and most notably goalkeeper Tony Norman. The centre pages displayed a picture of 'the men who carry Hull City's hopes for 1980/81', resplendent in a classy new Adidas playing strip, which remains another of my all-time favourites.

The previous season's league fixture had attracted 14,000 to Boothferry Park. Although some way short of that number, there was a good crowd of 5,056 present to see Deacy's 31st-minute header settle things for City. It was the Welshman's first goal at home and only his second since joining the club in

February (ironically, his first had also come against Grimsby in the league the previous season). *Hull Daily Mail* match reporter Simon Redfern said City fully deserved their win over the Third Division champions, one that gave them 'the perfect start to their 1980/81 season and the Anglo-Scottish Cup group programme'. It was enough to prompt me to state an intention to see every home game that season. That lasted about as long as City's new-found confidence. The Tigers exited the competition following defeat at Sheffield United and a draw with Chesterfield. The Spireites went on to edge out Notts County in the last final.

* * *

Another cup exit was soon forthcoming, courtesy of an emphatic loss to Lincoln in the League Cup. I was there for the 2-0 home defeat which completed a 7-0 aggregate win for the Imps but have long since erased it from memory. For one supporter, however, City's start prompted him to pen a letter to the match programme. Gavin Bennett requested that some form of 'special voucher' be introduced for the 'loyal supporters' among the 'paltry' 2,933 at the Lincoln game, as a reward to be used 'when the Tigers do get into the First Division pulling capacity crowds'. Worryingly, in his reply the editor stated that 'in fact 16,000 are required each home game to stabilise the boat'!

Eleven home games came and went before I passed through the turnstiles again, during which City managed just one win in 17 league matches. By the time of my visit, for the FA Cup first-round tie against Fourth Division Halifax Town on 22 November, they'd trebled that figure but even so Smith still appeared no nearer to sorting out his team's problems. Former England under-21 defender Paul Haigh was sold to Carlisle, to be followed out the door before Christmas by the popular Gordon Nisbet. Making these departures worse for supporters was the calibre of the players Smith brought in to replace them. As David Goodman writes, 'The likes of Billy Whitehurst, Brian Ferguson, Steve Hoolickin and Stuart Eccleston appeared to be worse than the players leaving.' As such – and despite victory over Millwall the previous week – the mood among the Boothferry faithful at kick-off wasn't great. Halifax had famously dumped Manchester City out of the FA Cup the previous season and many regarded them as favourites.[44]

In yet another change of matchday companion I went with Al, four years older than me and the only other would-be rockabilly in the village (more of which later). We spent the morning shopping – or rather, in my case, watching Al shop – for records. His purchases duly secured in a station locker, we boarded the train for Boothferry Halt. Being a time when the FA Cup still captured the imagination, the 4,024 attendance that day was higher than for any of the previous five home league games. It included a sizeable visiting contingent in the Kempton, segregated by police from City fans intent on claiming the stand for themselves. Al and I opted for Bunkers, where we stood low down behind the goal, me in full 'Christmas tree' mode of City scarf and one of those awful-but-all-the-rage eight-panel caps (which were orange rather than amber) and Al slightly more dapper in his 'trendy' ex-Italian army parka. From there we cheered a brace from 'King' Edwards that helped eke out a nervy 2-1 win.

The draw for the second round brought non-league giantkillers Blyth Spartans to Hull for what turned into an epic tie. The Colliers boasted several England non-league

44 Goodman, David, *Look Back in Amber* (Manchester: Parrs Wood Press, 2005) p.63

internationals and were in good form, unbeaten in their last seven matches in which they had scored 25 goals. They fancied an upset and according to striker Les Mutrie they should have caused one. 'Blyth should have won every one of those games,' he told Richard Gardham years later in *The Decade.* They certainly dominated play at Boothferry Park, where 6,050 spectators watched a pulsating clash. Edwards fired City ahead after just nine minutes but Blyth battled back and Alan Barker and Tony Boylan both hit the woodwork. At the other end, Stuart Croft and Nick Deacy hit the bar as City sought a second. Instead, just ten minutes from time, Mutrie swept home an equaliser. The Tigers – without a win in 34 games on the road – faced a tricky Tuesday trip to the north-east for the replay.[45]

It proved to be another cracker, described on the Blyth Spirit blog as 'one of Croft Park's all-time great games'. A crowd of 5,870 saw Mutrie give Blyth the lead with 'a superb solo goal'. This was cancelled out by Craig Norrie's stooping header only for Ray Young to restore the hosts' advantage before the break, courtesy of 'a stunning strike' from 18 yards out. Again both teams struck the woodwork and Spartans held on to their lead until five minutes from time 'when Edwards beat Tommy Dixon to a long ball down field to fire home an equaliser'. The drama continued in extra time when Tony Norman brilliantly saved a Mutrie penalty before reacting well to keep out Paul Ross's follow-up. Mutrie suffered further disappointment two minutes later when his potential winning goal was ruled offside. The teams would have to do it all for a third time. I would be there to see it.

---

45 Gardham, Richard, *The Decade: Ten Years that Transformed Hull City AFC* (Self-published, 2019) p.36

22 December 1980
FA Cup Second Round Second Replay: Hull City 2 Blyth Spartans 1

Elland Road: Gelderd End Kop; no ticket; programme 20p

The neutral ground selected for the second replay was Elland Road. It constitutes my first City road trip, an early Christmas present of sorts (on Dad's birthday) and one that 'Cottingham Tiger' recalls as going down in supporters' folklore. This was on account of the 'infamous British Rail football special with its unofficial stop and pick-up at Hessle Road flyover', along with 'the scenes at the final whistle and on the motorway as we all celebrated a small piece of overdue success'.[46]

The train carrying City supporters to Leeds arrived late, prompting 'the tie to be held up 11 minutes', according to *Daily Mirror* reporter Colin Diball. Fanzine contributor 'Bladerunner' remembers it having 'Echoes of *Von Ryan's Express*', 'This hi-tech marvel travelled at walking pace as far as Hessle Road flyover before conking out leaving 14 crowded carriages of Tigers followers somewhat disappointed. Memorable scenes ensued, including passengers walking the length of the train along the tops of the carriages to "discuss" the situation with the driver, and a large influx of non-paying passengers from a Hessle Road hostelry. The Leeds police wisely decided to delay kick-off to accommodate the arrival of spectators from this train.'[47]

Along with Al, I travelled door-to-door courtesy of Simon Gray's coach out of Easington. Simon remains something of a cult figure among a generation of supporters, due partly to his trademark red-and-white jacket but mainly for his insatiable appetite for organising away match travel, often regardless of

46 *Tiger Rag* fanzine (Issue 3, February 1994)

47 *Look Back in Amber* fanzine (Issue 1, September 1992)

demand. As a non-driver, the operation that first began with a coach to a 3-0 defeat at Blackpool in 1978 has enabled him to follow his team almost anywhere ever since. Given that these coaches weren't always even half-full (reportedly the fewest ever was 13 passengers to a Friday night game at Aldershot in 1982) it's impossible to say just how much this must have cost him over the years. I'd heard tales of these trips from Jim, one of the brothers from the Fulham game. Being a tad more streetwise than me, he'd already done a handful of 'aways' across the past two seasons to Walsall, Carlisle, Colchester, Peterborough, and 'Bloody Rubbish Mansfield'. These tales, which often involved the antics of those on the accompanying 'City Psychos' bus, filled me with a mixture of dread and excitement – a feeling I'd come to experience regularly over the next few years.

Simon's coach to Leeds was full and everyone was in good spirits as we arrived at Elland Road. That is everyone except Simon, whose walk across the coach park was interrupted by someone I later assumed was probably 'Mad Eddie', referred to in Shaun Tordoff's hooli-lit offering as bus driver for the aforementioned 'Psychos'. Not in the mood for niceties, he proceeded to accuse Simon of having shopped him to the police for allegedly drink-driving to the first replay on Tyneside. The nearby presence of the local constabulary ensured that it amounted to nothing more than a vocal assault but even so it was some introduction to away games – and these two were supposed to be on the same side! Suffice to say that for Simon, the episode took the gloss off what proved a rare City away win.[48]

Inside the ground it was something of a surreal experience. For a start only the Gelderd End was open, segregated between

---

48 Tordoff, Shaun, *City Psychos: From the Monte Carlo Mob to the Silver Cod Squad* (London: Milo, 2002) pp.129–142

the two sets of supporters in a crowd of just under 6,000. Here I was stood on the Kop end of my boyhood heroes with over 3,000 Hull City supporters for a game against a bunch of Geordie part-timers in a stadium that was far too big for the occasion. But it was a fantastic experience, a 'BLYTH CUP CRACKER' as headlined in the following day's *Daily Star*. Leading up to the game, City fans had hoped that their nemesis Mutrie wouldn't be available due to a long-standing hospital appointment. Instead he again played his part in a humdinger.

It was past the hour-mark when Norrie exchanged passes with Steve McClaren before firing City into a lead they held until just four minutes from time, when Blyth were again awarded a penalty for McNeil's foul on Johnson. Up stepped Mutrie again only to hit the ball wide. Fortunately for him, the referee deemed that Norman had moved and ordered a retake. This time the striker made no mistake and the game went to extra time. Therein the teams again couldn't be separated until McClaren crossed for Stuart Croft to head the winner just six minutes from time. 'CROFT HEADS TIE-BREAKER' boomed the *Hull Daily Mail*, the Tigers marched on, Blyth returned home with reputation enhanced and Smith, in perhaps his best decision as manager, immediately signed Mutrie for £30,000.

The Tigers' reward was a home third-round tie with Yorkshire rivals Doncaster Rovers, managed by Billy Bremner. It drew the only five-figure gate of the season to Boothferry Park, which again included Easington's only two rockabillies. City struggled for much of the game but won it with the only goal; a Nick Deacy header ensuring my season ended the way it had begun. The somewhat fortuitous win earned a glamorous away tie at Tottenham Hotspur. I wouldn't be going to that one. Several thousand did, braving missiles, violence and late, late heartache on an afternoon that still regularly gets talked about. Despite coming into the tie on the back of more woeful league form, City came close to creating a real upset. In the *Sunday Mirror*, Ken Montgomery wrote, 'Hull's gallant little fishing fleet had their 2000/1 Cup hopes scuppered by super sub Gary Brooke.' The '19-year-old East Ender', on for the 'tiring' Ossie Ardiles, met a Steve Archibald pass 'to torpedo' an 83rd-minute goal past Norman before starting the move from which Archibald added a second. Two goals inside the last eight minutes had decided matters, just as 'Spurs were spluttering to a midweek replay'. They would go on to win the FA Cup that year. City's season would take a rather less glamorous route.

* * *

Defeat at White Hart Lane ended what had been a welcome relief from the woes of the league. Although their gutsy performance initially prompted back-to-back victories (at Exeter and at home to Blackpool) a sequence of 11 games without a win ended all hopes of survival. In the spring of 1981 'Mike Smith's Super Black-and-Amber Army' slipped ignominiously into the bottom tier of English league football for the first time. There were acrimonious scenes along the way: protests from the newly formed Hull City Action Group, Deacy giving 'a double V-sign to the Kempton when substituted against Blackpool' and 'King' Edwards throwing his shirt at his manager in disgust after being substituted against Brentford. It was a reaction the player later admitted was 'immature' but one that at the time prompted the *Hull Daily Mail*'s Simon Redfern to suggest that the 'unsettled' striker 'may never play for the Tigers again'.

Club legend Raich Carter dubbed them 'the worst Hull side I have ever seen, apart from the lad, Edwards'. Heavy defeats at Chester, Newport, Barnsley and Huddersfield supported his view and six games from the end of the season relegation was confirmed via a midweek goalless draw with Swindon, watched by a record low attendance of 2,789. Many of those hadn't stayed to the end. Malcolm Richardson reported in the following night's *Hull Daily Mail*, 'Flag-waving members of the [Hull City Action] group appeared at the four corners of the ground as signal for disillusioned fans to leave the stadium.' These fans then assembled – somewhat ironically – in the social club underneath the North Stand for a meeting that attracted exposure on the back page of the following night's local paper. It was the start of a sustained campaign to 'bring to the nation's attention that Hull City AFC was dying on its feet'.[49]

In somewhat #TypicalCity fashion, the Tigers responded by then taking three points out of four against the top two. They beat Huddersfield 2-1 at home on Easter Saturday before drawing at Rotherham on the Bank Holiday. In his report of the first of these matches for the following Tuesday's *Huddersfield Daily Examiner* Paul Clark described how the visitors had 'produced their worst display of the season … against the worst team in the Third Division … and lost!' He added, 'Hull City, to whom defeat has become a way of life, somehow contrived to win.'

I wasn't at the game but I remember it for events later that evening. With the local caravan sites having opened for business, some of the 'Comforts' had tied in a weekend at the seaside with the football at Boothferry Park. As a group of inebriated Town fans made their way home from the village

---

49 Clark, Gary, *From Boothferry to Wembley* (Hull: Riverhead, 2008) p.37; Edwards, Keith (with Andy Pack), *Edwards … One-Nil!: The Keith Edwards Story* (see Sources) p.97; Clark, Gary, *From Boothferry to Wembley* (Hull: Riverhead, 2008) p.38

pubs and passed our new abode on Seaside Road, they entered into the full repertoire of Terriers songs. Opening my bedroom window to its fullest extent, I gave them a short, sharp blast of 'The Ti-gers' to send them on their way before quickly ducking my head back inside before they could work out from which house it came. Luckily, Mum and Dad had the telly on that loud downstairs they didn't hear any of it and this particular 15-year-old was left in hysterics at the absurdity of his actions.[50]

City and Blackpool finished seven points adrift at the bottom. With typical gallows humour, fans could claim they had gone down in style. Some weeks later, long after relegation had been confirmed and two days after a 22nd defeat of the season (away at Reading), the Tigers were due to entertain Grimsby in a match arranged to celebrate the long-awaited opening of the Humber Bridge. Paul Brooks recounts the tale of how ahead of the date, commercial manager Gordon Dimbleby asked Martin Tyler of Yorkshire TV if the occasion would be televised. He was told not, as the camera was needed that day to film an episode of *Emmerdale Farm*. Even a 'sleepy soap' now took priority over the toothless Tigers.[51]

---

50 Match report, *Huddersfield Daily Examiner* (Tuesday, 21 April 1981)

51 *Tiger Rag* fanzine (Issue 10, March 1996)

5

Rock This Town

HMV, Whitefriargate: Early 1982

I'm flicking through the LPs in the 'Rock 'n' roll/Rockabilly' section. I come to The Gene Vincent Singles Album, *a retrospective compilation on Capitol Records. As I stand browsing the cover, thinking how fucking cool I look and how much I almost resemble one of the late singer's backing band The Bluecaps, I'm suddenly aware I'm not alone. They're either side of me. From the calf-length DMs, bleached jeans and green MA1 flying jackets that have appeared in my peripheral vision, I know they're skinheads. I feel a sudden tightening of my arse muscles. Then one of them speaks. 'I wonder what Gene Vincent's doing today?' His mate laughs. There's a pregnant pause in which they await my response. None is forthcoming except for a wry smile as I continue to study the sleeve notes, even though I'm by now reading the same sentence over and over without actually taking in what it says. After what appears an age, both of my would-be tormentors move off to annoy another unsuspecting punter out looking for his vinyl fix. I heave a sigh of relief and, after discreetly checking the coast is clear, I head out the door and across town to Syd Scarbs.*

* * *

The look adopted by many football fans in the late 1970s and early 1980s is one of the most distinctive there has been. It was the period in which 'casual' came to the fore, with lads dressing to impress for an afternoon at the match. As part of my coming-of-age period it may well have offered me a real chance to get assimilated with the self-styled 'elite' among City's support. But that would've been far too easy. Instead, I opted for a style that would make me even more conspicuous than my 'hick from the sticks' appearance already did. Hence, while cool kids across the north wore the clothes later replicated by Elvis and Carty in *Awaydays*, and Londoners followed a path charted by *Faded Lois Dreams* hero Rich, I was rocking a niche look that stood out for all the wrong reasons.[52]

My musical tastes were honed at secondary school. The period 1978–1984 was what Simon Reynolds later chronicled superbly as the post-punk era. I didn't fully appreciate how lucky I was to be a teenager at this time. It's only when setting the sheer eclecticism of sounds against the blandness of much that followed that you see just how exciting it all was. Even Withernsea High presented a microcosm of it all. There was Tomesy, the fifth-form Ted from my first year, and Sue B, the first punk in my class (later to be credited on the debut release by Hull band Les Zeiga Fleurs). There was the sixth-form mod collective, getting down en masse front-of-stage as a band called the Internationals belted out 'Geno' at the 1982 Christmas disco. The Keyingham contingent of 2-Tone kids, complete with newly cropped heads and Harrington jackets and, by way of contrast, the local grebs who extolled the virtues of Saxon while dreaming of their own wheels of steel.

Individually, high school 'muso' Nibs (RIP) provided an education all of his own thanks to an almost Reynolds-like knowledge of post-punk while Toddy, the first Danny Zuko-

52 *Awaydays* is Kevin Sampson's 1998 book about Tranmere Rovers hooligans, made into a film in 2009; *Faded Lois Dreams* is Andrew Vaughan's 2014 book set in London in the mid-1980s

style 'grease-back' in my year, provided all the encouragement I needed for my own eventual choice. And of course there was the graffiti that adorned the books, the desks and even the classroom walls, providing an A-Z of rock and pop from AC/DC to Ziggy Stardust. It was a wonderful curriculum and I learned fast. By the time I left school it wasn't just with a clutch of A- and O-levels but also as one of very few Hull City season pass holders sporting a flat-top and a passion for rockabilly.

Yet prior to arrival in Form 1EJ, music came some way down a list that peaked with classic war films, westerns, *Starsky & Hutch* and *The Sweeney*. Like many kids my age, what tastes I had were shaped by ITV's *New Faces* and *Opportunity Knocks* (the *X-Factor* or *Britain's Got Talent* of the day). The former spawned Showaddywaddy, whose 1974 eponymously titled debut album became the first LP I ever owned. Meanwhile, Hughie Green faves Paper Lace's chart-topping single 'Billy Don't Be a Hero' was the first song I learned off by heart. I also liked Mud and Darts, I listened to Stewpot's *Junior Choice* on the radio and I loved the hit singles of my TV hero David Soul. At home the soundtrack was country and western, courtesy of Dad's cassette collection and a weekly local radio programme presented by the only bloke in Hull called Tex. I was in serious need of musical education.

It was provided in 1979, the year of landmark albums such as Joy Division's *Unknown Pleasures*. Owen Adams, writing in *The Guardian* 30 years later, described 1979 as a musical 'revolution' that 'negated the tacky glam-pop formula' before 'the counter-revolution of Stock, Aitken and Waterman in the mid-80s turned pop back to meaningless manufactured mush'.[53] In 2014 Bernadette McNulty termed it a 'vintage period' when BBC1's weekly *Top of the Pops* attracted a

53 https://www.theguardian.com/music/musicblog/2009/jul/24/1979-last-great-year-pop, *The Guardian*, 24 July 2009

record 19 million viewers: 'It was a moment when the show reflected one of the most diverse chapters in the British charts, a time of a luminal sound clash, where cheesy pop stars such as the Nolan Sisters rubbed shoulders with dogged rockers Motorhead. Next to them, snarling punks like the Buzzcocks were being usurped by the sardonic attacks of Elvis Costello and XTC, disco pioneers such as Chic fought it out on the dance floor with ska rude boys Madness and proto-electro pop star Gary Numan, while the reggae princesses of lovers' rock such as Janet Kay grooved next to country queens like Lena Martell.'[54]

This musical mix was replicated on the street by what *The Sun* listed as 'The Seven Tribes of Britain', 'rockabillies, heavy metal, new psychedelics, punks, new romantics, skins and mods'. Alwyn W. Turner recalls that two years later the *Birmingham Post* was still telling its readers, 'Today youngsters divide very clearly into cults – punk, skinhead, heavy metallers, mod or Ted.' Hull boasted examples of them all and as mentioned previously, the corridors of Withernsea High also bore evidence of the new youth movements. Pioneering punk Sue became 'Sid' overnight and was followed soon after by would-be rockers, soul boys/girls and new romantics, each struggling to carve out a new identity within the constraints of the school uniform.

By far the most noticeable were the mods and rude boys. This was the time of *Quadrophenia*, The Jam's first top-ten hit 'Eton Rifles', and Secret Affair's anthemic debut 'Time for Action', signalling what Adams termed a 'mod revival in full flow'. Alongside it, the 2-Tone label 'fully reared its head' on 8 November with the appearance of three bands on the same

---

54 https://www.telegraph.co.uk/culture/music/10617395/Why-Orange-Juice-still-sound-fresh-after-all-these-years.html, *Daily Telegraph*, 5 February 2014

Top of the Pops bill. When Jimmy Savile introduced Madness performing 'One Step Beyond', the Specials' 'A Message to You Rudy' and 'On My Radio' by the Selecter it was enough to convince the doubters that being sent to Coventry wasn't a bad thing at all! Some of my mates not previously known for their musical knowledge began sporting smart haircuts, wrap-around shades, button badges and RAF roundels. The arrival of the fishtail parka and tonic suit signalled the start of something new at Withernsea High. The sound of the suburbs had come to the seaside.[55]

Well, perhaps not the whole seaside. A few miles down the coast, Easington remained immune to any youth cult that didn't involve long hair, leather and loud guitars. The only new wave on show in my village was what *Sounds* termed the 'New Wave of British Heavy Metal'. The denim 'cut-off' became almost obligatory, scented with Patchouli oil and adorned with big sew-on patches bearing the names Motorhead, AC/DC, Iron Maiden, Saxon, Whitesnake, Judas Priest and Rainbow, along with dad-rockers Status Quo. I flirted with it briefly and even had a bit of air guitar going on at the local youth club.

But I soon craved something different. With hindsight (and having spent subsequent years rediscovering the sounds of the era) I should have gone with the 'in-crowd'. But not for the first time in my teenage years I took a wrong turn. I opted for another band and genre from that '2-Tone' *Top of the Pops*. The band was Matchbox, the genre was rockabilly and the catalyst for my conversion was Al (the older kid I'd attend those FA Cup ties with the following season). Here was a modern-day British band playing the music of my dad's era but, unlike 'plastic Teds' Showaddywaddy, one that wasn't (yet) mocked by *real* Rock 'n' roll fans. Not stopping to think of the reaction

---

55 Turner, Alwyn W., *Rejoice! Rejoice! – Britain in the 1980s* (London: Aurum, 2010) p.60

of my peers, I soon decided I'd become a 'Rockabilly Rebel'. That's if Mum and Dad didn't mind, of course.

* * *

Enjoying its original heyday in the mid-1950s, rockabilly music made an unlikely return to the UK charts in March 1976 courtesy of Hank Mizell's number three hit 'Jungle Rock', a track he'd recorded 18 years earlier. Teddy Boys suddenly found themselves back in vogue, with the *NME* printing a cover story in April that featured celebrity 'King of the Teds' Sunglasses Ron Staples, along with British bands Flying Saucers and Crazy Cavan and the Rhythm Rockers. Images of the 1950s could be found on both the big and small screen – from the 1973 films *American Graffiti* and *That'll Be the Day* to TV sitcom *Happy Days* and a Pepsi-Cola ad featuring a Fonz-like star called Eddie who was 'such a hit with the girls'. A national lobby campaign earned Stuart Coleman a weekend rock 'n' roll show on Radio 1. Compilation albums from the legendary Sun Records were reissued and labels such as London's Chiswick/Ace Records suddenly found a burgeoning new market. Specialist magazines such as *New Kommotion* were launched to cater for the new demand.

In June 1977, fights between Teds and Punks on the Kings Road made national news headlines and within two years the Edwardian originals had been joined by a second generation of fans who were discovering rockabilly for the first time. The result was a fully fledged revival, which even included a return to prime-time TV for Jack Good's *Oh Boy!* music show, originally aired in 1958. The 1979 version featured one of its original stars in Joe Brown, along with retro rockers Alvin Stardust (returning to his Shane Fenton roots), Les Gray of Mud and a Welshman called Mike Barratt (more of whom later). The music press were quick to jump aboard the bandwagon, with the *NME* of 16 February 1980 running another cover feature, headlined 'Rockabilly The Kid – The Bop That Just Won't Stop'.

The 1950s were back in vogue. 'Midnite Dynamos' gave Matchbox a second substantial hit and they would continue to chart for a couple more years. However, when set against the happening young things of mod, 2-Tone and new romanticism they were already beginning to look past their sell-by date. What the rocking scene – and I – really needed was a hot young pin-up act to cash in on the music's new-found popularity. Step forward the Stray Cats, a teenage trio from Long Island, New York, who landed in Britain in the summer of 1980.

Although resented by some, the Stray Cats were a godsend for the music press simply by virtue of being American. Their first *Top of the Pops* appearance in November (a fortnight after they'd appeared at Hull University as part of their first UK tour) created quite a stir and the band's first two singles, the 'punkabilly'-dubbed 'Runaway Boys' and the more traditional-sounding 'Rock This Town' went top ten, with the third, 'Stray Cat Strut' peaking just outside. I loved them and I can remember racing home after buying their debut single, desperate to alert the neighbourhood to the new-old sound of the 1980s. 'Turn that racket down, the whole street doesn't want to hear it,' Mum would shout upstairs. But it was my belief they did. Rock 'n' roll from the 1950s was here to stay again and I took great pride in being one of the few disciples of it to be found in the school corridors – despite the unwanted attention that being so sometimes brought.

I advertised my conversion courtesy of a pair of black leather brothel creepers (the first of several purchases over the years from Furman's shoe shop in Hull) and a new hairdo.

Inspired by Toddy (the only Elvis fan in my year), I initially played it safe with a basic 'grease-back' look and to this end I asked Mum to procure some Brylcreem. She got me Brilliantine instead. I shouldn't have been surprised; it was cheaper. The new-look thatch, which was basically my normal hair slicked back off my forehead and round the ears, made its debut to much derision from many of my class-mates. If school was the start, the village disco was the real place to show off one's finery. My brand-new creepers were partnered with a checked shirt, neckerchief and turned-up jeans, atop of which was initially a denim or donkey jacket (depending on the time of year), complete with the obligatory Confederate flag. The south was rising again – in Easington. What I needed now was a band to see live.

2 June 1981
Shakin' Stevens | The Jets
Hull New Theatre: Ticket £3.50

Probably relieved I wasn't sticking safety pins through my nose, Dad indulged my new-found passion. Budget-priced LPs were bought and original hillbilly tapes of the likes of Hank Williams and Hank Snow were dug out for my enjoyment on the back of films like *The Last Picture Show* and *Hud* showing on the telly. He also entrusted me with his prized programme from Buddy Holly and the Crickets' 1958 show at Hull Regal and followed it up by buying me the *20 Golden Greats* album, which was advertised on the telly. A few months later, Shakin' Stevens's third solo single 'Marie Marie' became my first-ever 7in purchase from Woolworth in Withernsea. Yes, that's right, Shakin' Stevens!

Recording with backing band the Sunsets since the late 1960s, Mike Barratt – for yes it was he – got his big break when recruited by Jack Good to play the lead part in the West End production, *Elvis!* This spawned those TV appearances on *Oh Boy!* and follow-up show *Let's Rock*, along with a solo recording contract with Epic and a UK top 30 hit with 'Hot Dog'. In October 1980 he entered the top 20 with 'Marie Marie' (undoubtedly helped by my purchase from Woolies). Within a year his cover of Rosemary Clooney's 'This Ole House' topped the charts and he was on his way to pop mega-stardom. Few rock 'n' roll fans begrudged him his success. Follow-up single 'You Drive Me Crazy' had just peaked at number two when 'Shaky' played to a sold-out Hull New Theatre. Undoubtedly, his crossover appeal helped but although David Blows acknowledged that 'lusting' girls comprised a large percentage of those 'crammed' into the venue, his *Hull Daily Mail* review also acknowledged that the audience represented a broad cross-section, 'from bouncing toddlers to ageing teddy boys and suburbia's respectable, wallowing in an overdose of nostalgia'. They weren't disappointed, as the singer and his band belted out 'non-stop up-tempo rock and roll like it's meant to be played'. As expected, the biggest reaction was reserved for his recent hits, the songs that have 'catapulted the Welshman to the top of the charts after years of slogging away and getting nowhere fast somewhere near the gutter of the music business'. Blows' review wasn't without its criticism. The length of set ('about 50 minutes') meant the performer 'didn't give full value for money', while the sound quality of the backing band was also called into question. But none of this mattered to me, appearing at my first genuine gig.

Support act were the Jets, three teenage brothers from Northampton – Bob, Ray and Tony Cotton. Their first single 'Rockabilly Baby' b/w 'James Dean' on Soho Records was recorded in 1978 and received regular airplay on John Peel. It is now a collector's item and I happen to have it thanks to Al's penchant to sell singles on to me after he got bored of them! The Jets were among the cluster of UK bands snapped up by a major label on the back of the Stray Cats' success. On this particular night, Blows said they 'got to grips with the frenzied beat for around 45 minutes and set the scene well, although their impetus was lost long before the main course'. I begged to differ!

However, as much as I loved their sound it was visually that the Jets made a lasting impression on me. Here were three young Englishmen dressing like American college kids of the 1950s. It was a look replicated by many of the younger 'hepcats' in the audience and one described by Robert Shelton in a 1983 article, 'Cat clothes and the Curtis cut': 'Box jackets, mostly with broad shoulders and one button (but shorter than the Teddy Boy look), peg trousers fairly pleated at the waist and tapering slightly to turn-ups; flashy satin, Hawaiian or checkerboard shirts; narrow ties; blue satin on shawl collars and pocket flaps; and slip-on shoes or loafers.'[56]

Now realising that I no longer looked the bee's knees in my rockabilly rebel look, I was desperate to revamp my wardrobe. A few weeks later I was on my way to doing so, courtesy of an authentic US varsity jacket, sourced by mail order from All-American Boy, followed in time by a neat pair of grey-flecked peg pants, a second-hand box jacket and a pair of penny loafers. Over the next few years, in my ongoing attempt to resemble some of the hip young hepcats adorning most of my album covers, I'd trawl Hull's alternative boutiques: Vipers Den on Spring Bank, Chris's (later Beasley's) in Trinity Market Square, The End (later X Clothes) on George Street and both Changes and Furman's in the city centre. With a growing number of like-minded souls at school, we soon began to look like a Holderness *Happy Days* ensemble.

---

56 Shelton, Robert, *History of Rock* (Volume 1 Part 6) (Orbis Publishing, 1981–1984) p.116

The other thing that needed addressing was the hair. The simple grease-back had to go, to be replaced by a flat-top or 'Mac Curtis' cut. As Neil 'Razor' Smith writes, 'It used to be said you weren't a real rockabilly until you'd had your first Mac Curtis haircut.' Shelton describes it as 'close-cropped hair, short on the sides and at the back with a distinctive flat top' and sometimes 'a fractionally longer clump at the front'. After trawling the city centre barbershops, including one in the station that asked if 'Sir' wanted 'anything for the weekend', I settled on Paragon Arcade where the younger of the two barbers himself sported a neat quiff. Out went the Brylcreem, in came the Cossack. Such a style wasn't universal. As Shelton writes, 'Brian Setzer of the Stray Cats sported dyed-blond locks with a cascading quiff almost covering his eyes.' Thankfully, I resisted the temptation to try and emulate the singer's reported use of sugar and water in order to form this wonderful bouffant. I did have one dabble, at home not in public. The results weren't great. They were even worse for Paul D (another would-be high school hepcat) who tried a 'recipe' that involved margarine and sugar. Instead of trialling it first he sported his new look at school. By lunchtime he'd been forced home for a rethink, having seemingly attracted every flying insect in Withernsea.[57]

17 July 1981
The Blue Cats plus Rock'n'Roll Disco

The Goodfellowship, Cottingham Road: Ticket (autographed) £2

The Shaky show gave me a first taste of the live rock 'n' roll experience but the chances of repeating it any time soon appeared

57 Smith, Noel 'Razor', *Crazy Man Crazy: Teds vs Punks & Other Gang Wars* (London: Rocket 88, 2016) p.143; also Robert Shelton's quote from same reference as [56]

remote. As a very young-looking 15-year-old I had little chance of conning my way into the Hull pubs and clubs, while the one local venue where I might have stood a chance didn't put on the bands I liked. The Grand Pavilion in Withernsea boasted a strong pedigree of live shows and was also popular for its Friday night discos. With a big local 'greb' fraternity, the venue played safe when hosting Def Leppard (with Magnum), Iron Maiden, Vardis, Praying Mantis and the Tygers of Pan Tang. It also ventured outside this comfort zone with gigs by the Revillos, the Vapors, Sham 69, the Beat (supported by the Akrylykz), the Lambrettas and Secret Affair. The latter saw an invasion of mods ferried in on Hull Corporation double-deckers, which went down well with the locals! Sadly, rockabilly wasn't catered for at 'Pavil'. So imagine my delight when the *Hull Daily Mail* brought news of a new weekly alternative, a rock 'n' roll revival that was 'swinging its way through Hull' courtesy of Friday nights at the Goodfellowship Arms on Cottingham Road. A crowd of 'about 230' attended the first event, with some having to be turned away. Those present 'dressed in style, with swirling skirts and slicked back hair much in evidence', despite many not being old enough to remember the era. Hull-based group Revival provided the live event, backed up by a rock 'n' roll disco.

Event promoter Mike Conway rated the evening a huge success and expressed his intention to attract some of the top bands in the country. When one of them was duly announced, I simply had to be there. A phone call to the pub landlord, a little white lie about my age (I added a year on) and a promise that I wouldn't so much as sniff the barmaid's apron got me in. I still regard it as one of the best calls I've made. That said, I felt really self-conscious as I stood in the queue waiting to get in. Not only was the doorman a very imposing character but standing among some of Hull's happening young things,

I felt completely out of my depth. Not that any of them did anything to make me feel that way – they achieved that by just looking so fucking cool! Finding a table tucked away in a corner, Al went to the bar and returned with the drinks (coke for me of course) and we sat back to enjoy the evening's entertainment.

The Blue Cats had been high on my radar since Garry Bushell had chosen 'Wild Night' as his single of the week in *Sounds*, 'Alive, a laugh, and as dynamic a slice of rip-roaring body-swirling rock 'n' rollin' dynamite as you'll find this side of post-Army Elvis … a steaming hot groover that's catchier than Asian flu in Southall High Street.' Meanwhile, Clint Bradley's lead vocals were 'so cool you could store a leg of lamb in that gob for two years without it going off'. In conclusion, the track was summed up as 'unavoidably danceable, compulsively singalongable, totally teenage and tirelessly essential for the endless summer of '81'. It's as spot-on a review as you could hope to read and if you don't believe me, the song is easily accessible on YouTube. I've still got the original Charly Records release, which along with the Stray Cats' debut remains my favourite track of the time.

Three months on from that rave review, the south London combo came to play at the Goodfellowship and, thanks to that phone call, I was there to see it. As I studied those in attendance that night, ranging from a few first generation Teds to kids only a couple of years older than me, I made mental notes of what my contemporaries were wearing. A couple of lads (Lee and Mike) particularly caught my eye with the most garish pairs of peg pants you could imagine, one in pink the other in lime green. Bright colours were the order of the day but these two seemed to be taking it a touch too far! In future years, Lee and I would become firm friends as would several others who I saw for the first time that night. There were no gaudy colours to be found among the Blue Cats' attire but by God did they ooze style. They looked *and* sounded the part. This was music that went beyond pure revivalism (it would later be termed 'neo-rockabilly') and had already gained them support slots with the likes of The Clash. They went down a storm, with 'Wild Night' raising the roof. My ticket duly signed, I went home convinced of three things: that ticket would be worth a fortune in years to come; Clint and the boys were a shoo-in for *Top of the Pops* in the not-too-distant future; and neo-rockabilly was to be *the* sound of the 1980s.

Just over a month later, the Jets were back in Hull for Conway's second sell-out gig of the summer. The intimate nature of the venue, with a low stage allowing the crowd to gather just feet away on the dance floor, made this the best of the three gigs I would see by the Cotton brothers. Although by now a major label signing with EMI and soon to get the TV exposure and chart success they craved, this was the Jets at their raw, rocking best. Rolling out their singles, including excellent cover versions of Herschel Almond's 'Let's Get It On', Johnny Jay's 'Sugar Doll' and The Genies' 'Who's that Knocking?' they delighted the assembled throng. Previously David Blows had described them as 'not a brilliant band, musically or vocally' but one that simply got on with the job. It was certainly some job they got on with this particular night. As Al and I headed home, having first dodged the customary post-gig trouble with the 'townies' outside, it was in the belief that we really were on to something big.

* * *

Over the next two years many tried to emulate the Stray Cats' chart success and several bands breached the hitherto ultra-conservative playlist of daytime Radio 1. Dave Phillips and the Hot Rod Gang enjoyed *Breakfast Show* exposure with their cover of 'Tainted Love', as did the Fantoms ('Five Foot Two Eyes of Blue') and the wonderfully named Shakin' Pyramids ('Take a Trip' EP). Perhaps the band that came nearest to being 'the next big thing' was the Stargazers. Adopting a more traditional sound, they signed to Epic Records and received plenty of daytime exposure for 'Groove Baby Groove', 'Hey Marie' and 'Ain't Nobody Here but Us Chickens'. Kids' TV got in on the act. *Get It Together*, a junior pop show co-hosted by Hull City fan Roy North (of *Basil Brush* fame), featured Marney Webb and his hugely impressive hairstyle on 'Still Searchin'', along with the Deltas, whose album *Boogie Disease* was one of my early faves. In 1982 came teen drama series *Jangles*, set in a fictional nightclub, starring Hazel O'Connor and a quiffed Jesse Birdsall and featuring the Fantoms playing live in one episode. On BBC1, *Grange Hill*'s latest bully 'Gripper' Stebson sported a fine flat-top as he made his fellow pupils' lives a misery. As Max Décharné writes, 'Rockabilly was so well established in Britain by 1981 as one of the country's recognised youth movements that London Weekend Television devoted an entire programme in their *20th Century Box* series to explaining its distinguishing features. By this stage it was clear that many old-school Teds had little time for the largely younger rockabilly fans, and the feeling was sometimes mutual.'[58]

In the programme, fans told the young Danny Baker of their concern that the scene was being diluted by its popularity. They needn't have worried. Within a year it was retreating underground. Just a few weeks after the Jets' sell-out show at the Goodfellowship, a gig by the Polecats to open Hull University's new Assembly Hall 'attracted only 210' despite the band's recent chart success. Such 'flops' gave licence to

58 Décharné, Max, *A Rocket in My Pocket – The Hipster's Guide to Rockabilly Music* (London: Serpent's Tail, 2010) p.291

reviewers like the *Hull Daily Mail*'s Alan Burgess who dubbed it 'a doubtful revival anyway'. A tad harsh perhaps but on the evidence of my next gig, he had a point.

21 May 1982
The Jets | Coast to Coast

Hull City Hall: Ticket £2.50

Nine months on from their successful Goodfellowship show, the Cotton brothers came back to Hull to play the City Hall. It was some step up in terms of size and would prove the city's swansong as far as the rockabilly revival went. Although the Jets arrived on the back of top-30 album success with *100% Cotton* and *Top of the Pops* appearances for their covers of Johnny Ray's 'Yes Tonight Josephine' and Andy Williams's 'Love Makes the World Go Round', Hull's appetite for such sounds was on the wane. Despite plenty of airplay, latest single 'The Honeydripper' failed to chart. In his 'Mailbeat' column under a headline 'Jets gig to backfire?', Angus Young feared that the promoters' gamble 'in plugging a strictly limited-appeal brand of music at a 1,800-seater venue in a city notorious for slack support' would not only backfire but 'could be the biggest pop concert blunder for years'. He opined that 'the Jets will be lucky to pull 300 on the night' and cited 'the recent Stray Cats disaster in Grimsby, when only 120 punters turned up' to support his view.

Young did concede that the band – whose tour also included 'the massive Birmingham Odeon' – had recently played to an audience of 1,200 in Ireland. But he wasn't convinced that they could get anywhere near that figure this time round. Even the band weren't sure that their gigs would sell, vocalist Bob Cotton telling Young, 'That's what we have been asking ourselves, we just don't know.' Even the announcement of support act Coast to Coast, whose cover of

Roy Milton's '(Do) The Hucklebuck' had gone top ten, failed to do the trick. 'Hucklebuck' was a year in the past and a year is an awful long time in pop music. In the event, the venue was less than half full and, despite being an excellent gig, I left with the feeling that the good times were well and truly over. The aforementioned HMV encounter with a couple of skinheads a few weeks later reinforced that view. I appeared to be part of a dying breed. Perhaps I should've gone mod after all.

6

Tip-Toe Through the Kempton

Ferensway: Saturday, 19 September 1981

'Oi! You lads going to the football?' He's looking straight at us. By us I mean Tom, Chris and me. Tom is the eldest of the two brothers I'd accompanied to the Fulham match six years earlier and Chris, also 16, is a Hull lad who's been staying at his parents' caravan. Both Tom and Chris are Grebs. I'm the young 'un, albeit only by a year and sporting my rockabilly rebel look. We've just got off the lunchtime Connor & Graham service bus from Easington and have ambled down the side of the Prospect Centre towards the station intent on getting a bus or train up to City. Coming on to Ferensway, we're met by a large group of lads under police escort. As we pause to suss things out, the copper's clocked us. 'Yeah,' we reply. 'Get in here then,' he says, and before we can argue we are ushered into the sullen-looking group. As we pass more lads at a bus stop, I catch sight of the word 'Blades' embroidered on a scarf draped over one bloke's arms. I tap Tom on the shoulder, 'Eh, they're Sheff U at that bus stop.' His reply is stinging in its delivery. 'Shut the fuck up! Who do you think this lot are?' I suddenly feel very scared and very, very conspicuous.

* * *

Probably because I hadn't experienced the rancour that accompanied relegation, I'd enjoyed my little run of cup games during Hull City's 1980/81 campaign. I'd got a real buzz from the fact that I'd been able to go unaccompanied by any 'guardian' – although in Dad's eyes I suppose Al inadvertently fulfilled that role. The fact that we strutted around town beforehand before heading off to Boothferry Park to stand with 'the lads' (after lunch with Al's mum at The Gainsboro first, of course) gave those days guaranteed kudos when regaling my pals at school with tales about 'going to City', especially to those who went with their dads. However, with Al's interest cooling over the summer, my plans for continued attendance the following season rested on like-minded souls at school, such as Gary, Carmo, Col M and Douggie P. Going with your mates was the logical next step on the matchday ladder and at least we were starting in the Fourth Division. But if we reasoned that because crowds would be so small there'd be no serious bother, we would soon stand corrected.

Regardless of league status, Boothferry Park was no stranger to matchday trouble – even among members of the home support as witnessed during some of the Action Group protests. Being a working-class port city and a collective home to the 'school of hard knocks', fighting came as second nature to some in Hull. Inter-gang rivalry was something many lads got into from an early age and for a time at the football this appeared to be the only thing holding City back when hooliganism first reared its head. That changed, first in the late 1960s with the skinheads of the Monte Carlo Mob, then a decade later thanks to the City Psychos. With the team now languishing in the football basement, the club was seen as a 'big fish' (no pun intended) to its rivals despite the small crowds. Meanwhile its hooligan firm was by now gaining itself a reputation as one that – literally – punched above its weight. There had been trouble against Bradford pre-season and in the first home league game, as well as reports of running fights away at Torquay of all places. In September they were about to be put to their biggest test in what just happened to be my first game of the season.

19 September 1981
Football League Fourth Division:
Hull City 2 Sheffield United 1

Boothferry Park: East Stand Terrace; no ticket; programme 30p

The Tigers made a solid start to life after relegation. They recovered from defeat at Torquay to beat Bradford and a point at Northampton put them in relative good heart for the visit of the promotion favourites. The Blades had accompanied City down, having wrongly believed that a point at Boothferry the previous April would be enough to save them. It wasn't; a dramatic late defeat at home to Walsall on the final day ensured they joined Colchester, Blackpool and City in having the letter 'R' inserted against their name on *Grandstand*. Not surprisingly they were favourites to make a swift return and they arrived unbeaten for what Mike Smith termed 'a very important game [even] at this early stage of the season'.[59]

Given its importance, this probably ranked as my first genuine 'not to be missed' match. I didn't miss it, although I spent much of the afternoon distracted by events taking place off the pitch. Long-time followers of City often spoke about the edge that accompanied a game against the Blades. A notorious Tuesday night fixture from March 1971, referred to by the *Hull Daily Mail* at the time as 'The Battle of Bramall Lane', was thought be the start of the rivalry. The Tigers had come from behind to win a feisty encounter in front of a crowd of over 40,000 inside the three-sided ground which at

59 Match programme (Hull City v Sheffield United, 19 September 1981)

the time still played host to Yorkshire cricket. It was seen as a pivotal result in the Second Division promotion race; instead #TypicalCity never built on their win and finished fifth. The Blades went up. It was to prove the Tigers' last win there for 39 years.

Crowd trouble became common at subsequent games, with one Friday night home fixture in September 1976 seeing police horses used to clear the terraces. City's 3-1 win three years later was another game marred by violence, while in the aforementioned meeting the previous April, Nick Deacy's fourth-minute opener had prompted a mass pitch invasion from the away end. There's little wonder that for City supporters of a certain generation, the chant of 'we only hate Sheff United' still holds true.

Keith Edwards would become the dominant character in so many encounters with the side from the red half of Sheffield, basically because he seemed to yo-yo between the two clubs, polarising opinion as he did so. In a 1995 fanzine article, Stephen Hodgson illustrates how popular the striker was with both sets of fans. He refers to the 'King Edwards' graffiti that 'appeared between Priory Road flyover and Ideal Standard', which was 'further evidence of his unofficial status within the city' and also the banner unfurled by away fans at Boothferry Park, following his transfer to Hull, which defiantly proclaimed, 'Keith Edwards – Blademan'. But it's a fine line between love and hate; in his autobiography, Edwards remembers his warm-up in that April game being accompanied by taunts of 'you're going down, we're not' from the away contingent. He doesn't say whether he enjoyed the eventual irony.

Edwards's effect was such that over the course of the next few years, I and many others would either help raise the roof of the Kempton in praise of the player, or be part of orchestrated chants aimed specifically at him. In return he would mark each goal he customarily scored by running to either celebrate *with* or *at* us, depending on the colour of his shirt at the time; from 'King Edwards' to 'king Edwards so to speak! In his two separate spells at Boothferry Park, Edwards averaged almost a goal every two games, finishing just three short of his century. He was the most natural finisher I've ever seen at Hull City.[60]

* * *

All week at school I'd been bigging myself up for 'Sheff U at home' and I was relieved I had door-to-door companions (had I been alone I'd have had to try and meet the other lads at the station). Despite this, I didn't feel that big now, in among the mass of Blades. The initial blur of seeing our plans altered had been replaced by genuine fear of what came next. There wasn't even another quiff to be seen in among the mob, many of whom were what I would come to know as casuals. That's all I needed, another reason to attract unwanted attention. Despite the warm September sunshine, my donkey jacket (complete with Confederate flag) was soon fully buttoned to hide my City shirt. My increasingly sweaty brow was playing havoc with my quiff, while inside my turned-up Falmers (Wranglers were out of Mum's price range) there was a 'whole lotta shaking going on'. Excitement had turned to anxiety and was bordering on panic when Chris's local knowledge came to the rescue. Beckoning us out of line and into the side streets near the flyover, we made our way to the ground in a rather more leisurely – if roundabout – manner. At last I could unbutton my jacket.

At the insistence of Chris, it was the first game I would watch from the Kempton and proved to be an amazingly

---

60 *Tiger Rag* fanzine (Issue 5, March 1995)

high-octane experience. A *Yorkshire Post* article in September 2001 entitled 'Welcome to the theatre of hate' described the Kempton as 'what football used to be about, a seething mass of energy, spitting vitriol at the opposition, lavishing praise on the home heroes'. In his brilliant book on Boothferry Park, Nicholas Turner writes, 'Despite its unassuming appearance, the humble Kempton produced prodigious levels of noise, a fact not lost on younger supporters in the early 1970s. From Bunkers Hill, they heard the vocal support generated in the low covered enclosure by sometimes only a couple of hundred visiting fans and for a time switched their habitual "end", before returning to Bunkers Hill.'[61]

Turner describes how this 'most basic of structures, anonymous and unambitious … betrayed the spectating experience to be enjoyed within its confines'. The low-roofed darkness stimulated 'a cosy and raucous atmosphere, difficult to generate elsewhere in the ground' where, as the *Yorkshire Post* writes, 'Football fans swayed, surged and roared their abuse in unison from the ageing terraces.'[62]

Given the above description and the anticipated chance of aggro, it was no surprise that many of what Turner dubs the more 'colourful' City fans opted for the Kempton. Standing within a few feet of the away fans helped crank up the atmosphere, which given a good couple of thousand from South Yorkshire in a crowd of 7,397 was far better than any I'd previously come across. Even with a new, secondary metal fence in place to supplement the five-foot-high, wooden-clad partition that previously acted as segregation, such 'exuberance' would struggle to be held back.

---

61 Turner, Nicholas, *Hull City – The Boothferry Park Years* (Thatcham: Dolman Scott, 2018) p.119

62 *Yorkshire Post* (29 September 2001)

The results were predictable, especially when a group of Sheffield fans were escorted around the pitch having 'infiltrated' Bunkers Hill. As they reached the massed ranks of City fans in the Kempton these interlopers were met with a hail of abuse and missiles. It didn't stop there. The resulting surge and trouble led to the match being held up for six minutes as fans spilled on to the pitch. The following Monday's *Hull Daily Mail* reported, 'Two fans were carried out on a stretcher and at least three United fans were escorted from the ground. St John Ambulance men attended to several fans on the edge of the pitch.' With 'small disturbances' reported before the game and mounted police called in to break up crowds on North Road immediately afterwards, the paper reported a total of 16 arrests accompanying what it termed the day's 'shameful' events.

On the pitch City won 2-1, although given other events that fact almost passed me by. Left-back Dennis Booth accepted a gift to give the Tigers a 24th-minute lead when United defender Neville could only divert Edwards's cross into his path. A minute before half-time the visitors deservedly equalised with a goal I remember well, mainly for the delayed but nonetheless raucous reaction of those to my right. The scorer was Bob Hatton, slotting home from close range after Charles's 25-yard shot had come back off the post. Hatton's status as a 'Hull-born Blade' earned him Hodgson's tag of 'a more detestable footballer I cannot imagine' in his aforementioned fanzine piece. Thankfully, Hatton's first goal in four games against his hometown club counted for nothing. With just ten minutes remaining – and against the run of play, it has to be said – Edwards raced on to Booth's cross-field pass before 'letting fly with a blistering right-footer into the top of the net', as described in that evening's *Hull Daily Mail Sports Mail*. David Goodman noted that the scorer's goal celebration was 'distinctly cool' although that wasn't apparent to me at the time. I was too busy dancing around to notice.[63]

Predicting what might happen at the final whistle, Chris had ushered us across to Bunkers for the final ten minutes, in order to make a quick exit. Many others were of the same idea and as such we got a great behind-the-goal view of the dramatic winner. Bunkers erupted as did the Kempton to our right – or rather the few hardy souls remaining in what only recently had been a packed home section. I wondered what was keeping them there. 'City Psychos,' said Chris, 'they won't be seen to run.' Fucking idiots, I thought to myself. They're gonna get battered. I had a lot to learn. At the final whistle we exited Bunkers and turned left, heading away from where things were already beginning to kick off and instead catching a bus back to the sanctuary of the station and our transport home. The whole experience had been one hell of an adrenalin rush even without ever getting really involved.

My first taste of the Kempton had been the perfect eye-opener for a young fan feeling his way into things. This was several steps up on what I'd witnessed against Fulham on my debut and even those FA Cup ties the previous year when the stand had seemingly been given over to away supporters. For the first time I'd seen football hooliganism first-hand at close quarters. But the threat of getting a clout aside, the exhilaration of being in such a densely packed enclosure was something else. The Kempton at its best provided a type of experience that will almost certainly never be seen again in English football grounds. Simply celebrating a goal could find you some distance from where you'd previously been standing, while anyone who couldn't be arsed to work his way to the toilets would prompt another clearance of the masses and wet

---

63 Goodman, David, *Look Back in Amber* (Manchester: Parrs Wood Press, 2005) p.66

clothes for those too slow to get out of the way! It soon became my new home.

* * *

The Hull City team that beat the Blades included several players I would come to revere over the next few years: goalkeeper Tony Norman, midfield duo Garreth Roberts and future England boss Steve McClaren, along with the post-Edwards front pairing of 'Sir' Les Mutrie and 'Big Billy' Whitehurst and flying winger Brian 'Bunter' Marwood. It was the defence that concerned most City fans though, with only the popular Dennis Booth usually escaping supporters' ire. Despite these failings, these were players I was desperate to now get to see on a regular basis – if life didn't get in the way. That autumn I'd entered the fifth form at Withernsea High, termed the most important year in a child's education. Dad was on my case, exams were the priority and with only a meagre paper round income to play with, not only were midweek matches ruled out but hopes of following City every Saturday were similarly slim. I was gutted, especially as such things didn't seem to prevent most of my mates from going.

Hence it was another month before I was back at Boothferry. League newcomers Wigan Athletic were the visitors, ultimately bound for the Third Division under new manager Larry Lloyd. The Tigers on the other hand were in trouble. Victory over the Blades had been followed by a five-match winless run in which the only points had come from home draws with Peterborough and Mansfield. A home defeat by Oxford at the start of October saw skipper Micky Horswill dispatch a bucket of water over protesting fans in The Well. Later that month, another defeat by Aldershot was accompanied by what the *Hull Daily Mail* termed a 'macabre "funeral march" to mark the death of Hull City'. Recalled in some detail by Hull City Action Group press officer Gary Clark, the march involved 'more than 50 members' carrying a plywood coffin with a flag draped over it reading 'Hull City RIP'. Starting out from Chalk Lane Club, they proceeded along Hawthorn Avenue and Anlaby Road to the car park at Boothferry Park. The *Hull Daily Mail* reported how 'to a beating drum the group clapped and chanted "Smith out!" "Needlers out!" and "We want a football team" in the half-hour procession'. Although some City supporters took exception to the protest and scuffles broke out along the route, the march achieved its objective with national coverage in the following day's *News of the World*.[64]

If protests weren't bad enough, City fans also suffered the bombshell news that the North Stand was to be demolished having apparently failed a safety certificate. Meanwhile, on the pitch, Edwards's goal against Sheffield United had proved to be his last (for now) in City colours and his immediate return to Bramall Lane for a laughable fee of £95,000 left a huge void that Mike Smith had hitherto failed to fill. Wigan added to the woes with a fifth league win, while the visitors were also rumoured to have got the better of things on the car park before kick-off. Thankfully, I was already in the ground by then and managed to avoid getting caught up in it (although of course I omitted this detail when recounting the tale at school).

Next up came an entertaining 4-4 draw at Humber rivals Scunthorpe, followed by further damaging defeats against Aldershot and Port Vale. City finally tasted victory again on 3 November with a 2-0 home win over York, before being edged out by the odd goal in five at home to high-flying Colchester. Inconsistency was their only consistency.

---

64 Clark, Gary, *From Boothferry to Wembley* (Hull: Riverhead, 2008) pp.43–44;

21 November 1981
FA Cup First Round: Rochdale 2 Hull City 2
Spotland: Pearl Street End Terrace; no ticket; programme 25p

November saw two rare occurrences. The first was England qualifying for the World Cup finals for the first time since 1970, courtesy of Paul Mariner's winner over Hungary at Wembley. The second, a week later, was me going to a 'proper' City away game. It was a trip long in the planning owing to my meagre income and eventually came down to a choice of games at two Lancashire rivals. We could either do the FA Cup first-round tie at Rochdale or the following week's league game at Bury. It seemed a no-brainer. Dale, perennial strugglers, only two places above City and the chance to sample the 'Magic of the Cup'; or their high-flying neighbours the Shakers, second in the league and unbeaten at home where they had scored 28 goals in just eight games.

We didn't allow for the #TypicalCity factor and plumped for Rochdale. Unlike the Blyth game, I felt brave enough to venture to the back of the bus where I sat with the regular Withernsea out-of-towners, which included schoolmates Gary, Carmo, Col M and Doug who'd all been to the Scunthorpe game a few weeks earlier. Among the older Withernsea lads were Dave Iley and Al Hewitt, who are both sadly no longer with us. The fact that they knew most of the others on board, including the large 'greb' contingent from the Holderness villages, helped ease us in and all was jolly on the way across the Pennines and on entering the ramshackle away end at Spotland. As I perused the rather basic match programme, in which manager Peter Madden's notes unusually appeared at the back rather than in the customary place towards the front, my attention was suddenly drawn to the opposite end of the ground, where scuffles were taking place. The fighting spilled on to the pitch, culminating in several dozen City fans being escorted around to where the rest of us were housed. It was an incident I'd become familiar with over the next few years and this particular one was recounted by 'Bladerunner' for a 1992 fanzine piece: 'Don't ask me why, but I remember counting among the Tigers fans on the pitch, no fewer than 11 casuals all wearing the blue and beige reversible hooded Pixie coat. And that was just on the pitch! It gives you some idea of the manic, mad scramble to be at the cutting edge of this week's fashion that was of epic proportions 11 years ago.'[65]

The pre-match trouble helped ignite the crowd and set the scene for a terrific experience. This new-found sense of camaraderie felt when tightly packed in together at one end made for a cracking atmosphere (even in a crowd of only 2,722). It was something Mike Smith acknowledged in his programme notes a week later, describing the 'special' following and the vociferous support so evident throughout the game, which he said had been appreciated by the players. Unfortunately our vocal efforts were not rewarded with a win. Despite McClaren in the 16th minute and Whitehurst in the 72nd twice putting City in the driving seat after the hosts' defence had failed to 'plaster over the cracks' (as Madden had urged), they hit back both times to earn a replay. One of Dale's goals came courtesy of a certain Terry Dolan. It wouldn't be the last time City supporters would come to rue that particular name.

* * *

Rochdale away provided a gentle introduction to the various forms of 'etiquette' to be followed when travelling on Simon Gray's coaches. The main one appeared to involve observing

65 *Look Back in Amber* fanzine (Volume 2, Issue 1, October 1993)

the unofficial seating plan – woe betides you if you sat in a slot reserved for a regular. Whatever alcohol restrictions were in place on coaches at this time were totally ignored and the soundtrack across the M62 was an all too familiar one involving the snap of ring-pulls, the hiss of bottle tops and the regular calls emanating from the back: 'Any chance of a piss stop, drarver?!' I don't suppose the planners took into account the drinking habits of football fans when deciding upon where to put service stations. Many found relief where they could. The sight of dozens of blokes standing on verges emptying their bladders became a trademark of Saturdays on the road.

Meanwhile, for those of us incapable of bringing our own beer, accepting someone else's could be fraught with risk. Thankfully I never suffered the ignominy of drinking a fellow passenger's urine – but I saw several who did! Being invited to drink piss was only one of several pranks an unsuspecting newcomer could expect to have played upon him. Storing anything in the overhead luggage racks was a risk but not as risky as falling asleep, especially if said sleep was heavy due to drink. From having an item of footwear removed and dispatched out of the skylight to the non-surgical removal of an eyebrow, it could prove an expensive kip. As I soon learned, it wasn't only the opposition fans to be wary of on these early jaunts.

As with Blyth, it took three attempts to beat Rochdale. I made a rare midweek excursion to Boothferry to the first replay and was on my way out of the ground feeling dejected when Gary Swann's spectacular last-gasp 30-yarder clinched a 2-2 draw and forced another Elland Road decider. Fortunately, I'd stopped at the top of Bunkers in expectation of seeing another City attack fizzle out when Swann struck. Lesson learned: never leave early.

Between the first and second replays, #TypicalCity won at Bury. Goals from McClaren and Roberts secured a first away victory of the season in which a 2-0 scoreline flattered the hosts. By all accounts the Tigers were terrific and according to Smith 'should have won the game by at least four goals'. Missing it was another lesson learned.[66]

Bolstered by burying Bury, two nights later City disposed of Rochdale thanks to McClaren's extra-time winner at a sparsely populated Elland Road. Mocks revision prevented my attendance; not that understanding of the Treaty of Versailles could compete with the local radio. Studying was near impossible when, as Nick Hornby describes, the crowd are much quicker than the commentators, every opposition shot really does sound as if it's heading for the top corner, every cross does create panic and every free kick awarded to them always appears to be 'right on the edge of the area'. Making matters worse for City fans, the local commentator was usually Dave Gibbins, who intentionally or not appeared to have little time for the Tigers. None of us could remember him ever getting excited about a City goal, a perceived bias we put down to his reputedly being a Hull FC supporter. Even Elliott Oppel had *wanted* City to win! Anyway, who cared what Gibbins thought, 'Mike Smith's Super Black-and-Amber Army' were in the next round of the FA Cup and Richard Lusmore of Form 5FD was on his way to ensuring he got an O-level in history.[67]

The following Saturday, Mutrie's solitary strike beat a Crewe side that included the 'ageless Ian Callaghan'. Unbeaten in six, the Tigers were on a roll only for the weather to intervene, wiping out the cup tie against Hartlepool and the

66 Match programme (Hull City v Crewe Alexandra, 5 December 1981)

67 Hornby, Nick, *Fever Pitch* (London: Victor Gollancz, 1992) p.118

remaining three league fixtures of 1981. It proved to be the coldest December since 1890 and the snowiest since 1878. Dominic Sandbrook writes of an amateur meteorologist in Shropshire who 'found the thermometer reading minus 29.8 degrees centigrade, the lowest reading in Britain's history'. Mike Smith had his players in training on Christmas Day, only for the Boxing Day trip to Darlington to be called off. This was probably a blessing as the club was reportedly struck by a flu bug. According to the manager, those deemed fit enough were forced to train on a variety of surfaces, from frozen grounds to powdered snow. A return to playing on grass appeared some way off.[68]

9 January 1982
Football League Fourth Division:
Bradford City 1 Hull City 1

Valley Parade: Midland Road Terrace; no ticket; programme 30p

The weather broke in time to allow the Tigers to beat Hartlepool on Monday, 4 January and belatedly progress to the FA Cup third round. I was in the crowd of nearly 5,000 that saw Marwood and Mutrie earn an away tie at Second Division Chelsea. I thought about going, but only briefly. A more realistic proposition than a school-night trip to Stamford Bridge was the weekend league 'derby' at promotion hopefuls Bradford, which would be played out in front of Yorkshire TV's cameras for *The Big Game*. 'Welcome to Hull City, paying their first visit to Valley Parade for a league match for 21 years,' read the Bantams' programme. It also added, without hint of irony, 'Many believe that Hull City's rightful place is in the First Division.'

---

68 Sandbrook, Dominic, *Who Dares Wins: Britain, 1979–1982* (London: Allen Lane, 2019) p.691

Here, on another difficult pitch, frozen underneath with a covering of snow, City's players wore 'special winter boots' acquired for them by assistant boss Cyril Lea on a recent trip to London. They proved very useful in enabling Garreth Roberts to convert Mutrie's gem of a flick to give the Tigers the lead. It was left to the prolific Bobby Campbell to earn the Bantams a point. We were situated below the cameras in the covered Midland Road terrace that ran the full length of Valley Parade, opposite the ill-fated old Main Stand. The noise from the travelling support came over loud and clear on the following day's highlights, a point again picked up by Smith in his next notes.[69]

Bradford was another fixture that had me both excited and a tad nervous beforehand, not surprisingly given the recent history between both sets of fans. In the event the day highlighted the good and bad when it came to following City at the time. The good was the raucous support and also the reaction of one local bobby when our over-subscribed coach unloaded its inhabitants, many of whom clambered down from the luggage racks in which they'd been housed for the whole trip along the M62. 'How many more are there?!' he enquired, after the allotted 53 seats had already been emptied. Rumour has it Simon had over 80 on board (and that was one of three coaches he ran that day). No wonder we'd struggled uphill! The copper seemed quite impressed – and amused. The more unsavoury side to the travelling support surfaced as part of the sinister edge to proceedings inside the ground. Along with the usual threats of violence exchanged between rival fans, for the first time there was a noticeable racist tone to some of the songs and chants being aired, with Bradford full-back Cyril 'Ces' Podd a particular target. These were

69 Match programme (Hull City v Chelsea, 21 January 1982)

the days of Alf Garnett and *Love Thy Neighbour* on the telly, and a 'golliwog' on your jam jars. As such, having a go at 'the darkie' was almost seen as par for the course, especially by some fans of a club like Hull City who were then yet to field a single black player. It was a disturbing episode but, thankfully, one aspect of football in the 1980s that is (largely) absent 40 years on.

A return of winter meant nine days elapsed before City returned to action with a Monday night trip to Stamford Bridge. I'm not sure how many City fans were there in the crowd of 14,899 but they came close to seeing the Tigers create a real shock. The *Daily Mirror*'s Kevin Moseley said that 'only the acrobatics of 18-year-old goalkeeper Steve Francis' saved Chelsea from 'an embarrassing – and perhaps deserved – shock FA Cup defeat'. He added, 'Francis alone stood between Hull and their first ever win at Chelsea in 16 visits.' The keeper's most vital saves came late on, twice denying 'goal-bound shots from Les Mutrie' and a Dale Roberts header. Moseley highlighted 'defensive ace Nick Deacy' and 'the strong running of striker Billy Whitehurst' as instrumental in a 'determined' City performance that nullified the 'skill of Mike Fillery and [Kevin] Hales' for Chelsea. The Tigers' tenacious performance earned a money-spinning replay at Boothferry Park to be played just three days later, with a fourth-round home tie against Wrexham awaiting the winners at the weekend.

The timing couldn't have been better. On the Saturday prior to the game at Stamford Bridge the *Hull Daily Mail* front page ran a story about 'THE MAN WHO SAVED HULL CITY'. Underneath the headline, Simon Redfern detailed how chairman and principal shareholder Christopher Needler had been 'keeping the club alive since last April' by pouring in 'a staggering £325,000 of his own money'. His actions had 'prevented the club from being liquidated at a time when they are losing £7,000 a week'. A combination of relegation, a halving of the club's overdraft 'from around £700,000' and the 'incredible annual salaries paid to two employees' (believed to be Smith and Lea) had contributed to losses of £131,395 for the last financial year, with accumulated losses quoted as £970,116. Needler told Redfern, 'I have injected the money because the bank won't.' Along with a £200,000 advance from William Jackson's 'as part of the £1.5m scheme to turn the present car park into a supermarket and leisure centre', the chairman's 'interest-free loan' meant the Tigers remained just within their new overdraft facility at the bank. Needler now placed his faith in a continuation of the 'slight improvement in the club's playing results' that he hoped would in turn attract more spectators through the gates. The next game at Boothferry Park would be a start.

21 January 1982
FA Cup Third-Round Replay: Hull City 0 Chelsea 2
Boothferry Park: East Stand Terrace ; ticket (lost); programme 30p

Memories of 1966 were to the fore in the run-up to Thursday; grainy footage of Waggy's goals at Stamford Bridge and a crowd of over 45,000 to see Chelsea win the General Election day replay. While there wouldn't be anything like that number inside Boothferry this time round, a ban on Chelsea fans travelling to away games meant we had to purchase tickets beforehand. I can't remember how I managed to secure mine but, ominously, it would appear that many Londoners also managed to do so in City's biggest crowd in nearly two seasons.

As with that previous FA Cup encounter, the Tigers put up another valiant display but eventually succumbed to defeat. 'Tired Tigers Bite The Dust' boomed *The Sun*. Youngster

Brian Ferguson went closest to creating an upset, denied three times by Francis in what reporter Michael Morgan termed a 'private battle' as City dominated the first half. Chelsea came more into it after the break but Francis was again called upon to deny Mutrie with a 'brilliant reflex stop'. At the other end, John Davies 'pulled out two magnificent saves in as many minutes' to deny Alan Mayes and Colin Lee, with Dale Roberts also clearing off the line from the latter. But two goals inside the last 15 minutes, from a Mayes cross-shot and a John Bumstead header secured the visitors' passage to the fourth round.[70]

Unfortunately the night wasn't remembered solely for the football. With Chelsea fans having secured access to the home ends, scuffles broke out during the game in the Kempton and the South Stand seats, and afterwards down North Road where in the darkness, confusion spread among those trying to make their way home. Among them was me, attempting with increasing desperation to find the blokes I'd travelled with to the game but who hadn't accompanied me round to the Kempton. As I struggled to remember where the car was parked, I'll admit, I was 'bricking it'. All the side streets merged into one in the darkness, while all I could hear were the tell-tale sounds of aggro and the odd police siren. Even though I was heading away from it, the relief when I finally located my friends was immense.

It had been another ugly experience and the following night's *Hull Daily Mail* made for grim reading. It reported how 23-year-old PC Robert Young had been felled by 'a brick-sized lump of concrete' when trying to separate rival fans near Hayton Grove. A night that had begun with such high hopes then turned really sour when news came through of a bottle

70 *The Sun* (21 January 1982)

being thrown through the Chelsea team coach and nearly blinding Steve Francis. The local paper's front page screamed 'COWARDS' and in Jeff Postlewaite's report Mike Smith issued a public apology to Chelsea for the 'mindless' assault. It was a sickening end to a night that had started so promisingly. But for Hull City AFC worse news was just around the corner.

7

'We'll Support You Evermore!'

Boothferry Park: Saturday 23 January 1982

What a difference a couple of days make. On Thursday night there were over 13,000 here to watch the cup defeat by Chelsea. Where are those bastards now, eh? They'd have been here if it was Wrexham and not Torquay we're playing! The frustration is palpable among the hardy regulars as we rattle around a Kempton that was bursting at the seams two nights ago. Andy Flounders helps lift spirits by marking his first start with a cleverly taken goal at the end where the North Stand used to be. City win 1-0. Unfortunately, results on the pitch are becoming a lesser priority. For while the gate of 3,293 is respectable for the Fourth Division and par for the course for the season it is again well below the figure required in order to break even. Unbeknown to many, the Tigers' fiscal position is approaching breaking point.

* * *

I've often wondered how things might have panned out had City gained the win over Chelsea that their performances perhaps merited. Another decent gate the following Saturday, for an eminently winnable fourth-round tie against a Wrexham side bound for relegation from the Second Division, could have been followed by a mouth-watering home meeting with Liverpool in the last 16. The receipts from both games would surely have been enough to buy City a financial stay of execution. Not only that but who knows what knock-on effect a cup run might have had on the Tigers' already improving league form (with several of Smith's signings at last beginning to flourish). Receivership might never have happened, City might have made an immediate return to the Third Division and we might never have heard of Don Robinson.

Instead, as Chelsea played out a draw with Wrexham (taking three games to get past them before beating Liverpool) the Tigers were extending their unbeaten league run to five matches with a 1-0 win over Torquay. Goalscorer Flounders – who the previous season had become the youngest post-war first-teamer at 16 years and 296 days – was on his way to becoming an adopted hero, known to us as 'Cousin' Andy on account of a very tenuous family link that needs no further examination here! The first of his 63 goals in City colours – a neat, back-heeled winner – brought the smiles back to our faces and restored optimism ahead of the biggest away game of the season.

30 January 1982
Football League Fourth Division:
Sheffield United 0 Hull City 0

Bramall Lane: Bramall Lane Stand Lower Tier Terrace; no ticket; programme 30p

Sheffield United away was a fixture I'd been both looking forward to and dreading since September. I viewed it as my biggest test yet. For the first time I was likely to be part of an away contingent that would be dwarfed in size by the home support. What's more, those home supporters came with a fairly fearsome reputation. Playing on our thinly disguised apprehension, the trip down the M18 saw our group regaled with horror stories of days past by lads who had made previous visits to the Sheffield clubs and – apparently – barely lived to tell the tale. Some of them revelled in our obvious discomfort and my sense of trepidation wasn't eased as we approached the Steel City. If I'm being honest, I didn't have a clue what I'd do if it did kick off. I can't say September's experience was one I really wanted to repeat any time soon (even if just being there did wonders in terms of classroom credibility points). As we neared Bramall Lane, I had the combination of sweaty palms and racing heartbeat that comes with such a feeling of nervous excitement. This time I wouldn't be able to rely on someone familiar with the local side streets to bale me out should the need arise.

I needn't have fretted. Route-marched to the ground under escort, not only was City's support impressive in number and voice but there were plenty of 'handy lads' on show. It was highly unlikely therefore that our small group of country bumpkins would be called upon! To the football followers of the 21st century it's perhaps hard to comprehend the sort of thought processes we went through when attending games in the 1980s. Talk of lads who were 'game' and willing to 'go toe-to-toe' with like-minded rivals in what they saw as a defence of Hull's honour was quite reassuring to the more impressionable of us. It sounds pathetic doesn't it? But that's how I and countless others felt. As it happened, a smooth police operation ensured that the day passed off trouble-free and the jousting remained of a verbal nature only. There was a crowd of 12,612 inside, with the low roof above the lower tier at the Bramall Lane End lending itself to superb vocal support (if not the best view of the action). 'Our supporters again appeared to have the loudest voices,' wrote Smith the following week and once again I returned home from a match hoarse.

City were fully deserving of a point from Bramall Lane's first goalless draw of the season. Indeed, they should have had all three. Not for the only time at the ground were we left feeling we'd not had the rub of the green – the officials having missed a Billy Whitehurst header that was over the line, according to video evidence seen later by Smith. The manager also highlighted his team's defensive performance at the promotion favourites. He wrote, 'Nick Deacy and Dale Roberts completely blotted out Bob Hatton, who has a high goalscoring record against us and any other threat.' I'm guessing that the 'any other threat' was Edwards who adorned the front cover of the programme. By choosing not to name him, Smith perhaps betrayed just how much the striker's move had rankled with him!

* * *

While my chosen means of away match travel offered the advantage of a door-to-door service, albeit one with regular early starts, home games didn't always allow for a lie-in either. When money allowed, I had plenty to fit in before meeting my mates at Hull Station. In fact the bus to the game would often be my third of the day, having come in early to get the flat-top trimmed and a few records bought before a bus home, quick change and another bus back to town. After such a hectic start my day would then involve a wait for Carmo, Col and Doug coming in from Withernsea. I'd stand near the old blue tuck shop hut, a vantage point from which to check for any sign of trouble across at The Green Gingerman, the nearest hostelry for fans arriving by train.

On arrival of the 76 EYMS we'd stroll on to Anlaby Road and make our way to the ground. Sometimes we'd linger a few minutes at the top of the flyover to take in the rugby union or cricket action down below us at The Circle. If Hull FC were at home, we might see some of the 'Old Faithful' making their way to The Boulevard. In fact, their early kick-offs often meant we'd hear them. Post-match we'd look to catch one of the numerous double-deckers parked outside Boothferry. Otherwise we'd retrace our steps back along Anlaby Road, a walk that would leave me with just enough time to pick up the 'Green' *(Hull Daily Mail Sports Mail)* from the dishevelled-looking vendor in the Debenhams doorway before boarding my bus home. The interaction between said vendor and his geriatric 'runner' Wally (whose speed in delivering the freshly printed paper hardly merited the term 'hot off the presses') was hugely entertaining if far from complimentary. It all added to an enjoyable matchday experience. But by February 1982 it was one that was under serious threat.

20 February 1982
Football League Fourth Division:
Hull City 5 Hartlepool United 2
Boothferry Park: East Stand Terrace; no ticket; programme 30p

The draw at Bramall Lane extended City's unbeaten run to eight games but by the time Hartlepool arrived in Hull, things had taken a turn for the worse. First up was what Smith termed an 'awful' home defeat by Northampton. The City boss was then left bemoaning a combination of missed opportunities and Whitehurst's dismissal in the 3-0 loss at Peterborough. At Tranmere it was his team's apparent inability to 'cope with the physical challenges' that left Smith frustrated after a 2-2 draw. Light relief was again hard to come by, although I do recall enjoying a letter in the Northampton programme, which heaped praise on one of the coach drivers' actions after a brick had been thrown through the back window at the Sheffield United game. But it was the 'PS' that caused much mirth among our group: 'There was one other thing that spoilt a good game for me, that was the chanting some of ours did about Keith Edwards' wife. I was never one of his ardent supporters but I felt a lot of the remarks were uncalled for.'[71]

In his reply, general manager Gordon Dimbleby urged, 'The sooner the laws of the land are amended to those of the [19]30s the sooner the louts can be given the punishment they so richly deserve.' I'm fairly sure by this he was referring to those responsible for the brick-throwing and not those who sang about 'Chalky' and Mrs Edwards.

Despite a hamstring strain, Les Mutrie scored both goals at Tranmere. He went two better as a Hartlepool team featuring future Tigers boss Phil Brown were thumped 5-2 in what the following week's match programme dubbed 'Mutrie's Massacre'. It was City's highest league score for nine years. Mutrie's goals took his tally for the season to 18 and earned him a guest studio appearance on Sunday's *The Big Game*, in which he described the Tigers as 'man for man the best in the Fourth Division skill-wise'. The softly spoken Geordie heaped praise on his team-mates, including Roberts and McClaren ('who thread the needle') and strike partner Whitehurst ('who takes an awful lot of stick for me'). On his way to a club record of scoring in nine consecutive matches, 'Sir' Les was City's biggest good news story. In fact he was their only good news story – and things were about to get a whole lot worse.

The following Thursday, 25 February 1982, there was a shock awaiting me when I grabbed the 30-odd copies of the *Hull Daily Mail* that constituted my after-school paper round. The front-page headline stopped me dead in my tracks. 'HULL CITY PUT UP FOR SALE' it screamed, under which the strapline confirmed that the Tigers had made unwanted history: 'Receiver in as Needler withdraws aid.' Reporters Paul Williamson and Simon Redfern described how 'a survival

71 Match programme (Hull City v Hartlepool Utd, 20 February 1982)

plan to save Hull City' had been launched 'after a receiver was dramatically called in at Boothferry Park'. The 'shock news' had been announced at a morning press conference, at which Christopher Needler had been joined by financial director Trevor Thomas and Martin Spencer, of chartered accountants Casson Beckman. Captured looking grim-faced around the boardroom table, they had issued a club statement that read, 'Mr Needler, who has supported the club over the past years to the extent of some £325,000 with further bank guarantees of £225,000, has been advised that he should not, in all the circumstances, continue funding the club.' Spencer put it rather more succinctly: 'Effectively, Hull City has run out of cash.'[72]

This was stomach-churning stuff. Although clubs had gone to the wall before, Hull City had claimed an unwanted first by bringing financial turmoil into the Football League. Even as I read it I couldn't really believe it. In particular, the timing of the announcement appeared ridiculous, coming just five days after one of the best performances of the season. Unfortunately, 'Mutrie's Massacre' had been watched by only 2,825 spectators, bringing in receipts of just £1,700.

With the Tigers heavily in debt it was the final nail in the coffin. In his account, former *Hull Daily Mail* and *Yorkshire Post* reporter David Bond writes, 'It became clear that [Bob] Chapman and [personnel director Ian] Blakey, who had stepped down after relegation in 1980/81, overstepped the mark in financial terms. The management team were being well paid, it seemed that most of their new players were being well paid in comparison with players who had already been at the club and the gates had dwindled when the gamble had

72 Buckingham, Phil, https://www.hulldailymail.co.uk/sport/football/hull-city-for-sale-receivership-4005024, *Hull Daily Mail*, 31 March 2020

not paid off. Something had to give – and it did towards the end of February 1982.'[73]

The next day at school, City's demise was the talk of the cloakrooms. The expressions on the faces of us 'regulars' told their own story, while for others it all sounded like just another tired joke at the club's expense. You know the sort, 'I rang Hull City today to ask what time kick-off was. They said, "What time can you get here?"' Or, 'Did you know Hull City are taking up the train tracks near Boothferry Park? They need the points!' It soon became obvious that this was much more serious, partly on account of nobody really understanding what receivership meant. As David Goodman writes, supporters were left confused simply because this was an unprecedented situation. 'Was the club up for sale, was it going to be relegated, closed down, what?'[74]

The answer was to be found on the front page of Friday's *Hull Daily Mail* under another staggering headline, 'CITY PUT THE LOT UP FOR SALE'. According to Redfern, Martin Spencer had transfer listed the entire 23-man playing staff, including 18 full-time professionals. The higher-paid players, dubbed 'The Boothferry Seven' (John Davies, Dennis Booth, Nick Deacy, Brian Ferguson, Dale Roberts, Micky Horswill and Billy Whitehurst) were given until 15 March to find other clubs or face dismissal. Spencer was tasked with what Mike Peterson describes as 'restructuring the club on a sound financial basis that would allow it to be sold as a going concern'. Restructuring initially meant dismantling. Ironically, this was already physically taking place courtesy of the ongoing demolition of the North Stand. With contracts

73 Bond, David, *'Meet Me On Bunker's Hill' – A Revealing and Personal Look at the Hull City Story* (Hull: Tykesport, 2006) p.46

74 Goodman, David, *Look Back in Amber* (Manchester: Parrs Wood Press, 2005) p.67

already in place, that particular task could continue regardless of other events. The sight of this once famous structure coming down appeared quite symbolic. The club was being taken apart before our very eyes.[75]

27 February 1982
Football League Fourth Division: Hull City 2 Mansfield Town 0

Boothferry Park: East Stand Terrace; no ticket; programme 30p

The two days between the announcement and the home game against Mansfield saw City attract unprecedented national publicity. News teams descended on the ground and Needler and Smith regularly appeared for interview, along with skipper Horswill and a young McClaren. For the first time, a story on Hull City AFC also attracted comment from Paul Barry of BBC's *The Money Programme*. It didn't make pleasant viewing. On *Look North*, Hull City Supporters' Club secretary Colin Smith said he hoped there would be 'five, maybe six thousand' present against Mansfield, 'despite the fact that unfortunately there's the local rugby on the telly tomorrow afternoon'. In the same feature, club legend Raich Carter outlined the way forward, saying, 'If you put it on the field the supporters will come, they'll still do it. The club may be dead but the fans are not. They say that the rugby has taken over here but I think football would come back with a real zip if they only put something on the field that is really worthwhile watching.'

In the *Hull Daily Mail*, Martin Spencer's message was somewhat blunter: 'It's up to the people of Hull not to support their club by looking at results in the paper, but to get off

75 Peterson, Mike, *A Century of City: The Centenary History of Hull City AFC, 1904–2004* (Middlesex: Yore Publications, 2005) p.74

their backsides and come to see a live game of football.' The first test of how much his words had resonated came two days later. ITN and BBC news crews were in attendance at Boothferry Park, with 'The fans who want to save Hull City' one of the lead-in headlines on the late evening edition. Some 2,000 extra spectators helped swell the crowd to 5,220. It actually felt a lot more than that with space in the Kempton at a premium. The atmosphere was excellent and we were rewarded with a morale-boosting 2-0 win, courtesy of a great strike from 'Cousin' Andy and a penalty scored by 'Sir' Les who again played despite his persistent hamstring problem. I think this was the game in which I first heard the shout 'you're bloody rubbish Mansfield' and it would become a familiar part of City supporters' matchday armoury for years to come – regardless of who the opponents were.

Smith's 'From Within' piece in the match programme (printed prior to receivership) heaped praise on Mutrie and the whole team for their display against Hartlepool. He wrote, 'With performances like those last week, it must be just the start for the rest of the season and our players must set higher and higher standards.' Wise words – but for the manager, it was nearly the end. His final notes appeared in the supplement used to accompany the programme for the following Tuesday's rearranged home game against Halifax Town. As always he was full of praise for his players and the supporters. Describing recent events as 'confusing, disappointing, sad and in some way inevitable', he said that receivership 'had knocked the players very flat'.

To then battle so hard to beat Mansfield was 'to their credit'. Even more important was that 'the crowd was boosted by more than 2,000 people' who kept the team's morale 'going all the time'. He concluded by saying that the same approach was required for the Halifax game 'and with the help of our magnificent supporters' it 'must be the most important game of the season'.[76]

Smith concluded by thanking 'all those supporters who have wished us well. I can only ask them to keep on wishing us well.' He added, 'Whatever happens, this club is too important to go out of business.' They were the last words he penned as City manager. Two days after the Halifax game, which City again won 2-0, Smith became the first significant 'cutback', along with Lea and commercial manager Dimbleby. It appeared to have taken him by surprise. 'SMITH SNARLS AT SACKING' was the *Hull Daily Mail* headline, with the outgoing boss quoted as saying, 'I'm very angry.' He had support among the players. Billy Whitehurst, by this time a firm fans' favourite, was disappointed. Years later he told Richard Gardham, 'I felt sorry for Mike Smith. The nucleus of that squad that went on to be so successful was down to him. Colin Appleton [Smith's eventual permanent replacement] reaped the rewards of Mike's work to a certain extent.'[77]

The day prior to the Halifax game, the *Hull Daily Mail* had printed the Action Group's '20-point plan to save the Tigers'. Ironically, the first of which was for 'City manager Mike Smith, assistant boss Cyril Lea and the whole board of directors to recognise they have failed to bring success to Boothferry Park and resign forthwith'. Others included hopes for a consortium to come forward 'with a basic knowledge of football', a wish for the club to 'never again be controlled by an individual family or individual company' and an immediate rejection of 'any idea for City to share the Boulevard'. They appealed for the players to remain loyal and for supporters to 'bring a neighbour, a relation or

---

76 Match programme (Hull City v Halifax Town, 30 February 1982)

77 Gardham, Richard, *The Decade: Ten Years that Transformed Hull City* (Amazon, 2019) p.37

a friend' to the Halifax game. Interestingly, they also floated the idea of 'Hull FC and Kingston Rovers to play a game at Boothferry Park to raise funds for City' while suggesting that City consider switching to 'playing Sunday afternoons when neither Rovers nor Hull are playing'. Tellingly they urged people to back the official supporters' club's 'Save the Tigers' fund, having buried the hatchet with their erstwhile rivals in the wake of receivership. They ended their note, 'TIGERS WE LOVE YOU'.

* * *

In the immediate wake of Smith's dismissal, City turned to youth development officer Bobby Brown (whose salary was immediately halved) to run the team, assisted by 'goal ace' and club icon Chris Chilton, who had hitherto been looking after the juniors. They instilled a spirit of togetherness that would serve the club well. Although their first game in charge resulted in a narrow loss at leaders Wigan, they oversaw an excellent run of form. Prior to defeat for an injury-hit City at Darlington on 23 March, the Wigan reverse was the only blot on a run of seven straight wins. It was a sequence that saw Mutrie complete his record; his tally of 14 goals in nine matches ending with one of the three that beat Port Vale. Seemingly galvanised by uncertainty, the Tigers stormed into the top ten.

I missed the midweek home win over Scunthorpe and the away trip to Aldershot which yielded a resounding 3-0 win, with City scoring three times in ten minutes. Dennis Booth recalled the players in the bath afterwards, singing 'on the dole, on the dole'. They were certainly enjoying themselves, as Whitehurst explained to Richard Gardham: 'It wasn't a worrying time. We were winning games. We were still getting paid, even though some of that was coming from the fans, which was tremendous. I thought they were great days. We had great camaraderie. We all got together and rolled our sleeves up. It brought us closer together. We were great mates in that team.'[78]

The loss at Feethams was followed by a 2-0 defeat at Colchester, an occasion that marked Nick Deacy's last game for the club. Along with captain Micky Horswill he had agreed to join Hong Kong side Happy Valley the following week. They were the first of the so-called 'Boothferry Seven' to depart and the Welshman didn't go quietly. In a *Hull Daily Mail* article headlined 'Deacy slams City board', the defender launched a 'bitter attack on the club's directors' and in particular their 'handling of the current crisis'. Talking to Simon Redfern, Deacy 'claimed that the directors had misled the players and the public' when dismissing a consortium of prominent local businessmen (one that included Ian Glenton and Paul Dixon) with the club 'in such a desperate plight'. He also warned of more player departures 'if plans to bring in wage cuts went ahead'. Deacy had come to the conclusion that 'the same board are going to be in power next season and I don't want to be part of it'. He wasn't the only player to go public with his criticism of the way things were being handled.

Towards the season's end, with still no news on the club's long-term future, five players whose contracts expired in July – Flounders, McNeil, Norman, Swann and Whitehurst – were notified that they were not to be offered new terms. The manner in which this was done, with letters being handed out in front of the other players, prompted Norman to speak out and express his disgust. Thankfully, rumours of a move to Birmingham City came to nothing and the goalkeeper

---

78 See [77]

remained at Boothferry Park. These issues aside, the players thrived in the face of adversity. This was probably because, as Norman said, 'When you're in the bottom division and the receiver is called in, you can't get much lower. In fact it was rock bottom.' The response it triggered 'proved there was a bit of bounce left in the club'.[79]

Bounce was something City's attendance figures were experiencing too as fans rallied to the cause. The *Hull Daily Mail* used the crowd of 6,952 as the headline for its report of the Halifax game (rather embarrassingly a figure that again didn't include me; night games were still a real problem). A similar figure (6,121) attended the Scunny match, the 'huge following' at York formed almost half the total of 4,771 and the atmosphere generated by the 5,506 against Port Vale was among the best I'd experienced (especially when Booth netted from the halfway line).

There's little wonder that the memories of those spring days of 1982 remain among my favourite. There was a special bond between players and supporters of the like I don't think I've ever experienced. On Sunday, 28 March, along with what the programme referred to as '250 loyal and ardent City supporters, accompanied by several of the club's staff and their families', I took part in a ten-mile sponsored walk from Boothferry Park across the Humber Bridge and back, as part of the Save the Tigers fundraising drive. I can't remember how much my individual contribution to the fund was but I do recall how proud I'd been to take my sponsor form around school, especially when teachers who remembered watching Waggy and Chillo were only too keen to pledge their support. I felt I was doing my bit for *my* team. A week later, prior to kick-off against Hereford, Dave Dewberry and

79 Bond, David, *'Meet Me On Bunker's Hill!' – A Revealing and Personal Look at the Hull City Story* (Hull: Tykesport, 2006) p.49

four other members of the Hull City Action Group completed a 24-hour marathon walk around the Boothferry Park pitch. Bobby Brown was fulsome in his praise, saying how much he 'admired their efforts'. It was, he added, the 'type of activity' that was 'more likely to gain support of all those interested in the future of the club'.[80]

Undoubtedly the best way of pulling together of course was via the turnstiles. To this end the home crowds were by now being bettered only by the three teams in the promotion race (Sheffield United, Bradford and Wigan) and it was enjoyable to watch City again. What's more, the Tigers looked more than capable of competing with them. Booth was perhaps stretching things a bit when describing the performance at Aldershot as being 'like Real Madrid' but the back-to-back wins I'd watched against York (ironically, midweek away games were an easier operation for me than getting to Hull and back) and Port Vale were accompanied by some of the best football I'd seen played in a long while.

The York game in particular could well have been the perfect away-day experience had it not been for a moment that to this day still makes me cringe. It occurred when a bloke in front of me on the packed away terrace turned round and asked the time. On observing my smaller-than-average digital watch face he exclaimed, 'That's a *girl's* watch!' To make matters worse he proceeded to tell all and sundry this, ensuring that within minutes I had what appeared to be over 2,000 City fans queuing up just to have a gander at my timepiece. It served to put a real downer on an otherwise excellent evening.

---

80 Match programmes (Hull City v Hereford United, 3 April 1982; Hull City v Darlington, 10 April 1982)

14 May 1982
Football League Fourth Division:
Halifax Town 2 Hull City 2

The Shay: Stand not known; no ticket; programme 30p

Amid constant rumours about potential takeovers, City lost just five of their last 23 league games and finished a very respectable eighth. Prominent among some of the other matches were the 'What a winner Whitehurst' five-goal thriller at home to Bury and the midweek solitary goal away win at fellow 'crisis club' Rochdale. The latter was memorable for two things. Firstly, there was 'Sir' Les's goal celebration, which involved swinging on the inside of the net in front of the City support that consisted of two coach-loads and a Psychos minibus. Secondly, the final whistle prompted an away fans charge across the pitch towards the Sandy Lane End, which seemed to be orchestrated by a lad with a false leg wearing a white butcher's coat! Flushed by the success of scattering the home fans from their kop, it was a triumphant-sounding away contingent that was then escorted back to our vehicles. The locals didn't take too kindly to such arrogance and promptly bricked our coach as we left Rochdale. It was the first time I'd experienced such an event and, apparently, the first time one of Simon's coaches had ever been done. It wouldn't be the last.

On that walk back to our coaches, we'd chanted, 'If you're all going to Stockport clap your hands.' I'd joined in even though I had no intention of going – my second Spotland trip of the season had cleaned me out financially. True to form, #TypicalCity again upset the odds to win 2-1 at Edgeley Park and briefly keep alive their faint hopes of going up. These were eventually ended by draws against lowly Crewe and in the Stockport return fixture. Gates fell back to around 3,500 and when we travelled to Halifax on a Friday night in

May, there were lingering fears that it could still prove to be City's last-ever game. Another sizeable away contingent saw a 'Bunter' Marwood brace earn a 2-2 draw and the final whistle brought emotional scenes. The players threw their shirts into the crowd, which appeared symbolic as none of us really knew if we'd ever see this group together again. They might not have been the finest team ever to have worn the famous black-and-amber but by simply staying on to see the season through they were guaranteed hero status. The following day came the news we'd been desperate for. The *Hull Daily Mail* front-page headline announced 'TIGERS TAKEOVER' and 'New boss named: Boothferry Park future assured'. The Tigers were saved from extinction. I'm not ashamed to say I shed tears at the news – the first time I'd cried over City since Chris Green had told me his dad didn't have room to take me to that Oxford game back in 1978.

In total I'd clocked up 21 matches over the course of one of the most dramatic seasons in the club's history and after a slow start I was by now a regular at Boothferry Park. This increased attendance had helped boost my fledgling programme collection, which included an issue from all but one of my half-dozen away games (only the York one eluded me). These were carefully stored away, along with the newspaper match reports. I had just turned 16 and now regarded myself as a proper supporter of my local football club. I was lapping up the camaraderie that came with being part of the 'Black-and-Amber Army'. And with a new saviour in the shape of Don Robinson, things were set to get even better.

8

'Tigers, Tigers, Roar, Roar, Roar!'

The Old Showground: Friday, 15 October 1982

The prospect of a Friday night in Scunthorpe wouldn't usually have me giddy with excitement. But this one does. It's provided City with an away game at another team above them in the table and one that has just posted a club record nine-match unbeaten start to the campaign. Given its importance, there is also that possibility of extra spice off the field – what in police parlance would be referred to as 'potential for disorder'. The fact that City fans, as well as the players, see this as the perfect opportunity to make a statement to our closest neighbours and the rest of the division has the adrenalin going as we cross the magnificent Humber Bridge. This is a Hull City team on the up.

* * *

In the spring of 1982 there was one non-football story that briefly turned my attention away from Hull City's post-receivership dramas. On 19 March, Argentinian forces occupied the island of South Georgia in the southernmost waters of the Atlantic Ocean. Within a month they had raised their national flag in Port Stanley, capital of the Falkland Islands, a British Overseas Territory. The response involved what many critics saw as the UK Government's last great imperial venture and 74 days later the Falklands were British again. What Graham Stewart termed the 'last good-old-fashioned war' appeared like something straight out of my childhood *Commando* and *Warlord* comics

Notwithstanding the fact that people were actually dying, it got my 16-year-old juices flowing in a way that watching *A Bridge Too Far* at Hull's Tower Cinema had done a few years before. And not only mine. The Falklands War inspired patriotic outpourings across the country of a type last seen at the previous year's Royal Wedding, Botham's Ashes and *Chariots of Fire*. For people accustomed to cheering modern-day 'chariots' Seb Coe and Steve Ovett, described by Dominic Sandbrook as 'throwbacks to a lost age of sporting empire', the images of victorious British soldiers stood atop Mount Tumbledown harked back to empirical dominance of another kind. Where one was the image of 'patriotic young men, raising the Union Jack over the stadiums of the world' the other showed their military counterparts fluttering it from backpack radio aerials and eventually high above Government House. At times it bordered on near-jingoism, feverishly whipped up by tabloid headlines such as 'Stick it up your Junta' and 'Gotcha!' But for many, it simply stirred the British 'bulldog spirit'.[81]

Within days of victory in the Falklands, the World Cup in Spain offered another chance for Brits to feel good about themselves. With England there for the first time since 1970 (as part of a three-pronged Home Nations assault) hopes were high. Unfortunately, the expedition mounted by Ron Greenwood's squad at España '82 didn't prove as successful as the one Margaret Thatcher had sent to the South Atlantic.

---

81 Stewart, Graham, *Bang! A History of Britain in the 1980s* (London: Atlantic, 2013); Sandbrook, Dominic, *Who Dares Wins: Britain, 1979–1982* (London: Allen Lane, 2019) p.628

The Three Lions returned home early, albeit undefeated. It was a start of that stomach-churning cycle – in which hope and optimism turns to disappointment and despair – that I would soon experience on a regular basis. Sort of #TypicalCity but on a national scale.

World Cup disappointment couldn't dampen the spirits of City fans that summer. Don Robinson's arrival was all we needed, even if he did begin by warning everyone that the following season would be difficult. It didn't matter. Gone for good were rumours of a possible merger and ground-share with Hull FC, a scenario that had appeared unpalatable to large sections of both clubs' support. Instead, the preferred choice of rescue involved a foundation set up by Harold Needler's widow Hilary, which aimed to secure Boothferry Park as a sports venue, clear the massive debts and provide compensation for the outgoing management (who had recently launched a legal case against the club). By July, the Tigers' flirt with extinction had already become Bob Carver's fish and chips paper, eclipsed by events in the Midlands where the once-great Wolves also called in the receiver, following relegation to the Second Division. It was the start of what Dominic Sandbrook describes as 'the most catastrophic decline in British football history'. Barely four months on, City's demise was already old news.[82]

Scarborough-based Robinson was a former wrestler (appearing as Dr Death) whose only previous sporting connections with East Yorkshire came via a short-lived playing career for Hull KR between 1957 and 1960. 'I wasn't very good,' he told the *Hull Daily Mail* in 2012. He'd made his name (and money) at Flamingo Land and the Royal Opera House. Along with manager and former schoolmate Colin

---

82 Sandbrook, Dominic, *Who Dares Wins: Britain, 1979–82* (London: Allen Lane, 2019) p.225

Appleton – who he immediately installed as new City boss – he'd also transformed Scarborough FC into one of the richest clubs in non-league football, helped by two FA Trophy Final appearances at Wembley. Although stressing the need for his new club to get its house in order, Robinson brought much-needed positivity to Hull City. As David Goodman writes, 'He said that he was a winner and only wanted other people who thought of themselves as winners to play for the club.' His rhetoric was relentlessly upbeat and he pledged to 'hand over to somebody else in two years' time' if he had not made the club financially viable *and* successful on the field. Skipper Garreth Roberts described to Goodman the refreshing approach that Robinson brought: 'Don was so enthusiastic. It was his first step in the league arena but he was such a showman, such as when he rode around the edge of the pitch on horseback! Also he threw sweets to the crowd and got us to kick footballs into the crowd, dead cheap plastic footballs, but it was great. We went to hospitals, did charity work, and got noticed around town.'[83]

Robinson's enthusiasm and often ebullient showmanship made his partnership with 'the quiet and resilient' Appleton one that Mike Peterson terms 'a strange blend'. But it was to prove extremely effective. His first move on becoming chairman was to appoint a new board, before calling the players in one by one to explain his hopes for the coming season and to ask them to take a cut in appearance money. Chris Chilton was retained as assistant manager, with Bobby Brown returning to the club in a part-time capacity as youth liaison officer.

The chairman also announced big plans for Boothferry Park. Since the demolition of the North Stand, City had

---

83 Goodman, David, *Look Back in Amber* (Manchester: Parrs Wood Press, 2005) p.74

effectively been playing in a three-sided ground, with only contractors' boards behind the goal at the car park end. Original plans for a sporting and leisure complex had been kyboshed by receivership, with the exception of the new supermarket. Now Robinson announced plans to make Boothferry Park 'into the outdoor entertainments centre of the north', according to Simon Redfern in the *Hull Daily Mail*. Instead of the 'two-storey sports complex' originally envisaged by Bob Chapman, the North Stand would incorporate 'a Hollywood Bowl-type dome and social club' capable of hosting major pop concerts as a means of bringing in more revenue. There would be a new stand for supporters but one that didn't include as many executive boxes as first envisaged. Sadly, such plans never came to fruition; a supermarket, new club offices and a small open terrace was all that materialised. But to even announce such ambitious ideas was refreshing given the doom-mongering that had gone before. The 'Robinson Renaissance' was in full swing and the fans had belief again.[84]

One of the chairman's changes not received so enthusiastically was the inclusion of the colour red for the first time in the new City kit. This came via the pinstripes on the predominantly amber shirts, as part of the trim on the black shorts and as the primary colour of the socks. The new, Admiral-supplied affair signalled a radical change from its classy and more traditional Adidas predecessor but at least this one was available for fans to buy. Red was also used on the programme cover and as part of a makeover of the ground. It was seen as a nod to Robinson's previous Scarborough and Hull KR connections, although the man himself said it was to symbolise the blood the players should be willing to shed in

84 Peterson, Mike, *Farewell to Boothferry Park* (Hull: Arenasport, 2002) p.49

the cause. Blimey. Despite my reservations, I placed the new shirt on my Christmas wish list.

The Tigers' squad retained the nucleus of players who had battled through adversity the previous campaign. Norrie, Eccleston and Ferguson had departed, while returning to Boothferry was the popular Pete Skipper. Released to Darlington two seasons earlier on a free transfer by Smith (a move he later admitted was his biggest mistake as City manager), Skip had made no secret of his desire to return to his hometown club. He did so courtesy of a £10,000 fee paid by the supporters. Also 'new for '82' were former Middlesbrough duo Billy Askew and Billy Woof. Left-sided midfielder Askew is generally regarded to have been one of the club's shrewdest free-transfer signings ever. Appleton now proceeded to blend these new arrivals with the core of youngsters already at the club.

My first game of the new season was the goalless draw against Bradford City in the Football League Trophy. The Tigers had kicked off their campaign with a 2-1 win at Hartlepool in front of just 923 spectators. A few hundred more then saw them lose at Halifax. In his first 'Colin's Column', in the programme, Appleton thanked all those whose help over the summer had ensured the club had managed to hold its annual open day and get everything fit for the new season. He said that his 'first impressions within the club were of disappointments with the position Hull City find themselves in, and yet one of hope and optimism'. The Bradford game did little to set the pulse racing and the result signalled the end of the club's first silverware hunt of the new era. Despite this, a goalless draw against a side promoted the previous season was enough to convince the 3,202 present that Appleton's hopes weren't misplaced.

The Wembley of the North. Boothferry Park, August 1971 looking towards the North Stand (top) and from the opposite direction (Alamy Stock Images)

First cut. Chris Galvin celebrates Vince Grimes' goal against Fulham on 20 September 1975 (Hull Daily Mail)

King Edwards. Striker Keith Edwards, pictured signing autographs at the club open day in 1979, was the one shining beacon in difficult times (Lindsay Walters)

Sunnier climes. City manager Mike Smith meets the fans at the club's annual open day in 1980 (Ian Lees)

Up for the Cup. The Tigers edge past Halifax Town in the FA Cup first round on Saturday, 22 November 1980. City are defending the old North Stand end (Keith Middleton)

My mate Al and I can be seen at pitch level on Bunkers Hill, to the right of Keith Edwards (9) scorer of both City goals (Keith Middleton)

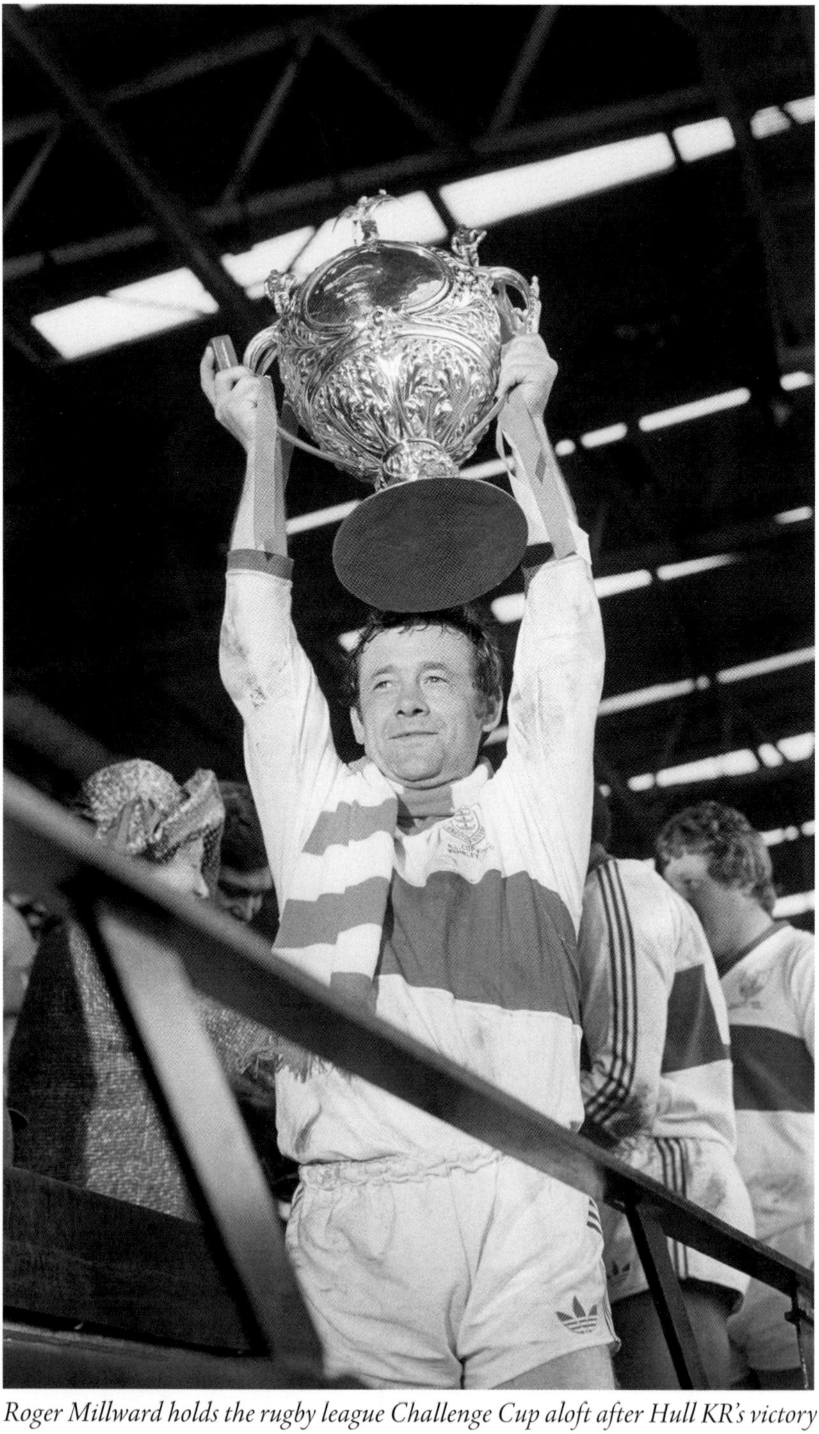

Roger Millward holds the rugby league Challenge Cup aloft after Hull KR's victory over Hull FC at Wembley in May 1980 (Alamy Stock Images)

Hull Vikings in speedway action at the Boulevard (Matthew Nicholson)

Yorkshire entertain Glamorgan at The Circle in cricket's Sunday League. Note the modular pavilion to the left, which replaced the Victorian original (Author's photo)

Boothferry Park, pictured in 1982 after demolition of the North Stand, a sight that was indicative of a club being dismantled (David Featherstone)

Fans heading across the main car park during the early-1980s. Note the close proximity of the home and away entrances to the Kempton, which often made for interesting pre-match entertainment (Roger Hill)

Scarborough entrepreneur Don Robinson stepped in to save the club and predicted that City would one day play on the moon

Robinson's first managerial appointment, Colin Appleton, didn't quite guide the Tigers to the moon but he did oversee City's climb from the basement (both pictures Hull Daily Mail)

The Tigers draw 2-2 at The Shay on 14 May 1982 in a game many supporters feared may be the club's last (Keith Middleton)

A year later, on 4 April 1983, City returned to Halifax en route to promotion to the Third Division (Keith Middleton)

Some well-known City interlopers are pictured here in among the 'Bloody Rubbish' Mansfield away following prior to our 'promotion party' on 2 May 1983 (Roger Hill)

A year later, on 12 May 1984, a packed Kempton looks on frustrated as City fail to beat Bristol Rovers and ultimately fall short in their pursuit of a second successive promotion (Lindsay Walters)

The travelling City support pictured on the Spion Kop at Northampton's former County Ground home watching a Fourth Division game in March 1983 (David Featherstone)

City fans being escorted to the Second Division game against Sunderland in October 1985, part of 'the largest contingent of visiting fans seen at Roker Park' that season (Gary Jones)

4 September 1982
Football League Fourth Division:
Hull City 1 Wimbledon 1

Boothferry Park: East Stand Terrace; no ticket; programme 30p

The school bus felt different that September. The summer holidays had marked the end of an era. Unlike many of my mates, I'd opted for the safety net of two more years, during which time I hoped the job outlook would improve. I also needed the sixth form to atone for some of my O-level failings as well as hopefully adding a couple of A-levels to the CV. Seeing City get promoted would be an extracurricular bonus. To that end things didn't begin well, Flounders scoring in a narrow defeat at newly relegated Bristol City on the opening day. Marwood was sent off as another loss followed at Sheffield United in the League Cup and there was suddenly a dip in those raised expectations.

Next up was Wimbledon, another relegated team, for the first home league game on the last Saturday of the school holidays. It was a low-key affair, played out in front of City's lowest-ever opening-day home crowd of 3,674. The attendance wasn't helped by a small away following, which included a young skinhead with a 'Wimbledon'-emblazoned Union Flag tied round his waist, who I bumped into coming out of Paragon Station that lunchtime. The fact that I remember this incident so vividly perhaps tells you all you need to know about the game. 'Cousin' Andy was again on target, 'ramming home a close-range header' on 39 minutes to cancel out a Dean Thomas piledriver for the Dons five minutes earlier. According to Simon Redfern, Flounders was also guilty of passing up the best of City's numerous other chances in a 1-1 draw against the eventual champions. My only other memory of the day comes from the curtain-raiser between a Holderness

& District Boys League Under-14s representative side and a Hull Schools XI. Two of my Easington mates, Clarkey and Maccer, featured for Holderness, with a certain Dean Windass in the Hull ranks.

Tucked away in the 'Commercial Corner' of the match programme for the league opener was another revolutionary Robinson idea. First revealed in the *Hull Daily Mail* as 'a drink to boost City', Tigercola was the result of a tie-up with Scarborough soft drink firm Clarke's. The deal, which would see the manufacturers 'donate 1p to City for every can of Tigercola they sell', was set to 'boost the Tigers' finances by at least £10,000' according to Simon Redfern's report. The Don told Redfern he thought it was 'one of the biggest sponsorship deals for a soccer club' and, in typical fashion, added that having been in receivership a short time ago, City 'have now finally gone pop'. A million cans of Tigercola were initially produced and I can remember them being readily available on Simon Gray's away coaches. In 2012 Robinson told the *Hull Daily Mail* that when launching the drink he'd been threatened with legal action by Coca-Cola over breach of copyright. 'Of course I was a little upstart and told them where to go,' said the City chairman. The club saw the drink as a winner. They marketed it as 'the fizz that makes the Tigers roar' and urged fans to 'Support the Can that Supports the Club'. It might've helped had the stuff not tasted absolutely revolting!

Although underwhelming, the Wimbledon result kickstarted a ten-match unbeaten run for City. Three nights later, Flounders (again), a Mutrie brace and a goal from McClaren yielded a 4-0 home win over York. I wasn't there, my night match logistical problems again proving insurmountable. According to Appleton, I missed some 'terrific football'. I also missed the 'encouraging' win over the Blades in the League

Cup second leg – accompanied by the usual shenanigans off the field – as well as away performances at Aldershot (won 2-1) and Colchester (0-0). These performances convinced the manager that his team had 'enough of the basic things right'.

Typically, the next game I did get to see was the 'frustrating' 1-1 draw with Hartlepool, although Appleton's view that you had 'to be there to believe it' suggests an air of dominance in City's display. Torrential rain is my one abiding memory of the goalless affair against Swindon, a result that left City 11th in the table after eight matches, six points off leaders Torquay who were due to visit Hull the following week. Despite Appleton hailing the 'extra people' who were attending games, the crowd of 3,786 against Swindon was still on the disappointing side. Six wins in the next seven matches would help address this, with the first one sending out a real message to the Tigers' rivals. In front of 4,128 spectators, Mutrie bagged a brace and both Dale Roberts and Pete Skipper were on target as the table-topping Gulls were culled. City won 4-1, setting things up nicely for a Friday trip across the Humber.

15 October 1982
Football League Fourth Division:
Scunthorpe United 0 Hull City 1

The Old Showground: Doncaster Road Terrace; no ticket; programme 30p

It's fair to say that City supporters have often looked on Scunthorpe in the same way that Leeds look on Hull but in the early 1980s there was a proper local rivalry, helped in no small part by the hosts' manager John Duncan hardly ever having a good word to say about the Tigers. He did, however, have a real feel for this particular occasion. In his programme notes he described the two matches in store that night as 'the one on the field and the one off it, to decide which supporters can give the most encouragement'. He added his hope that 'both contests will be competitive but never violent'.[85]

In the same publication, Martyn Girdham's 'Showground Snippets' reflected on the Iron's recent record-breaking win at Peterborough, which had taken them up to third. It had been filmed by Anglia TV for their Saturday night highlights show, leaving Girdham to bemoan the fact that the Yorkshire TV region didn't boast its own equivalent. Instead YTV took the Granada edition, which was 'supposedly serving the north of England' but rarely even mentioned the lower leagues. I knew what he meant. Back then we had to rely on the *Calendar* local news magazine programme for anything City-related.

Scunny's excellent start had been achieved wearing a new kit that harked back to their origins as North Lindsey United. After a decade playing in all red, they now sported a classy sky blue number with claret pinstripes and bold claret 'V' on the chest. My kit-geekery cap was well and truly doffed to that design. I was equally impressed by City's attire. It was the first chance I'd had to see the new away strip and it didn't disappoint. White shirts, red shorts and white socks with neat black-and-amber trim throughout. It looked even better in close-up on 'Sir' Les as he celebrated in front of more than 3,000 of us in the 'Donny Road end', having 'coolly rounded' goalkeeper Joe Neenan to slot home the slickest of winners and settle a pulsating game just five minutes from time. As Simon Redfern wrote, City had 'lowered the colours of the Fourth Division front-runners' for the second successive week. Not a bad way to spend Friday night after all!

* * *

85 Match programme (Scunthorpe United v Hull City, 15 October 1982)

The Scunthorpe win got everybody excited, not only on account of the result but the gate at The Old Showground (7,483) was the division's highest of the season to date, comfortably surpassing that which had seen City lose at Bristol on the opening day. The Tigers were the biggest draw in town. Ahead of the following weekend's home game with Northampton, Appleton was full of praise for his players and the travelling fans: 'For those supporters who were able to be with us at Scunthorpe, we must agree that occasion was something to be enjoyed. The team performance in attitude and so many good individual performances were a delight and of course, the winning goal coming the way it did, with Les Mutrie scoring in the cool, clinical way he can. Of course, it was tremendous to learn there wasn't any terrace problems, in fact the comments were something we don't hear very often about supporters and that behaviour was complemented [sic] in all areas.'[86]

Ahead of the Cobblers' visit, City lost 'a very fast end-to-end game' at Hereford, their first defeat since August. Edgar Street was a delight I'd have to wait to experience but my next ground tick came ten days later. Before then Marwood (two), Whitehurst and Flounders scored the goals that dispatched Northampton with ease in front of 4,317. The following Saturday, on the same day as 26,771 crammed into Boothferry Park to watch Australia beat Great Britain 40-4 in the first Ashes rugby league test, I headed west along the M62 to help form part of a crowd of just 1,568 at Prenton Park, Tranmere. It was a day that reminded us all of where City stood at the time in Hull's sporting pecking order.

At least the 200 or so of us at Tranmere were well rewarded as McClaren's only goal of the game brought another away

86 Match Programme (Hull City v Northampton Town, 23 October 1982)

win against another team experiencing financial difficulties. Appleton described it as 'much nearer to the required type of patient, controlled performance I have been trying to develop and the players have responded tremendously in their application'. McClaren's winner notwithstanding, the most exciting part of the day happened on the way home when I again experienced the unwanted sensation of broken glass on a coach. This time there was no brick involved; just two lads larking about on the back seat and pushing against the rear emergency exit door, resulting in the full pane falling out and shattering on the middle lane of the M62. Fortunately it did so without causing damage to any vehicles around us, but it meant a rather draughty ride home for those of us near the rear.

Tuesday brought new leaders Bury to Boothferry Park for a game that saw the unveiling of the 'artistic work' on the South Stand seats, part of Robinson's drive to 'improve the image of the ground'. More significantly, it pitted the Tigers against a team boasting a formidable unbeaten away record. Games under floodlights always seem to take on an extra-special feel and this would live up to its billing as goals from Marwood and Skipper clinched a 2-1 win. Bury didn't give up their record without a fight and the last quarter was described as proper 'edge of your seats' fare before City finally clinched the win that moved them to within three points of their opponents.

It was the best game of the season thus far and watched by the biggest league gate (6,101). The figure didn't include me, again forced to follow events by radio. How I cursed everything and everyone, from public transport to where I lived, from the fixture schedulers to Dad's lack of interest and even the timing of my actual conception. Sometimes, just sometimes it was shit being a 16-year-old hick from the sticks. I had again missed the 'not to be missed' and it was everybody else's fault but my own. 'Colin's Column' for the weekend visit of Peterborough didn't help: 'Congratulations to everyone associated with Hull City Football Club on your commitment on Tuesday night against Bury. I don't see why coming together at a football ground shouldn't always create that tingling expectation without going over the top, with players and public working together to enjoy their entertainment. We don't have to be drawn in by the disruptive minority, do we?'[87]

So, according to Appleton, I wasn't 'committed' to Hull City; not in the way that Gary, Carmo, Col and Douggie were. I could sense their smugness as they too digested the manager's notes. Perhaps Appleton was right. I mean, Simon Gray lived out our way and despite not being able to drive he still got to midweek games. Granted, he didn't have any homework to do, being several years my senior. Granted, too, he didn't get to see the full game due to his bus home leaving Hull station at 9.30pm. And not forgetting also that he was left with completing the last four miles courtesy either of a timely lift, a taxi or – more often than not – a lonely walk along dark, country lanes. But surely, if I was really committed I could do the same? Even if my walk home was another two miles further?!

Peterborough United visited Hull the following Saturday. It was 6 November. I never liked matches around Bonfire Night. Dark, covered terraces were often the chosen venue for some amateur fireworks show and the sound of 'crow-scarers' going off in among packed-in supporters is one of the few aspects from the old terrace days that I have no desire to see return. By this time my mates and I had a regular matchday

---

87 Match programme (Hull City v Peterborough United, 6 November 1982)

position, about halfway up and some ten yards or so from the segregation barrier to our right. Thankfully it wasn't quite high or dark enough to be a pyrotechnic's preferred choice. But whenever one went off – as it did in this game – it caused quite a stir. City produced their own fireworks on the pitch in front of a crowd of 5,535. 'Bunter' bagged a brace, Billy Woof scored in his last game before departing overseas and a Posh own goal completed the tally in a 4-1 scoreline. But it's the sound of that bloody firework that I always associate with the day.

Because of our usual position, several of City's 'faces' were now well known to us. We were in or around Wally and the 'Kempton choir' and as such were familiar with the words to most of the songs and chants. We were even brave enough to try and start the odd one, if we felt the atmosphere was going flat. This could happen quite often due to the small number of visitors, although some away followings would compensate for lack of numbers by level of volume. Peterborough's was one such example and they kept up their vocal backing despite their defeat. They also weren't averse to fronting up at the Kempton partition, which was credit to them given the numbers involved. They wouldn't be the only ones.

The win was City's fourth in a row but the rest of November proved much trickier. First up was a painful introduction to the bleak open away terrace at Vale Park. Seemingly miles away from the action, the atmosphere consisted of little more than the taunts of the home fans as the Tigers went down to the only goal. It was another big game, billed by Vale boss John McGrath as a 'top-of-the-table' clash (in reality it was fifth versus third although only four points separated the top seven). It was the third City fixture in a row watched by a crowd of over 5,000, with about a fifth of that figure having travelled down from East Yorkshire. Vale's star man was new striker Bob Newton, signed for £15,000 from Hartlepool. He was the top scorer, cover star of the day's programme and *Match Weekly*'s Fourth Division Man of the Month for September. But it was centre-half Phil Sproson who stole the headlines with the winner. Appleton described his players as 'deeply disappointed' not to have returned 'with at least one point' from the game. Some City fans felt the manager had approached things too cautiously and that the team hadn't had a real go. There was much frustration on the way home, with opinions varied as to where we'd gone wrong. For my part I came home convinced that the whole Port Vale experience possessed few redeeming features save for their kit, which resembled a white-and-black version of the Scunny template. Wisely, I didn't share this geeky observation with my disgruntled fellow passengers.

The big games kept on coming. A crowd of 9,102 welcomed Sheffield United in the FA Cup, with that pre-match feeling that always accompanied a visit by the Blades. Even Appleton noted, 'It is hoped that any off the field activities don't take the headlines.' Along with their sizeable following, United also brought Edwards. In his autobiography, the striker maintains that any abuse City fans gave him was slight compared to that received from Blades followers. That's not how I remember it, nor Stephen Hodgson in *Tiger Rag*: 'Edwards the former hero was now the villain and abuse rained down on him from Kempton. As ever he had the perfect answer, an early strike to put United 1-0 ahead. He celebrated by running straight for Kempton and I can still remember the feeling as my feet were lifted off the terraces by hundreds of City fans surging downwards. Edwards retreated to the centre circle as City fans spilled on to the pitch.'[88]

---

88 *Tiger Rag* fanzine (Issue 5, March 1995) p.29

For a long time it appeared that this solitary strike would see the Blades through but a Tony Kenworthy own goal late on brought the house down and earned City a deserved replay. I didn't join my mates in going (there's that lack of commitment again) but I could've predicted what would happen. What always happened back then at Bramall Lane. City got shafted. Those Wembley dreams dashed 'for another year'; another cup exit at the hands of the Blades, another defeat at Bramall Lane and another reason to sing, 'We only hate Sheff United!' Even Appleton alluded to such feelings in his next notes, which began, 'So Sheffield United have done it again.' Describing the first meeting as 'quite special' he labelled the replay performance as 'the most disappointing' since he had been at the club. Enough said.[89]

* * *

Given that modern managers can be heard bleating about 'fixture chaos' and 'player burn-out' when asked to play three times a week, it's quite staggering to think that back in 1982 in the midst of a gruelling promotion campaign and with a squad of only 17 first-teamers, Don Robinson arranged a couple of 'prestigious' friendly fixtures to coincide with the busiest part of the season. In the run-up to Christmas, either side of a tough-looking test at Blackpool in the league, Soviet side Dynamo Kiev and Kevin Keegan's rejuvenated Newcastle United were both scheduled to visit Hull. In the event the latter game was postponed until the season's end but the Kiev one went ahead as planned, giving fans a taster of the European nights we could dare to dream about in the future once Robinson's plans really took off.

89 Match programme (Hull City v Chester, 27 November 1982)

29 November 1982
Friendly: Hull City 0 Dynamo Kiev 3

Boothferry Park: East Stand Terrace; no ticket; programme 30p

Hosting a club of Dynamo Kiev's stature was arguably the most prestigious game seen at Boothferry Park since Hungarian giants Vasas had visited in 1954. Ranked (somewhat inaccurately) 'the top side in Russia', Kiev were the first Soviet team to win a European trophy when lifting the Cup Winners' Cup in 1975 and had again reached the European Cup quarter-finals in 1980/81, where they had lost to Aston Villa. They were managed by Valeriy Lobanovskyi, recently also appointed national team coach and their squad included 1975 European Footballer of the Year Oleg Blokhin. Eight of the side had been in the Soviet Union's 1982 World Cup squad, of whom five – Baltacha, Demyanenko, Bal, Bessanov and Blokhin – had played. For those with a programme, reading the visitors' team sheet was quite a contrast to the one they'd read two days previously, which had listed the players of Chester City.

Hull had beaten Chester 2-0 to arrest their recent winless run. They could now enjoy themselves against opponents who'd lost narrowly to Newcastle and had won at Hearts. Despite this, Appleton fielded almost a full-strength side, with John Davies deputising for Tony Norman in goal. Young keeper Len Findlay would gain a first senior appearance when coming on as one of five second-half substitutes. It was a bitterly cold night and Kiev scored early through Yevtushenko to ensure it was also a testing one in front of what at the time was Boothferry Park's third-highest home gate of the season (6,901). Further strikes from Khlus in the 66th minute and Dumanski in the 77th ended City's 17-match unbeaten run at home and gave the Tigers what Simon Redfern reported as 'a lesson in taking chances with a minimum of possession'. All in all, the game was seen as a worthwhile exercise. Far from treating the fixture as an unwanted distraction, Appleton said the experience of playing against 'a difficult type of opposition … should be invaluable to our young team'. Robinson, who had hosted Dynamo at The Grand Hotel in Scarborough, told the *Hull Daily Mail* that the visit of such a 'top-class side' was a 'great privilege' for City before – in his usual style – predicting that the next time the two teams would meet would be in the European Cup Final. When set against the backdrop of the Cold War the two clubs had given British and Soviet politicians what the local paper termed 'a lesson in Detante'.

One player who didn't feature in the Tigers' line-up was Justin Fashanu, the Nottingham Forest striker having reportedly demanded an 'outrageous' £1,000 appearance fee after his manager Brian Clough had given permission to play. In the *Hull Daily Mail*, Robinson commented, 'I would be wanting to buy him for that!' It was an embarrassing episode that at least finished amicably, courtesy of Clough's reported offer to bring his Forest senior side to Hull for a friendly later in the year – 'for nothing except travel expenses'. Appleton said it was a mark of 'a generous man'. Another forward unavailable to Appleton was former City favourite John Hawley, whose short-term loan from Arsenal hadn't been confirmed in time. Taking what the local paper termed 'a substantial cut in wages', the striker told David Goodman that the club he returned to was 'one of the most bizarre set-ups I'd ever seen', due mainly to the Robinson-Appleton axis. He was introduced to the crowd at half-time, although not 'waving my arms about' in the way his chairman had wanted. 'That just wasn't me,' said Hawley.[90]

90 Goodman, David, *Look Back in Amber* (Manchester: Parrs Wood Press, 2005) p.79

Hawley's acquisition brought some much-needed experience ahead of the weekend trip to Blackpool. Applauded warmly on the Monday, five days later the Withernsea-born striker got a hero's welcome from the travelling support at Bloomfield Road, before playing a part in the Mutrie goal that earned a point. Appleton termed City's opponents 'very useful'. Not according to a popular call-and-response chant of the time, aired just prior to kick-off:

'I said Blackpool.'

'I said SHIT!'

'I said Blackpool.'

'I said SHIT!'

'I said FUCKING Blackpool.'

'I said FUCKING shit!'

While this would normally have been a well-received chant among the travelling support, on this occasion it was rather less so, the reason for which can be found in the *Hull Daily Mail* of Monday, 6 December 1982. Under the headline 'Tigers boss slams fans' it describes how a 'perturbed' Appleton was 'rightly critical' of a section of the away support 'who chanted obscenities during the minute's silence in memory of former Blackpool president Albert Parkinson'. Appleton added, 'If anyone starts thinking that it helps the team as far as letting them know they are there, they are off track. That is not the way to do it.' In fairness, I'm not sure that anyone was aware of the pre-match commemoration but even so it was another regrettable incident involving supporters of Hull City.

According to Mike Peterson, John Hawley had once stated his ambition as being 'to hit the North Stand clock' at Boothferry Park. He found the more desirable target of the back of the Colchester net a week after his debut. 'Cousin' Andy bagged a brace in a 3-0 win. A similar scoreline away at Crewe had the Tigers in the top three at Christmas.

The Yuletide fixture list of four games in eight days was a thing to behold. Of course the club hierarchy loved it, on account of the bigger crowds over the holiday period. On Bank Holiday Monday, 27 December, I was among a reported 10,042 spectators inside Boothferry left largely frustrated by Halifax goalkeeper Lee Smelt in a 1-1 draw (it was a figure amended to 9,692 in subsequent records but was still comfortably the best crowd thus far). The following evening I joined the big City contingent that virtually turned Darlington's Feethams into a home ground. 'Thank you very much for Peter Skipper' was sung with particular gusto as part of a noisy vocal repertoire and our reward came via a 2-1 win; goals from Marwood and Askew prompting a celebratory pitch invasion. The Tigers' unbeaten run stood at six matches and victory over Rochdale on New Year's Day took them top – as playfully demanded by The Don before jetting off for a Yuletide break in Florida. Marwood, rapidly becoming the talisman, and Garreth Roberts were on target in another 2-1 win in front of another bumper crowd of 9,059. It was a very Happy New Year at Boothferry Park.[91]

91 Peterson, Mike, *Farewell to Boothferry Park* (Hull: Arenasport, 2002) p.21;

9

The Tigers Are Back!

Sealand Road: Saturday, 30 April 1983

The players are up above us in the directors' box and they're getting a great reception from the fans on the pitch. I've hitched a lift on Carmo's back to get a better view. I'm already fantasising about the scene back home when Mum spots me on this week's Calendar Sport, *or rather she spots the hand-knitted amber-and-black woollen 'tea cosy' perched upon my flat-top. It was a gift from Dad's mate Henry and is a relic of the Raich Carter era. In the spirit of The Don, I'd got Mum to remove the bobble to give me a sort of cool Dexy's/Bowery Boys look. In truth it's nearer a complete cock look. But I don't care. A year ago I wasn't even sure I'd have a football team anymore. Now, here I am, celebrating promotion. The Tigers are back!*

* * *

January 1983. Despite the cold, I opted against a jacket while standing in Easington village square awaiting the out-of-towners coach. Mansfield away and my Christmas present, a brand-new City shirt, was making its debut. It was short-sleeved and I was freezing my nuts off but I was determined to advertise who I supported and where I was heading. I needn't have bothered. Aside from a couple of blokes walking their dogs I didn't see another soul and the two I did couldn't give a toss what I was wearing or where I was going. I felt sorry for them and their ignorance. The impending trip to Field Mill would surely see City build on their New Year ascent of the Fourth Division summit.

By half-time I'd somewhat revised this view. Not for the last time in my City-supporting career, a 'sea of black-and-amber' on the old Quarry Lane away terrace stood motionless and gobsmacked by what was unfolding in front of our eyes. City were three down by the break, rainswept and ripped apart by a team that despite its league position were far from 'bloody rubbish'. It was a scoreline the Tigers contributed to with what Simon Redfern referred to as 'two gifts' in a 'catastrophic spell'. After Gary Nicholson had swept home the Stags' first on seven minutes, John Dungworth capitalised on a Garreth Roberts slip to make it 2-0 three minutes later before hammering home the third from the penalty spot just past the half-hour mark, following Skipper's foul on him; and all this despite City having 'the majority of play'. Bunter's 78th-minute reply barely constituted a consolation and was received as such by the '2,000 or so City fans in Mansfield's best gate of the season'. It was all so #TypicalCity.

The bad news wasn't restricted to the field of play. Tuesday's *Hull Daily Mail* reported, 'Angry shopkeepers at Mansfield were still clearing up … after gangs of soccer hooligans, many from Hull, rampaged through the town centre smashing shop windows, worth hundreds of pounds.' The report claimed that '32 Hull fans, nine of them juveniles, were arrested and bailed to appear before court at a later date'. Being 'detained all afternoon' and therefore missing the match was probably a blessing for them.

Despite the defeat, the Tigers remained top on goal difference from Bury. They bounced back the following week with an excellent away win at rivals Wimbledon. Dave Bassett's side were experiencing the Manager of the Month curse in which they lost four of the next five league games. A rare Dale Roberts goal and another from Whitehurst secured City a 2-1 success in front of 2,766 at Plough Lane. The league table in the next home programme had Hull City printed in bold atop the Fourth Division. 'Colin's Column' made pleasant reading: 'It is a major credit to the players that we find ourselves in the top position of the Fourth Division, and of course the publicity that their success attracts can only be good for all concerned ... [However] there is still another mountain to climb and although we must savour the present situation, we must also be realistic in the fact that our task is only just beginning.'[92]

The manager's caution was underlined by a tense afternoon against Bristol City in front of another decent gate of 6,835. 'Sir' Les popped up 11 minutes from time to settle the contest and keep the Tigers at the summit. Pole position was maintained with a point at Hartlepool combined with Port Vale's surprise defeat at Chester, and as City prepared to host Stockport, Appleton expressed his delight at still being top after five games of 1983. He was even happier by the end of the afternoon. The Tigers went goal crazy against their hapless visitors, completing a magnificent 7-0 rout. 'Cousin' Andy grabbed his first hat-trick in league football, with Mutrie, Askew, Skipper and Garreth Roberts also on target in the club's biggest win in 18 years.

Bizarrely, even on this most momentous of afternoons I managed to find something to get miffed about. It came via the sight of two lads stood near me in the Kempton who I knew from school were not City supporters. I remember

92 Match programme (Hull City v Bristol City, 15 January 1983)

feeling aggrieved that they should be enjoying such a stunning display on what I automatically assumed to be their first visit to the ground all season. And there they were, celebrating along with the likes of us who'd been to Mansfield, to Darlo, and to Tranmere. What right did they have to see City at their imperious best? My indignation was such that it was hard to stop myself from going over to these upstarts and accusing them of being mere 'bandwagon jumpers'. Thankfully, I thought better of it – as I would 25 years later when such feelings resurfaced at Wembley. Who was I to criticise anyone anyway? There are enough skeletons in my own cupboard for me to be in no position to begrudge others a chance to bask in black-and-amber glory. It's worth remembering that we all have to start somewhere. These two just got luckier than most.

* * *

After years of ridicule, the Tigers were at last making headlines for all the right reasons. The Stockport result confirmed them as the form team in the division, Appleton was named January Manager of the Month and a couple of weeks later, they were even featured in popular magazines *Match* and *Shoot!* They were also the subject of a special feature on *Calendar* ahead of the local derby at York, scheduled for Saturday, 12 February. Robinson and Appleton had taken the players to Scarborough for a couple of days of training on the beach, before heading back to a snowy Hull in preparation for the game. Understandably, the mood among the players and management was relaxed and in some cases buoyant, although Chris Chilton offered wise words of caution when asked by John Helm if the 'people of Hull … really believe you can go into the Third Division'. The assistant manager's reply was typically down-to-earth, 'Whether they believe it or not, we've still got to prove it … I'll believe it when we're four points clear with one game to play.' In contrast, the City chairman wasn't holding back in his view as to where his club was heading. It was during an interview in Scarborough with a young John Shires that The Don came out with the quote that City fans would often hark back to years later, 'We're after getting into the Third Division next year, the Second Division after that and the First Division, playing in the European Cup and if there's going to be a team playing on the Moon, we want Hull City playing up on the Moon.'[93]

Robinson then heaped praise on the club's support, pointing out that City were the only club in the league to have 'more than doubled' their attendances and that the support from the fans has been 'absolutely tremendous'. This support manifested itself in different – and sometimes unusual – ways. In February the club even released its own song, 'The Tigers Are Back', written by City fans Henry Priestman and Mark Herman. Priestman was an acclaimed musician later to achieve fame as part of The Christians, while childhood friend Herman was a film producer, with later credits to include *Brassed Off*, *Little Voice* and *The Boy in the Striped Pyjamas*. Taking a tune ('Out of Touch') first used by Priestman's former band Yachts and adding new lyrics, 'The Tigers Are Back' was 'thrown together very quickly', according to Herman, 'with the help of the (slightly bewildered) squad … and of course new chairman Don Robinson'. The day after the Stockport game the players were in the boardroom back at Boothferry Park to add their own vocals to a new club anthem. In September 2018, Priestman told the *Hull Daily Mail*'s Phil Buckingham that they 'didn't want to be there': 'It was a Sunday and they'd been dragged in to sing on this song. Don Robinson, who has a larger than life character, had

93 From *Calendar* (Yorkshire TV, 11 February 1983) via the TigerTube YouTube channel

insisted. All the players were looking at me thinking, "Who's this ginger idiot?"'[94]

However, with Dennis Booth's 'enthusiastic conducting' the players soon got into the swing of it. The song was released at the end of February on Don Records with a catalogue number COL001, hence a tribute to both the chairman and manager. All proceeds went to the players' pool as a reward for their efforts. It proved hugely popular, temporarily replacing 'Tiger Rag' as the team's song to run out to and knocking Duran Duran off top spot in the charts – the Syd Scarbs charts that is.

It's easy to forget what halcyon days these were for the club. As Herman told the *Hull Daily Mail*, supporters felt a belonging that hadn't been there for some time. And it wasn't just City. The Hull rugby clubs were at the height of their success too. Appleton wrote, 'Hull City AFC are in a position to add to what would be a super 1982/83 for the sporting public in Hull and District.' He urged us to 'concentrate all our energies to make those dreams come true'.

Colin Appleton's Manager of the Month award was announced ahead of the visit of Aldershot, which therefore made it almost inevitable that City would slip up. Indeed, it would prove to be a frustrating February. The Tigers were held at home by the Shots and away at Torquay, while the derby at York was one of many games to fall foul of the wintry conditions. The month closed with the eagerly awaited home game against Scunthorpe. The two points lost at Plainmoor meant City's lead at the top had been cut to a single point by virtue of Port Vale's win at Hereford. The visitors were a further 11 points back but had three games in hand and

94 Buckingham, Philip, https://www.hulldailymail.co.uk/sport/football/football-news/hull-city-tigers-song-duran-1982059, *Hull Daily Mail*, 8 April 2020

remained very much in the promotion picture. They were also under new management. Allan 'Casper in a Suit' Clarke had replaced John Duncan, controversially sacked in January after an FA Cup third-round defeat by near neighbours Grimsby – a club he'd allegedly been speaking to about their own managerial vacancy.

26 February 1983
Football League Fourth Division:
Hull City 1 Scunthorpe United 1
Boothferry Park: East Stand Terrace; no ticket; programme 30p

The Humber derby was easily the most attractive game in the division and the *Match of the Day* cameras rolled into town. The six-minute-long special feature on their Sunday afternoon highlights show did a decent job of promoting the positivity oozing out of City at the time: the redevelopment plans for the North Stand, 'The Tigers Are Back' and even Tigercola. Presenter Tony Gubba – who interestingly (given future events) referred to the club as 'Hull Tigers' in his intro – accompanied Don Robinson for a drive across the Humber Bridge. The Don was in full PR mode and talked about the expanded catchment area that the bridge had opened up. Gubba quoted the day's crowd as 14,252, although it would subsequently go down as 11,933. There were several possible reasons for the adjustment. It may be that the 'three or four thousand' Robinson had predicted would cross the Bridge that afternoon failed to materialise. Or perhaps it was tied in with the players' pay agreement at the time, which saw them receive an extra bonus for every 1,000th fan through the turnstiles. Or of course it may simply have been a case of one-upmanship, initially designed to send a message out to those who still viewed Hull as a 'rugby town'. Hull FC's Challenge Cup tie at The Boulevard, taking place at the same time, attracted a crowd reported by Gubba to be 12,189 (it would subsequently go down as 11,197).

City's mascot was eight-year-old Nicholas Barmby of Appleton Primary School but the future City player and later manager shared the disappointment of many as Denis Leman's shot deflected off Askew's head to give the visitors a 33rd-minute lead. Only Norman's superb save from Steve Baines's header prevented a second after half-time. But with just over six minutes left, Mutrie's excellent footwork created the chance for Marwood to steer home the equaliser. Appleton described the result as 'a little disappointing' but the *Match of the Day* piece finished with him, Clarke and both chairmen toasting a hoped-for joint promotion come May.

The Scunthorpe result allowed Port Vale to go top by virtue of a 2-1 win over Halifax. It provided a timely kick up the backside, and three days later, City travelled to Bury for the customary thriller. The five-goal affair was settled by a wonderful Flounders winner. Gary maintains it's the best game he's ever seen City involved in. It would be. Again I was left regretting missing out on a trip to the home of the black pudding. Instead I was probably finishing an essay on Cardinal Richelieu and I'm not sure Mr Twinning would have accepted my being at 'the best game I've ever seen' as a justifiable reason for not handing it in. I could only hope Northampton away the following Saturday would match it.

Midweek results saw the Tigers return to the top and their position would have been even better had Port Vale not levelled late in a 2-2 draw against Hartlepool. Still, Vale's weekend involvement in a local derby against Crewe offered City the opportunity to kick on at the County Ground, perhaps the quirkiest venue I'd yet visited. Prior to its replacement by the

Sixfields Stadium in 1994, this was the last remaining three-sided venue in the Football League (an honour it had shared with Sheffield United up until 1974). The Cobblers shared it with Northamptonshire County Cricket Club and the local bowls club, and even Town supporters described it as the worst ground and playing surface in the league (a reputation earned due to it being used as a spectators' car park in the summer). It was also unusual in having Spion Kop as the name attached to the away terrace, an open affair that only stretched as far as the goal. From there to our right was the old Main Stand, which would be demolished in the wake of the Bradford fire disaster of 1985. To our left was a line of advertising boards that formed the barrier to the cricket pitch, with the pavilion in the distance beyond.

The poor pitch certainly didn't help City and Gage fired the Cobblers ahead early in the second half. With time running out and somewhat against the run of play, Askew's equaliser appeared to have claimed a draw that the Tigers' performance hardly merited. Then, with just ten seconds remaining, Garreth Roberts played a through ball for Flounders to run on to. 'Cousin' Andy was perhaps fortunate still to be on the pitch following an off-key performance. Appleton's decision to keep him on now paid the most handsome of dividends as the man described by *Hull Daily Mail* reporter Keith Perry as 'Hull City's incredible young striker' ran on and thumped the ball into the roof of the net from just inside the box.

It's another goal I can remember quite vividly as it was scored at our end and sent the City fans on the Spion Kop into raptures. Moments later, to the tune of 'Here we go', chants of 'You've been robbed' were being aimed at the understandably disgruntled home supporters. Our celebrations were topped off when The Don climbed aboard our coaches to personally thank us for our efforts. Appleton wrote, 'I'm sure the players make your journeys worthwhile.' They certainly had that day, especially when coupled with the news that Port Vale had been held by their neighbours. Advantage City.

* * *

My away trips were by now being worn as a badge of honour in the classroom and after each one I'd go into school with my recently acquired match programme on full show. As a member of the lower sixth form, one of my lunchtime responsibilities was policing access to the computer corridor, which was restricted only to the nerds with the correct passes (and usually glasses). This otherwise mundane task was often brightened up by the visit of several fourth- and fifth-form would-be City 'casuals', only too keen to share tales of the latest away games with the kid with the dodgy haircut manning the doors. As there was no official recording of away followings one of our themes was guesstimating it, based on the number of coaches, size of the away end, etc. I became almost obsessive in my pursuit of the numbers following City at the time. Perry did his best to oblige, referring in his match report to 'at least six coach-loads of fans [having] made the 150-mile trip down the M1' to Northampton.

In his next programme notes, Appleton expressed his appreciation of the travelling support but also warned, 'We also must realise we are only as good as our next game.' Somewhat presciently as it turned out; Mark Ferguson's 77th-minute winner for lowly Tranmere the following week ended City's 22-match unbeaten home record in all competitions. Wimbledon – back on track following their new year blip – had cut the Tigers' lead to three points. Ominously, both the Dons and Port Vale (losers to Blackpool) also had two games in hand. Perusing the *Sports Mail* and the Sunday papers cast something of a shadow over my 17th birthday celebrations. Were we going to blow it?[95]

City organised a 'British Rail Excursion' (aka 'Football Special') to Peterborough the following Saturday, priced at £7 and leaving Hull just before lunch. It helped ensure another excellent away following in a crowd of 3,805. I opted for the door-to-door convenience of Simon's coach, making the same trek south as that of a fortnight earlier. In the hosts' programme, Paul Richardson of the *Peterborough Evening Telegraph* described just how tight things were at the top end of the division. In his view 'the top eight all have a reasonable chance of going up'. Posh sat ninth.

The low roof at London Road's Moy's End made for incredible noise. And our efforts were amplified even more by the perceived injustice of seeing Askew dismissed after only 17 minutes for a foul on Mario Ippolito. The City fans channelled their disgust at the decision into some of the most rousing away support I've ever been a part of. In fairness, our heroes didn't just shut up shop – they took the game to their hosts. And when Mutrie capped his 100th Football League appearance for the Tigers by heading Marwood's wonderful cross in off the post on 51 minutes, it simply encouraged those of us behind the goal to even greater efforts. One particular rendition of 'Appleton's Black-and-Amber Army' seemed to extend for almost the whole second half. Willed on by this wall of noise, City were within just two minutes of a memorable win. But as the sound of 'We shall not be moved' boomed out from the away end, Micky Gynn's deflected 20-yard shot wrong-footed Norman who despite getting hands to the ball couldn't stop it bouncing in. There was a split-second silence before that sickening sound of three sides of the ground

95 Match programme (Hull City v Tranmere Rovers, 12 March 1983)

erupting in celebration. I felt completely crushed; I imagine the players even more so.

The following Friday's *Calendar Sport* showed the briefest highlights in its weekend preview slot (it had been Anglia TV's featured game). They couldn't even begin to do justice to the drama and spectrum of emotions experienced. In his next programme notes, Appleton described his team's performance at London Road as one 'full of character and determination and skill for young players'. He added, 'We hoped through playing in a positive manner, that Lady Luck would be with us, but it was not to be, and two points were lost.'[96]

Wimbledon benefited from that late Posh leveller to go two points clear at the top of the Fourth Division. City's next opponents, Port Vale, were a place and a point behind the Tigers but had two games in hand. The Valiants' visit was a proper 'six-pointer' and the game was another to garner television coverage, via Granada TV's Saturday night *Match Time*. This time there was no background build-up piece, just seven minutes of edited highlights, with John Helm at the, well, helm. The highlights accurately reflected a match that City deservedly won in the 67th minute when Marwood finished a sweeping move involving Booth, Whitehurst and Mutrie to net his 14th goal of the season. He was then denied a second by Vale keeper Barry Siddall's fine stop, while Jim Steel missed the visitors' best chance of a late reply. Earlier Whitehurst had passed up two good opportunities for City. Meanwhile, former Liverpool skipper Emlyn Hughes – signed from Rotherham to add experience during the run-in – went close to capping his first match in the Fourth Division with only his fourth goal of the season, courtesy of a decent long-range strike

96 Match programme (Hull City v Port Vale, 26 March 1983)

that would have silenced the 'Big Fat Emlyn' chants from the away section![97]

Marwood's clinical finish in front of the under-construction Grandways store at the old North Stand end had the home fans in raptures. The crowd of 15,615 (later amended to 14,410) was Boothferry Park's biggest for six years and the sixth biggest in English football that day. Appleton later recalled how prior to the game he'd spoken to a reporter at the *Hull Daily Mail* 'about the importance of loud vocal support from what promised to be the largest home game at Hull for many a day'. Perhaps unsurprisingly, Don Robinson wasn't afraid to milk this latest success and he did so, appearing with Marwood on Monday night's *Calendar*. It was therefore a given that when struggling Darlington arrived a week later, #TypicalCity blew the chance to strengthen their title grip by dropping points in a 0-0 draw. A packed Quakers defence and an excellent display from their reserve keeper Fred Barber ensured a frustrating afternoon.

4 April 1983
Football League Fourth Division:
Halifax Town 1 Hull City 2

The Shay: South Stand Terrace; no ticket; programme 35p

Easter Monday and almost a year on from the last emotional night at The Shay, I was back in West Yorkshire as part of a massive travelling support. Our previous visit had been accompanied by some anxiety that we might just be watching our club's final game. Almost one year on and those same fans were back in even bigger numbers hoping to see virtually that

97 During the 1982/83 season Yorkshire TV only produced five editions of their own show *The Big Game* due to having no top-flight representatives (following Leeds United's relegation). City v Port Vale was therefore one of several games for which highlights were submitted to Granada's regular *Match Time* programme.

same City team get their promotion push back on track. Prior to proceedings, Town boss Micky Bullock publicly thanked The Don for his 'kind gesture' in presenting two crates of champagne following his team's wins over City's rivals Bury and Colchester. He joked that the pair hadn't agreed on what the present would be should his side add the Tigers to the list! Thankfully, Robinson wasn't called upon to present anything as Billy Woof, recalled in place of Whitehurst for his first senior game for over six weeks, and Brian Marwood scored the goals that earned an invaluable 2-1 win.

Initially, though, it appeared the game might go the same way as Darlington with City frustrated in their early efforts and Lee Smelt replicating his Boxing Day heroics. But right on half-time, Woof met Neil Thompson's cross to send the ball looping in. And after Martin Nuttall had stabbed home an equaliser on 54 minutes, Woof sent Marwood racing clear from halfway to score his 15th goal of the season 12 minutes later. It proved the winner although the Tigers were thankful for a brilliant Norman save near the end to confirm it. The game was played in front of 5,011 spectators which, given that the average Halifax gate was about 1,700, gives some idea of the size of the travelling City support. It was a fact not lost on Appleton who wrote the following week, 'It seemed as if there were only Hull supporters at Halifax, no one there doubting one bit they can contribute to the success of their team – they kicked every ball for the players on the field – took all the knocks – frustration and enjoyment in what was a vital win.'[98]

Blackpool were next up for a meeting of the recently judged third- and first-placed clubs in the National Programme Awards. In the bronze-winning edition, the City manager was in reassuring form after admitting that he had 'experienced

98 Match programme (Hull City v Blackpool, 9 April 1983)

some doubting Thomases' but that 'at least when we needed a boost at Halifax we got one'. City scored after just 43 seconds against Blackpool, they were two up inside three minutes and eventually won 3-1 (with two more from Marwood). Their next victory, 1-0 at Swindon was described by Appleton as a 'sign of the players' determination to achieve something'. Three wins on the trot meant that everybody was up for the short trip to York the following Tuesday. Despite this being the day we returned to school after the Easter break there was no way even I was missing this one, although I didn't take that bloody watch with me!

York's biggest crowd for seven years, 9,909, included 'around 5,000 of who were Hull fans' according to Simon Redfern in the *Hull Daily Mail*. It was the biggest away following I'd yet been part of. A repeat of the previous season's impressive win would do nicely thank you. But on a night of controversy, which began with Appleton's omission of the fit-again Mutrie, John Byrne put a massive dent in City's title hopes with the only goal of the game just before the hour. Redfern's view that he 'looked offside when netting Brian Pollard's lob from almost on the line' was shared by most City fans present. Both Marwood and Billy Woof hit the bar, while Redfern also pointed to the 'ridiculous 41 free kicks awarded against the Tigers by Burnley referee David Scott' as further evidence of a night in which the odds seemed stacked against them. Completing a night of misery for the visitors was the dismissal of Dale Roberts for foul and abusive language in the tunnel after the final whistle.

Although Don Robinson awarded the players their winning pay despite the result, saying, 'The way they fought was a credit to the city. They were the Tigers last night,' the real winners were Wimbledon whose 3-2 success against Crewe returned the Dons to the top of the table. Meanwhile, yet again a disappointing result was accompanied by news of more trouble around an away ground. Sadly, as seen at Mansfield at New Year, it was becoming a predictable downside of taking such big numbers away. Once again the *Hull Daily Mail* carried stories of City fans causing damage to residential areas and, at the behest of The Don, the following Saturday's home match with Crewe saw a bucket collection that raised £135 to be sent to the victims.

30 April 1983
Football League Fourth Division:
Chester City 0 Hull City 0

Sealand Road: Popular Side Terrace; no ticket; programme (no price)

If asked beforehand, the home of Chester wouldn't have been many City fans' choice of venue at which to seal the deal. Still, this was the scenario facing us after Askew's solitary strike clinched a nervy 1-0 win over Crewe the previous week. Victory at Sealand Road would therefore confirm promotion and even a point would suffice should Bury fail to beat Scunthorpe. Around 1,000 of us made the trip, almost doubling our hosts' average gate in the process. A certain surreal air was lent to proceedings prior to kick-off when I opened the match programme only to read Chester boss John Sainty's preview of the Northampton game, played a fortnight earlier. The correct manager's notes then appeared further on in the publication, on the visitors' pages. I suspect the printers were subject to a refund request the following Monday.

As for the game, it was all a bit of an anticlimax with promotion confirmed courtesy of a rather boring goalless draw, while Bury became the latest victims of Scunthorpe's belated charge for the fourth promotion spot. At the final whistle we all streamed on to the pitch and I was on Carmo's back when the players and management came out into the directors' box. Indeed, I took great delight in pointing myself (and Henry's hat) out to all and sundry when the pictures appeared on the front page of Tuesday's *Hull Daily Mail* alongside the slightly underwhelming headline 'TIGERS ARE BACK – IN DIVISION 3!' Sadly, my hoped-for TV appearance never materialised.

Promotion euphoria attracted 8,735 to Boothferry Park on May Day. City's opponents were Mansfield, which in itself was slightly poignant given that the Stags' last visit had been the first post-receivership game. Now they were providing the opponents for the first post-promotion game. Print deadlines prevented Appleton sharing the supporters' celebrations, instead saying he hoped 'we will know our fate for next season' by the time his notes appeared. He went on to describe the season as 'one of encouragement', adding that producing a combination of promotion, enjoyment and entertainment along the way was all that could have been wished for back in the summer of 1982. It was a 'credit to both team and supporters, because all along we were aware that we need to do things together'.

There were still three games to go and going on to win the championship would now provide 'the icing on the cake'. Disappointingly, more dropped points in a 2-2 draw with Askew and Marwood scoring ensured that the title would be Wimbledon's. Given their run of just two defeats since January it was hard to begrudge the Londoners their success. Further frustration followed as Port Vale's win at Stockport the following Friday lifted them over City too. Limping up in third was not what was expected of the best-supported club in the division.[99]

---

99 Match programme (Hull City v Mansfield Town, 2 May 1983)

With the final game away at Rochdale not scheduled until 14 May, the week off brought light relief by way of another Wembley defeat for Hull FC. It was a shock one too, the red-hot favourites beaten 14-12 by Featherstone. Not surprisingly, many City fans took great delight in this latest failure beneath the Twin Towers. The following Monday, City hosted Newcastle in the rearranged friendly. Over 9,000 came to see Kevin Keegan's high-fliers beaten 3-2. Suitably buoyed by their display against a team heading back to the First Division, City capped off a terrific season with a 3-1 win at Spotland. Coupled with a surprise home defeat for Port Vale it was enough to clinch second place behind Wimbledon. Appleton termed it 'a dream of a season': 'We would have settled for promotion before the season started so we can't be too hard on not winning the league. There have been so many memorable individual occasions and the increase in support created a terrific atmosphere – particularly when the potential of the stadium wells to the noise of "The Tigers are Back".'[100]

Making the moment sweeter was the fact that this was by and large the same group of players who had experienced the darkest of times only a year before. They were now a group with real potential, as Matthew Rudd alluded to in a 2013 piece for The Two Unfortunates blog's 'Great Football League Teams' series. Tony Norman was 'a behemoth in goal, a model of consistency, agility and fitness that made him irreplaceable'. The central defensive partnership of the 'composed' Dale Roberts and the 'fearless' Skipper provided the base from which 22-year-old captain Garreth Roberts and his fellow 'production line midfielders' McClaren and 'the gifted Marwood' could supply what Rudd termed the 'spine-chilling duo' of Whitehurst and Mutrie up top. In fact, given

100 Same as [99]

Marwood's 19 goals as a 'marauding winger' and Appleton's regular use of 'nippy youngster' Flounders (13 goals), City could actually be said to have a potent attacking quartet, one that contributed to the club's highest league goals tally since 1967. Making City's achievement all the more remarkable was the size of the squad. In addition to those named, throw in full-backs Booth, Bobby McNeil and Gary Swann, the sweet left foot of Askew and what Rudd terms, 'the odd kid or loanee when the time demanded it' it was all Appleton had to work with. 'And he made it work,' proving wrong those who doubted his ability to step up to full-time management.

There's no denying that the City team of 1982/83 were blessed with consistency of availability, which allowed six of them to play 40 or more league games, ten to play over 30 with bit-part duo Flounders and Swann topping 20. As Rudd writes, 'Not only were Appleton's best players very good, they were also handy at not getting injured.' In justifying their inclusion in the blog's series, he adds, 'The truly remarkable achievement was that there was never a lull in form – not once did they lose two games in a row, and never did they go more than two without a win. The team spirit was the kind that could earn its creator a fortune if it were ever to be processed and sealed in a jar.'[101]

Rudd quite rightly suggests that none of those who played a regular role in that promotion season need ever be concerned about their status with supporters to this day. And if success at first-team level wasn't enough, the campaign also ended with City's reserves victorious in the North Midlands League for the first time. The future was bright; the future was black-and-amber.

---

101 *The Two Unfortunates* website: http://thetwounfortunates.com/great-football-league-teams-45-hull-city-1982-3/

10
'Yawk-sher'

Easington: Sunday, 11 September 1983

It's just after 3.30pm and the game has been abandoned. I cheer as the TV pictures show the players celebrating in the rain. In the afterglow of City's promotion, the summer of '83 has been a belter, the hottest July on record soundtracked by the hottest pop record ever made. To cap things off there's even been some long-overdue success for Yorkshire County Cricket Club. Or 'Yawk-sher' as the rowdier elements of the crowds at Headingley, North Marine Road and today at Chelmsford would acclaim them. Led by the veteran Ray Illingworth, the Tykes are crowned Sunday League champions. And back in May I'd been in Hull at one of the wins that proved crucial in helping it happen.

* * *

Although Bradford-born writer J.B. Priestley once described Hullensians as 'not quite Yorkshire but not quite anything else', the city boasts a rich history of hosting the county's cricket club. The Tykes played their first match in Hull in June 1879, a County Championship fixture against Surrey on the old Argyle Street ground. The Circle (on the site of City's current home) hosted its first championship match in July 1899 and continued to stage at least one game a year right up until July 1974. The Tykes boasted a decent record there, winning 48 and losing only seven of the 88 first-class matches staged at the venue. Referred to as 'the county cricket ground, Hull' it also hosted City games in 1905/06 before the Tigers moved into their adjacent Anlaby Road home the following season. In later years The Circle enjoyed visits by three touring Test teams – the South Africans in 1904 and 1929 and the Australians in 1909 – and the site would later act as 'winter' home to Hull & East Riding RUFC and West Hull ARLFC.[102]

It was at The Circle in 1937 that legendary pair Herbert Sutcliffe and Len Hutton put on 315 for the first wicket, the only opening partnership on the ground to top 300 runs. Other notable feats included Maurice Leyland's 263 against Essex in 1936 and Johnny Wardle's 9-48 in an innings against Sussex (as part of match figures of 16-112, Yorkshire's fourth best of all time). In 1968 a Yorkshire side described by John Arlott as 'the strongest, best balanced and best directed team in the country' were crowned county champions at the venue, but only after what was termed 'the most famous game to have taken place in Hull'. Having been held up by a 105-run seventh-wicket Surrey partnership, Yorkshire required three wickets with only 15 minutes remaining. Just five minutes were left when Don Wilson trapped last man Robin Jackman lbw and Yorkshire had won by 60 runs, thus clinching their 29th championship and completing a hat-trick of titles for the first time since the 1930s. It would prove their last for 33 years. Six years later, the last three-day match at The Circle saw Basil D'Oliveira hit a hitherto championship career-best 227 in the first innings for visitors Worcestershire. The first one-

102 From an *Edinburgh Evening News* report of David 'Soldier' Wilson's transfer from Heart of Midlothian to Hull City circa 1905 (via The Early Tigers & Hearts Heritage on Twitter)

day match Yorkshire played in Hull was in 1969 and with the exceptions of 1976 and 1985 they played a Sunday game there every year until 1990 when a pitch deemed unsatisfactory and a downgrade in facilities signalled the end of the city as a county venue.[103]

* * *

Dad encouraged my love of cricket from an early age and although there was no organised team in Easington, there was enough interest to ensure the stumps came out regularly across the six weeks' holiday. And of course, it never seemed to rain! Admittedly, participation for cricket was never as great as for football. To some lads it didn't seem the most attractive proposition, especially when someone like Clarkey decided to 'dig in' Boycott-style for the afternoon. Frustration increased when having finally dismissed him, you went in to bat and got out first ball. I was more of a bowler back then, a left-arm over of some considerable pace which I actually had to rein in at times. Honestly. On one occasion our game had to be abandoned when I was chased back my full run-up and over our garden fence by a bat-wielding Jim, after I'd uprooted all three of his stumps with an absolute peach. He accused me of chucking and was aiming to emphasise the point with the size six Gunn & Moore he was holding.

Cricket could also be found on television throughout the summers of the 1970s and 1980s. Not only did the BBC show all England's home Test matches in their entirety, but it would also broadcast the annual Roses fixtures in the County Championship. We had the John Player League on Sunday

---

103 From https://www.theguardian.com/observer/osm/story/0,,543993,00.html, *The Guardian*; Also from Yorkshire CCC website, https://yccc.production.parallax.dev/news/view/8426/throwback-thursday-hull, 16 April 2020

afternoons, featuring the unmistakeable tones of Arlott and Yorkshireman Jim Laker (who Dad informed me had once played cricket in our village during the war). A familiar ritual would see Dad come in from his 'Sunday Club' at The White Horse, have his lunch, pop the telly on for the cricket and fall asleep almost before the end of the first over. Despite snoring loud enough to all but eclipse what Frank Keating termed Arlott's 'articulate, leisurely, confiding countryman's burr', he had this strange ability to wake up immediately should I dare switch over to *Football Special*. 'Eh, I was watching that,' would be the riposte from the prone figure on the settee. The dial would immediately go back to BBC2.[104]

Although the 40-overs format was designed partly to attract a younger audience, it was usually only the last ten of the game that got the juices flowing courtesy of a tense run chase. However, if Yorkshire were involved then I'd be quite prepared to sit through the full afternoon and indeed, by the game's climax, the whole family could well be gripped, especially if the Tykes were in with a shout of victory. Not that this was often the case during the early 1980s. As with Hull City, I was discovering a team whose better days already looked behind them.

* * *

My first trip to The Circle was in June 1979 when Dad took Phil and me to see Yorkshire play Surrey, historically the Tykes' greatest rivals after Lancashire. Actually, Yorkshire's greatest rivals at this time appeared to be themselves. Between 1968 and 1986 the club was ripped apart by a succession of internal disputes, chronicled superbly by Stuart Rayner. At the centre of it all was usually Dad's hero whose previous

104 Swanton, E.W., *Barclay's World of Cricket: The Game from A–Z (2nd Edition)* (London: Collins, 1980) p.136 (via Wikipedia)

appointment as captain not only failed to bring success but instead served only to heighten the sense of acrimony within the ranks. Boycott turned his back on England in a last-ditch attempt to concentrate on leading Yorkshire to success. It never came and in 1978 he was removed in what Rayner describes as 'the cruellest of sackings'. Still on the playing roster, his personal feud with Ray Illingworth would have far-reaching consequences. Appointed team manager in 1978, Illingworth hoped that having only Yorkshire-born players in the side would create a 'team spirit' able to overcome anything. It would prove forlorn.[105]

Despite their problems, Yorkshire had arrived at Hull unbeaten in any format of the game and the Surrey fixture would maintain that run of good form. It was a low-scoring affair with Boycott making only 13 runs in Yorkshire's reply to Surrey's 128, before offering a catch to Allan Butcher at slip off the bowling of David Thomas. Dad was devastated. A knock of 48 from skipper Jackie Hampshire and a fifth-wicket stand between Jim Love (13 not out) and Kevin Sharp (25) saw the hosts home for the loss of four wickets, with four overs remaining. The Hull crowd was happy (or even happier in the case of those who'd spent the afternoon in the beer tent). Dad tried convincing Phil and me that Sir Geoffrey's 13 had proved decisive and I went home having seen Yorkshire victorious in my first live match. All in all it had been a good day. But as with most of Yorkshire's good days at that time, they tended to be few and far between.

Having enjoyed this rarest of events – a dads' and lads' sporting day out – it became an annual fixture on the family calendar over the next few years. Phil's presence made it even more surreal as the two of us shared very few mutual interests.

---

105 Rayner, Stuart, *The War of the White Roses: Yorkshire Cricket's Civil War 1968–1986* (Worthing: Pitch Publishing, 2016) pp.145–162

Mum didn't join us, although she was a keen watcher on television. Instead, some of the village elders would be our companions. These included Clarkey's grandad and a local ex-serviceman, Ken, who I would later discover had the touching habit of always ordering two halves of beer as opposed to a pint – one for him and one in memory of the pal he'd lost in the war. Such blokes' wry observations on proceedings were often as entertaining as the game itself.

Entertaining or not, the Hull fixture usually proved popular. In 1989 the groundsman, Walter Hillaby, explained the problems of finding accommodation for the 'unusually large crowd' attracted by Yorkshire's visit. He was quoted as saying, 'At Hull, we generally have to make room for between 5,000 and 6,000.' This crowd was accommodated in just two permanent seating areas, Yorkshire members being able to watch from the picturesque pavilion, built in 1874, while others could find shelter – if required – in the rugby stand that had been erected to replace the original grandstand, damaged during the Hull Blitz. The rest of us were either on the temporary stands erected around the boundary, on the 'Hull Hill' (a small grassy knoll that also formed part of the perimeter) or in the beer tent. Hillaby's hopes for the annual visit were simple enough, consisting of 'glorious weather' that should set things up for 'a good day's cricket'. He also referred to the oft-criticised wicket at The Circle, saying, 'I plan to prepare a good "strip" although, here at Hull, the wickets are generally slow and, if anything, the bounce tends to be low.'[106]

The wicket belied its reputation to produce some real crackers, too. The somewhat dour 1979 affair was followed a year later by a cracker against Gloucestershire, in which Pakistan opener Zaheer Abbas hit a century in an imposing

106 From *County News* (official programme & scorecard, Yorkshire v Glamorgan, 25 June 1989)

total of 232/4. The unlikely hero of Yorkshire's reply was Sheffield-born opener Peter Ingham, who carried his bat for an unbeaten 87 as the hosts reached their target with two overs to spare. It was his highest score in 13 one-day matches and enabled him to join a select band of Yorkshiremen who can claim to have enjoyed their greatest day at The Circle.

In 1981, thanks to 'Beefy' and the 'miracle of Headingley' cricket was back in the national spotlight. But several weeks prior to 'Botham's Ashes', the crowd at The Circle for Yorkshire versus Glamorgan learned of a shattering loss in the first Test at Trent Bridge; disappointment compounded by Yorkshire's narrow defeat unfolding in front of them. The following summer a Nottinghamshire side that included Hull-born Mike Bore were the visitors for what proved the only high-scoring tie ever seen at the ground. Bore endured a difficult day at his former club ground, with 1-52 off his allotted eight overs as Yorkshire made 232/6. Jim Love struck six sixes in a top score of 70, backed up by solid knocks from Chris Old (45) and opener Kevin Sharp (40). Sir Geoffrey, meanwhile, had come in down the order at eight, scoring a couple not out at the close. With some justification, Dad again pointed out that they were the two most important runs of the innings. Clive Rice's 82-run batting masterclass formed the bulk of the Notts reply, backed up by 45 from John Birch and a career-best unbeaten 28 from Mark Fell that enabled the visitors to finish on 232/8.

Given that I'd witnessed a piece of history, my third visit to The Circle should have stuck long in the memory. Unfortunately, it was eclipsed three days later by seeing Bryan Robson score for England after just 27 seconds of the World Cup opener against France. My main cricketing highlight of 1982 instead came at the start of August when Dad took

Phil, me and my mate Gary to Headingley. It was my first taste of 'County HQ' and in particular the Western Terrace, a part of the ground that hasn't always covered itself in glory. The atmosphere was fairly restrained on this particular day, largely thanks to Yorkshire having the game effectively won while people were still queuing for their first pint.

It was a quarter-final in the NatWest Trophy, cricket's equivalent of the FA Cup. Opponents Essex were at that time one of the most consistent sides in the country. But as so often happened at Headingley, form went out of the window on the toss of a coin. A typically muggy morning saw the Tykes opt to make first use of traditionally bowler-friendly conditions – and how they used them. England opener Graham Gooch (10) was the only one of the top eight batsmen to reach double figures as Essex reeled from 18/4 to 36/7 and 51/9, before Stuart Turner (50 not out) and Ray East (33) put on 81 for the last wicket to set their hosts 133 to win. Ex-Manchester United central defender Arnie Sidebottom (3-21) and Graham Stevenson (3-25) did most of the damage. The second half of the Essex innings was played in gorgeous conditions but storm clouds were gathering as Yorkshire began their reply. Dad later told me he would have left as soon as Boycott was out for 14 but agreed to stay so as not to disappoint Gary. So when the rain finally forced the teams off the field and into what we thought would be a premature end to proceedings, we were forced to undertake a very wet walk back to the car. All four of us were soaked to the skin by the time we found sanctuary and it proved a fairly quiet drive home. As we headed eastwards, the return of blue skies behind us allowed Yorkshire to knock off the remaining runs without further loss. Martyn Moxon's unbeaten 78 and 33 from Bill Athey saw them through to the semi-finals. Therein they would lose to Warwickshire. The wait for silverware went on.

Illingworth had replaced Chris Old as captain midway through the 1982 season. A stalwart of the Yorkshire side that had dominated the game in the late 1950s and early '60s before leaving to lead Leicestershire to success, his return to playing at the age of 51 prompted more than a few raised eyebrows. But as Rayner writes, even at this age 'Raymond Illingworth was still a brilliant captain'. His effect on the Tykes appeared immediate. Derbyshire were beaten by 19 runs, with Paul Jarvis becoming the youngest player to take a hat-trick in the Sunday League two days before his 17th birthday, and the *Bradford Telegraph & Argos* reporting, 'For the first time this season Yorkshire were a well-drilled unit with Illingworth leading, Boycott giving unselfish support and everyone else trying his utmost!' If that praise summed up how bad things must've been prior to his appointment, there was at least what Rayner terms 'cause for cautious optimism' the following summer. It was to prove justified as Illingworth did what no Yorkshireman had done for a decade by leading his county to a major trophy. Unfortunately, even this achievement would be overshadowed by a disastrous County Championship campaign and another Geoff Boycott controversy.[107]

22 May 1983
Sunday (John Player Special) League Cricket: Yorkshire beat Middlesex by 6 wkts

The Circle: Temporary seats; no ticket, programme or scorecard

The game against Middlesex at Hull was only Yorkshire's third scheduled Sunday League fixture of the season. It came on the back of a six-wicket opening-day win at Warwickshire and an abandoned draw in Leeds against Surrey. For a time it

---

107 Rayner, Stuart, *The War of the White Roses: Yorkshire Cricket's Civil War 1968–1986* (Worthing: Pitch Publishing, 2016) pp.223–224

appeared the weather would also thwart the conclusion at The Circle. Indeed Phil and I had to cajole Dad into attending, following heavy downpours in the morning and an uncertain forecast. Thankfully our pressure paid off and we were there to see Yorkshire win on a faster scoring rate, the predecessor to the much-maligned Duckworth-Lewis method.

Batting first, the visitors were bowled out for 127 in 39 of their allotted 40 overs. At one stage they subsided from 40/2 to 53/6, with only a 52-run partnership between Wilf Slack and wicketkeeper Paul Downton helping them to a competitive total on a damp track. What was really interesting was the composition of the wicket takers. Yorkshire's attack was spearheaded by youngsters Paul Jarvis and Graham Stevenson but they took just three wickets between them. Jarvis removed skipper Mike Gatting and the dangerous Roland Butcher without scoring. Stevenson had to settle for tail-ender Wayne Daniel. Instead, it was the unlikely duo of Illingworth (4-6 in eight overs) and Boycott (3-15 off four) who caused the bulk of the damage. As Rayner writes, the captain 'had proven that whatever his birth certificate said, he could still excel in professional cricket, even after three and a half seasons in retirement'. Even Dad was impressed, although not as much as he was by his hero's feats. Not only did Sir Geoffrey take a trio of wickets but it was his catch, off Illingworth's bowling, that got rid of England off-spinner John Emburey.

In reply Boycott made only six before Emburey claimed his revenge, lbw. And as in the Middlesex innings it was the spinners who came to the fore. Emburey took 3-19 and Gatting 2-21 as Yorkshire lost wickets regularly. They eventually reached 80/6 off 24 overs before the rain returned. Only three players reached double figures, with Kevin Sharp top-scoring on 26, but on the way home Sir Geoffrey's bowling was the only topic up for discussion. In fairness, as Rayner points out, it would prove a bigger contribution to his team's eventual title success than his batting (he would later be dropped at Cardiff after a succession of bad scores): 'Three times he opened the bowling, and the 42-year-old sometimes came back to use his nous in the crucial "death" overs.'[108]

Yorkshire went top in July but as Rayner says, no one was getting carried away. They were two points clear with two matches remaining but nearest rivals Somerset had games in hand. The first of these, at Lord's, was won so even when the Tykes snatched an unlikely looking win against Derbyshire at Bradford Park Avenue, thanks to an injured Bill Athey seeing them home, Somerset remained favourites. However, when the latter then lost by 55 runs at Worcester, it left the Tykes needing only to avoid defeat at Chelmsford on the final day, regardless of what Somerset did at home to Warwickshire. In the event the rain proved decisive. While Somerset chased down 175 to win at Taunton, 'in Essex Yorkshire, backed by a huge army of fans, watched the rain come down'. Play was abandoned at 3.30pm with the award of two points each and despite having a worse run rate than the West Country side, Yorkshire were crowned champions by virtue of more away victories during the season. It would prove to be the Tykes' only Sunday League title win, their first piece of silverware since 1969 and the last trophy that they would win while sticking to their policy of only selecting players who were born with the county boundaries.[109]

Illingworth was quite rightly proud of his side's achievement and his own part in their success. An ever-present throughout the campaign, he finished top of the league's bowling averages and was the most economical too, in addition to bringing

---

108 Same as [107] p.224–226

109 The Cricket Paper: https://www.thecricketpaper.com/features-and-columns/996/where-are-they-now-yorkshire-sunday-league-winners-1983/

his tactical ability to the fore. Reflecting back on the season in 2015 he described it as 'interesting' – something of an understatement given that Yorkshire combined winning the Sunday League title with finishing bottom of the County Championship for the first time. He is quoted as saying, 'The trophy meant a great deal as the club hadn't won any silverware for a number of years. It was also a massive effort as every other county had two to three overseas players, but we were all Yorkshire-born ... despite the disappointment of the County Championship, it was satisfying that we still had guts and character to pick up some silverware.'[110]

Unfortunately, the Sunday League title barely served to paper over the cracks. Two days later, defeat by Essex condemned Yorkshire to the foot of the County Championship. For many 'creekit' fans in the Broad Acres, no amount of 'trivial' trophies or success at 'tap it and run' could compensate for that. In mitigation, the league placing didn't tell the full story. As Rayner writes, 'Poor weather handicapped Yorkshire from the start, and they were bottom in early June after drawing five badly weather-affected games at a time when there were no championship points for draws.' In total, Yorkshire lost the same number of games (five) as champions Essex, 'Yet they were never higher than 15th. The difference was that they only won once.'

Despite it being a World Cup year there were still enough overseas players in the county game to 'put Yorkshire to the sword', while the Tykes' antiquated selection policy, overwhelmingly upheld at the 1982 AGM, meant they had no such weapon to call upon. A lack of cutting edge was put down to the dearth of genuine pace bowlers. Although Jarvis was undoubtedly an exciting prospect who skidded the

---

110 Same as [109]

ball through with considerable venom and Stevenson was dubbed 'Yorkshire's Botham' on account of his proficiency with both bat and ball, the Tykes could never count on a Courtney Walsh, Malcolm Marshall, Michael Holding or Colin Croft to intimidate the opposition and clean up the tail. However, *Wisden* editor David Warner suggested it wasn't just quality that Yorkshire lacked. Rayner quotes him as saying, 'Apart from Simon Dennis [Len Hutton's nephew], who is an outstanding exception, the pacemen have lacked the heart for the battle and have too easily gone down with one injury or another.'

As for the batting, Boycott was again at the centre of controversy when reprimanded for slow scoring against Gloucestershire at Cheltenham. He was also cited as 'having everything to do' with Athey's decision to join the West Country club within a month of the end of the season. It would eventually lead to the committee voting to release their former skipper despite having already awarded him his testimonial. What Anthony Clavane called the 'Boycott Wars' were about to enter their most acrimonious stage.[111]

During the off-season of 1983/84, Yorkshire would find itself in both the news and sports headlines, courtesy of a soon-to-be nationwide industrial dispute (the miners' strike) and a full-blown rebellion among its cricket club membership. While the former, which officially began in March 1984, would last a full year, the fall-out from the latter would linger even longer. It began when what Clavane described as a spectacular *coup d'état* saw members of 'the pro-Boycott Reform Group sweep to power in a series of rancorous

---

111 Rayner, Stuart, *The War of the White Roses: Yorkshire Cricket's Civil War 1968–1986* (Worthing: Pitch Publishing, 2016) p.227; Clavane, Anthony, *Moving the Goalposts: A Yorkshire Tragedy* (London: Riverrun, 2016) pp.62–67

elections, bringing their beloved leader back – as committee member as well as player'. Their success was complete. In Rayner's words, 'Yorkshire really had become Boycottshire.' The following summer Yorkshire not only again struggled in the County Championship but also finished second-bottom in the defence of their Sunday League crown. In 1986 a 'counter-revolution' at committee level finally saw the departure of Boycott and a halt to the internal strife. What it didn't manage to end was the wait for that elusive County Championship.[112]

* * *

While I continued to attend county games at The Circle throughout the 1980s, my memories of them are vague. This is possibly due to the fact that City's resurgence relegated all other sporting interests to sideshow status, especially when they yielded little success themselves. By the end of the decade the crack of leather on willow would also have Hull KR, Easington United and even an insatiable appetite for live music gigs to compete with in my attention bank. Meanwhile, my active support of the club (or chasing a lost cause as it might be seen) soon took me off to several other venues, both in Yorkshire and beyond. Such masochism would also extend to following the hapless England Test team of the time at home and abroad. None of which need concern you now.

By this time, Dad had stopped attending The Circle with me, perhaps because such events had become an extension of Saturday night for my drinking mates and me. His lack of attendance may also have had something to do with the departure of Boycott, although he continued to follow the club's fortunes with interest and a couple of years later we got

112 Clavane, Anthony, *Moving the Goalposts* (London: Riverrun, 2016) pp.62–63; Rayner, Stuart, *The War of the White Roses: Yorkshire Cricket's Civil War 1968–1986* (Worthing: Pitch Publishing, 2016) p.239

to enjoy a lovely day out together at the historic Scarborough Cricket Festival. Of those Sundays spent at The Circle, the 19-run loss against Nottinghamshire in May 1984 was one of ten suffered by the reigning Sunday League champions. The next game, in July 1986, was far more pleasurable and included my first Yorkshire century at The Circle, courtesy of Jim Love's unbeaten 104. Combined with a thumping 64 from Phil Robinson it helped steer the Tykes to a total of 255/6 and an emphatic 102-run win over those same Nottinghamshire opponents.

The 1987 season proved a non-event as far as Hull was concerned, with August's scheduled fixture washed out without a ball being bowled. A photo of me taking a leak under the Anlaby Road flyover provides the somewhat embarrassing proof that, along with the usual crowd, I actually made it to the ground before trudging back into town, a fact made more frustrating given that I'd only got back to Easington from Manchester's legendary Haçienda nightclub in time for breakfast! However, that season did at least bring some more long-overdue success, in the form of the Benson & Hedges Cup. Frustratingly, despite getting to Leeds to see the quarter-final rout of Hampshire and the majority of the rain-affected win over Surrey in the semis, I wasn't at Lord's to see Love clinch a dramatic win by blocking out the final ball of the game. I did get to welcome the players home the following day, courtesy of a Sunday League win over Middlesex at Scarborough, but it was poor consolation.

Sadly, 1987 was also the year that Humberside County Council ordered demolition of the old Circle pavilion, which had been declared unsafe. It was replaced by a rather charmless modular prefab and a planned upgrade of the facilities never materialised. It was the end of one piece of local cricketing history and the beginning of the end of another. I have no recollection of the six-wicket win over Leicestershire in July 1988, which would suggest that my first view of the new-look ground was delayed until Yorkshire's game against bottom club Glamorgan on Sunday, 25 June 1989. An unbeaten 92 from Richard Blakey helped the hosts to a 49-run win, with the Welshmen's reply undermined by a wonderful return of 3-4 by Sidebottom and three wickets also for occasional spinner Martyn Moxon. Unbeknown to us at the time, it was the Tykes' penultimate visit to Hull.

In that 1989 interview Walter Hillaby had admitted, 'Although I enjoy having the county here, I'm glad when it is over.' I assume he didn't mean permanently but a year later that's what happened. On Sunday, 10 June 1990, eight years after Huddersfield's Fartown had been the latest 'out ground' to be dropped, Hull hosted its last county game. As with the first fixture in the city back in 1879, the opponents were Surrey and in what might be termed – for the purposes of this book at least – #TypicalCity fashion, Yorkshire signed off with a loss. Adding another predictable postscript was the fact that I wasn't there to see it, having opted instead for a night in Norwich in support of a Hull band. In truth, given my increased attendance at Headingley and Scarborough, as well as the occasional away trips, I saw no real need to say goodbye. Similar to speedway at The Boulevard, I suppose I never truly appreciated what I'd had until it was gone.

11

A City Psycho(billy)

Hull Dingwalls: Thursday, 24 March 1983

This is not the playful scene of two years earlier. This is not Psycho Steve sliding down the bannister of the Goodfellowship's stairs shouting 'M-e-e-t-e-o-r-s!' at the top of his voice, much to the amusement of his mates. And this is not the friendly dance floor that sees the same Psycho Steve – complete with peroxide-bleached 'rim' haircut, a box jacket that looks about two sizes too big and the most lurid pair of tartan peg pants from which hangs a ridiculously long cat-chain – rolling around the floor to a track called 'Graveyard Stomp', while those same mates pretend to kick the shit out of him. That had been my introduction to Psychobilly. But this, happening in front of my eyes right now, is something completely different. The Rezillos' 'Somebody's Gonna Get Their Head Kicked In Tonight', which heralds the band on to the stage, sounds like a threat as well as a promise.

* * *

By 1983, my enthusiasm for City was matched only by an ever-growing appetite for music. Countless weeknights spent in the company of Radio 1's self-styled 'Rhythm Pals' Kid Jensen and John Peel were attuning my ears to a rich seam of eclectic sounds, from my staple rockabilly diet through classic early soul and original ska to indie faves, dub-heavy reggae, bizarre German industrial mash-ups and even incomprehensible Cossack folk music. It was thanks to this nighttime fix that I first fell in love with 'The First Picture of You' by the Lotus Eaters, quite simply the finest pop single ever recorded. Elsewhere, Peel's playlist introduced me to names as diverse as Aztec Camera, Jerry Butler, Chameleons, Cocteau Twins, Sisters of Mercy, Sophie and Peter Johnston and Xmal Deutschland. It was the first time I'd encountered the Smiths, while New Order's 'Temptation' and seminal *Power, Corruption & Lies* album would eventually lead me in a whole new musical direction.

As a bonus, many of the bands Peel championed were soon to be seen live on the box courtesy of Channel 4. The new station came into being in November 1982 and among its first programmes was a weekly live music show called *The Tube*. At the end of its first series in March 1983, its replacement *Switch* adopted a similar format. For some reason, unlike its forerunner (which lasted for five series), *Switch* only saw out the summer. The Stray Cats played live on the show in August but, due to those hours of nighttime listening, it was the appearance of bands from outside the rocking genre that really enhanced my musical education. Thanks to *Switch*, by the start of the new football season I'd added Bow Wow Wow, Spear of Destiny and even the Style Council to my list of liked bands. Of course I kept this to myself at the time.

Back in the rocking world, every week would find me scanning the music press for news of upcoming releases while also awaiting replies to my regular correspondence with the various bands and record labels. Indeed, such was my correspondence with Nervous Records owner Roy Williams that we could almost be classed as pen pals. Restless, the Sharks, the Pharaohs, Red Hot 'n' Blue and John Peel faves

Fireball XL5 all emerged as possible contenders, while the return of the Stray Cats to our TV sets to promote the '(She's) Sexy and Seventeen' single from third album, *Rant 'n' Rave*, offered the prospect of another retro wave to ride the back of. But when it came it wasn't a rocking one. Instead, it was the pop/soul/swing sounds of JoBoxers and Roman Holliday that found their way into the *Top of the Pops* studio. Meanwhile, an acapella group from New Jersey called 14 Karat Soul also created quite a stir when hitting the UK. Playing to full houses, they recorded a stunning session for Kid Jensen as well as appearing on Channel 4 programmes *Switch*, *Loose Talk* and *The Tube*. As someone who'd come to love old doo-wop compilations, I was blown away and couldn't wait for the vinyl release that would surely follow. Unfortunately, it never did. [113]

The constant hunt for vinyl meant most Saturday mornings were spent in Hull's numerous record shops – the legendary Syd Scarbs under the City Hall, Shakespeare Records in Paragon Station, Sheridan's second-hand shop on Anlaby Road and HMV on Whitefriargate. A few years later Andy's Records joined them and the likes of WH Smith, Woolworth and Hammonds of Hull also had music sections that occasionally merited a browse. But Syd Scarbs was always my favourite. Not only did it have a great rockabilly album collection on the ground floor, but the basement singles section was a veritable treasure trove catering for devotees of all genres, as well as being a meeting place for some of the coolest characters in town. The *Hull Daily Mail* was right to call it 'an institution' for many people growing up in the area, right up until its closure in 2001.

* * *

113 JoBoxers were fronted by Dig Wayne, formerly 'Buzz Wayne' of New York rockabilly band Buzz & The Flyers

Psychobilly was a genre I'd first become aware of at the Goodfellowship two years earlier. Its so-called 'first wave' peaked between 1983 and 1985 though that didn't mean it went mainstream. In September 1984, Radio 1's Steve Wright – the polar opposite of John Peel when it came to musical tastes – described it live on air as 'a mixture of mindless thug music and rockabilly'. This came a day after fellow DJ Bruno Brookes had displayed similar ignorance when using the term to label 'Long Black Shiny Car', the new single by neo-rockabilly band Colbert Hamilton & the Hell Razors.

Thankfully, Craig Brackenridge has since provided a far more knowledgeable examination of this strange hybrid mix in his 2007 book. He termed psychobilly 'the bastard of all music genres, and a bastardisation of many', drawing its influences from rockabilly, rock 'n' roll, '60s garage punk and even '70s glam rock. It was a sound first brought to the media's attention by US band the Cramps, though they always refuted the suggestion they were the first psychobilly band. That title has tended to be bestowed on homegrown combo the Meteors.

Both were soon represented in my fast-growing record collection. I even tried to use the monthly village disco – the highlight of my teenage social calendar – to introduce psychobilly to a wider audience, Psycho Steve-style. A compliant DJ, a couple of joke shop blood pellets and a group of mates only too willing to pummel fuck out of me brought 'Graveyard Stomp' to the masses; well, the 50 or so kids inside Easington Church Hall at any rate. It certainly created a stir and was well received, or so I thought until a particularly attractive young lady pushed her way through the throng, leant over close to me and said, 'Get up you silly bastard!' Perhaps Easington wasn't ready for psychobilly after all. Thankfully, Hull was and what's more, it had a new venue in which to host it.[114]

Situated on George Street and with capacity to hold 470 people, Dingwalls opened in January 1983. It was the ideal size for groups who otherwise would not have been catered for, especially following conversion of The Tower to a nightclub. What's more, the brand boasted a pedigree as one of the best-known venues in London, having hosted live music in the heart of Camden Town since 1973. In late 1982 its owners Peter Gross and top promoter Harvey Goldsmith embarked on an ambitious expansion project, aiming to take the venue's self-styled brand of 'Rhythm and Booze' around the country. Hull was one of six provincial locations chosen. Under the management of Paul Mayo it took over the former Hofbrauhaus building, underneath the Odyssey Discotek, a venue remembered for its table-mounted telephones that were designed to help with the dating process. Although the experiment was ultimately doomed to failure and Hull Dingwalls was initially beset by teething troubles, it was seen as a welcome and much-needed addition to the city's nightlife.

Cabaret act Beano may have been a strange choice to open the venue on Wednesday, 19 January but the following Saturday brought the first sell-out gig, courtesy of Peel favourites the Farmers Boys. Bands as diverse as Amazulu, Aztec Camera, Big Country, the Damned, Dr Feelgood, Durutti Column, Eurythmics, Orange Juice, Sisters of Mercy and the Undertones graced the stage over the course of its short-lived existence. Local acts were catered for on Monday and Tuesday and there were also plenty of retro nights – the Polecats, Roman Holliday, soul stalwarts Zoot and the Roots and blues master Bo Diddley. Dingwalls also hosted a regional

---

114 Brackenridge, Craig, *Hell's Bent on Rockin' – A History of Psychobilly* (London: Cherry Red, 2007) p.11

heat of the UK Rock 'n' roll Dance Championships, with the Flash Cats and BBC radio's 'The Big Bopper'. It was a venue made for me, especially given its 10.30pm throwing-out time, which allowed the catching of the last number 76 bus. The only obvious drawback was that not only was I underage but I very much looked it (no cosy arrangements with the landlord this time). Still, nothing as trivial as age was going to keep me away the night the Meteors hit Hull.

* * *

Formed in 1980, the Meteors' harder-edged sound and stage act that often involved singer P. Paul Fenech spitting chicken blood out over the audience soon set them apart from their fellow rockabillies, as well as alienating them from the traditional rocking circuit. Fenech played down any style distinction: 'The sort of music we play, the papers call it psychobilly, I don't really call it psychobilly, it's just rockabilly to me. It's just that we don't sing about the same things the Polecats sing about, pink clothes and Cadillacs cos that stuff doesn't interest me. I sing about really 'orrible stuff cos, basically, I'm a really 'orrible person.'[115]

Regardless of any ostracism, the Meteors soon built up a loyal following. Initially known as The Crazies or Zorchmen, they were what Brackenridge calls 'a motley collection of ex-punks and rockabillies looking for something more rowdy'. They quickly became renowned for 'going mental' at gigs, their term for an all-elbows affair that would come to be known as 'chicken dancing', 'slam dancing' or simply 'wrecking'. Not surprisingly, injuries could easily be sustained. I know of at least two lads hospitalised at Meteors gigs in Hull, although this possibly had more to do with the changing

---

115 From Channel 4's *Whatever You Didn't Get* (March 1983)

face of the band's travelling fans. As both the Wreckin' Crew and the infamous Kattle they brought a far more aggressive feel to what had hitherto been an 'essentially good-natured' experience.

The band gained national exposure in 1981 when a short B-movie-style promo film, *Meteor Madness*, was chosen as the supporting flick to feature-length ska-revival movie *Dance Craze*. On the back of this came a debut single, radio airplay and a session on John Peel, followed by a TV appearance on Thames TV's *White Light* show and the front cover of *Sounds*. By 1983 the band had undergone several line-up changes, with Fenech the only surviving member. Still, the immediate future looked bright. Their reworking of John Leyton's 1960 number one 'Johnny Remember Me' was easily their most commercial release to date. It not only proved a big indie chart hit in 1983 but thanks to daytime airplay on national radio also came close to breaching the UK top 40. The B-side, 'Wreckin' Crew', was more representative of the band's live sound. It was the title track of their second album and the first with the new line-up. No album had had such an effect on me since Stray Cats' debut offering two years earlier and I wasn't the only one. Loaning it to some of my mates attracted a favourable reaction. My first live experience was to prove equally as exhilarating.[116]

24 March 1983
The Meteors
Dingwalls, George Street: Ticket £2.50

The crowd at Dingwalls reflected the changes taking place in the local rocking scene. Many others who'd been swept along by the 'Cat' revival of 1981 were now getting into psychobilly.

---

116 Brackenridge, Craig, *Hell's Bent on Rockin' – A History of Psychobilly* (London: Cherry Red, 2007) p.22

Brackenridge goes some way to explaining how many of these new devotees (me included perhaps) were often ignorant about the original influences, '[They] gained their love of rock 'n' roll not from lovingly collecting 25-year-old 45s tracked down in dusty American record stores but by watching *Grease* and *Happy Days* alongside seeing Matchbox and Stray Cats on *Top of the Pops*. This was a generation weaned on *The Wanderers*, *Lemon Popsicle* and stacks of low-rent, TV-advertised rock 'n' roll albums.'[117]

Members of the new crowd weren't taken solely from among the old rockers either. 'There were also a first generation of psychobillies who had appeared from punk, mod or skin backgrounds and had no real appreciation of rockabilly beyond knowing who the Stray Cats were.' Brackenridge could easily have been describing many of my mates. This new crowd's look reflected the new sound. It was a fairly standard format, as depicted by the Meteors on the *Wreckin' Crew* album cover. Gone was the exaggerated play on the 1950s peg suit (as worn by Psycho Steve) to be replaced by a look summarised by Brackenridge as 'one associated (rightly or wrongly) with violence and a certain amount of boneheaded activity'. The 'essence of menace … was undeniably part of the attraction'.[118]

The haircut was the first obvious difference between the psychobilly and his more traditional forerunner. The short flat-top of the rockabilly revival was still in evidence but the length and height of the top began to take on ever more exaggerated proportions, 'often from a modest inch at the back to 5–6 inches at the front then eventually from nowt at the back to as much as hairspray could control out front'. This would often be dyed or bleached, with the sides and

117 Same as [116] p.14

118 Brackenridge, Craig, *Let's Wreck – Psychobilly Flashbacks from the Eighties and Beyond* (Retford: Stormscreen, 2nd Edition 2005) p.41

back shaved to a number one or totally bald. As time moved on many psychos opted for an almost mohawk look, while another variation was the totally shaved head with just a 'rim' of a flat-top running all the way round. Steve Rowe at Classic on Jameson Street was my preferred choice of barber. At three quid a go he wasn't cheap but he was bloody good, hardly ever reaching for the spirit level or Afro comb as he sculpted the perfect flat-top.

The early standard psychobilly uniform was T-shirt, a tartan or plaid (checked) overshirt, jeans and Doc Martens or biker boots (although Furman's also did a stylish line in leather buckle-fashioned shoes that fitted the image well). From this – as with football's casual movement – certain short-lived fads followed. Ski jumpers and baseball/college jackets were items that had at one time been the choice of the traditional rockabillies but were now adopted by the psycho crowd. The most common form of outerwear, however, was either the skinhead's green MA1 pilot jacket (a facet of the crossover scooterboy movement) or the leather bomber/biker jacket, the latter usually adorned with some decent artwork on the back. I had both items in my collection, with my leather carrying a confederate flag complete with skull in the centre and the words 'Mutant Power' daubed across it. Even smarter was the Guana Batz logo that appeared on the arm of my MA1, courtesy of a mate who fancied himself as an artist. It was good but when combined with close-shaved flat-top, tie-dye bleached jeans and Furman's psycho shoes or DMs, I must have looked a right twat.

Winter would see the old donkey jacket rolled out, or a long black trench coat of the style worn by Fenech, although my prized item of winter wear, bought a couple of years later, would be a genuine leather and sheepskin RAF surplus flying jacket. It also served me well on the terraces. Meanwhile the arrival of summer (and new band Guana Batz) heralded a penchant for Bermuda shorts. Brackenridge also refers to the clamour for dungarees (also popular with the traditionalists) and the pyjama fad, as popularised by the band Restless, who I would get to see at Hull University in 1985.

A month before their Hull appearance the Meteors featured in the glossy, pop-orientated *Record Mirror* and then on Channel 4. Along with the earlier quoted interview with Fenech (conducted while having another piece of artwork applied to his already heavily tattooed arm) the band were recorded live at the Brixton Ace. This was the Meteors' third line-up (there would be many more). Performing 'Hills Have Eyes', a speeded-up cover of 'Wild Thing' and the anthem 'Wreckin' Crew', it showed us what to expect at Dingwalls.[119]

I was accompanied to the gig by City regulars Carmo and Doug, the latter a heavy rock fan tagging along out of curiosity. The nervous excitement I felt on the bus that night was of the sort normally reserved for a big game. Safely through the door, things began quietly enough but as soon as the band arrived on stage, the mood darkened. 'Fancy paying money to get your 'eads kicked in,' said Fenech, and within seconds of them opening up with a cover of the Surfaris' 'Wipeout' I knew this would be no good-natured Goodfellowship scene. This was something altogether more sinister, with a real 'edge' apparent between the locals and the London mob, one of whom was dressed in undertaker's top hat and looked every inch the top boy.

The area in front of the stage was turned into a seething mass of bare torsos and flailing arms and I soon realised that

---

119 The Channel 4 programme was *Whatever You Want*, a youth magazine show presented by Keith Allen, which ran from November 1982 to March 1983. The final five episodes (including that which featured the Meteors) were retitled *Whatever You Didn't Get*

staying around the edges was the safest option. Unless the lasses there gave you a shove back in! As the night wore on and the pace barely let up – 'Lonesome Train', 'Wreckin' Crew', 'Graveyard Stomp', 'Mutant Rock', 'Blue Sunshine' – that Rezillos introduction appeared more and more prescient. Lee (minus his pink peg slacks these days) was taken to hospital with a broken collar bone. I was amazed he was the only one. It was at times brutal and, along with a future Meteors gig at Retford Porterhouse, was easily the most violent dance floor experience I've witnessed. On the bus home, we agreed that the adrenalin rush had been akin to that of matchday and we simply had to see the band again. We wouldn't have long to wait.

25 July 1983
The Meteors
Spring Street Theatre: Ticket £2.50

My final visit to Dingwalls was on Friday 8 July for a rock 'n' roll night, starring London's Dynamite Band. Featuring young saxophonist Ray Gelato prior to him forming the Chevalier Brothers, their sound was 'big band British rock 'n' roll' as far removed from the Meteors as could be. It was music that the original Teds in evidence in the small crowd had no doubt danced, scrapped and slashed cinema seats along to back in the day. But although I found it entertaining enough, it didn't provide anything like the same rush felt on my last visit to the venue. The Meteors gig had left its mark and, in ten days' time I'd get to do it all again – or so I thought.

On 18 July the *Hull Daily Mail* reported that Dingwalls was to close each of its regional franchises with immediate effect. It was a huge blow to music fans in the city – not to mention the 13 people who lost their jobs in Hull. Although there had been teething problems – cancellations by the likes of Wilson Pickett and Paul Young (twice), complaints from Odyssey's management about the noise and the refusal of magistrates to grant a late licence – Hull had been the only one of the six reported to be making a profit. Within a month the doors were locked and within a year the building was demolished, having been damaged by a fire that began in Odyssey and gutted both buildings. Rumours as to what caused it would continue to circulate for years afterwards. Of more immediate concern to me was the fact that the Meteors were due to play a return gig at Dingwalls at the end of the month as part of their ET Went Home tour. Thankfully, along with Killing Joke, this gig was rescheduled for Spring Street Theatre. Other shows were not so lucky, among them what would have been the Hull debut of the Smiths (scheduled for August) and Paul Weller's Respond Tour.

The Meteors' tour took its name from the departure of Dave 'ET' Bass. Perhaps due to feedback from the previous show, there was a sell-out crowd in attendance at Spring Street – and thankfully no broken bones. This time I avoided getting caught up in the front-of-stage frenzy. Although not as numerous as at Dingwalls, the Kattle were still in evidence and there was a feeling that some locals might use the night as an opportunity to settle scores. In the event, I used my noggin and enjoyed the gig from the raised platform of the seating area aisles, only occasionally entering the fray and even then I remained on the periphery. This built-in defence mechanism was one I'd honed at the local village discos, particularly at Burton Pidsea where the combination of unfamiliar faces, a licensed bar and a small number of beleaguered flat-tops was often a recipe for a night fraught with risk.

Over the coming years, my 'don't look now but their boys have just come in' line would become a joke rolled out in the pub on many an away-day. Little did my mates know the sweat and toil that had gone into perfecting such an adept early warning system. As well as sussing out 'bovver', I was also fairly fleet of foot and could clear potential hotspots should the need arise. This wasn't necessarily something to be proud of but if the only alternative was to stand and get my features rearranged then 'on my toes' I went. At pace too, as one particular sprint down a street in Chester would illustrate. It was enough to earn me the nickname 'Linford Lusmore'. I've been called a lot worse. Thankfully, on this particular night no trouble materialised but needless to say the prospect of 'doing a Lee' and ending up in A&E wasn't one I wanted to contemplate. I was content to observe from a distance – even though the demeaning glances from the females in the audience were akin to being handed a white feather.

On first viewing, the home of the Hull Truck Theatre Company had appeared a strange choice as the natural replacement for Dingwalls but it actually worked very well. Indeed the night proved such a success that the venue subsequently announced the launch of a new Sunday night live music club starting in September. Imaginatively entitled The Street, none other than the 'Undisputed Kings of Psychobilly' were invited back as opening-night headliners.

18 September 1983
The Meteors | The Nerve Blocks

The Street @ Spring Street Theatre: Ticket £2.50

Two months later, the sound of PiL's 'This Is Not a Love Song' heralded the arrival of The Street. The *Hull Daily Mail* described it as filling the void left by closure the previous year of the Humberside Theatre (Spring Street's forerunner), which for over a decade had provided Sunday night live music. The Street was to take up where Groucho's and Clouds had left off. It was hoped that giving opening night to the Meteors would guarantee a repeat of their July attendance. In the event, 'Theatre administrator Mr Barry Nettleton said about 300 people turned up.' It was the third time I'd seen the band in Hull inside six months and on each occasion there had been new faces in attendance, wanting to witness this latest 'fad' for themselves. Again they weren't to be disappointed as Fenech and co. put on another blistering live show. Sadly the same couldn't be said of Hull punks the Nerve Blocks, playing their final gig but whose style was lost on what was essentially a rock 'n' roll crowd.

Set to follow the Meteors at The Street during that September and October were Hull band Poor Howard supported by the New Politans; '7-piece rhythm band' Mumbo Jumbo with support again in the form of a local act, Fun and Frenzy; York band Toned F; and finally 'London's top punk band Sex Gang Children', supported by Hull outfit Les Zeiga Fleurs. With jazz act the Stan Tracey Octet and Brotherhood of Breath also set to play the venue, the diversity of talent available for the Hull public to catch live was there for all to see.

Despite a lack of daytime exposure on 'the nation's favourite radio station', psychobilly's popularity continued to grow. Various compilation LPs helped spread the word but it was 1984's first *Stomping at the Klub Foot* live album that acted as a real catalyst. Located in the main ballroom of the now-demolished Clarendon Hotel in Hammersmith, the Klub Foot became the centre of psychobilly universe. For those unable to get there, the live albums gave a taste of what we were missing. Also helping me to stay abreast of the rapidly expanding scene were the compilation cassettes I began recording, with sounds captured largely from John Peel's show. I soon had over 50 C90 tapes full of the legendary DJ's dabble into the world of flat-tops and checked shirts. For the duration of sixth form (and beyond) my tape deck remained permanently set on play/record. 'Doing my homework' had never proved as rewarding, even more so on Thursday, 26 July 1984 when Peel dedicated the Meteors' 'Deep Dark Jungle' session track to the East End Ruffabillies (the day after my Rockabilly Top 20 had appeared in *Sounds*). I was becoming a media whore!

23 April 1984

'These Cats Ain't Nothin' But Trash' All-Dayer

Nottingham Palais: No ticket; entry £4

By early 1984, with Carmo possessing some wheels the *NME* gig guide had become as important to our upcoming activities as City's fixture list. As such, instead of taking in the Easter Bank Holiday home game against Rotherham, five of us squeezed into his Vauxhall Cavalier bound for the Trash Bash All-Dayer at the Nottingham Palais. Nominal headliners were Finnish band Hanoi Rocks but going by the haircuts on show they weren't the ones most people had come to see. Guana Batz were certainly the top attraction for our little crew, with the Sting-Rays, the Tall Boys, Thee Milkshakes and the Prisoners completing an attractive-looking line-up. It was like a Klub Foot northern version. Never had I seen so many flat-tops assembled in one place.

The show was filmed and released as *Nothing But Trash*, highlights of which can be found on YouTube. Its title was taken from the new kid on the block, a genre that brought elements of 1960s US garage punk and psychedelia into the rockabilly mix. I'd first come across it via a 1983 Big Beat album entitled *These Cats Ain't Nuthin' But Trash,* which featured the Sting-Rays, Milkshakes and Cannibals. The latter weren't present at Nottingham but there were still plenty of diversifying influences on show in the remaining line-up.

First up were the Prisoners (featuring a pre-JTQ James Taylor on Hammond organ) whose slick 1960s-influenced sound failed to win over the flat-topped masses. Fellow Medway band Thee Milkshakes were also met with indifference despite a heady blend of mutant surf punk, retro pop tunes and witty putdowns from main Milkman Billy Childish. The Tall Boys were always going to be on a winner, simply on account of their Meteors roots, but it was the Sting-Rays who really brought the crowd to life with their own unique brand of anarchic high-energy rock 'n' roll. This meant that by the time Guana Batz took the stage we were well up for it. Pleasingly, Feltham's finest didn't disappoint. The latest darlings of the psychobilly scene were already an accomplished live act, with 'King Rat' and a speeded-up version of the *Joe 90* theme tune guaranteed to inspire a proper wreck-fest on the dance floor. Throw in the witty on-stage patter of frontman Pip Hancox and here was a band whose wagon I could jump on. All in all, it was the type of show that was even worth missing a 5-0 City win for.

12

Up For It!

Boothferry Road: Saturday, 27 August 1983

It's when a pint glass lands and smashes on Carmo's car bonnet that I truly realise the new football season is upon us. Not just a new season but a different type of season, which will pose different challenges to the two spent in the league basement – both on and off the field. Thankfully, the fact that we are inside the car means we aren't swept up in the ensuing mass of bodies seeping across the road from Silver Cod as City and Burnley fans exchange pleasantries. It's a Bank Holiday weekend and for once the sun has come out to greet it. Burnley, a team whose mid-1970s home shirt ranks highly in my kit geekery table, are about to bookend the most heartbreaking season of my City-supporting life.

* * *

In July 1983 London 'style bible' *The Face* belatedly lifted the lid on football's casuals, giving wider exposure to a scene that had been steadily exerting its influence over the terraces since the late 1970s. Its history has been documented extensively and dare I say definitively in Phil Thornton's *Casuals* and Bill Routledge's *Northern Monkeys* publications, along with a host of books dedicated to individual club firms (among them Shaun Tordoff's Hull City offering). My first recollection of it at Boothferry Park was during that Sheffield United game in 1981, something reinforced by the self-styled 'Bladerunner' in a fanzine article he penned over a decade later: 'As anyone who was there will tell you, City had an extremely large casual following from about autumn 1979 to 1986, although the golden years were 1981 to 1984.'[120]

'Bladerunner' anointed the casuals as the natural successors to the 'City Psychos' whose ranks had included 'beer boys, punks, normals, thugs, thieves, hitchhikers, Simon Gray rejects and anyone else who enjoyed a rowdy day out following the Tigers around on a big blue-and-white double-decker bus'. He described how attending Northern Soul all-nighters in the late 1970s began to influence the dress sense of those making the weekly pilgrimage from Hull; a dress sense somewhat at odds with that of your stereotypical football hooligan. Beginning with the basic Adidas cagoule and rainwear look, his personal history of the Hull Casuals proceeds on a course through the 'sportswear habit' – Barcelona replica shirts, Le Coq Sportif (especially Saint-Étienne tops), Lacoste, Patrick cagoules, Bundeswehr tracksuits and Russian fleece efforts – to the short-lived fads for sheepskin flying jackets and accompanying Biggles-style leather flying caps, or Belstaff outdoor wear, especially the Dalesman jacket. In *City Psychos*, Tordoff examines the fad for labels and how 'everyone had their own personal favourites: Pringle, Lyle & Scott, Tacchini, Armani, Fila, Hugo Boss, Valentino, etc.' Then there was the unlikely sudden craze for Farah slacks – a must-have item for the smartly dressed fan back in the day.

When *The Face* revisited the casual scene with a 1993 feature entitled 'The revenge of the likely lads', it highlighted Hull's individual stamp on the original scene, which

120 *Look Back in Amber* fanzine (Volume 2, Issue 1, October 1993)

apparently came via the wearing of Puma Vilas trainers from 1980–'83 and Lois Jeans (worn inside out!) in 1981. When considering City's league status at the time and given that the only other teams and places mentioned were 'Manchester, Liverpool, Glasgow and Leeds', 'Bladerunner' felt the *Face* article 'speaks volumes for the dress sense of City supporters, that their sartorial elegance was deemed so noteworthy even ten years later'. The joke among non-believers at the time was, 'Here they come, the lads from Prem,' although 'Bladerunner' was adamant that the Anlaby Road store was one shop definitely *not* on the recommended list. Instead, trips would be made to Manchester's Arndale Centre and to Harrods Sports Department, while in Hull itself any Army & Navy stores or the sports shop down Newland Avenue offered rich pickings. Later in the decade, 'James Wright – Master Tailor' of Anlaby Road would be a preferred choice. As well as disregarding certain stores, 'Bladerunner' also touched on what he viewed as fashion 'mistakes', one of which was apparently stretch jeans of 'any make, any year' – 'narrer arrers' as they were colloquially known in Hull.

Dubbed elsewhere as 'Dressers', 'Scallies' and 'Perry Boys', in Hull these 'likely lads' were initially labelled 'Trendies', a name 'Bladerunner' attributes to '13-year-old fat girls, dressed in white court shoes and cheap two-tone black-and-white gear'. Among my mates they tended to be referred to as 'Totty's Mob', although this was perhaps a sweeping generalisation for a group known to have disparate strands, often according to the various housing estates they hailed from. Having come more to the fore during the previous season's promotion campaign, their numbers increased in line with the club's overall growing support. They were certainly out in force on the opening day of the new season.

27 August 1983
Football League Third Division:
Hull City 4 Burnley 1

Boothferry Park: East Stand Terrace; season pass; no programme

In the summer of 1983, buoyed by seeing my first promotion campaign, I became 'Hull City AFC Season Passholder Number 970'. This newly acquired piece of card granted me access to the 'Ground (Except Well)', which for me meant the Kempton. At 17 I felt on the cusp of something special. I was about to start my final year of full-time education and the following March I'd be legally allowed to drink in pubs; my efforts over the next nine months would go a long way to determining whether or not I could actually afford to. The carefree days were on their way out but not before there was a bank holiday to be enjoyed – one that coincided with City's first game back in the Third Division. Excitement abounded.

The bookies didn't appear to share our optimism. The Tigers were 25/1 outsiders for a second successive promotion. Pre-season favourites were John Bond's Burnley, newly relegated and City's opening-day opponents. Colin Appleton's main concern over the summer had been strengthening his squad following promotion. He made two acquisitions, striker Steve Massey from Northampton and left-back Mick Hollifield who joined from Wolves on the recommendation of Emlyn Hughes. Departing the club was Bobby Brown, the man who'd helped oversee team matters during the receivership period and who'd done an excellent job as youth development officer. It was a move that upset many fans along with Brown himself who was said to be 'a very disappointed and disillusioned man'.

Boothferry Park had enjoyed something of a makeover in the summer, courtesy of the small Grandways Terrace at the north end. This was the place initially chosen by the new 'likely lads' element among the home support and ensured that away fans were now sandwiched in the north-east corner between two vocal elements – the old-style Kempton kop to their immediate left and the 'young trendies' to their right. It all made for what Appleton agreed would be 'more atmosphere for the players and especially for the goalkeepers who were standing alone last season', even with crowds of less than 10,000. In future seasons, the Well and even the Best Stand seats would become the preferred choice for these new casuals in their attempts to be close to the action, both on and off the pitch. Along with the Grandways terrace there was also a new steel cage around the away section, erected 'after a few Middlesbrough fans got a bit over-excited in a pre-season friendly', as City fanzine *On Cloud Seven* later termed it. A Monday night fixture, it saw what the *Hull Daily Mail* described as '140 so-called fans … left behind by their angry Teesside coach drivers whose vehicles were damaged on the journey to Hull'. The report termed the subsequent incidents during the match as 'some of the worst crowd trouble recorded at Boothferry Park', prompting Don Robinson 'to look into erecting barriers around the visiting supporters' terracing'.

As expected, it wasn't only the bookies who had Burnley well backed. Their support was big and loud behind the new fencing, helping create a fantastic atmosphere among the 9,764 present (a figure later adjusted to 8,394). Despite an encouraging pre-season in which City had remained unbeaten against four teams from higher divisions, including First Division Ipswich, not even the most blinkered fan could have imagined such a start against a team including five former internationals. Neither, I suspect, could the Burnley supporters. Big Billy set things rolling on ten minutes, lifting the ball over the advancing Roger Hansbury. Four minutes later it was 2-0 courtesy of debutant Massey's crisp left-footed finish. Kevin Reeves reduced arrears shortly afterwards but City secured the points with two second-half goals. Massey converted from close range on 47 minutes before Whitehurst 'lunged forward to head in Garreth Roberts's pinpoint left-wing cross' 14 minutes from time. City had sizzled in the sunshine. The Clarets' tag of favourites was blown away in emphatic style and defeat signalled the start of a season of mid-table mediocrity. We took great delight in sending them on their way. It was therefore perhaps inevitable that they would gain their revenge in the cruellest manner some nine months later.[121]

* * *

In his notes for the following Tuesday's League Cup tie against Lincoln, Appleton asked supporters, 'Did the team justify your optimism? Did they help to make your holiday weekend?' My answer on both counts was a resounding yes. On a cautionary note, however, he added, 'One swallow doesn't make a summer, and we now know success doesn't just happen, it has to be worked for.' He was right to temper expectation – City were largely uninspiring in a goalless draw that night and would eventually exit 3-1 on aggregate.

Midfield duo McClaren and Roberts had been at the forefront of the opening-day win. Unfortunately, they wouldn't be paired together again for a month after the former sustained serious burns when removing a cap off his car radiator. McClaren's absence was felt at Gillingham where City backed up their initial success with what Appleton termed a 'fortuitous' 2-1 victory. Marwood and Mutrie were on target, with future Tiger Ray Daniel missing a penalty on

121 Willie Donachie, Kevin Reeves, Brian Flynn, Billy Hamilton and Tommy Hutchinson (from Issue 3 of *On Cloud Seven*, November 1989)

his Gills debut. It was a victory celebrated by what Appleton referred to as 'a large following' of City fans.

The team's travel to Kent had been sponsored by the Tigers Supporters' Association (TSA), a group formed from the old Hull City Action Group. But it was one of the other Kent-bound coaches that made the front page of Monday's *Hull Daily Mail* after police 'swooped on about 60 youths boarding a coach in St Stephen's Square, Hull, at 12.30am on Saturday'. Among the 'small armoury of items recovered' was 'an air rifle barrel, a rounders bat, knives and razor blades'. Suffice to say, the coach didn't make it to Priestfield. Neither did I and nor was I at Valley Parade three nights later where City supporters made up 'a third of the crowd' of 3,391. The Tigers fought out a goalless draw, with Appleton saying, 'It was ironic that a better all-round team effort produced only one point by comparison with the performance at Gillingham.'

10 September 1983
Football League Third Division:
Hull City 5 Millwall 0

Boothferry Park: East Stand Terrace; season pass; programme 30p

City's unbeaten start set things up nicely for the following Saturday when Millwall were set to visit Hull. It was the day my cousin Melvin got married. I remember that because when the invitation came out he'd made a point of telling Mum 'not to worry' if I opted to watch City instead of being there. As a football fan himself (and a bloody good player too at local level) he appreciated how much my Saturdays meant to me. I'm glad he did, although given City's opponents, I did – briefly – flirt with the idea of using his wedding to my advantage.

This was to be my first live introduction to Millwall and their infamous followers. Like most football fans, I'd seen the

Panorama programme 'F-Troop, Treatment and the Halfway Line'. I was familiar with events at the 1978 FA Cup quarter-final against Ipswich and, closer to home, I'd heard plenty of stories from past encounters locally. One of these involved Paul D (he of Stray Cats hairdo infamy) telling his mates, 'Leave me to die,' as he was literally dragged to safety by the hood of his snorkel jacket. Another tale involved brothers Steve and Ian T reputedly employing different tactics to dodge a Millwall charge through Paragon Station, the former busting a gut to flee his pursuers while his older brother calmly stepped into a phone kiosk, picked up the receiver and pretended to make a call. Cap doffed for that one.

Such stories prompted another knot in the stomach ahead of a game that City won 5-0. The scoreline didn't tell the full story; the Tigers scored from all five attempts on goal, while the visitors hit the woodwork four times. At least the Millwall supporters lived up to their reputation. Taunted by the Kempton to the tune of Malcolm McLaren's 'Double Dutch' ('The Millwall die and the Millwall die'), the response of the visiting fans was to try and dismantle the new segregation fences. It was an action lost on the far side of the ground where The Don, sitting in the directors' box, later judged them to be the 'Best Visiting Supporters' that season. Perhaps their fighting spirit resonated with the former Dr Death who'd once 'needed four stitches in a hand wound when trying to break up some fighting on the terraces' during a friendly between Scarborough and City in July 1972.[122]

Thankfully, the rest of the game and my journey back to town passed off quietly and I was on my service bus in time to catch the chairman on Radio 2. The win had taken City top of the table and gave Robinson the platform he craved. He

122 Bond, David, *'Meet Me at Bunker's Hill!'* (Hull: Tykesport, 2006) p.48

didn't let us down, repeating his claim of the previous season about City playing on the Moon. We lapped it up – most of us would have settled for promotion. In his next programme notes, Appleton took a more pragmatic view, saying that while 'it has to be better to have the points in the bag' his team required luck with injuries and to avoid a change of attitude. 'Players can become complacent, supporters can become too particular and both can get things out of perspective.'

Ironically, by the time these notes appeared, City had been knocked off the top by virtue of dropped points at Deepdale. Tony Norman proved the hero in a goalless draw by saving a John Kelly penalty. Back-to-back home wins returned City to the summit. I remember the 2-0 home win over Lincoln not so much for Big Billy's brace but more for the away following, many of whom arrived late, all wearing sponsored red baseball caps and intent on 'having a go'. There was no trouble three nights later when Whitehurst was again on target to account for third-placed Wimbledon. Boothferry was becoming a fortress. Appleton cited the gates, which had doubled 'since last season at this time', as a big factor in his team's good home form. Attendances at Boothferry Park were certainly impressive, even allowing for the match programme appearing to add a thousand to what would later become the official figures. The last three home wins had seen a week-on-week climb: 6,537 for the Millwall game, 7,523 for Lincoln and 8,133 for a game against the Dons that attracted few visiting fans.

The Tigers were on a roll. Unbeaten in seven games, they were two points clear of second-placed Bristol Rovers and three above Sheffield United. When Steve Taylor sent Tony Norman the wrong way from the penalty spot in the 74th minute to earn Wigan a point at Springfield Park, it was the first goal conceded by City in 568 minutes of league football.

Earlier the game had seen 'a minor pitch invasion in the home penalty area on nine minutes' as City supporters maintained their tradition for kicking off in Wigan. In fairness, Taylor's penalty – cancelling out Andy Flounders's opener just two minutes earlier – was the least the hosts deserved. The *Hull Daily Mail* headline 'Norman is Tigers hero' said it all, with the Welshman producing 'a string of sparkling saves'. The result allowed Oxford to take pole position but City remained well in touch. Robinson was happy enough as he announced in the *Hull Daily Mail* that he was doubling the players' draw bonus from £10 to £20, an act which prompted a note to the Football League – seemingly from someone within the club – asking if such a move was legal 'just like the champagne given to Halifax last season'.[123]

8 October 1983
Football League Third Division:
Hull City 4 Sheffield United 1
Boothferry Park: East Stand Terrace; season pass; programme 30p

If the Millwall result was impressive, the one gained against Sheffield United was outstanding. The two teams began the day separated by one point and a couple of places but the second-placed Tigers ran out emphatic winners. It was certainly the 'one to remember' that Appleton hoped it would be beforehand. Along with informing supporters of the midweek acquisition of Steve Osbourne on professional forms and Ian Davis's return home following an operation, the manager enthused about the contest in store. Describing as 'super' some of the recent matches between the two clubs, he wrote, 'But at each there has always tended to be an element

123 *On Cloud Seven* fanzine (Issue 3, November 1989)

of doubt about the reactions of the supporters on the day. It is nice to think that we are going to watch a good attractive game with three to four hours' smooth-running entertainment and the police in very little evidence. However, because of the past encounters, spectators may be looking for things which may not occur, therefore let's all concentrate on getting to and from the game, channelling our energies to supporting the teams. These should be occasions to remember, so let's make it right ... Hopefully, my few words will fall on some of our younger supporters' ears, and they realise what they do can either help or hinder the players a great deal. Let them be an enthusiastic help to Hull City.'[124]

They certainly were a help, comprising the bulk of what the *Hull Daily Mail* termed City's 'biggest crowd for seven and a half years'. The attendance was quoted as 16,728 at the time, though this was later downsized to 14,775. Whatever the figure, it generated hitherto record gate receipts of £28,725, a figure that, according to Phil Braund in the *Sunday Mirror*, delighted Robinson who 'hauled himself up the 45 steps to the press room' to declare the amount before adding, 'And, thank God, we keep it all.' In fairness, the piece (entitled 'Don's Boom Boys') did go on to quote the City chairman as admitting, 'Taking three points from United has thrilled me even more.' Me too. I hadn't known Boothferry to be as full or as noisy as the Tigers maintained their 100 per cent home record courtesy of a thumping 4-1 win, shattering the Blades' unbeaten start in the process. Similar to the Millwall game, the scoreline doesn't tell the full story, with the outcome in doubt until what the *Hull Daily Mail*'s headline termed a 'Late Blitz'. Three goals in 12 minutes sealed City's success.

---

124 Match programme (Hull City v Sheffield United, 8 October 1983)

On a rain-soaked afternoon the game started with a bang, McClaren seizing on a slip by United left-back Joe Bolton before fooling goalkeeper Keith Waugh and sliding home. The visitors were level within six minutes courtesy of a Colin Morris penalty after Dale Roberts had handled a Kevin Arnott cross. And that's how it stayed until the 79th minute when, according to Simon Redfern's match report, Marwood 'seized on a woeful back-pass from United centre-back Mick Henderson, before curling the ball round Waugh and into the net off a post'. When 'Marwood pounced again after 86 minutes', latching on to Askew's pass and sprinting half the length of the field before beating Waugh for 3-1, the points were assured. Even so there was still time for Mutrie to 'put the icing on an already very tasty cake' (as described six years later by City fanzine *On Cloud Seven*) when 'waltzing' from near the south-east corner flag into the penalty area and beating a couple of defenders before stroking the ball 'past the bemused Keith Waugh'. It was a goal of real poise, befitting of a player of such class. Mutrie himself described it to Richard Gardham as 'one of my favourites'. Given his predecessor Keith Edwards's place in the opposition ranks, Mutrie's goal carried extra credence with supporters, as noted by Stephen Hodgson: 'Oh yes, arise Sir Les, bye-bye Edwards.'[125]

Unsurprisingly, Appleton's pre-match words hadn't resonated with the visiting fans and they began hurling seats from the Best Stand on to the pitch. The final whistle brought its own problems and for reasons I can't recall, I found myself alone for the walk to town. The challenge now was to get as far down Anlaby Road as possible before the delayed release of the Sheffield contingent. In the event I was almost at the flyover by the time their advance guard was making contact with the

125 Gardham, Richard, *The Decade: Ten Years that Transformed Hull City AFC* (Self-published, 2019) p.40; *Tiger Rag* fanzine (Issue 5, March 1995)

City stragglers. The procedure was simple: keep walking, avoid any eye contact and whatever you do, *do not* arouse attention – hard as that might be for a kid with a daft haircut. What I didn't need was to be spotted by Paul D, minus his legendary snorkel jacket and up above me on the flyover. 'Eh, Luzzy, how good was that?' he shouted back, while proceeding to wave his City scarf in delight. Oh fuck! The chase was on! Thus my first visit to Hull Fair was an unplanned, impromptu affair that allowed little time to sample the food stalls on Walton Street. Somehow I managed to avoid a good kicking and got back to town in time to catch the bus home. I promised myself I'd avoid Paul at all future City games.

29 October 1983
Football League Third Division:
Oxford United 1 Hull City 1

The Manor Ground, Cuckoo Lane End Terrace; no ticket; programme 40p

City stuttered slightly after seeing off Sheffield. Points were dropped in successive draws at Brentford and Bolton. I'm guessing lack of finance was the reason I missed both, although seeing King Kurt's 'Destination Zululand' single reviewed by celebrity chef Delia Smith on *Saturday Superstore* provided some consolation for missing the 1-1 draw in west London. Three nights later, Appleton praised his players for performing 'heroically in atrocious conditions' at Burnden Park. Frustrated that 'such commitment' had yielded only a point, the City boss wondered 'what lies around the corner'. His answer came by way of a shock home defeat at the hands of Plymouth. Tommy Tynan scored twice for the visitors and Marwood missed a second-half penalty in front of the *Match of the Day* cameras. City's first loss of the season meant they dropped to third ahead of the visit to leaders Oxford, a team fresh from dumping Kevin Keegan's Newcastle out of the League Cup.

As with all away games, the Tigers were well backed at Oxford. A mixture of official and unofficial groups headed south by various means. Underlining their need to be different, the casuals were by this time arranging their own independent means of travel. This came in various forms, including bus, train and sometimes Luton furniture van. Similar to how their Psychos forerunners had operated in the 1970s, flyers were used to advertise upcoming trips. Under the banner 'Delta Travel Services' and entitled Away Travel with Hull City Season 1983/84, one resurfaced on a City supporters online forum in 2017. It makes for fascinating reading: 'It is proposed for the coming season that the elite section of Hull City supporters who would expect to travel with us should become more organised than they have been in previous seasons. We do not expect the term "elite" to cover persons with a multitude of scarves, hats, badges, patches, banners and flags, neither do we expect people wearing largely flared trousers or Haircut 100 groupies to consider it right to travel with us.'

I'm not sure whether I was seen as a follower of Nick Heyward's chart faves but I was certainly one of those 'other people' that the flyer referred to who might choose to travel on 'a coach where the organiser will sit at the front (possibly in a red jacket) and sells crisps, sweets, soft-drinks and lemonade'. No prizes for who he was referring to! The document also offered advice on the carrying of alcohol ('coach drivers cannot see through holdalls, etc.') as well as highlighting methods undertaken to avoid what it termed police 'harassment'. These included not always travelling straight to the destination, along with giving passengers the option to 'take advantage of the stops on the way and continue the journey by service train'

– it advised 'regular supporters' to 'purchase a rail card'. Prices were to be 'basically the same as Hull City Supporters Club and the "Lottery Ticket and Crisps Appreciation Society" coaches' (poor Simon took a bit of a battering from this new 'elite'). Deposits were required up front and if demand wasn't sufficient for a coach then vans could be organised. If this was also not feasible then the deposits would be returned. Notice of trips was to be posted in the Personal (Business) column of Wednesday's *Hull Daily Mail.* As with their forerunners, the casuals subscribed to a similar mantra: 'It's our team and our right to express our support in whatever way we choose.'

Ironically, the first trip arranged as part of the new service was the ill-fated one to Gillingham referred to earlier. But on those journeys when the destination *was* reached, those aboard would again underline their need to be set apart from their peers. Instead of the away terraces, they chose the more expensively priced seating areas, whether they were designated for City fans or not. It was a move fraught with risk, as would be seen on this occasion. It all began quietly enough as I joined the bulk of the 'guesstimated' 500-strong City following on the open Cuckoo Lane End. Discussion centred on the upcoming stern test of the team's post-Plymouth defeat recovery powers. Just prior to kick-off we became aware of something happening to our right. The rush of police soon told us that some of City's 'elite' had taken up seats in the Main Stand above a paddock in which were housed their Oxford counterparts. A rendition of the national anthem, accompanied by some stiff-arm salutes only served to further antagonise their more multiracial audience below. After a fair bit of posturing on the part of both groups, a forced ejection ensued, with the 30-strong City contingent being relocated to our terrace. Fighting then broke out at the opposite end of the ground, later reported in *City Psychos* to have been caused by West Ham fans with connections to Hull (referred to at the time as the 'ICF Cockney Tigers'). It was all 'going off'.

Against this feisty backdrop, City – with Flounders replacing the injured Mutrie – began as brightly as the autumn sunshine. They were rewarded when Marwood latched on to Whitehurst's knockdown to fire home in the 18th minute. The Tigers then spurned several chances to increase their lead and when 'Chicken' George Lawrence slammed home Brock's left-wing cross to level matters just past the hour, it constituted City's sixth successive away draw. Despite a creditable result, there was little chance of applauding the players for their efforts. The final whistle brought further trouble with those of us in the away end being subjected to a hail of missiles from home fans, some of whom had come across the pitch and others who'd made their way around the ground and were firing their barrage from behind the stand. It all made for a pretty hairy walk back to the coaches. There was an overwhelming sense of relief when we were finally clear of the city boundary and heading back home.

Appleton described the result as 'the little boost needed', adding that his players' response had shown 'what good tradesmen they have become'. Despite this the following Tuesday's home draw against Walsall extended the winless run to five matches. That it didn't become six was only thanks to a late Mick Hollifield goal (his first and only for Hull) in a 3-2 win at Bournemouth. City remained in the top three. Appleton was by now employing a 5-2-3 formation, which he didn't change the following week even after visitors Newport County had seen John Aldridge sent off for what the fanzine *On Cloud Seven* would later term 'persistent Scouse whining'. The game remained goalless, meaning City had drawn half of their 16 matches to date. A narrow home win over Orient was offset by a first away defeat of the season at Exeter and the Tigers were in need of a run of wins to underline their promotion credentials.

* * *

The Oxford game was an eye-opener. I now realised it didn't matter where you travelled to watch football; every town and city had its fair share of lads looking for a ruck. Trouble simply came with the territory. The other factor I was becoming aware of was the apparent rift that the casuals' emergence was creating in the ranks of the travelling City support. Already an obvious target for 'banter' on account of my Gripper Stebson haircut and garb, the fact I travelled to games with a largely 'greb' element put me on one side of an increasingly fractious divide. There was a growing resentment among those on Simon's coaches towards the 'new kids on the block'. Although there were a few casuals on board (local lads, well known to us all) they stood out like I did among the old-school bikers, bootboys and what would otherwise be regarded as straights or scarfers. Many among the latter shared the view that these 'Trendies' had no real interest in City and were only there to pose and fight. Matchday for these lads was 'about territory, honour, not losing face, a primal reaction to somebody invading your space or coming on to your manor and taking liberties'. In truth, the two sides were more similar than they thought. For one thing, many of the 'elite' had been following City for years and, flipping the argument on its head, many among my out-of-towner mates weren't always there just for the football, being equally as interested in the day as a whole, particularly the drinking. Indeed, some of them were former 'bovver boys', not averse to having a go with rival supporters. In short, the only thing setting them apart was image.[126]

---

126 Bannon, James, *Running with the Firm* (London: Ebury, 2013) p.160

I didn't share my fellow supporters' disdain towards the casuals, despite their often leering attitude towards me and my ilk. In fact, I had a grudging respect for them not least because their involvement in any aggro often meant the rest of us didn't have to join in! I also had several mates among their ranks, some of them local lads who I'd known from school as well as 'Townies' whose acquaintance I'd made through either City or work (or both). There was also 'Dill', whose Mohican haircut and punk-inspired fashion set him slightly apart from those he travelled with and made for instant recognition when weighing up friend or foe. All of which only made this almost toxic matchday atmosphere even more uncomfortable. Thankfully, for all the sniping, it only occasionally boiled over into anything serious inside the grounds. More often than not the simmering tension came to a head in the city centre pubs, notably the legendary Trog Bar where the Saturday night clientele was split down the middle between the biker crowd and followers of what would now be called Hull's 'fashion circuit'. It was just a shame that what was becoming a great time to watch City on the pitch was in danger of being tainted by in-house aggravation off it.

19 November 1983
FA Cup First Round Proper: Penrith 0 Hull City 2
Southend Road; no ticket; programme 30p
The draw for the first round of the FA Cup sent City to Penrith of the North West Counties Football League, a tie for which Mutrie was omitted following the first of several disagreements with Appleton. A trip to a non-league team was always an attractive proposition and the Tigers were well backed in Cumbria, 'taking over the town' according to one of numerous posts on a Facebook page dedicated to memories of Boothferry Park when the game cropped up as a topic some 37

years on. Whenever such memories are revived, tales emerge that again reinforce the joys of following your team in the early 1980s (regardless of whether they've grown legs with age). The Penrith tie provided a rich seam of such stories, including from some who never even made it to the match, such as the '22 lads' aboard a Luton van pulled over by the police on the way out of Brough just west of Hull. When the boys in blue discovered what one of the lads described as 'a barrel of beer monsters' on board and notified the van hire company the trip was officially off. The local constabulary didn't have such success when trying to detain a coach carrying some of City's 'elite' near the ground, only to be informed by the organisers that such detention laws only applied to Football League grounds and as such they had no right in holding them. A few minutes later they were on their way, leaving their frustrated would-be escort behind.[127]

For some reason the game itself had an early kick-off time of 2.15pm. Many pubs in the town were shut, possibly due to Manchester City being at nearby Carlisle in a Second Division fixture. This fact didn't deter those Hull fans in desperate need of a drink. One of my standout memories of the day involves being sat on our coach at traffic lights and watching with great amusement as a group of lads attempted to enter a swanky-looking hotel bar one by one through its revolving door, only to reappear seconds later by the same means, followed by the footman. Others had more luck. One supporter on Facebook recalled nipping out at half-time for a pint then getting back in for the second half! The police also thought it was safer to have City fans inside the ground despite the regular outbreaks of trouble in the covered terrace that ran the full length of one side, which housed both sets

127 Hull City AFC Boothferry Park Photos/Memories Facebook page

of supporters. Another supporter on Facebook remembered 'getting slung out in the chaos only for an inspector to tell his PCs to sling me back in again'. Indeed, one of our regulars, John B, was twice ejected for fighting only to be back in the ground for a third time to celebrate a place in the next round.

Penrith came into the tie in good form. With only one defeat in their last ten matches, they sat just behind leaders Stalybridge Celtic in Division One and were looking for a repeat of their previous first-round appearance two years earlier, which had resulted in a win over Chester. It wasn't to be. 'City lay their cup jinx' was the *Hull Daily Mail*'s headline to Simon Redfern's report as the Tigers 'reached the second round of a cup competition for the first time under Colin Appleton's leadership'. Well backed in a crowd of nearly 2,000, City 'produced a thoroughly professional and disciplined performance' to overcome their hosts 'far more easily than the scoreline suggests'. Only 'tame finishing, a post and brave Penrith defending' ensured the tally stayed at the two goals scored inside a 12-minute spell towards the end of the first half. Skipper Roberts opened the scoring just past the half-hour with a 'blistering 20-yard snapshot' and Big Billy doubled the lead when he 'soared above home keeper Paul Kirkbride' to head home a Marwood cross. To compound the disappointment for the home full-back who bore a rather unfortunate resemblance to Peter Sutcliffe, he was subjected to chants of 'there's only one Yorkshire Ripper' whenever he happened to touch the ball. The humour of football fans in the 1980s knew no depths.

City's reward was a trip to struggling Rotherham but before then came the aforementioned league matches against Leyton Orient and Exeter. The Londoners were beaten 2-1 thanks to a Big Billy brace but despite a rare goal from Bobby McNeil the long trip to Devon proved fruitless as the Grecians triumphed by the same scoreline. And so to Millmoor, a ground in which the low roof at the away end made for a fabulous atmosphere. As always at Rotherham the City following was raucous and as so often at Rotherham, we came home disappointed. Initially it appeared we were in for a good day when 'Cousin' Andy swept home a Billy Askew cross to give City a deserved lead. I still maintain it's the loudest cheer I've been part of when celebrating a goal. Unfortunately, the home side hit back. A Kevin Kilmore brace turned the game on its head and our dreams of Wembley were again ended before the big boys had even entered the competition. Ah well, at least we really *did* have the league to concentrate on.

13

Sounds of the City

Easington: Friday, 2 December 1983

Friday night means tea on a tray upstairs, the portable's on and like every other 'groovy fucker' I'm tuned to The Tube. *Tonight's edition begins with a 'Hull Bands Special', which opens with presenter Jools Holland sitting on the deck of former Humber ferry the PS* Lincoln Castle. *Over the next 20 minutes or so, along with his Squeeze band-mate (and Hullensian) Johnny Bentley, Holland treats us to sights and sounds as diverse as Red Guitars, the toilet beneath the King Billy statue in Lowgate, Indians in Moscow, white telephone boxes, the Luddites and punk-poet Swift Nick. The piece concludes with Bridlington band International Rescue performing live at Spiders nightclub. The song 'This Town' is one they've been asked to write specifically for the show and the feature concludes with Holland asking, 'Is this the Humber Sound?' I'm not sure but after watching this I'm determined to find out.*[128]

* * *

At the same time as the city's football club was coming out of the shadows, Hull's music scene was also battling around the

---

128 'Be there or be un-groovy fuckers' was the term used by Jools Holland prior to a show in January 1987. This led to a three-week ban and the show was eventually pulled in March the same year

lower leagues, striving for that one big hitter whose success might pave the way for other purveyors of what local music 'zine *Zig-Zag*, in one gig review, termed the 'Humber Sound'. When Channel 4's cult music show *The Tube* arrived to film a feature on the sounds of the city, to be broadcast in December 1983, it opened the door for some much-needed exposure.

For the young Richard Lusmore, by now making his first tentative steps into a musical world beyond the cocoon of the '50s rocking scene, it was to act as something of an eye-opener. For a start I didn't appreciate just how much talent there was within the city. At the time pub rockers Revival were the only local band to have remotely caught my interest. Most other stuff simply passed me by. *The Tube*'s visit helped change that. For those not old enough to have watched it first time round the feature is available in its entirety on YouTube. Indeed, as with many things, the internet is a great starting point for anybody wanting an introduction to the Hull bands of the time, with a designated Hull Music Archive website and a couple of great Facebook pages. Back in 1983, however, I didn't have that luxury.[129]

The Tube's feature on what David Blows (in his weekly *Hull Daily Mail* 'Mailbeat' column) termed 'the Hull area and its huge, as yet untapped, potential' shone a light on names I'd previously come across on the flyers and posters displayed in city centre record shops. Foremost among these was Syd Scarbs where the basement in particular became a place to keep abreast of local happenings. But it was only in 1990 and Ian Mowforth's retrospective article for the debut issue of City fanzine *From Hull to Eternity* that I fully realised just how vibrant the scene had been. Later conversations with the

---

129 *Zig-Zag* review of a gig by Red Guitars and The Luddites; http://www.hullmusicarchive.co.uk/, Hull Music Archive | Facebook, (1) Hull and East Yorkshire Music scene, 70's and 80's | Facebook

likes of Kari Brown (aka Kari Kool of Cool to Snog fame) and Tony Menzies (once of COUM Transmissions and Throbbing Gristle, and 'a reservoir of memory' with regards to the era) also helped join the dots. Between Mowforth, Brown, Menzies and the internet I've managed to grab a glimpse of what following Matchbox's urge to be a 'Rockabilly Rebel' in 1979 had cost me in terms of musical education. Not that my sources shared a common view of who deserves most credit among the movers and shakers of the local scene. As in football, music is also about opinions and even 40 years on strong views are maintained as to which bands deserve their place in Hull music's hall of fame. So let's go back to the beginning. Well, sort of.

Like many provincial towns and cities, Hull was still home to punk long after the demise of the Sex Pistols. Ian Mowforth's piece began by paying tribute to 'nurtured' punks such as Z-Men and Born BC, the latter 'driven by the harsh vocals of Ranus and guitaring from the Broadie brothers'. He wasn't as complimentary about the 'instantly forgettable' Wires Die and Nerve Blocks while original Hull bands Foeticide and Strangeways failed to even get a look-in. Fronted by Pete Stitt, the latter opened up for the Exploited at The Tower in November 1981 just a week after recording their one-and-only single, '(I Don't Know) Who She Is' b/w 'Years of Pain' on Reif Records. Released in March 1982, it provides the band with their own claim to fame in the Humber Sound story – according to Stitt, it became 'the most highly valued single in Hull's musical history' when copies of it sold for £80 on eBay some 26 years later.[130]

In 1979, Tony Menzies returned to the city and immediately set about promoting gigs in Bestobel House (a

130 From the 2008 feature on Strangeways on www.boredteenagers.co.uk

student bar) and then at the Wellington Club. There he also performed with the Defectors who in 1980 released their three-track 'Target Baby' EP on Louder Records. It was recorded and mixed in a 12-hour session at Cargo Studios in Rochdale on 8 October 1979 (the same date – as remembered by Menzies – that Siouxsie & the Banshees played Hull City Hall, supported by the Cure and the Associates). The Defectors were just one of several Hull bands spawned by Section 60, an outfit formed in 1978 and considered by Kari Brown to be 'very important' to what followed, not least by virtue of their members (including 'underrated genius' Paul Moller) subsequently popping up in various other acts that followed in their wake. Ian Mowforth describes the Odds, the Mountbattens, Blitzkrieg Patrol and the Akrylykz as having 'led the way until 1982' when 'they were then joined by a welter of bands including London Boys, Moscow, Tee-Hee-Tee, Bushfire, Neopolitans, Wine Gums, Attic Art, Screaming Cataleptics, Dorien Gray, Hellfire Club, Shower Attachments, Neo Classix, Abstraxt, Cruel Garden, Monitors, Righteous and World Service. Kari disputes the right of the 'not significant' Mountbattens to be placed in such company and also takes issue with Mowforth's descriptions of the sounds created by My Silent War and Discobolisk as 'acoustic music … fed by Hull Uni students Everything But The Girl'.

Hull music, eh – it's all about opinions!

One of the bands seemingly with universal appeal locally was pop/mod ensemble the Odds, even if they are remembered by some for the far-from-warm reception they were afforded as late replacements on the support bill at the Damned's 1979 Hull City Hall gig. In 1981 they released a catchy self-funded single ('Fool in the Crowd' b/w 'Nails and Knives') as prelude to a tour of Germany and Sweden. They eventually morphed into Moscow (later Moscow for Pleasure) who became firm favourites of 'Mailbeat'. Meanwhile, saxophonist Stuart Matthewman went on to forge a very successful career as part of chart-toppers Sade. He was joined there by fellow Hullensians Paul Cooke and Paul Denman, previously of the Posers who, according to Paul Simper, were credited by Matthewman as being 'the only band in Hull trying to do something new' at the time.[131]

Another local lad who went on to bigger and better things was Roland Gift, who in 1985 would achieve pop stardom with Fine Young Cannibals. Before then, it appeared that he might find fame and fortune closer to home. Previously a member of the Blue Kitchen, Righteous and World Service, in 1979 Gift joined some fellow students at the Hull College of Art in punk/ska band Akrylyk Vyktymz (later shortened to the Akrylykz), originally as saxophonist. When Kari Brown and her friends went to see the band's launch gig she recalls, 'We wet ourselves to see Roland as front man' before adding, 'The joke's on us now!' The band recorded the double A-sided single 'Smart Boy'/'Spyderman' for Red Rhino Records of York. Released in 1980, it was picked up by Radio 1's Mike Read and John Peel who described the band as having 'caused a large ripple in the music pool'. By the time the second single appeared, Polydor had bought out Red Rhino. Entitled 'JD' b/w 'Ska'd for Life' it was the first 'local' release to find its way into my record collection but unfortunately not into the charts. A third single never materialised after the band's manager reputedly did a runner with the cash advance and the demo tapes.

The Akrylykz also provided the backing band for the legendary Desmond Dekker on his 1980 *Black and Dekker* comeback album, which included the hit single 'Israelites'.

---

131 Simper, Paul, *Pop Stars in My Pantry* (London: Unbound 2017) Extract via https://shapersofthe80s.com/tag/pop-stars-in-my-pantry/

Sadly, however, they weren't required for his subsequent TV appearances. [132]

The main venue for bands like the Odds and the Akrylykz was the 500-capacity Wellington (or 'Welly') Club on Beverley Road. It first opened in 1913 but, as described in the *Yorkshire Post,* it wasn't until many years later, under the stewardship of 'no-nonsense secretary Doreen Wilson' – and thanks largely to Tony Menzies – that it came into its own as a live venue. Kari remembers that the Welly 'had no three-phase power and so Tony had to connect it all himself'. Many Hull gig-goers would be eternally glad he did so. The Welly was 'strictly conventional' down below but it was in the upstairs lounge bar where Mrs Wilson's 'empathy with the underdog' began to bear fruit. Many local bands used to come to her and say, 'Mrs Wilson, we've got nowhere else to go.' As a result, Kari began organising Tuesday night gigs by local bands in the upstairs lounge bar, which she rather incongruously renamed The Basement Club.[133]

Downstairs, the concert room played host to some of the biggest names around, with Menzies-promoted gigs by the Beat and the Specials in 1979 offering the Akrylykz their first real break. The band soon became the staple support act for shows promoted by Kari – Magazine, Psychedelic Furs, Monochrome Set, Echo and the Bunnymen – before later headlining the same stage to a packed house. Notable support slots were also bagged with the Beat and UB40 at Hull University, the Clash at Bridlington Spa and Dexy's Midnight Runners at the Music Machine in London, alongside extensive gigs in their own right. One of these came at the

132 From a 2009 interview with band member Piotr Swiderski for www.boredteenagers.co.uk/akrylykz.htm

133 The Newsroom, https://www.yorkshirepost.co.uk/news/welly-goes-back-rock-roots-celebrate-100th-year-1859540, 22 August 2013

Sheffield Mecca where an upcoming local band by the name of ABC provided support. Nationwide press coverage came via the *NME*, *Sounds* and even *Smash Hits*. But a year later the band split, citing the usual 'musical differences' as one of the reasons. Their demise and that of the Defectors and the Odds signalled the end of what Kari calls the 'three key Hull bands' of that era, the only ones seriously 'courting record label interest'.[134]

While Gift went on to eventually become a pop star, fellow ex-Akrylyk Nik Townend set up the Vital Records label, another player in any search for the Humber Sound. In 1981 the label's third release (and first album) was the now-legendary Hull compilation *Mrs Wilson's Children*. Compiled and produced by Kari Brown, it featured 12 regulars from the Welly Club roster, including her own band and the aforementioned Defectors. Other offerings came courtesy of the London Boys (who *Sounds* described as 'a dance sound based on a 12-bar rhythm and blues structure with modern influences'); Nyam Nyam and the Vets (more of whom later); the highly rated Blitzkrieg Patrol; 'Ferriby funksters' the Ashtrays; *NME* competition winner Johnny Solo; the seemingly forgotten Faux Pas; three-piece home recording artists Psychologic; Human Zoo ('Hull's most talented and imaginative pop group' according to the *Hull Daily Mail*); and Sons of the Pope whose closing track (and title of the album) 'epitomises the spirit of the Wellington Club'. Kari explains the album's origins: 'Every Thursday night one of the bands we read about each week in the *NME* took to the stage supported by one of the very many members of the Hull music scene. At some point we decided these bands should be celebrated. Spurred on by the success of Sheffield's *Bouquet of Steel* and Brighton's *Vaultage 78*, we went in search

---

134 Same as (133)

of 12 bands. The title of the album was provided courtesy of the Sons of the Pope, the youngest of all the bands and the ones who were often at the sharp end of Mrs Wilson's tongue, the spirit of her lament being, "You wouldn't do that in your own home."'[135]

Initially, a lack of funds threatened to stop the album in its tracks after Kari had done all the groundwork in terms of master tapes and artwork. Thankfully, Paul Trynka of Nyam Nyam stepped in and 'stumped up the cash' and this landmark recording finally saw the light of day. Trynka says, 'It was the start of a beautiful time when you'd be listening to John Peel and your own record would come on, maybe with a couple of words of approval, little moments that felt life-changing.'[136]

In February 2014, Kari recalled a similar feeling when interviewed for the Only Death Is Fatal blog, 'Cool to Snog was one of the three bands he chose to play on his show. It was the thrill of my life, certainly. "And here all the way from Hull is Cool to Snog."' A few years later, in an interview for *SFX* magazine, Peel told her it was 'one of the best names for a band' he'd ever heard. Even those who were critical of the quality acknowledged its importance. In a 1981 piece entitled 'Hull: There's Life East of Leeds', esteemed Liverpool fanzine *Bop Eye* described it as 'drab and average' but described the bands involved as part of 'a new breed' in the city who 'actually want to be good!' Three decades later, *Mrs Wilson's Children* earned a CD re-release as part of the Welly's centenary celebrations. A one-off gig was arranged with several of the original bands lined up to play. Once again it was all overseen by Cool to Snog's founder.

---

135 From Nyam Nyam blog: https://nyamnyamhopeofheaven.wordpress.com/2012/10/26/mrs-wilson-and-other-personalities/

136 Same as [138]

Other Hull venues of the era included Dingwalls on George Street; the University Union; Hull Tech College (host to the Skids, the Dickies and Magazine in 1979, as well as an infamous Adam and the Ants gig that reputedly had to be abandoned when someone set fire to the stage!); the Blind Institute on Beverley Road (Crass, the Au-Pairs, Delta 5); Desolation Row at Spiders; New York on Anlaby Road and the Spring Bank Community Centre on Wellington Lane. The latter was remembered by 'Junk Monkey' online as 'probably the most horrible place you could ever wish to see a band … a concrete shed … sweat dripping off the incredibly low ceiling … ludicrously low stage'.

Kari Brown disputes this. 'It was brilliant,' she says, before also taking issue with Ian Mowforth's opinion that 'undoubtedly the crucible of Hull music venues was Clouds'. Housed at Spring Street Theatre and run by Paul Tognola (of local heavy metallers Ethel the Frog and Salem) and Steve Larkman (the Crack), it is also remembered by Townend as having 'a good stage and a top-rate lighting rig'. Mowforth compared it to the legendary Eric's in Liverpool, saying: 'Clouds rapidly became the place to be.' Cue Kari again: 'Really? I don't think so. Welly Club all the way! This Clouds stuff seems a bit weird; we certainly didn't call it that, colloquially it was known as just Hull Truck.'[137]

Hull music, eh – it's all about opinions.

In 1981 another important venue came into use. The Tower was built as a 1,200-capacity cinema in 1914 and after closing in September 1978 was restored to near-pristine condition as a venue for music and boxing. Between 1981 and 1983 (when owner Wally Mays oversaw another change of purpose to a nightclub) the Grade II-listed building hosted

137 Comment by Junk Monkey on interview with Nik Townend, (5 January 2009) www.marcoonthebass.blogspot.com

regular live concerts. While I was bopping in the aisles to Shaky at the City Hall, the city's really cool kids were catching the likes of Bow Wow Wow, Depeche Mode, Theatre of Hate, New Order, Bauhaus, Orange Juice and Stiff Little Fingers at The Tower. Hull had 'woken up', according to *Bop Eye*: 'Compared with London or Liverpool it's still a "sleepy town", but compared to three years ago things are definitely healthy … Hull is no longer 12 months behind the rest of Britain. There is now a proper venue – The Tower, which allows people to see name bands without travelling all over the country. A club scene now exists – The Silhouette Club (there were two but The Roach Club is now closed) which is frequented by Hull's "fashion and music set" who are proving life exists east of Leeds.'[138]

This 'fashion and music set' soon became part of what Mowforth termed a 'contemporary community … developing its own notions of cool and sense of critique', indulging in street chic courtesy of The End (previously 5-4-3-2-1 on George Street), Transvaal, and Changes (*Bop Eye* had listed The End, Changes, Next and Backstage as Hull's 'four good fashion shops'). By 1983 the aforementioned Spiders on Cleveland Street had joined Spring Bank's Silhouette Club as a cool place to be seen after dark, a fact acknowledged by London 'style magazine' *i-D* in its March issue. A piece entitled 'Heaven or Hull' highlighted the newly opened Dingwalls and Thursday's Desolation Row night at Spiders, where 'bands such as Everything But The Girl [and] Urban Shakedown' could be seen.

Perhaps bizarrely, the likes of the Cameo and Victoria coffee clubs and Ocean 11 were also listed, albeit with the warning, 'GO IF YOU DARE!' The piece formed part of an

138 Source, 'Silhouette Club in Hull, Spring Bank 1980s' Facebook page (25 May 2020)

'innovative' photo-documentary-style regular feature ('The Straight Up') that included a short question-and-answer session with a local subject or two. Hence the reader got to know that Mandy was wearing an Anne Smith outfit from The End and liked Hull's 'famous' fish and chips but disliked 'doing what the boss says', while friend Sarah (also kitted out from the same cool boutique) liked 'partying down' at the Silhouette. So there you go.

Meanwhile, in sleepy Sutton, Jill Pullen launched *Kindred Spirit*, a music fanzine dedicated to Hull. Originally planned as 'an outlet for budding poets', Jill's idea was launched in the classifieds section of the *NME*. Her online blog tells the story of how the responses helped form the bulk of the first issue, which came out in late summer 1983, priced 30p. A proper homemade affair produced 'using my portable typewriter – with a good supply of Tipp-Ex and hand drawn artwork', *Kindred Spirit*'s debut issue also featured live reviews of Killing Joke at Clouds and local music event Sounds 83, held at Burton Constable Hall. The fanzine lasted for four issues before 'life got in the way'. It included local bands International Rescue, Punctured Tough Guy and Les Zeiga Fleurs (Issue 1), Red Guitars and Lady Jane (Issue 2), Cold Dance (Issue 3) and Quel Dommage (Issue 4). Jill's younger brother Jeff would later take up the fanzine baton when getting involved in the City publications of the late 1980s.[139]

* * *

With so much happening by 1983, what this burgeoning Hull scene needed was a bit of national media attention. It came courtesy of the telly. Channel 4's *The Tube* – almost a successor to the BBC's 'youth' programmes *Something Else* and

139 From 'Kindred Spirit – The Story of a 1980's Hull fanzine' blog

The Oxford Road Show – soon became the perfect way to kick off the weekend. It ran from November 1982 to April 1987 and was a showcase for emerging bands. Having your home city featured was massive. Not that the choice of bands was ever going to please everyone – especially in Hull, it would seem. The Luddites' inclusion surprised Mowforth, given that at their Clouds debut the previous year the singer and guitarist had performed the whole set with their backs turned to the audience. But with a new singer on board, the Luddites recorded the 'Strength of Your Cry' EP, from which the track 'Doppleganger' was featured on *The Tube*. It became their biggest hit, achieving a decent indie chart placing and a slot in John Peel's acclaimed Festive 50.

Synth-pop outfit Indians in Moscow were formed in 1981 by keyboard players Pete Riches and Stuart Walton (formerly of Hornsea band the Most). Mowforth termed their sound 'not unlike early Human League and Heaven 17, with also a Kraftwerk influence' but 'by far their biggest attraction' live was lead singer Adele Nozedar. 'Carrying a witch's staff onstage,' writes Mowforth, she proceeded to 'tease and trash her audience with equal aplomb'. Unsurprisingly then, her performance of the band's debut single 'Naughty Miranda' probably garnered most attention, as recounted in the Punk Girl Diaries blog: 'Adele looked and moved around like the missing link between a bleached blonde slightly deranged Siouxsie, and the future troubled pixie Katy-Jane Gartside from Daisy Chainsaw.'[140]

Despite Peel reputedly calling it the worst record he'd ever heard, 'Naughty Miranda' was an indie chart-topper and the band subsequently moved to London in search of success. But despite a few acclaimed singles and an album release on

140 From Adele Nozedar, https://punkgirldiaries.com/adele-nozedar-indians-in-moscow/

Kennick Records, they eventually fell into obscurity. Punk Girl Diaries suggests they were probably guilty of 'confounding their audience with their ever-shifting, mutable identity, [making them] impossible to pigeon-hole'. They disbanded in 1985, reforming in 1998 but minus their original singer.

A mere 15 seconds of mimed action was hardly the best introduction to International Rescue. For many people they were the best of the local bands to be seen live. Fronted by the charismatic Steve Skinner, Mowforth described them as 'entertainment with a capital E' and added, 'The band's professionalism and musicianship should never be underestimated.' Selling out every gig and with adoring fans wearing the green-and-red Rescue T-shirts, their popularity led to tours of Spain, France and Belgium, where debut single 'You Need Shoes' went to number six and eventually earned them a recording contract with Polydor. Unfortunately, despite all this (and their brief television exposure), commercial success didn't follow. Instead, due to a managerial dispute their planned debut LP *Another Whig* never saw the light of day. The band bounced back, gaining a support slot on the gigging circuit with Orange Juice. However, according to Mowforth, two accompanying singles ('Shoes' and 'Life in an Elevator') didn't do them justice and when Skinner was persuaded to join Orange Juice as guitarist in 1984, things were never the same again.

Hence it was Red Guitars from among the *Tube* quartet who went on to enjoy the greatest success. Formed originally as the Czechs, this all-guitar band belied their 'traditional rock' conception, combining 'African-rock-style-guitaring with early R 'n' B to create something of a uniquely sounding result'. Undoubtedly political but without the in-your-face approach of the likes of Billy Bragg and the Three Johns, songs such as 'Good Technology' and 'Steeltown' provided what Mowforth termed 'an unparalleled insight into the life and times of the early 1980s'. Debut single 'Good Technology' in particular became a phenomenal indie success, selling 20,000 copies. 'I do think that's an excellent record, I must say,' was John Peel's reaction and the single gained plenty of Radio 1 airtime, topped the indie charts and earned a Festive 50 place. Subsequent radio sessions for Peel and David 'Kid' Jensen, along with appearances on Annie Nightingale and TV's *The Old Grey Whistle Test*, hinted at a sudden rise to stardom. Follow-up singles 'Marimba Jive' and 'Be with Me' both topped the indie charts but their debut album *Slow to Fade* 'almost came too late and, with the sudden shock departure of vocalist Jerry Kidd, their unique style as personified by "Marimba Jive" dissolved'. Replacement vocalist Rob Holmes helped the band 'maintain their topicality' but although songs like 'America and Me' and 'National Avenue' reached new heights of critical acclaim this wasn't matched by sales. Holmes finally went solo and out of the ashes of the Red Guitars emerged the Planet Wilson.[141]

* * *

The Tube opened my eyes and ears to the sounds and sights on my doorstep. From that moment on, when listening to John Peel, names of Hull bands would also demand my attention. Yet, as Mowforth suggested – and both Kari Brown and Tony Menzies would testify – the programme had barely skimmed the surface. Nyam Nyam and the Vets weren't even mentioned on the show but were rated just as highly.

Originally comprised of Paul Trynka (guitar/vocals), Trevor Simpson (bass/guitars) and Dave Jones (drums),

141 From https://www.redguitars.co.uk/johnRowley.php

Nyam Nyam were featured in *Bop Eye* alongside Tee-Hee-Tee and International Rescue. Therein Simpson described their music as 'atmospheric, moody, sort of gothic but not as gloomy'. Formed from the ashes of Mental Block (Hull's first punk band) their first gig as Nyam Nyam was supporting the Rezillos at the Welly in December 1979. Three months later they recorded their debut single, 'Knowledge', described by Trynka as 'minimal, with spookily simple drums'. It became their contribution to *Mrs Wilson's Children*.

Jones left the band after an 'infamous' gig at Hornsea Floral Hall, to be replaced by Jock Lurie, while on occasional keyboards was Tim Allison, who I'd later become mates with through Spiders and City. Lurie and Allison appeared on the second single, 'When We Can't Make Laughter Stay' b/w 'Knowledge (Chapter II)', released in August 1981. Along with John Peel, it received airplay on Peter Powell's Radio 1 drive-time show, a move that not only reportedly prompted 500 extra sales but also nearly forced Allison to crash his car: 'I thought, oh my God, what the fuck, that's us!' But it was Nyam Nyam's next release that really caught the eye. 'Fate' was produced by New Order bassist Peter Hook and released on Factory Benelux in 1982. The 12in version 'Fate/Hate' was dubbed an 'electro classic' and went top five in the *NME*'s dance chart. By this time a third drummer, Steve Jessop, had replaced Lurie. Further changes would see Allison leave ('we weren't seeing eye to eye, it was probably over really stupid things') and the arrival of What Katy Did Next's Paul Moller on sax/violin.[142]

The band's growing reputation was enhanced by live support slots with New Order, the Chameleons and Happy Mondays and in 1984 they recorded their debut LP.

142 From https://nyamnyamhopeofheaven.wordpress.com/2012/10/26/mrs-wilson-and-other-personalities/

Entitled *Hope of Heaven*, it was released on Situation Two/ Beggar's Banquet Records (although Hook reputedly told the band that, had they asked, Factory 'would've done it for more!'). It received critical acclaim. Hook described it as 'the sound of the '80s', Chris Roberts in *Sounds* termed it 'a great white hope', while in *Melody Maker* Colin Irwin wrote, 'If this were to sell in huge quantities, pop music would never be the same again. Sadly it won't, and it will.' For Mowforth, *Hope of Heaven* is 'one of the finest undiscovered albums of the decade', with sales crippled by a lack of airplay. In his *Swing* fanzine of winter 1984, Allison cited Peel's refusal to play it 'for personal reasons' as 'particularly disappointing'.

Along with underwhelming sales of the album, Mowforth bemoaned the fact that the band 'never seemed to endear themselves to the Hull music scene, possibly because their ambitions were far greater'. For his part, Trynka told *Bop Eye* that the band didn't consider they were a part of the Hull scene, suggesting that other bands 'just spend their time slagging each other off. We're not interested in back-biting.' This is a shame given that when Irwin revisited the album for *Mojo* magazine he describes how the city played a big part in the band's sound. Indeed, Trynka is quoted as saying that 'the band was an escape from a psychological place rather than a geographical one'.[143]

Ironically, according to Moller, the support Nyam Nyam did attract was more in keeping with the main theme of this book, 'I got in with the wrong crowd, Taff, Simms. Nutters. Going into the pub getting paralytic, next thing you're with Nick Turner running down the road knocking on every door – City psychos. That was more or less the nucleus of

143 From the feature 'Buried Tresure' (*Mojo*, November 2012)

the Nyam Nyam following. A bunch of nutters. But we were pretty young. They were good times.'[144]

After releasing an EP, 'The Architect', in 1985, Nyam Nyam finally called it a day, with Trynka going on to edit *Mojo* before becoming an acclaimed biographer. In 2012, 'having been unjustly overlooked for three decades', a remastered 18-track *Hope of Heaven* was released by LTM Records, which included the singles and one new track 'Doubt'. Irwin's review considers this to be yet another case of what might have been.

Formed in 1976 and still on the go over 40 years later, the Vets began life playing Sex Pistols covers and supporting punk band the Z-Men. They hailed from the seaside resort of Hornsea and were labelled 'Hull's answer to the Cure', a tag that Mowforth felt didn't do justice to their originality. An early one-off single release on Epic ('Fly' b/w 'Contrix') was described as 'bizarre' but was played twice by John Peel and helped attract a cult following. But it was the release of the next single, 'World in Action' on the Deck Chair label, that really saw the band take off. Peel described it as 'an absolute classic', playing it 'a total of 17 times over the next few months' according to the band's bio. The DJ even travelled up to Hornsea and played a gig with the band at the Floral Hall. Fronted by Roy Bickenson's 'emotional and tense vocals', the Vets' live performances 'were as compelling as any early Joy Division gig'. Mowforth describes guitarist Neil Scott as 'the epitome of the 1980s musician' who in late 1979 added the 'atmospheric synthesiser sound' that would become the Vets' hallmark. Scott went on to feature with a number of other bands, among them Everything But The Girl. In 1983 the Vets appeared on the BBC's *Bubbling Under* TV show. Becoming firm friends with International Rescue (helped by

144 Author of several City books including *'Hull City – The Boothferry Park Years'* (see Bibliography)

an interchange of members), the two bands gigged extensively together, including what at the time appeared to be their final show, with Moscow completing the bill. Regarded by Mowforth as 'the finest Hull-area band ever' it was the Vets' departure from the scene, coupled with the closure of Clouds that in his opinion signalled the end of an era in Hull music.[145]

* * *

If *The Tube* offered one way of attracting national recognition, some Hull bands employed less conventional means in order to try and do so. Issue 2 of *Swing* magazine in the winter of 1984 carried a cover picture of a scantily clad Sharon, lead vocalist with goth band Les Zeiga Fleurs (LZF). Under the headline 'Sex or Sexism?' *Swing* told the story of how Sharon was set to pose naked for men's magazine *Mayfair*, purely in order to gain some extra publicity for the band. 'Local girl bares all for the sake of a Hull pop group' was how 'Mailbeat' headlined it. The decision was defended by band leader Ingo Dewsnap, another man who played a big part in the Hull scene of the 1980s.

In comments now removed from his website, fellow musician Nick Clay recalled how Dewsnap recorded a large number of local bands at 51 Stepney Lane on his four-track portastudio. As such he deserves credit for being the first to record the Housemartins, and for getting a local scene going. Although Clay wasn't exactly gushing with praise for LZF – 'Hairspray; Booming doom-laden bass lines; Extra-big drum kit; Funereal set; No fun; Black clothing de rigeur; No summer songs to lift your hearts' – compliments were to be had elsewhere. The band's 1983 cassette release *Good Men Die Quietly* received a favourable review in the debut

145 Bio from the Vets | ReverbNation

issue of *Kindred Spirit*, Jeff Pullen describing it as 'a good first offering'. But let's face it, what are a few kind words in a hometown fanzine when set against the prospect of thousands of blokes buying your records on the back of having seen your main assets?[146]

The same edition of *Swing* also referred to the 'minor controversy' caused by Punctured Tough Guy's cover for their *Warped Houses* cassette album. It depicted a picture of Wensley Lodge, an old people's home in Hessle where 11 elderly residents died in a fire that was originally – and wrongly – attributed to Hull serial killer 'Daft' Peter Dinsdale (Bruce Lee, as he became more notoriously known). The magazine suggested that to have two local bands on the same label (Xcentric Noise) courting publicity in what might be termed unseemly ways perhaps wasn't mere coincidence. That said, Punctured Tough Guy's 'dark, disturbing music for the ill at ease' came highly rated. They were ranked among *Swing*'s 'Five of the Finest' locally. Not for long. After releasing the three-track 'Acid Rains' EP they disappeared for good, with guitarist Dave McSherry later to resurface as one half of famed Hull dance duo Fila Brazillia.

Punctured Tough Guy weren't the only band among *Swing*'s 'Five of the Finest' whose name might be remembered only by the keenest Hull music aficionado some four decades on. Quel Dommage (whose guitarist was Xcentric Noise creator Andy Thompson) also failed to get noticed despite their 1984 debut single 'Bright Lights', getting Peel playlisted and prompting the 'inevitable Joy Division, Cure comparisons'. Poor Howard, described by *Swing* as 'the east coast of the USA meets the east coast of the UK', didn't even have the satisfaction of Peel appeal for their 'Maybe Tomorrow' single

146 From Pink Noise and other crap Hull bands from the 80's (karoo.net)

(on Self Drive) after the Radio 1 DJ returned it to them, following what band member Ian Priestman described as 'a failed PR trick'. Their vocalist Rob Holmes later joined Red Guitars. As for the fourth outfit, the Desperate Men, even the aforementioned specialist internet sites would appear to have erased all memory. But at least *Swing* wasn't wrong in its final choice, thanks to a cassette album *Themes for the Well-dressed Man* that was described as 'an absolute must … a neat pop sound that could easily be integrated into any musical idiom of the last 30 years'. The band behind it would soon need no introduction, even outside the city of Hull. Their name was the Housemartins.[147]

147 *Swing* magazine (Issue 2, Winter 1984)

14
Coming Up Short

Turf Moor: Tuesday, 15 May 1984

It's a surreal feeling. We've won but we've lost. The supporters to our immediate left have lost but are taunting those who've won, and to the far left, behind the goal, is a sizeable number of supporters with affiliation to neither team. They're celebrating more than anyone. Directly in front of me, City's players are applauding us as we acclaim their efforts over the season and in particular the 90 minutes we've just watched. If what I'd felt at the previous two games was mere frustration, this is sheer dejection. I'm struggling to keep my emotions in check. Football can be fucking cruel at times.

* * *

Several months before the never-to-be-forgotten, ill-fated trip across the Pennines, Port Vale were City's scheduled opponents at Boothferry Park for the final game of what Simon Redfern in the *Hull Daily Mail* termed 'a great 1983'. The Valiants' visit would bring the curtain down on what had been a memorable year for the Tigers. But despite coming into the game on the back of three straight wins, not all was rosy in the City camp. For a start, many fans were unhappy to see

Les Mutrie loaned out to Doncaster Rovers following what was termed 'a personality clash with Appleton'. Then, just before Christmas, the manager himself had visited Swansea to have talks about a possible managerial move – one he would eventually turn down due to his wish to finish the job he'd started at Hull. The fact he even entertained the possibility of such a move given the success he was enjoying seemed strange. Not as strange as my plans for the final game of 1983 though; I was planning to take a *girl* to a football match. In the end, I took two.

31 December 1983
Football League Third Division:
Hull City 1 Port Vale 0

Boothferry Park: East Stand Terrace; season pass; programme 30p

And before anyone accuses me of being a sexist dinosaur, it's worth remembering that as a rule of thumb girls didn't go to football back in the early 1980s. With few notable exceptions, Saturday afternoon was a 'men only' thing. Only very rarely was a female seen on our away coach and there certainly weren't many to be spotted in the Kempton. In fact, I'd yet to meet any girl who either fancied going to a match or who I actually wanted to take! That all changed in line with City's resurgent fortunes. With the team being talked about in glowing terms, it perhaps wasn't surprising that several of the girls I knew began enquiring as to what 'going to City' was like. As I was very keen on one, I offered to provide first-hand experience. Unfortunately she insisted on bringing a 'plus one' along too.

The Tigers came into the game in tremendous form. The week after their disappointing FA Cup exit, two Garreth Roberts goals helped clinch a thumping 3-1 away win at promotion rivals Bristol Rovers. Single-goal successes were then secured on successive days. A season's best Boxing Day crowd of 15,461 (originally listed in the programme as 18,421) saw a Scunthorpe side including *the* Ian Botham beaten by Steve Massey's solitary strike. The following day Pete Skipper secured the points at Rotherham (and some revenge for our FA Cup exit) in front of another noisy away contingent in a Millmoor crowd of 6,298.

The Tigers therefore welcomed bottom club Port Vale to Hull on the last day of the year looking to make it four wins in a row, with the expectant attendance of 9,431 (later downsized to 8,736) swelled by a couple of inquisitive 'chicks from the sticks' accompanied by their gallant host. It was a win-win situation; or rather it was after City had escaped punishment for Dennis Booth's apparent trip on Vale's Young inside the box on 71 minutes. Two minutes later, Roberts won the game with a wonderful goal. In the *Hull Daily Mail*, Simon Redfern described how the City skipper 'waltzed round Tartt and Hunter' before driving home from 20 yards. The Kempton erupted and in the ensuing chaos I found myself on my back with the object of my desire on top of me. It was easily the best goal celebration I'd yet experienced. Like the skipper, I'd bagged a beauty of my own. How I longed for City to add to their tally so we could do it all again! Alas, it remained 1-0 and the moment was forever frozen in time. Nearly 40 years on I need to consult my scrapbook for details of that goal. The celebration, on the other hand, is remembered with the greatest clarity.

Due to injury to Steve Massey and the failure to gain Alan Taylor's international clearance in time (following the former FA Cup winner's arrival on trial from Vancouver Whitecaps), Appleton handed 19-year-old non-contract striker Andy Saville his senior debut against Port Vale. Two days later it was the other young Andy who starred as City backed up their New Year win with a 2-2 draw at Southend in the first game of 1984. Flounders scored both goals at Roots Hall before a winter whiteout brought a halt to proceedings. The postponement of two home games dashed hopes of any more cavorting in the Kempton. In truth, they'd gone before Big Ben heralded in the new year; my decision to head out with the lads instead of hammering home my Kempton advantage, so to speak having proved costly. Just like City, my 1983/84 was to be a case of so near yet so far.

January brought with it an incident that would have far-reaching consequences for the Tigers' promotion hopes. At the same time as Radio 1 *Breakfast Show* host Mike Read was causing something of a media storm by refusing to play 'Relax', the 'suggestive' debut single by Frankie Goes to Hollywood, a meteorological one was affecting the British Isles. A combination of snow and ice forced postponement of the January home games against Gillingham and Preston but it was the aborting of the trip to Burnley on the Saturday in between that would prove pivotal. Gale-force winds added to the wintry chaos on the 13th – a Friday – leaving six people dead and the transport network paralysed. The following morning, the forecast of more of the same prompted many fans to set off earlier than normal for the trip to Turf Moor. Simon Gray didn't do 'early' so we set off at the normal time. Atop the Pennines conditions were inclement; what David Goodman describes as 'a combination of snow, wind and ice'. They were bad enough to force City's team bus to 'swerve from side to side more than once on the hazardous journey'. David Bond recalls a darkly humorous anecdote from Garreth Roberts, which referred to the fact that Steve McClaren had dropped out of the squad on the morning of the match: 'You hear about these disasters when someone escapes because of a twist of fate. The way we're going, Steve McClaren might be the only one left by Monday, so he may have to take over as manager.'[148]

Goodman also uses a quote from the City skipper, in which he remembers that 'players were trying to convince the bus driver to turn around because it was too dangerous' and then finding out that having got the game called off, they 'then found that quite a few supporters had got there and it wasn't that bad once you were over the top of the Pennines'.[149]

Our coach was one of those that had ploughed on regardless, the usual pre-match cocktail of drink and debate rendering many of us largely oblivious to what was going on. The first we knew that something was amiss was when we met the team coach and some of those who'd departed earlier heading back eastbound on the other side of the M62. It later transpired that Colin Appleton had phoned John Bond from Hartshead Moor Services and informed him that he and his players would not be completing the trip but were instead turning round and heading home. This despite being told that the weather in east Lancashire was better and the pitch was playable. In the following weekend's Preston match programme notes, Appleton wrote, 'With regard to the recent events against Burnley, whatever inconvenience I may have caused, I hope you will all bare [sic] me in that decisions were discussed and decided by both parties and once the full facts are known, those who travelled to support us should at least be aware that they were probably the first consideration.'[150]

---

148 Bond, David, *'The Hull City Saga: The Seesaw Tale of the Tigers'* (Derby: Breedon Books, 1999) p.34

149 Goodman, David, *'Look Back in Amber'* (Manchester: Parrs Wood Press, 2005) p.81

150 Match programme (Hull City v Preston North End, 21 January 1984)

Unfortunately, more bad weather meant it was April when these notes finally saw the light of day (the original programme being reissued alongside the one for the rearranged game). By then – and by way of apology – the still-on-holiday Don Robinson had offered to meet Burnley's match expenses of £1,300. He also offered to buy 1,000 match tickets for City fans who could prove they'd made the trip. Meanwhile, the Football League launched an inquiry into the events. They eventually fined the club £2,500 but inflicted no points deduction. Perhaps they should have done – the Tigers' ultimate punishment at the season's end would be far crueller.

Most fans felt the club had got off lightly and those of us who'd travelled to Lancashire were far from happy. Our mood was soon darkened further by the sale of Les Mutrie to Colchester. It was a move that few of us could understand. He was one of the most gifted strikers to have graced Boothferry Park, a fact acknowledged by partner Billy Whitehurst when interviewed by Richard Gardham: 'Les Mutrie's touch was as good as anyone I've played with. He had the ball on a string.' The striker himself, contributing to the same book just a few weeks before his tragic premature passing, had his own thoughts on why his time at City was up: 'Colin picked me regularly in the side until he realised I could not, at my age, track up and down the field then show my skill and flair when given the chance, which is when he resorted to a back five, leaving out a forward, which was usually me.'[151]

On Cloud Seven remembers 'Sir Les' leaving with a final parting shot at Appleton: 'If you have opinions you've got to go – and I'm afraid I have opinions.' Despite success on the pitch, it was clear that the manager was beginning to polarise opinion among supporters. Mutrie's sale came on the back of

151 Gardham, Richard, *The Decade: Ten Years that Transformed Hull City AFC* (Self-published, 2019) p.36

dubious team selections and an overriding defensive mindset. The Burnley debacle simply gave further ammunition to the doubters.[152]

28 January 1984
Football League Third Division: Millwall 1 Hull City 0

The Den: Ilderton Road End Terrace; no ticket; programme 40p

If January had arrived on the back of a rather amusing tick in my book of firsts, the month was brought to a close with a much more challenging one, courtesy of a maiden visit to The Den. Millwall away was another date in the diary I'd had noted for some time. It was seen as the sort of rite of passage that had to be passed before I could be classed as a proper City fan. Writing for the *Amber Nectar* fanzine in 2017, Matthew Rudd summed up why: 'In the 1980s [The Den] was at its most seething, spitting, nasty, hateful and perilous.' I wasn't the only one who was aware of its significance. For the first time since I'd started doing away games, Dad cast some doubts about my going to one. Even with his limited football knowledge, he knew that Cold Blow Lane rarely offered a warm welcome.

Ours was one of a handful of coaches to make the trip and Carmo was my sole companion, Gary having been stopped from going due to mocks revision. As we wended our way through the mean streets of south London I began wishing I'd used that same get-out clause. Some light relief was provided by the identity of the coach we were on. Simon Gray had swapped Connor & Graham for Hull-based outfit Good News Travels. The nature of the 'Good News' in question came via

152 *On Cloud Seven* fanzine (Issue 3, November 1989)

the religious mottos across the back. Making this choice even more amusing was that they were also the coach operator for City's 'elite' travelling to the same game. As such, anybody in the vicinity of The Den in the hour or so before kick-off would have been confronted by the rather surreal sight of two coaches of football fans with 'Jesus Saves' emblazoned across them. I'm not sure such holy thoughts were uppermost in the minds of the passengers, especially on the casuals' coach.

In an episode recounted in *City Psychos*, those on board alighted about a mile from the ground and made their way on foot in what they felt was a show of strength. Surprisingly, they remained unchallenged and must have felt quite pleased with themselves as they entered the ground without as much as a hair out of place. Only later did they learn that the anticipated reception committee were some distance away, apparently meeting old rivals West Ham in a prearranged affair.

Not being as bold on our coach, we remained on board as it made its way along what the author Simon Inglis termed 'the perfect setting for a Jack the Ripper horror film', before pulling up on the 'sinister dark unsurfaced car park on top of a disused railway embankment'. This formed the approach to the Ilderton Road End. It was grim and once inside the ground there wasn't much by way of light relief. Even allowing for the expected heavy police presence it wasn't somewhere you were ever going to feel at home. The Den carried an air of permanent menace unlike perhaps any other in the league. The three sides of high banking terraces, with a pitched roof only covering the rear third of each, contributed to the air of intimidation. Little wonder then that it was said to be hated by visiting players, supporters and journalists alike. Even manager George Graham's programme notes alluded to the sort of thing that might occur if things didn't go the hosts' way, citing an incident in the recent 'derby' against Brentford that had seen one person run on to the pitch 'to confront an opposition player'. Graham also referred to the 'remarkable game' up at Boothferry, the outcome of which he hoped would give his players 'a little extra incentive' this time round. It did. Teddy Sheringham marked only his third league start with the game's solitary goal.[153]

There were around 300 away fans inside The Den, housed in a glorified cage tucked away in the corner. Our view was partially obstructed by the huge concrete base supporting the floodlight pylon that 'rose out of the terraces'. It added to our sense of being unwelcome and unwanted. The total crowd numbered 3,996 but when that mournful chant of 'M-i-i-i-i-w-w-a-a-a-a-w' rose up round the ground, it bristled. It had me imagining how the real John Chard and his men must have felt at Rorke's Drift when hearing those Zulu war songs ringing out. I'm ashamed to admit it but I was almost relieved that City didn't equalise; the locals went home happy and we were allowed to escape without a hair out of place. Even so, I think it was Leicester Forest services before my heart rate returned to normal. Ironically, The Den would become one of my most frequently visited grounds with City. In total I made six trips there, two of which came at night. I think the term is 'masochistic'.

11 February 1984
Football League Third Division:
Lincoln City 1 Hull City 3

Sincil Bank, South Park End seats; no ticket;
programme 40p

I've seen some amusing sights during my time following Hull City and by coincidence two of these came during the away

---

153 *The Millwall History Files*: www.millwall-history.org.uk/the_den.htm

game at Lincoln, which took place a fortnight after defeat at The Den. The Tigers travelled to Sincil Bank having moved back up to fourth courtesy of Brian Marwood's winner at home to Wigan. Walsall still sat atop the division but having played more games than Wimbledon, Oxford, City and Sheffield United. Lincoln had become a bit of a rival and games there always attracted a decent turnout of lads. This latest trip had added spice, not only due to City's ongoing promotion push but also on account of the Imps fans' antics at Boothferry back in September.

Once again we were travelling courtesy of Good News Travels, this time on a double-decker. Jim used to regale me with tales of the original City Psychos travelling to places like Lincoln on the standard Corporation Transport 'deckers' normally used on service routes. This was much different, a luxury effort that made for a very enjoyable ride. Just outside Lincoln, the police pulled us over along with several other City coaches. But it wasn't just coaches. Right in front of us were at least four Luton removal vans, which when the back doors were rolled up revealed themselves to be jam-packed with casuals.

An old workmate of mine, Mark, was in one of them. He said the secret was to either get a seat in the cab or one of the places above it on the shelf in the back. Otherwise you were simply a sardine for the duration of the trip! I don't think the local constabulary could quite believe just how many passengers each van held. And if all this didn't provide enough amusement to while away the time spent at the side of the road, we were then treated to the even more bizarre sight of a passing hearse, complete with Hull City favours trailing from each windscreen. Apparently it belonged to an undertaker from Withernsea. As some wag put it, City fans were dying to get at Lincoln.

The game itself made the use of such unorthodox transport worthwhile. City produced their best performance of the season to win 3-1 and claim their first victory at Sincil Bank since 1961. They did so the hard way, trailing at the break to a Phil Turner piledriver despite having dominated the half. Two minutes after the restart Marwood raced on to McClaren's pass to score via the post. Nine minutes later 'He's here, he's there, he's every fucking where' Gary Swann hooked home number two and on 76 minutes the same player completed the turnaround when diving to head home a wonderful Bobby McNeil cross.

It was a result befitting of a massive City following that was again spread over different parts of the ground. We'd opted to join the 'elite' in the seats behind the goal, from where a constant barrage of noise was maintained. One of the customary chants on such occasions was, 'Naa-na, naa-na, he's from 'ull and he's from 'ull', with the accompanying pointing of fingers at strangers intended to communicate to our hosts the incredible size of our support (interestingly, we hadn't felt the need to do this at Millwall). Most amusing of all was the half-time interval when the several hundred among the seated contingent converted the call-and-response/stand-up-sit-down chant 'Appleton's black-and-amber army' into 'Simon Gray's red-and-white jacket' in irreverent tribute to our coach operator. Continued throughout the break and into the second half, it looked and sounded fantastic, capping one of the best away-days yet.

A potential blank weekend due to the FA Cup was filled with a friendly against a Grimsby side enjoying a 16-match unbeaten run in the Second Division. The Tigers lost 3-2 but bounced back to beat York in the Associate Members' Cup (AMC) before going down to defeat on their return to league action at Plymouth. Tommy Tynan struck twice in front of a

10,023 crowd lured to Home Park by tickets for the Pilgrims' upcoming FA Cup quarter-final against Derby. They were the only team to complete a double over City that season. Three nights later, another big crowd of 11,192 was at Boothferry to see City lose again, this time by a solitary goal at the hands of leaders Oxford.

And when Bolton left Hull with a point the following weekend, the jitters were full-on.

Games were coming thick and fast. McNeil notched a rare goal in the midweek win over Bournemouth as City settled into a fixture pattern of Saturday-Tuesday-Saturday. A seven-game unbeaten run put them back on track. Included among it were two wins in the AMC, the one over Bury coinciding with my 18th birthday. Among the others was a lively 2-2 draw at Bramall Lane, played out in front of 15,374 spectators, including a large and vocal City contingent, which according to both my memory and the manager provided 'rousing support'. Simon Redfern left readers in no doubt as to where he thought the praise should go. Under the *Hull Daily Mail* headline 'Worthy City draw was Taylor-made' he wrote, 'With the transfer deadline just five days away, Hull City's trialist striker, Alan Taylor, made a firm bid for a permanent contract on Saturday. He engineered both City's goals in their entertaining promotion tussle with Sheffield United at Bramall Lane, which gave the Tigers their third draw in the last four league games.'

It was from Taylor's 'perfect right-wing cross' that McClaren drove home from 15 yards on 34 minutes. And after Kevin Arnott and Edwards (of course) had turned the game on its head, Taylor provided the pass from which Marwood drilled home an equaliser nine minutes from time, firing through Waugh's legs in front of a delirious away end. Redfern said 'a draw was the least City merited, because sweeper Stan McEwan [a February arrival from Exeter] was desperately unlucky to have a 45th minute "goal" disallowed for handball by Taylor' when his half-volley brushed the striker's arm on its way into the net. The Tigers were also left to rue the post that denied Askew on 26 minutes and referee Malcolm Heath's rejection of a penalty appeal when Ray McHale appeared to bring down Massey in the box. Contrasting City's near-misses with Norman's relatively quiet afternoon, Redfern concluded, 'It is clear which side was the most menacing.'

Despite the positive reaction to the performance, City remained sixth, 12 points off the leaders albeit with games in hand on all the teams above them. After Brentford were then dispatched by goals from Marwood and Dale Roberts, a Tuesday night defeat at Walsall provided the only blip in a run of six straight wins that resurrected City's title challenge and also saw them reach the AMC quarter-finals.

7 April 1984
Football League Third Division:
Wimbledon 1 Hull City 4

Plough Lane: North Stand; ticket (no price); programme 50p

It was this win at what the match programme acclaimed as the home of 'the league's leading goalscorers' that convinced me that City were on for a second successive promotion. What's more, it had me believing we were going up as champions. The Tigers were irrepressible, sweeping aside their third-placed hosts in style. A deflected Marwood shot, Flounders's far-post header following Skipper's flick-on from a Marwood corner, a 20-yard Garreth Roberts special and a McEwan penalty had the Tigers four goals to the good before Glyn Hodges' consolation goal five minutes from time. Little did we know, as we ironically cheered this late strike, the great significance it would have in the final scheme of things.[154]

We watched the game from the North Stand seats, which although populated by plenty of City fans wasn't segregated. Thus every time I stood up to celebrate a goal I inadvertently clipped the Dons-supporting bloke next to me. By the time of the third goal I felt I ought to apologise and did so, to which he replied, without hint of malice, 'Yeah, it's getting a bit annoying now!' In fairness to him, just before the final whistle, as he and his pals made an early exit he shook my hand and wished me 'all the best in the Second Division'. He said he didn't think he'd be seeing us there. Unfortunately he was right, but not in the way he probably envisaged.

Appleton described the win as 'worthy of praise of the highest grade'. The bonus of defeats for Sheffield United, Bristol Rovers and Walsall added to the celebrations and there was a party atmosphere inside Boothferry just 24 hours later as City entertained Tampa Bay Rowdies in the first leg of the Arrow Air Anglo-American Cup (don't ask). The Don donned the full cowboy gear and rode round the pitch on a horse. City triumphed 3-0 and we all appeared to have backed a winner. The feeling was reinforced with league victories over Preston and Exeter, and even though Gillingham left Boothferry with a point from a frustrating goalless draw, we were in high spirits as we packed into The Old Showground at Scunthorpe on Easter Saturday.

Once again we were treated to the sight of City fans being escorted back round the ground to our end, having infiltrated the home stands. But more importantly we were made to feel how Millwall fans had when they'd come to Boothferry. The Tigers hit the woodwork four times (including Gary Swann

154 Match programme (Wimbledon v Hull City, 7 April 1984)

striking the bar from about a yard out) in stumbling to a 2-0 defeat at the hands of their relegation-threatened neighbours. Garreth Roberts was reported as saying the ball must have had splinters in it. Derek Bell, with a controversial penalty after what many considered to be a non-existent push by Mick Hollifield, and the prolific Steve Cammack compounded our disappointment.

* * *

The situation was becoming unbelievably tense. 'Bunter' scored after just 17 seconds in a 5-0 win over a poor Rotherham team in a home game that I missed due to attending that 'Trash Bash' in Nottingham. The result lifted City to fourth, a point behind the Blades with a game in hand. Oxford were as good as up and Wimbledon not far behind. It was all about that third promotion spot now.

The rollercoaster continued. A week later, despite taking the lead, the Tigers lost 3-1 at Leyton Orient while Sheffield United won 1-0 at Southend thanks to an 88th-minute goal. Just a week earlier they'd overcome Rotherham with a 90th-minute strike. Spawny bastards. But when City beat Southend 2-1 at Boothferry and Wimbledon beat the Blades by the same score at Bramall Lane, the ball was back in the Tigers' court. Positive results against Port Vale and Bristol Rovers would confirm a second successive promotion.

The mood on our Bank Holiday Monday night trip to Vale Park was one of cautious optimism, fuelled by news of a Sheffield United defeat at Bolton that afternoon. The sight of dozens of Blades coaches returning home was wonderful, especially given the fact that many of them held newspapers up at the windows to ensure they couldn't see us goading them. There was none of their mocking 'Targers, Targers, ra-ra-ra' chant now. Those same Tigers were now in the box seat. On entering the ground, John Rudge's programme notes cheered us even more. The Port Vale boss wrote of a campaign that had been 'largely a tale of woe' and a season of 'lost opportunity'. If ever a team was on the beach it was this lot. With memories of the previous season's defeat still fresh in the mind, the prospect of using Vale Park as the venue in which to place one foot in the Second Division was very appealing. Given the state our opponents were in it should have been a formality. But of course we hadn't factored in #TypicalCity and in particular the manager's craziest team selection yet. The 'general consensus was that Appleton had flipped' was how *On Cloud Seven* later described it, adding, 'Six were at the back from the start, but that didn't stop Mark Bright from scoring a superb goal for Vale. Whitehurst mysteriously had a goal disallowed, but there was only one reason why we lost the game – the manager's tactics.'[155]

I don't think I'd ever felt as annoyed by defeat as I did that night in the Potteries. We had passed up a massive opportunity and thrown our hated rivals a lifeline. Thank God we didn't have to pass those same Sheffield coaches on our way home.

The following Saturday, 9,857 spectators were inside Boothferry to see City attempt to get the win over Bristol Rovers that again would virtually guarantee promotion. If anything, this game proved even more frustrating than the Port Vale result. Things didn't go to plan from the start, with the visitors delayed due to their coach breaking down near Sutton-in-Ashfield in Nottinghamshire. Then two of their replacement taxis sustained punctures en route to Hull. On top of this, the players did their best to get changed while on the move but with only six of them present at 3pm, kick-off was delayed. This further increased the nerves among the

155 *On Cloud Seven* fanzine (Issue 3, November 1989)

expectant crowd. Manager David Williams, who arrived at 'two minutes to three' according to an interview he quickly gave *Calendar* outside the ground, was true to his word when saying, 'We'll get out there as quickly as we can,' and the game kicked off only four minutes late.

Once under way it was understandably all City. Chance after chance came and went. 'Cousin' Andy hit the bar then saw an audacious back-heel scrambled off the line. McEwan was denied by an excellent save from a free kick. It was simply not meant to be. When the final whistle blew, it was one point not three. Appleton remained upbeat, telling *Calendar*, 'We have to be optimistic. We needed four points from two games and we've just left it a little bit hard for ourselves with having to win by three clear goals at Burnley on Tuesday.'

15 May 1984
Football League Third Division:
Burnley 0 Hull City 2

Turf Moor: Longside Terrace; no ticket or programme

The days leading up to the game were like no other I'd experienced while watching City. David Bond quotes Garreth Roberts' description of the build-up as so intense 'because the situation gripped the whole city'. It preceded what the skipper termed 'probably the most emotional game I ever played in'. The number of City supporters making the trip to Turf Moor that spring evening in 1984 took everybody by surprise, especially Burnley FC and the Lancashire constabulary. The turnstiles struggled to cope with demand for access, leaving many fans still outside the ground when the game got under way. I was one of them and bounced along with the rest of the queue as news of an early City goal travelled along the line. Marwood had netted after a minute, crashing home from Taylor's knockdown. Once inside it was an amazing sight.

The huge travelling support had the away enclosure rocking and the noise was incredible. To our left, beyond the home section in the Longside and standing on the open Bee Hole End terracing were an impressive number of Sheffield United fans, which lent a rather surreal feel to proceedings.[156]

Five years later, City fanzine *On Cloud Seven* revisited the night's events as part of a review of the season. The article described how 'any City fan at Burnley will probably name that match as the most memorable they've ever seen'. I wouldn't argue with that. As the *Yorkshire Post* match report reads, 'Hull's attitude was marvellous: every kick was charged with fire.' With Whitehurst resembling 'a Centurion tank ahead of it all … Taylor and Marwood running fiercely in his wake' and Roberts and McClaren 'bolstered in midfield by the surging Swann' (preferred to Askew in the starting line-up), City appeared irrepressible. Sheffield United winger Colin Morris told Bill Mallinson of the *Daily Mail* it had been 'the worst 90 minutes I have ever sat and watched'. In truth, City could and should have achieved their target by half-time. Sadly, the second goal didn't arrive until past the hour and despite Morris admitting that he was 'so worried during the last 20 minutes', the Tigers rarely looked like adding to their tally.[157]

Dave Milns's piece for the *Hull Hell & Happiness* fanzine went into more detail and still provides painful reading nearly 40 years on. In particular the list of missed chances reopens old wounds: Swann's from seven yards out, Marwood just failing to pounce after Hansbury's fumble of a McClaren 25-yarder and, most agonisingly, Overson's knee diverting Roberts' 21st-minute goal-bound shot over the bar after Hansbury's

156 Bond, David, *'Meet Me at Bunker's Hill!'* (Hull: Tykesport, 2006) p.51

157 *On Cloud Seven* fanzine (Issue 3, November 1989)

parry of Marwood's drive. In addition, the forwards were guilty of spurning half-chances by firing over and wide. At the other end, Norman remained a virtual spectator. The second half proved a more even if no less entertaining affair as City understandably struggled to maintain their tempo. But after Whitehurst had rifled inches wide, Marwood combined with the burly striker to poke home his 16th goal of the season following Taylor's clever dummy. Perhaps it would've been easier had he missed. For as the game took its toll on the Tigers it became more and more obvious that they were going to fall short in their task.[158]

Many years later, Richard Gardham captured the memories of several of the players involved in the game for *The Decade*. Billy Whitehurst said City 'should have scored seven', conceding that he 'missed a couple of sitters' in a 'magnificent' team performance. Pete Skipper said, 'We couldn't have done any more.' Garreth Roberts used the term 'slaughtered' and physio Jeff Radcliffe opted for 'battered'. But ultimately, it wasn't enough.[159]

At the final whistle, City's players and supporters applauded each other with tears in their eyes and with emotions running high things were in danger of turning ugly. Those around me who weren't crestfallen seemed intent instead on trying to scale the fence and get at the gleeful home fans. I just wanted to get out of there and get home, indeed get anywhere away from the scene of what appeared to be a crime of the highest order. After all the highs of the past ten months I simply couldn't accept that it had ended like this. But if we the supporters were hurting, we could only imagine how bad the City players were feeling. Garreth Roberts described the

---

158 *Hull, Hell & Happiness* fanzine (Issue 3, March/April 1989) pp.32–33

159 Gardham, Richard, *The Decade: Ten Years that Transformed Hull City AFC* (Amazon, 2019) p.44

'awful' feeling in the dressing room afterwards: 'Everyone was so quiet and hardly anyone spoke for a long time. Some players just meandered off to find their own little space, collect their thoughts and try to put it all into perspective. It was so hard to believe that we'd lost our promotion chance by one goal after 46 games.'[160]

Colin Appleton told the *Daily Mirror*, 'It's bloody cruel. We'd done enough not to merit what we've had to endure tonight.' City and Sheffield United had both finished on 83 points but whereas the Tigers' miserly defence had only shipped 38 goals, it was at the other end of the pitch where the Blades' extra cutting edge had seen them narrowly home, scoring 86 goals to City's 71. Appleton said there should have been a play-off, adding, 'We've really merited promotion after coming up last season and the only difference between us and Sheffield United has been the goals of Keith Edwards.' How that last fact hurt Hull City fans.

Even now the drama wasn't over. Immediately after the game, Appleton resigned in order to take the Swansea job that he'd reportedly been offered at Christmas. 'Hull Boss Quits!' boomed the *Daily Mirror*'s back-page headline the following morning. Under it, Keith Meadows described how the manager had dropped his 'resignation bombshell … just an hour after his team failed to clinch promotion to the Second Division'. It quoted Appleton as saying, 'Even my chairman does not know yet, but I will not be manager of Hull City next season.' Interviewed for the following night's *Calendar*, Don Robinson declared himself extremely disappointed by the timing and manner of the move. Garreth Roberts put it rather more poetically: 'It was a kick in the balls followed by a kick in the teeth.'

---

160 Bond, David, *'Meet Me on Bunker's Hill!- A Revealing and Personal Look at the Hull City Story'* (Hull: Tykesport, 2006) p.51

That edition of *Calendar* made painful viewing. Chris Kiddey told viewers that 'the players involved in last night's epic battle were too upset to talk'. Only Chris Chilton could bring himself to be interviewed. He praised the players for their 'tremendous' performance and said, 'We couldn't have done any more last night.' Bemoaning the 'run of the ball', both at Burnley and against Bristol Rovers', Chillo finished by saying that for 'the last three hours of playing football Hull City as a team have done everybody proud'.

* * *

Unsurprisingly, City's run to the final of the inaugural Associate Members' Cup is largely overlooked when recounting the 1983/84 season. With no rotation back then, Appleton had little room for manoeuvre during a campaign that had begun back in February. Wins over York, Bury, Preston and Sheffield United meant that just three nights after the disappointment of Burnley, the Tigers hosted Tranmere Rovers in the regional final. There was a decent showing from the visitors in a crowd that included about 4,000 City fans who had seemingly either come to terms with their Turf Moor hangover remarkably quickly or were simply using the game as a cathartic experience. I hadn't and I couldn't. With Appleton gone, Chilton took charge for this unwanted finale and the players commendably rose to the task, winning 4-1 with two goals each for Taylor and Roberts. Had this occurred one year later, it would have earned the club a first trip to Wembley. Instead, in #TypicalCity fashion, plans to hold the inaugural final there were shelved. Phil Booth, writing several years later in the *Yorkshire Post*, explains, 'The football authorities doubted whether Hull and their opponents Bournemouth could muster enough fans to fill the national stadium. It was a kick in the teeth for two proud clubs, but protests were rendered pointless by the unlikely presence of the Horse of the Year Show. At the time that event was staged at Wembley, and caused so much damage to the pitch that it was deemed unplayable … So the clubs drew lots and Hull won the right to stage the game at Boothferry Park. Bournemouth won 2-1, and City's misery was complete. The Wembley mishap was later memorably described in the *Amber Nectar* fanzine as a dream being shelved by 'equine vandals and their jodhpured friends'. The jokes soon followed to rub salt in the wound, 'Come on lads. Why the long faces?' [161]

Only 6,197 were at Boothferry that Thursday night to see a rare Bobby McNeil goal prove in vain. At least the loss of Wembley and the subsequent defeat provided a fittingly anti-climactic epitaph to a campaign of glorious failure. As the now-defunct *Amber Nectar* online fanzine summed it up, 'In pretty much one fell swoop City had lost out on promotion, lost out on a visit to Wembley, lost out on a proper trophy and lost a good manager.'

Although Appleton's strange team selections and defensive mindset helped ensure that his departure wasn't universally mourned, his record spoke for itself. Mike Peterson sums it up when saying that his teams 'may not have matched the flamboyance of the chairman, but they were effective'. Looking back at his programme notes, it should be pointed out that he was also a manager who cared deeply for the supporters, especially those who travelled away. In his notes for the Plymouth game in October he'd praised the 'absolutely fantastic' fans who'd attended both the Brentford and Bolton games in 'atrocious conditions'. He bemoaned the 'present segregation system' that meant supporters were often denied

161 Article 'What the FA Cup really means to Hull fans', *Yorkshire Post*, https://www.yorkshirepost.co.uk/news/what-fa-cup-final-really-means-hull-fans-1841736, 15 May 2014

shelter from the elements when covered areas remained unused. Similarly he appreciated the economic problems of the time, stating after the away game at Bournemouth, 'When we realise that there are people travelling who are unemployed, then it is a must that we show our appreciation.'[162]

Appreciation was something that Hull City as a club had also gained from the wider football community. The Tigers finished fourth (behind Watford, Liverpool and Shrewsbury) in the Football League Executive Staff's Association Club of the Year award. Bobby Robson announced that they had won this honour 'for moving from near bankruptcy to Third Division promotion contenders and at the same time becoming one of the best-supported teams outside the First Division'. It was a wonderful accolade from one of the game's great gentleman – but it was no substitute for what had been missed out on.

162 Peterson, Mike, *Farewell to Boothferry Park* (Hull: Arenasport, 2002) p.49

15

Blessed Brian

The Baseball Ground: Saturday, 20 October 1984

The whistle has just blown and City's players are looking our way in search of reassurance. Fuck 'em. I can barely manage to raise my hands in applause. Quite simply we've been battered, blown away by half-time. Again. Why should I clap that shit? And now, we've got to face those fucking idiots outside wanting to have another pop. Fuck you City. And fuck you too Brian Horton. I said Chillo should've got the job.

* * *

Brian Horton was officially appointed Hull City manager on 12 June 1984, joining the club on their US tour in time to take charge against Tampa Bay Rowdies in the second leg of the Arrow Air Anglo-American Cup. City lost the game 1-0 but clinched the trophy 3-1 on aggregate. It meant nothing given what had gone before but at least it got the Tigers some sponsorship for their new kit.

With Horton at the helm, the team would immediately secure a return to the second tier of English league football and back it up with a brief flirtation with promotion to the First Division. A manager whose appointment I struggled to embrace would show me the folly of my initial scepticism by presiding over two very successful seasons. And thanks to some money in my pocket, I got the chance to fully enjoy them.

Initially, however, I struggled to raise any enthusiasm. The gloom of Turf Moor was slow to lift. Over the course of the summer my mind kept wandering back to that bloke at Plough Lane who'd congratulated me in April; how convinced we both were that day that City were as good as up. Then I re-ran the numerous 'what ifs': that ironic cheer when Glyn Hodges scored, Appleton's Bank Holiday selection at Vale Park, those misses against Bristol Rovers and even our failure to overcome a Newport side reduced to ten men. The list was in danger of becoming all-consuming. Throw in my lack of faith in City's new player-manager and I wasn't exactly busting a gut to get back to Boothferry. Even the new kit, which I regarded an improvement on the previous Admiral affair, failed to lift my spirits.

In addition to my self-pity and apathy, I was also faced with the prospect of weekend working at my first job, as a junior technical clerk on a major construction project at the nearby gas terminal. The bloke who'd interviewed me was called Jack Charlton. Like his famous namesake he was a Geordie, but unlike him this 'Wor Jackie' hadn't recently been linked with the City job. Indeed, he had no interest whatsoever in football, a fact he told me without invitation. It wasn't a great start but after a real grilling of an interview he told me, 'The job's yours, start next Monday … and you'll be expected to work weekends.' The likelihood that my Saturdays would now be spent carrying out quality assurance checks led me to abort plans to renew my season pass.[163]

---

163 Similar to the 1982–1984 kit, the shirts no longer carried a red pinstripe but two shades of amber, while the socks were in new 'candy-style' hoops in amber, black and red. I'd have preferred them without the red!

Thanks to the draw for the League Cup first round, three of City's first four games were against recent rivals Lincoln, whose manager Colin Murphy was another reportedly linked with the Tigers' vacancy. I actually got to the season opener at Sincil Bank, which ended goalless, but I missed City's return the following Tuesday in which they established a 2-0 aggregate lead in the cup with Whitehurst scoring the first of 24 goals in all competitions throughout the season. I was working the day Bournemouth were beaten 3-0 in the opening home league game, a third successive clean sheet for Horton's team. It was certainly better than I'd expected and I have to admit to being impressed when watching them thump Lincoln 4-1 in midweek to earn a second-round tie against top-flight Southampton.

Reassessing my priorities in the wake of such a showing, I missed only three more matches all season, two of which came in the Associate Members' Cup. All in all, not a bad effort. To achieve this, I arranged to work Sundays instead of Saturdays (for the same rate) and I booked unpaid holidays to cover the midweek trips. My basic take-home for that period was £82, a figure that with weekends thrown in could exceed £100 (the equivalent of over £300 today). A vast amount of this went on football trips. I never bothered to work out the total cost of seeing City achieve a second promotion in three seasons but I do know it was worth every penny.

8 September 1984
Football League Third Division:
Bolton Wanderers 0 Hull City 0

Burnden Park: Burnden Stand; ticket £3.65;
programme 50p

Despite the new manager, other close-season changes at Boothferry Park were kept to a minimum. Chillo retained the role of assistant boss in Horton's setup, with Dennis Booth becoming coach. Just the three new players were recruited – Lawrie Pearson, Mike Ring and Neil Williams – with most fans wondering which, if any, could fill the void left by the departing Brian Marwood (sold to Sheffield Wednesday for £115,000). Ring did his best with goals against Bournemouth and Lincoln. It was a promising start.

Appetite restored, I booked on Simon's coach for the trip to Burnden Park. On a typically damp Lancashire afternoon, I decided to accompany those who opted for the designated away seats in the covered Burnden Stand. It wasn't one of my better decisions. As our stand adjoined the open terrace behind the goal on which most of the travelling support was located, the paddock in front was the preferred location for the more unsavoury elements of the home crowd. Given that some of City's 'elite' had also chosen to sit, their Bolton counterparts' attention was soon diverted upwards and, after an uneventful goalless draw, things came to a head at the final whistle. Those from the paddock intent on trouble made their way on to the concourse at the same time as we came down from above. The result was predictable. In view of the numbers concerned it was probably as well that the police were not slow in arriving on the scene. However, in their rush to descend the stairs they knocked an old lady over, later said to be Brian Horton's mother (although I've never had that validated). Obviously in distress, the incident did little to improve the mood among the City support. It was another day on which I was relieved to make it back on the bus unscathed.

Tony Norman's third consecutive clean sheet kept City up with the early pacesetters and when Preston North End arrived at Boothferry, they were joined by the *Match of the Day* cameras. Writing some years later, Paul Brooks recounted events for City fanzine *Tiger Rag*: 'What a joy it was to watch the video again and see our heroes run out to the massive chart buster "The Tigers Are Back". How wonderful it was to hear Barry Davies patronise us on our terrific half-time entertainment. Did we really laugh at some pillock dressed as Charlie Chaplin trying to hit a ball with a walking stick? I think not, Barry. The star of the show, however, had to be the Kempton kop. Twice the Lancastrians took the lead in the Tigers' eventual 2-1 defeat and twice the song "You're gonna get your fucking heads kicked in" drowned out the commentary.'[164]

Having watched the game again courtesy of the wonderful TigerTube channel, I don't believe Davies was being patronising. Indeed, he seemed to have a genuine feel for what The Don was trying to achieve at City. Two other things stood out from the 17 minutes and 52 seconds of edited highlights: the quality of Preston's two goals and the quality of the Tigers' football.

After the game there were sporadic incidents of trouble on Boothferry Road, news of which reached those in charge at the club. In Horton's next programme notes for the visit of Gillingham, he wrote how pleased he and the players had been with the support both home and away but added, 'I hope that the few people who spoil it can turn their attention to watching the action on the field instead of causing trouble.' He would have no worries that night given a paltry turnout from the Medway. And those Gills fans who did make the trip went home disappointed thanks to a City win remembered mainly for Billy Askew's second goal. The *Hull Daily Mail* described it as 'magnificent': 'McEwan played an exquisite long ball down the right to Steve Massey and he passed perfectly into

164 *Tiger Rag* fanzine (Issue 4, January 1995)

the path of the ginger-haired midfielder who unleashed a 25-yard thunderbolt which Hillyard got a hand to, but could not keep out.'[165]

Next up was a return to Turf Moor, which had the potential to open old wounds, and indeed the home fans tried their best with various taunts. However, as Paul Brooks remembers, the travelling support was in defiant mood. Along with a rousing rendition of 'Al-an Tay-lor, is a wanker, is a wanker' after the former Tigers striker had missed a penalty, there was even more gusto in the mocking question we asked of our hosts: 'Where's your friends from Sheffield?' On the pitch a McEwan penalty earned City a deserved point that set us up for a midweek trip to the south coast.

* * *

Prior to Sky's grip on English football, the League Cup was a competition that could still whet supporters' appetites, even in the early stages. Thus when City were paired with First Division Southampton, it was a tie worthy of the term 'glamorous'. With the first leg away, I booked a couple of unpaid days off work and the trip to The Dell remains one of my favourites from that era. City went down 3-2, with future Tiger Steve Moran scoring twice either side of a Joe Jordan header for a Saints team that included six internationals. Dale Roberts levelled the first of these and when Garreth Roberts slid in to score with just ten minutes remaining right in front of us, the vociferous City following housed on the old Archers Road End terrace celebrated as if it was the winner. We sang our hearts out that night and the goal celebrations made it a memorable occasion. The 'idiot who hurled a brick through the coach window' referred to by

165 *Hull Daily Mail* match report (19 September 1984)

Simon Gray in his regular programme column was rather less fondly remembered.

Saints boss Lawrie McMenemy was full of praise for the Tigers: 'They were a hard-working side, but nothing less than we expected. They spread the ball around well, chased, harried and knew what to do against First Division opposition.' In his notes the following weekend, Horton described the support received at The Dell as 'tremendous' and said, 'It really lifted the players. To see as many Tigers fans travel that distance really shows the potential for football in Hull.' Hang on a minute; he was beginning to speak my language. But before we could dream about a potential giantkilling, there were three league games to be negotiated, which yielded a mixed bag of results.

3 October 1984
Football League Third Division:
Bradford City 2 Hull City 0
Valley Parade: Grandstand; ticket £4; programme 40p
I remember little of the goalless draw at home to Reading but the midweek trip to Valley Parade was memorable mainly on account of the awful weather conditions, which again had a bearing on our night as a whole. It was thoroughly miserable as my cousin Melvin drove me and two other lads, Steve and Kev, down the M62. The rain was 'siling it down' and having arrived just after kick-off we immediately made for the relative comfort of the Grandstand seats as opposed to the open away terrace. Relative comfort is perhaps an apt choice of words; Wikipedia quotes Simon Inglis likening it to 'watching football from the cockpit of a Sopwith Camel' due to its antiquated supports and struts. Still, at least we remained dry for the course of a suitably downbeat 2-0 defeat.

We weren't the only away supporters in what appeared to be non-segregated seats, although none of us made our presence known. With what appeared to be wannabe members of the Ointment thug firm trying to seek out possible interlopers, it was impossible to concentrate on the game. I felt like Richard Attenborough's character in *The Great Escape*, just waiting for one of my mates to drop us in it. But even Steve – a man not normally averse to having a row – kept schtum. Not that City's display gave us anything to be vocal about anyway. We returned to the car unscathed, blissfully unaware that the mild discomfort we felt that night would be put into stark perspective seven months later.

As we departed West Yorkshire, my commitment to making the following Saturday's seven-hour coach journey to Plymouth proved a source of much amusement among my fellow passengers. Several questions were asked about my sanity. 'It will be just like City to win,' I replied. And of course, this being #TypicalCity, they did just that. Flounders's solitary goal earned a first away win of the season and put the 200 or so of us on the Barn Park terrace in a positive frame of mind ahead of the return match with the Saints. It was still a bloody long ride home though.

There were a reported 16,000 spectators inside Boothferry Park the following Tuesday, the largest crowd of the night in the competition. Despite later being adjusted to 14,613 it was the biggest gate at Boothferry Park in nearly a decade. Among them were a host of club legends such as Raich Carter, Ken Wagstaff, John Kaye and many others. They watched the Tigers again go toe to toe with the same star-studded Saints line-up that had edged past them the previous week. In his regular programme column a week later, Dave King said of the club's VIP guests, 'I am sure that they must have been taken back "down memory lane" by the atmosphere which the crowd and the game generated. It was super to see a real crowd, to see the lack of spaces on the terraces, to see the rows of occupied seats and even to be jostled again.'[166]

Horton described the atmosphere as 'something I'd heard about … It lifted the players and everyone enjoyed it.' City matched their First Division counterparts every inch of the way – forcing 13 corners to Saints' three – but the lively Danny Wallace, who gave Dale Roberts a torrid time, fired Southampton ahead. Flounders doubled his tally for the season to level matters only for Moran to make it 2-1. City were then handed a golden chance to level matters but McEwan picked the worst possible time to record his first penalty miss. The Tigers continued to battle but Whitehurst's 86th-minute leveller came too late to prevent a brave exit on aggregate.

* * *

The miners' strike was in at its height when Doncaster Rovers visited Hull on 13 October 1984. Not for the first time, normal political sympathies were set aside as football rivalry took precedence. 'We all agree … dockers are harder than miners' was part of the Kempton's repertoire as the Tigers-supporting members of this particular Labour stronghold showed little solidarity with their brethren from the 'Socialist Republic of South Yorkshire'. On the pitch, strikes from Flounders, McEwan and Skipper had most of the 8,500 crowd in raptures as City raced into a three-goal lead. To their credit, Doncaster – managed by Billy Bremner – stuck at it and a late rally pulled two back to set up a tense finish.

Next up was Derby away, a fixture that had been eagerly anticipated by the hooligan element of both teams. Rumours were rife beforehand, with talk of leaflet drops by the 'Derby

166 Match programme (Hull City v Doncaster Rovers, 13 October 1984)

Lunatic Fringe' urging a decent turnout of locals in order to show Hull City who the real Third Division 'top boys' were. On the pitch the centenary-celebrating Rams did just that, with the game settled by the break. From a superb vantage point high up behind the goal, we watched in stunned silence for the majority of a 3-1 defeat. The Tigers slipped to 12th, their lowest position all season. Afterwards, the streets outside were again the scene of large groups of lads trying to get at each other, with police horses causing their own brand of mayhem among those not wishing to be involved. It wasn't a pleasant experience and to those of us still sceptical about Horton's appointment, it was all his fault!

A 14-match unbeaten run finally won us over. Ironically, it began with the return of the previous manager and his new Swansea team. Big Billy provided the required welcome courtesy of a brace in a 4-1 win. My only trip to Eastville (and a reminder of my old speedway days) was then rewarded with a deserved and hard-earned draw against second-placed Bristol Rovers. Whitehurst scored City's equaliser and a 'magnificent' Tony Norman save in the last minute secured the point, which always makes that long ride home just that bit more bearable. The following weekend's frustrating goalless affair at home to Rotherham ('more bloody miners') was played in atrocious weather conditions but three nights later goals from Flounders and McLaren saw off Cambridge. The Tigers were up four places to seventh. Next up was a trip to the Orient, one that has since gone down in City folklore.

10 November 1984
Football League Third Division:
Leyton Orient 4 Hull City 5

Brisbane Road: West Stand seats; no ticket; programme 50p

Things didn't start that auspiciously. With Simon only

running a weekender, options for getting to the game were limited. In the event our intrepid organiser paid for Gary, Mark (aka 'Tash Ward') and me to join the official supporters' club in order to get to the game – he clearly didn't want to lose us to the National Coaches-organised matchday competition! On arrival in east London we soon 'lost' our new travel companions in search of a beer. We found it in the King Harold in Leyton, where soon there was assembled a 30-strong rag-tag group that included members of the exiled City Southern Supporters' Club plus the usual mix of 'grebs', 'scarfers', a couple of 'Trendies' and a handful of West Ham fans who'd tagged along out of curiosity. We enjoyed a decent session before setting off on the five-minute walk to the ground, only to almost immediately be accosted by a van-load of police. My status as the token flat-top didn't endear me to them. After a quick frisk, we were allowed on our way but not before I heard one of the coppers tell his mate, 'Watch that cunt in the green jacket.' Charming.

Again eschewing the open away end we entered the seats in the old West Stand, where our number bolstered the City contingent to something approaching 100. With three times as many behind the goal it constituted another respectable away following. My sense of foreboding beforehand, evoked by bad memories of the previous April, looked spot on as Orient raced into a three-goal lead inside half an hour. Barry Silkman was the chief tormentor, setting up all three. With echoes of the recent Baseball Ground debacle growing, it was all we could do in the seats to keep up our vocal encouragement, which for the duration of the game included an ongoing rendition of 'I-C-F, Cockney Tigers' in honour of our matchday guests. Just before the break our support was rewarded when Askew's corner floated directly in. It was a lifeline.

We spent half-time discussing the need to score early if we were to get back in the game (while also making a note of the significant number of home lads congregating to our left; a prudent observation as events turned out). Our hopes for an early second-half strike were granted – but in the wrong net as that man Silkman made it 4-1 with a 25-yard screamer. The game appeared up.

What followed was one of the most remarkable turnarounds I will probably ever see at a football match. With 25 minutes left, Whitehurst's cross was turned home by Steve Massey who ended his lean spell with a close-range finish. He later told the *Hull Daily Mail*, 'I'm lethal from two yards!' Five minutes later, Askew's corner found Horton whose header was only pushed into the path of Flounders; 4-3. By now I was almost hoarse with excitement and there was a genuine feeling that more was to come. In the 77th minute Corbett handled a free kick in his own box and the Tigers had a penalty.

Amid all the excitement, we'd failed to notice the aforementioned 'daft lads' suddenly come charging across the seats. But nobody was going to spoil our day and they must have realised this as they came to a complete standstill just five yards away. This allowed one of our number (quite possibly 'Carlton Paul') to lunge forward and crack the main protagonist with the golfing brolly the guy had previously been posturing with. Attention now turned back to the pitch where McEwan blasted home from the spot. All square. A draw would have been a superb achievement but when 'Cousin' Andy smacked home the winner with just two minutes left, it was pure ecstasy. The *Hull Daily Mail* called it 'an unforgettable 23 minutes'. The scenes of jubilation at the final whistle were unreal, with the only disappointment for me being that Big Billy was the only player who bothered to come across to the seats where – in my opinion at least – our band of brothers had not faltered for 90 minutes, while those behind the goal had largely been found wanting.

City had moved level on points with third-paced York thanks to what Horton termed 'one of the most exciting games I've ever played in'. In his notes for the FA Cup first-round tie against Bolton, he quoted Chris Chilton's description of 'one of the craziest games he'd ever seen' and added that it had revealed 'the character that we have in the side … although with the players that we have, we should never really get into that situation'. He was right, of course, but had the players not done so I and several hundred other City fans wouldn't have had 'Remember Orient' as a rallying call for years to come.

* * *

The Bolton tie was another that carried an edge. The visitors made their intentions clear from the off when several of their number infiltrated the Kempton prior to kick-off. Soon spotted, they were subsequently dealt with and ejected, although I hasten to add I take no credit for this clean-up operation. Reunited with their sizeable following on the opposite side of the fence, those same Bolton fans must have thought their side had earned a return pop at their counterparts as the game drifted towards a replay. But then Trotters keeper Simon Farnworth inexplicably allowed 'Classy' Massey's toe-poke to crawl under him for another last-minute winner. Oh how we danced around the Kempton that afternoon! For the second week running City had played their 'Get Out of Jail' card.

The return to league action saw Newport County beaten 2-0, another game for which the away end stood almost empty. In contrast, City's away following was growing in size on a weekly basis, many of whom followed the casuals' lead in taking up a position in the seats. This was especially so at grounds like Wigan's Springfield Park, where the alternative was an open mud heap behind the goal. Spending extra dosh to sit down could be easily justified. Wigan also warrants a mention as it was one of the very few matches for which I was issued with a ticket when passing through the turnstiles. On the pitch Billy Askew scored in a 1-1 draw that kept City in touch with the leading group. I celebrated the fact by taking my life into my hands when accompanying Carmo to see the Meteors at Retford Porterhouse. But even this paled in comparison to what awaited me a week later.

As was becoming evident, choosing the seats by no means guaranteed a trouble-free afternoon, a fact that was illustrated vividly at Prenton Park where Tranmere Rovers provided the second barrier to City's FA Cup progress. Although this was some years before publication of Kevin Sampson's excellent *Awaydays*, much of the afternoon played out like a scene from it. I'd not seen any trouble at Tranmere on my previous visit but this was very different. Irked by rumours of pre-match incidents in the town, it soon became apparent that some among the home support were out for retribution (as were City's 'lads' who, according to Tordoff, made up a quarter of the 2,000-strong away following and for who the game provided a 'chance of revenge for a painful visit endured by the early Psychos in August 1978').

The rival groups positioned themselves either side of the thin yellow barrier tape used for segregation in the seats. Then it started. The football soon became secondary to the hail of flying seats and snooker balls. Missiles mixed with charges and counter-charges as both groups went at it for what seemed a good 20 minutes or so. I'm not ashamed to say at one point I wanted out, only to be met by a rather more resilient member of the travelling support who told me in no uncertain terms, 'Nobody fucking run!' I didn't need telling twice. I was lucky. When things eventually settled down I at least still had a seat to sit on – unlike Carmo who found his not only missing its back rest but with part of the seat itself also kicked away. Throw in memories of a coach backseat covered in 'a fine mixture of whisky, lager and urine' and the passengers being roundly entertained by John B's pissed-up rendition of 'Inky Pinky Parlez Vous' and you have a trip that wasn't to be forgotten in a hurry. Almost superfluous in view of the off-field events, the Tigers strolled to a 3-0 win and with it a place in the hat with the big boys. A week later Whitehurst's winner against Walsall stretched City's unbeaten run to double figures as we approached the crucial festive period. [167]

The last away game before Christmas was a Tuesday night trip to third-placed Millwall, a fixture brought forward from Boxing Day. Having broken my duck the previous season, I thought I knew what to expect. I didn't. This being a night game The Den took on an even more sinister air, especially given a smaller City following (there were only 18 of us on our 53-seat coach) and the fact that our driver somehow managed to pull up at the wrong end of the ground. As curious home fans came to have a closer look and a surprised – and suddenly very nervous-looking – solitary policeman tried frantically to contact reinforcements, the driver did his best to rectify his mistake, while surrounded by now highly amused spectators. I don't need to tell you how I and 17 others on board were feeling. Safely delivered to the away end at last, even the pre-match presentation of the 'Best Behaved Supporters' trophy won by Millwall the previous season failed to ease the tension.

This would be another 'I was there' trip to be worn as a badge of honour in later life, thanks mainly to more heroics on the pitch. Trailing to an early goal, an own goal brought City level only for them to then lose Tony Norman, forced off

---

167 Tordoff, Shaun, *City Psychos: From the Monte Carlo Mob to the Silver Cod Squad* (London: Milo, 2002) p.157

with concussion after a heavy challenge from John Fashanu. 'Cousin' Andy donned the gloves and was duly beaten just before the break. Many among City's support vented their spleen at Fashanu to such an extent that one police officer had to issue an ultimatum: 'Any more of that and you'll be all let outside!' Nobody needed telling twice.

Norman returned for the second half and City earned their reward for a gutsy display when Gary Swann smashed home a deserved equaliser. The delight among the 100 or so travelling fans didn't last long. Leaving the ground afterwards, for the second time that night our coach came to an unfortunate standstill, at a bus stop packed with Millwall fans. Anticipating the immediate shattering of glass, we all hit the deck; that is except Gary who, in his own words 'wasn't as quick to react'. Instead he recalls seeing 'a line of would-be F-Troopers pull their hands from behind their backs and then … gesticulate rather than chuck a brick!' Behind me, Bransholme bin man Stocksy was another who remained alert to what was going on: 'There's a bloke here suggesting I'm a wanker. I am, mate, I am. Anything you say.' Ah, we can laugh about it now.

Third place was City's following a 4-0 home victory over Brentford and 1984 was ended in fine style, thanks to Askew's winner earning the points on a 'heavily sanded pitch' at York in front of 5,000 travelling Tigers among a crowd of 9,665. After Keith Walwyn had cancelled out Flounders's first-half effort, City's flame-haired midfielder won it just eight minutes from time. The goal was described in *On Cloud Seven* as 'a perfect 40-yard chip from the wing which dipped into the top corner, and no it wasn't meant to be a cross, we are in the presence of genius here'. Again the trip to Bootham Crescent wasn't without its incidents off the pitch, with seats scattered at another away game.

While Horton's side finished the calendar year second in the table and were looking well placed to complete the job in the spring, I ended 1984 unemployed and zonked out on the settee following the end of my contract and a New Year's Eve that had seen me carried home before midnight. At least McEwan's reliability from 12 yards provided the perfect pick-me-up as City edged past Bristol City in front of a New Year's Day crowd of 9,753. Horton's Tigers were on the prowl.

16

'Targers and Sparders'

Spiders: Saturday, 9 February 1985

It's a blur, just one beautiful, cheap – nay, ridiculously cheap – alcohol-induced blur. So many people with smiles on their faces. So many beautiful people with smiles on their faces. So many friendly faces. And all sharing the same passion for music. Fucking good music that fills the dance floor. And I've been up there, I've been up there for everything, not just the rockin' stuff. Spear, Killing Joke, Jesus and Mary Chain, Smiths, The Fall, New Order, the lot. Jeez, he even dropped a bit of Booker T in there. And Louis Jordan. He's a fucking top man that DJ. They're all top fucking men. And top women. In a top place.

* * *

I was to be officially unemployed for three months. Prior to finding work again (ironically, on the other side of the Dole Office counter), I relied on my savings in order to follow City. It didn't always appear a sensible investment. The first excursion of 1985 was to Brighton in the FA Cup and yielded the Tigers' first defeat in 15 matches. A 1-0 scoreline on an ice rink of a pitch was hard to stomach in the temporary West Stand Extension seats. This wasn't only because City dominated proceedings but also due to the combined effects that a hangover, six-hour coach journey and the freezing weather had on my fragile constitution. City didn't win for five matches in the wake of their FA Cup exit. I was at all of them including both Mansfield games in the Associated Members' Cup, another icy south coast trip to Bournemouth (1-1) and a first visit to Reading's Elm Park that is recalled with more clarity than the 4-2 defeat merits. As such, you'd expect that the win that arrested this run would be one to be savoured. It was – but not entirely because of the football.

9 February 1985
Football League Third Division:
Hull City 2 Burnley 0

Boothferry Park: East Stand Terrace; no ticket; programme 30p

Unlike most 'memorable' games, I can tell you little about City's routine win over Burnley other than the facts as reported by Simon Redfern. 'A blizzard greeted the kick-off of City's first home league game since New Year's Day,' which left a sprinkling of snow on the pitch. Richard Jobson made his City debut following a £40,000 move from Watford, left-back Mick Hollifield played his first league game of the season, 'recalled right-back Bobby McNeil played his 150th league and cup game' and Tony Norman was up against his old club. City dominated matters against lowly opponents but had to wait until the 66th minute for any tangible reward, Billy Whitehurst sticking out a foot to divert a wayward McNeil shot home for his 14th goal of the season. The points were assured 11 minutes later when Whitehurst's overhead kick from a McClaren throw-in was lashed home by sub Steve Massey. The majority of the 6,478 in attendance went home happy and Brian Horton described the result as 'important in many ways', praising 'the mood and spirit shown by the players'. That's it. So why does the date and result of this fixture remain engrained in my memory? Because it pre-empted my first visit to Spiders.

In December 1983, the finale of *The Tube*'s feature showed Swift Nick putting his Hull accent to best use when beckoning people off a Hull Corporation double-decker with the words, 'Right lads, Sparders.' Moments later the viewer was inside the place that over the next decade or so would become almost as big a part of my life as Boothferry Park. Long before the City of Culture, Spiders was part of Hull's subculture and had a reputation that spread way beyond the city boundary. This was largely thanks to it becoming the natural weekend haunt of many of the city's student population and a magnet for misfits.

It hadn't always been that way. In 1979 Pete Tarbotton and Lynne Hangar bought half-shares in the Seven Seas Club on Cleveland Street. According to Andy Roe's anthology, the club consisted of 'an undersized bar area, a DJ box and a side room called The Lounge. It also came with a poor reputation and was in need of "some necessary surgery".' The venue required rebranding and a whole new music policy. In 2007 Tarbotton told the *Hull Daily Mail*, 'Gothic wasn't a word used then, but we wanted an alternative style and the name Spiders came up [in 1980].' The name was backed up with some iconic spider designs and dozens of interwoven, wrought-iron spider's webs.[168]

For a while things were hard as some of the old '*Saturday Night Fever* crowd tried to cling on'. It was difficult to get the word about that the club was changing. Up until 1981 Spiders played a style of music that was not the alternative sound we associate with the club today. What sparked the change

168 Roe, Andy, *Spiders: Tales from Behind the Web* (Self-published, 2017) pp.10–12

was Thursday's showcase for up-and-coming bands. Known initially as The Roach Club (later becoming Desolation Row) it also saw the club play 'more experimental music' – a move that prompted its listing alongside Silhouette Club in that *Bop Eye* article. Everything But The Girl (who famously took their name from a slogan above the windows of Turner's furniture shop on Beverley Road) played their only live set in Hull at Spiders, while the 'musical output, and the type of clientele that it quickly attracted, acted as a springboard for the future direction of the club'. Local bands were also given Friday nights for a time, while another new concept, a student night on Wednesday and Thursday (replacing the Roach nights), again kept the club's bank happy.

There are several reasons why the club eventually took off. Firstly it was cheap. Everything inside was reasonably priced, including the door charge and £1 membership fee that lasted for five years (the proceeds of which went to a local dog charity). From the start in 1979 it was a privately owned venue 'free of any bank or brewery ties', hence it could set its own bar prices that nowhere else in Hull could touch. With draught beer at around 50p a pint, shorts priced 30p and an incredible range of low-priced cocktails, what could possibly go wrong? In time I would become well acquainted with the 'Tyzer', 'Pink Pugsley', 'Green Gremlin', 'Brown Bomber', 'Tarantula' and the wonderful 'Pan Galactic Gargle-Blaster'. In the *Hull Daily Mail* Allison Coggan recounts her time spent sinking a pint of the latter 'as Joy Division grieved in the background'. Just £1.50 'of your dole money' would acquire you 'this concoction of cider, Pernod, vodka, Galliano, orange juice and blackcurrant'. No wonder the place was rammed.

Given all the above and the fact it was tucked away from the city centre, Spiders became popular with those wary of the busier fashion circuit of pubs and clubs. In addition, the stonking music policy also ensured it was a magnet for some of the area's really cool types. Spiders stuck fairly rigidly to Tarbotton's 'anti-dance theme', preferring – in its own words – to 'play music by talented artistes who sing, play and write innovative music'. Under this umbrella, punters could expect to hear 'punk, new romantic, new wave, rockabilly, psychedelia, goth, grunge and metal'. There was to be no 'cheesy music' and those into boy or girl bands were told the club was not for them. In short, Spiders achieved what it aimed for: 'Good music to listen to, in a genuine friendly atmosphere.' This anti-establishment music policy ensured it had a ready market of people to who it appealed, especially given Hull's university city status. A dress code of 'trendy clothes are out' and an encouragement to wear 'jeans and T-shirt' also set it apart from Hull's other clubs of the 1980s (although, somewhat peculiarly, tattoos were banned).

The real gauge of Spiders's popularity was that unlike many of its counterparts it never had to advertise. The fact that the owners were against billboarding helped but the club really did survive on word of mouth. Spiders had genuine credibility. I dare say it still has. All that the owners asked of their punters in return was that respect be a two-way thing; they didn't suffer fools gladly (God knows how my mates and I lasted so long there!). By 1983, although some might argue in favour of Silhouette, Spiders became known as *the* place to be seen, even for some of my cooler fellow students from the sticks.

* * *

My debut at this most iconic of Hull nightclubs was well timed. A bitterly cold January had seen me frozen out of my latest relationship and I was in need of a change of social scene. Staying local was no longer desirable. Ever since sixth form – and those Friday lunchtime discos up dancing to 'This Charming Man' – I'd had people urging me to check out Spiders. 'You'll love it,' they all told me. 'It's right up your street.' Tom B, a City regular and at 17 already a Spiders veteran, was the latest to try cajoling me. I'd twice come close to taking the plunge but both times there were obstacles or doubts I couldn't shift, involving either logistics (it wasn't exactly 'up my street' geographically) or the 'myths' about the place: from *having* to wear black to get in to the tales of violence and stabbings. Even Dad appeared unsure, placing a night at Spiders alongside a trip to Millwall! In the end, female rejection closer to home provided the necessary motivation.

Some four hours after City had moved back up to second in the table, I met Tom in the Queens pub on George Street. As I stepped through the door it was like that first night at the Goodfellowship all over again. Although black was predominant, there was also a plentiful supply of Brylcreemed quiffs, manicured flat-tops and outlandish psychobilly cuts – and not only on the lads! I immediately knew I was going to enjoy myself. A decent playlist had me almost not wanting the night there to end. But this was only the aperitif and when the music stopped and the lights came on it was time to head across North Bridge to the main event. Again, I wasn't to be disappointed.

After several minutes queuing, I was signed in and stood waiting to be served my first 50p pint of Sam Smith's bitter. King's 'Love and Pride' was blasting out through the PA system, to be followed immediately by Dead or Alive's 'You Spin Me Round'. Neither record would probably appear on most people's first-choice alternative compilation but since that night, both instantly scream Spiders at me whenever I hear them. As do the Redskins' 'Keep On Keepin' On', Killing Joke's 'Love Like Blood', Jesus and Mary Chain's 'Never Understand' and of course anything by the Smiths. This was proper music for misfits, whatever their creed. There wasn't a dodgy track or dodgy mullet to be found.

To my disappointment, I quickly learned that the Meteors were banned from the playlist as the dancing was deemed too violent. I found this quite amusing given the action when Spear of Destiny's 'Liberator' gained an airing. Still, there were enough quiff-based sounds to keep me and my mates more than entertained – the Cramps, King Kurt, Sammy Masters ('Pink Cadillac'), Benny Joy ('Spin the Bottle'), the classic 'Reet Petite' by Jackie Wilson and aptly titled 'Saturday Night Fish Fry' by Louis Jordan. Throw in a bit of surf-rock – the Ventures' 'Hawaii Five-O' and the Soup Dragons' 'Hang Ten' – and some belting 1960s garage classics and I was pretty much guaranteed to be soaked in sweat by the close (even before I'd been up to the indie stuff). Resident DJs Pete Ellis, Dave Prescott and Chris Von Trapp would soon become men to be relied upon to ensure the night went off with a swing – quite literally thanks to Frank Sinatra's 'New York, New York', which brought things to a close. It was the start of a beautiful friendship. Spiders would remain the preferred late-night venue for Carmo, Darren, Gary, Jonesy and me for the next five years. There within its wrought-iron décor countless long-term friendships were forged, several not-quite-so-long-term romantic relationships were enjoyed and, thankfully, very few enemies were made.

* * *

Back at Boothferry things moved on at pace, with City's fixture list bringing a run of games against their main promotion rivals. Horton dubbed the first of these 'the Third Division's match of the day' as leaders Bradford came to town. Nine points adrift with a game in hand, Hull really needed to win but even with Bantams keeper Eric McManus forced off early, thanks to a typically robust Whitehurst challenge, they were second best and beaten 2-0. A crowd of 14,762 was attracted to the game, leading to a great atmosphere inside the ground and the inevitable trouble outside, which according to Shaun Tordoff's *City Psychos* led to a couple of Bradford fans receiving knife wounds.

To Rotherham next. Their win over Bristol City had enabled them to leapfrog the Tigers into second. For the first time I opted for the seats in the Millmoor Lane Stand as opposed to the atmospheric away terrace. Whitehurst scored in a 1-1 draw played in front of over 7,000 with Horton feeling his side's 'entertaining football' had merited maximum points. Three nights later it was the long trip down to Gillingham, another side vying for promotion. Here the pre-match pub grabbed my attention as it appeared to be the watering hole of choice for the local psychobilly fraternity; therefore perhaps not the best place for my fellow Easington resident Tot to announce in the broadest East Yorkshire tones that the beer tasted 'like piss!' Unlike the beer, City fizzed for the first 45 minutes and Horton described it as 'perhaps our best football of the season'. Unfortunately it yielded no reward. Dave Mehmet's second-half goal sent most of the 6,051 crowd home happy and the Gills up to second. City slipped to fifth but Horton remained upbeat, saying, 'If we can continue to play as we have in our last two games we can achieve that final push towards promotion.'

Jobson's disappearance due to 'homesickness' was offset by a much-needed win over Bristol Rovers. Whitehurst and Flounders scored goals that Horton said 'deserved to win any game', with Norman producing a vital penalty save in a 2-0 scoreline. I celebrated by making a second visit to Spiders. Having had such a belting first night there, it perhaps seems strange that it took me three weeks to return. The reasons were financial; I was into my third month without work, my savings had expired and my dole was funding my Tiger-trekking. Spiders was cheap but getting to and from there wasn't. A taxi home cost between £12 and £15, the equivalent of almost half a week's benefits. There needed to be a bloody good justification for spending that amount of cash on a night out. 'Chasing skirt' was one. My second sortie came at the behest of a girl I'd known from school and who basically had me on a string. So what's a few quid when set against the fulfilment of one's desires? I should have known better. We shared a dance or two, a joke or three and a taxi home, even though it was miles out of my way. I played the gent, paid the bill and got a peck on the cheek. The wry smile on the cabbie's face said it all. Still, a City win and a good night at Spiders was a double I'd gladly settle for at the time. Anything else was just being greedy. Wasn't it?

City's form was shaping up somewhat better than my love life and the win over the Gas was the first of 12 in the next 15 matches. I wasn't one of the '100 or so loyal City fans' at Swansea on a Tuesday night to see what Horton called 'an all-round team performance that clinched a very much needed away win' against a team on a nine-match unbeaten run. He said his team 'created so many chances with sparkling attacking football', eventually rewarded by a first league goal for Neil Williams and a 'beautiful' Steve McClaren volley. Things were now set up nicely for the crunch home game against Derby.

9 March 1985
Football League Third Division:
Hull City 3 Derby County 2
Boothferry Park, East Stand Terrace; no ticket; programme 30p

The Derby game marked one of the last times that Boothferry Park Halt would welcome a 'Football Special' bringing away fans directly to the stadium. There were plenty aboard it. The Rams had temporarily taken over Sheffield United's mantle of our arch rivals. Given events in the earlier meeting at the Baseball Ground, what Horton termed a meeting of the 'two best-supported clubs in the league' was guaranteed to carry an edge. Many City fans who were there in a crowd of 9,782 still regard it as their favourite game.

That said, for most of it, the majority of another large crowd appeared set to be left disappointed – especially those of us in a packed Kempton. A Steve Buckley penalty and Trevor Christie's goal meant City trailed 2-0 at half-time and it remained that way into the final quarter. Standing near the partition in the Kempton, we took the brunt of the away contingent's gloating, including Rams boss Arthur Cox raising two fingers from the dugout in response to the away contingent's gleeful chant, 'Arthur, Arthur, what's the score?' Thankfully, another Orient was just around the corner. A tentative 69th-minute Whitehurst penalty in front of 'the young trendies' packed on the Grandways terrace raised hopes, only for Bobby McNeil to then be dismissed for stealing yards at a throw-in. In Gary Clark's words, 'The Kempton went mad, and this stoked City up to absolutely tear into Derby,' creating 'the hottest atmosphere imaginable' from the 'baying crowd'. A red for Derby's Mickey Lewis redressed the balance and this was immediately followed by a clever header from Flounders to draw level with 11 minutes remaining. When Big Billy then rose to meet Askew's injury-time corner with what Horton termed 'one of the best headers I have ever seen', pandemonium ensued, including an impressive-looking pitch invasion.[169]

---

169 Clark, Gary, *From Boothferry to Wembley: We'll Keep the Hull Flag Flying High* (Hull: Riverhead, 2008) p.53; Horton, Brian *Two Thousand Games – A Life in Football* (Worthing: Pitch Publishing, 2020) p.88

There's nothing beats a last-gasp winner, especially when it also caps a stirring comeback. As such, the Kempton was the place to be that day. It's hard to describe to non-believers the actual sheer physical effort it takes to celebrate a goal, especially when it is scored in such circumstances as that Whitehurst winner. The current term is 'limbs', although too much of it seems to involve using a phone. Not back then. I jumped about like a total fuckwit, hugging complete strangers (having lost my mates during celebration of the equaliser moments earlier) and actually thinking, 'I'm going to die here, my heart can't take it.' And although my mouth was wide open and the word 'Y-e-e-e-e-e-s-s-s-s-s-s' was being shaped, nothing was coming out; the previous goal celebrations and the venom with which we'd directed 'You're not singing any-m-o-o-o-re' to our rivals across the fence had completely wiped out my voice. It was one of those rare occasions when I went home really feeling I'd kicked every ball. People often joke that celebrating a goal is better than sex. Who was I to argue?

The Tigers backed up their Ram raid with a Doncaster double. In blizzard-like conditions, many among the City contingent that comprised the majority of the 5,942 crowd were still queuing outside as the Tigers built up a two-goal lead. As with the earlier meeting, Rovers rallied in the second half but again fell short. Horton said the win over 'such a good side' was 'a tribute to the players' attitude and ability'.

It was another occasion when events filled both the front and back pages of the *Hull Daily Mail* due to the tale of a City fan being scarred for life courtesy of a Stanley knife slash down his back. A solitary Neil Williams strike at home to a stubborn Lincoln on a snowy March night secured a fifth straight win before that man Tynan halted the run with the brace that secured Plymouth a point at Boothferry.

Celebrating a maiden goal for young Spiders-goer Andy Saville at Cambridge's Abbey Stadium was the standout element of City's 3-1 win at the bottom club, before the following Tuesday brought more home frustration as Bolton secured a point in another 2-2 draw.

Somehow in among all this on-field action I managed to successfully negotiate a job interview and acquire myself a new girlfriend. The job lasted considerably longer. The Tuesday after the Plymouth game, 26 March, I took up the role of casual clerical assistant with the Department of Employment, based at the Hull 'B' Unemployment Benefit Office in Essex House down the 'Land of Green Ginger' in the Old Town area. It wasn't the best-paid job but given the economic times it offered security, provided I got through the six-week 'parole period'. I did – and remained a civil servant for two years. By contrast my new belle was gone before my role became permanent. My new employment allowed me to once again fully indulge my passion for football and music, a passion I'd taken to recording in diaries; logging games and gigs attended, records bought, TV and radio highlights and, in particular, the nights out enjoyed. Nearly four decades on they make for amusing reading.

* * *

At Easter BBC's *Look North* programme focussed on the upcoming six-pointer against third-placed Millwall, with just three points separating the teams. The Don and his newly named Manager of the Month for March were interviewed and nautical jokes followed aplenty as Billy Whitehurst and Garreth Roberts were quizzed on the deck of the *Golden Hind*, berthed in Hull. Given such a big build-up, the Tigers defied #TypicalCity logic by starting strongly and taking an early lead through 'Cousin' Andy. At least a large percentage of the Millwall following avoided their team's early setback, for reasons explained by Nicholas Turner: 'During the course of the game an old engine rolled up from the Hessle Road direction, pulling some of the oldest most clapped-out carriages still in service. It was like a 1950s train. The ancient rolling stock had been allocated as it seemed to be the most expendable in case of damage. Predictably the wheezy old diesel pulling the wagons wasn't up to it, and struggled to get to Hull for the kick-off. Out of the ancient grimy carriages came a motley assortment of big tough characters, of the type that only Millwall can supply. Hundreds of them. Purposeful and determined, but not best pleased. Canny Don Robinson, to his credit, sized up the situation and made his way to the North Stand turnstiles to allow them to get in free as the game was well under way.' [170]

Many City fans took great delight in piling out the back of the Kempton on to the crumbling terracing to notify the visitors of the score. The tables soon turned when the Londoners levelled matters but another Stan McEwan penalty cooled their ardour and secured a vital home win in front of a superb 10,426 attendance. Horton called it 'a tremendous fighting performance by the whole team'. As the title race entered the final straight, it was becoming too tight to call.

The nine-match unbeaten run was ended two days later at promotion rivals Bristol City. In his programme notes, Robins boss Terry Cooper described it as a fixture his team had 'earmarked for about six weeks as the one which could really decide whether we have what it takes to get into the Second Division'. A Bank Holiday gate of 11,952 included a large following from Hull. After the long trip down, the last thing we needed was the goading of one particularly

170 Turner, Nicholas, *Hull City: The Boothferry Park Years* (Hull: Dolman Scott) p.126

objectionable Brizzle fan who stuck his nose through the gap in the partitioning gate behind the away end to hurl abuse at anyone bothered enough to look his way. Unfortunately for him, his protruding conk made an inviting target to Pozzy, arriving unseen from the toilets. Suffice to say the goading stopped. It was the only shot on target City landed all afternoon. 'Very disappointed' at missing out on the chance to end the hopes of one of his team's rivals, Horton decreed that every game 'must be treated as a cup final'. His players responded with another nap hand against Orient.

'Billy has a ball in Tigers romp' was the headline to David Lamont's *Hull Daily Mail* match report in which he described how 'Billy Whitehurst left Boothferry Park proudly clutching the match ball after his first hat-trick for the club had given Hull City their most emphatic win of the season against lowly Orient'. It had been a struggle early on and the visitors actually took the lead courtesy of a penalty. City were frustrated but in the lead-up to half-time a moment of individual brilliance from Whitehurst drew them level, the striker picking up a Roberts pass out wide before chipping the keeper from a difficult angle at the Bunkers end. The second half saw the Tigers totally dominant. A trademark McEwan free kick made it 2-1 before Big Billy took centre stage. First he converted Massey's cross 'with an unstoppable shot' before completing his hat-trick late on after 'Cousin' Andy had unselfishly laid on the chance. Flounders himself had stooped to head the fourth moments earlier.

A week later a single-goal success at Newport was earned by an early Gary Swann volley that we actually missed due to our coach arriving late, following a windscreen smash near Birmingham (another Simon Gray away-day classic). Thankfully, our disappointment at this was more than atoned for the following Tuesday.

Not all-ticket. A journey through time for the author: young, amber and black.

Brian Horton (left) arrived in the summer of 1984 and continued the club's post-receivership rise, assisted by City legend Chris Chilton and Dennis Booth (Hull Daily Mail)

Like the old days! A packed Boothferry Park for the League Cup tie against First Division Southampton on 9 October 1984 (a figure later amended to 14,613) (Lindsay Walters)

City fans outside a traditional pre-match watering hole, the Silver Cod pub on Anlaby Road, ahead of the top of the table clash against Bradford City on 16 February 1985 (Roger Hill)

City fans in the 'Grandways' stand (forefront) eye up their visitors from Bradford to their left, sandwiched in-between them and the City fans in a packed Kempton to the right of the picture'(Roger Hill)

A celebratory pitch invasion moments after City clinch a dramatic win over promotion rivals Derby County on 9 March 1985 (Roger Hill)

Chairman Don Robinson hands out free champagne to supporters in the Kempton prior to the game against York City on 6 May 1985 as City celebrate promotion to the Second Division (Lindsay Walters)

Despite the 0-2 defeat in the game, the players come out afterwards to take the acclaim of the crowd (Lindsay Walters)

The fans again invade the pitch in celebration (Lindsay Walters)

Hampden horror show. As these pictures might show, attending England's 1985 Rous Cup game against Scotland at Hampden Park was one of the most frightening matchday experiences I'd ever encountered (Karl Skirrow via 'Casuals from the 80's' Facebook page)

Rockin' the town: from Goodfellowship to Gatsby's and Spiders on Saturdays! A selection of shots mainly from the summer of 1985, featuring several of the Hull 'Cats', including Lee, Vince, Reggie, Corky, Andy H, Andy L (RIP), Jon and Mike among others...

Wrecking times. Top psychobilly band Guana Batz were regular visitors to the Adelphi Club, ensuring a sweaty night for Hull's flat-top fraternity. The author can be seen in the main picture sporting a nifty turquoise bowling shirt, bought from Chris's (aka Beasley's) in the old town (Ali Caldwell)

Our 'Caravan of Love' at the infamous game at Selhurst Park on 13 December 1986 saw City lose 5-1. 'Pozzy' is at the front, in the denim jacket. (Author's photo)

Another from the Selhurst Park game. Brian Horton sent off and our merry little band of 'Out of Towners' chased down the railway lines! (Author's photo)

A month later and a much more sedate affair away at Shrewsbury Town on 31 January 1987. A 2-1 win at Gay Meadow took the Tigers through to the FA Cup fourth round and a memorable night in Swansea (Gary Jones)

Sounds of the city. Spiders nightclub, Hull music fanzines, the Mrs Wilson's Children compilation and The Mighty Strike all formed part of the author's musical education (Pictures courtesy of Andy Roe, Ian Beharrell and Julia Brown)

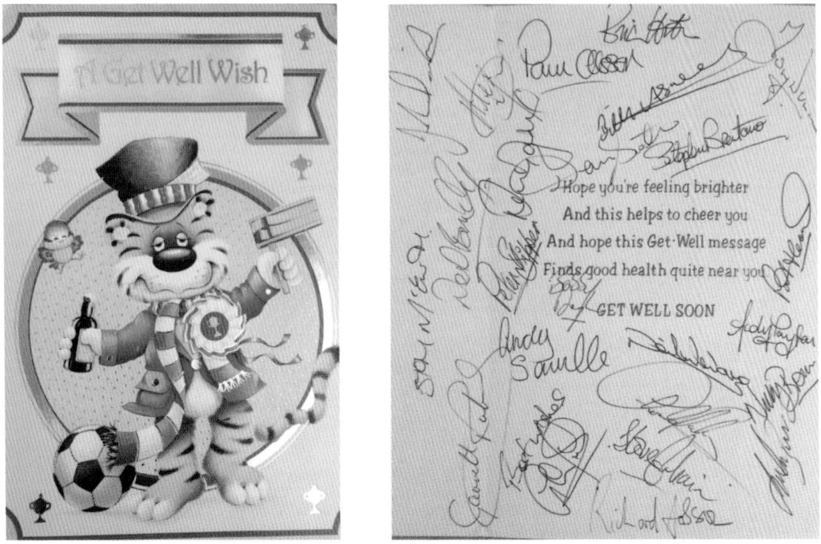

The 'Get well' card signed by the Hull City players and management on the occasion of the author's short stay in Castle Hill Hospital, March 1987

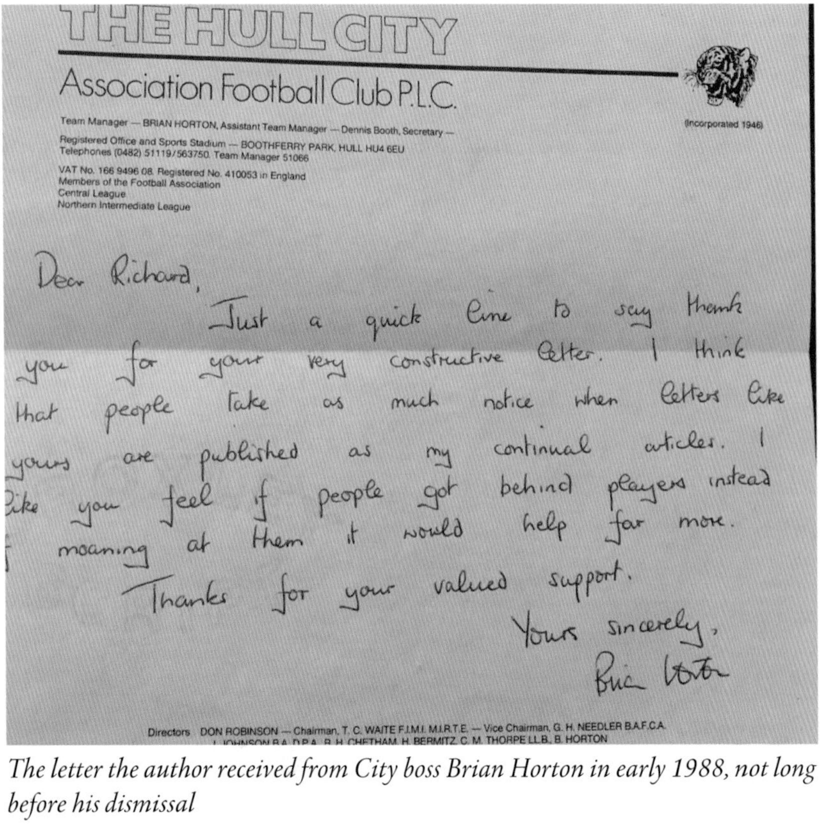

THE HULL CITY

Association Football Club P.L.C.

(Incorporated 1946)

Team Manager — BRIAN HORTON, Assistant Team Manager — Dennis Booth, Secretary —
Registered Office and Sports Stadium — BOOTHFERRY PARK, HULL HU4 6EU
Telephones (0482) 51119/563750. Team Manager 51066
VAT No. 166 9496 08. Registered No. 410053 in England
Members of the Football Association
Central League
Northern Intermediate League

Dear Richard,

Just a quick line to say thank you for your very constructive letter. I think that people take as much notice when letters like yours are published as my continual articles. I like you feel if people got behind players instead of moaning at them it would help far more.

Thanks for your valued support.

Yours sincerely,

Brian Horton

Directors DON ROBINSON — Chairman, T. C. WAITE F.I.M.I. M.I.R.T.E. — Vice Chairman, G. H. NEEDLER B.A.F.C.A.
J. JOHNSON B.A. D.P.A., R. H. CHETHAM, H. BERMITZ, C. M. THORPE LL.B., B. HORTON

The letter the author received from City boss Brian Horton in early 1988, not long before his dismissal

23 April 1985
Football League Third Division:
Preston North End 1 Hull City 4

Deepdale, Town End Terrace; no ticket; programme 40p

I knew it was going to be a good night as soon as I got to Baker Street. Never have I seen as much alcohol piled up ready to be put on board a bus. The driver agreed: 'Look lads, I'll have to put some of this in the boot for the way back, there's no way you can drink all that between here and Preston!' They would have had a good go – well it was St George's Day after all. As it was, the bus chassis visibly lowered with each crate packed into the luggage hold. And there was still enough on board to ensure a cracking pre-match atmosphere as we made our way across the M62.

Lack of toilet stops and the 'piss in a can' alternative on a bumpy coach meant the floor soon became a fluid mixture of spilt beer and who knows what else? Having opted for moccasins, I was grateful for the foot bar that ran along the bottom of each seat.

City's magnificent following was rewarded with an excellent 4-1 win that lifted them back up to second. Horton enthused about the support ('it sounded like we were the home side') and the performance. In particular he praised scorers Steve Massey and Andy Flounders who'd 'made their goals with their own hard work and persistence', Garreth Roberts for 'a fine opportunist goal' and Stan McEwan's tenth penalty of the season, 'which is a tremendous record'. In the *Hull Daily Mail*, David Lamont said, 'Hull City put themselves firmly in the promotion driving seat with their best away win of the season at Deepdale,' pointing to the fact that a draw between the two Bristol clubs had allowed the Tigers to move 11 points clear of the fourth-placed club with a thoroughly professional team performance.

Amusingly, even a memorable night such as this earned a place in Simon Gray's growing hall of shame after he left one poor fan at Hartshead Moor on the way *to* the game, as recounted years later in *Hull, Hell & Happiness*: 'The tannoy at Deepdale announced an urgent message for Simon and to cheers from the City fans present he set off around the ground.' The unfortunate passenger was picked up on the way home!

The following Saturday, goals from Whitehurst, McEwan and Massey helped City again come from behind to beat Wigan 3-1 at Boothferry Park. They were now within three points of promotion. All the previous season's heartache would be erased with victory at Walsall.

4 May 1985
Football League Third Division:
Walsall 0 Hull City 1

Fellows Park: Centre Stand; ticket £3.50; programme 40p

Five years on from that 'last one out' day at Wembley, another pivotal match in City's history was set to clash with Hull interest in a Challenge Cup Final. Thankfully I had no conflict of interests this time round. I was among the 2,500 City fans headed for the West Midlands. More precisely, I was on the Connor & Graham coach that flew a large number of City scarves from a rear skylight. Don't ask me why, but it looked bloody impressive as we sped down the M1. And our day was capped off when Pete Skipper rose unopposed in the 19th minute to head home Billy Askew's free kick and seal promotion. It should be said that had it not been for the newly elected PFA Third Division Goalkeeper of the Year, the one goal may not have been enough – Tony Norman produced two wonderful saves to deny the spirited hosts. The goalscorer acknowledged as much in an interview with

Richard Gardham for *The Decade*: 'We were battered by them, but we won. Tony Norman had one of those games, which he had quite frequently, where he saved everything. My goal came from a Billy Askew free kick. He put it in from the left-hand side. I managed to get above the kid who was marking me just inside their box, and headed it into the bottom corner. Ronnie Green, who was in their goal, dived over it and let it in. It was a great occasion.'[171]

The final whistle prompted a celebratory pitch invasion, with Skipper describing how fans were 'on the pitch trying to nick your boots and so on'. In the same publication, Garreth Roberts remembers being together with Gary Swann at the final whistle and simply saying, 'Good job, well done.' Unfortunately, as seemed all too common back then, the local constabulary refused to enter into the spirit of things and Carmo was unceremoniously chucked back over a perimeter wall by four coppers when trying to join the happy throng. Thankfully it couldn't spoil our overall enjoyment, which was further enhanced by news of yet another Hull FC failure at Wembley. Rugby town? Pah!

Writing in the *Hull Daily Mail*, David Lamont reported that City had 'immediately set themselves a new target – the Third Division championship'. That lasted three days. Any outside chance of pipping Bradford at the post was scuppered when York won at Boothferry in front of a May Day holiday crowd of 15,795. The champagne handed out by The Don to supporters beforehand had lost some of its fizz. Defeat also came at Brentford in the final game, where City supporters took over all four pubs on the corners of Griffin Park and Swann netted in a 2-1 reverse. However, on this occasion, our disappointment was soon put into perspective by the news

171 Gardham, Richard, *The Decade: Ten Years that Transformed Hull City AFC* (Amazon, 2019) p.48

filtering through on the way home. Firstly, we heard of the trouble between Birmingham and Leeds fans at St Andrew's culminating in a wall collapse that resulted in the death of 15-year-old Ian Hambridge. Even this tragedy was in turn eclipsed by news from Valley Parade where 56 supporters lost their lives after the main stand caught fire during what should have been a day of celebration for the champions. It was a disaster that would have far-reaching ramifications for football.

* * *

Before the summer arrived to bring some respite from the bad news, I had one more match to attend. Unfortunately this too would bring more unwelcome headlines to an already battered sport. Scotland versus England was a fixture that I'd grown up watching on the box and one I knew had the potential to get tasty. While seeing Wembley taken over by tartan-clad hordes every other year was old news, in recent times the number of England fans heading north had also increased. After some serious groundwork on our part, Simon was eventually talked into adding Hampden Park to his new ground ticks and organising a coach. The masochist in me meant I just had to be on it.

25 May 1985
Rous Cup: Scotland 1 England 0
Hampden Park, Glasgow: North Enclosure Terrace; ticket £4; programme £1
Following the demise of the annual Home International Championships, the Rous Cup (named after former FIFA secretary Sir Stanley Rous) was devised in order to preserve the oldest international fixture in the world, which dates back to 1872. It was a game guaranteed to whet the appetites of

supporters north and south of the border – as well as giving the police a real headache.

Wembley was chosen as the inaugural venue but this decision was reversed, ostensibly to avoid the Bank Holiday weekend down south. And so just after 6am on Saturday, 25 May I boarded a Connor & Graham coach in Easington bound for my first England away game. To say it was a mixed bag on board by the time we left Hull was an understatement. Along with a few City regulars, I had one lad with me experiencing his first taste of a live football match. Also on board were a couple of known faces from City's 'elite' (one of who recounts the trip in *City Psychos*). They shared a bit of banter with us on the way up but the air of menace was never too far away.

At the second of two service station stops, we ran into a coach of Manchester City supporters. One of them handed me a glossy sky blue calling card, which read 'You've just been tuned in by the MCFC Mayne Line Motorway Service Crew'. He shook my hand and wished me well before cheerily informing me that should he ever need to leave me another card it wouldn't be delivered in such friendly circumstances. Encountering other groups from Leeds and Stoke reinforced our feeling that there was to be a sizeable England contingent heading to the game. I began to look forward to the atmosphere that would be created when we were all congregated together. I should have known better.

My choice of attire for the trip, which was done as much with Spiders in mind on our return, was to be found as wanting as my segregation hopes. Within minutes of arrival at Hampden, the persistent drizzle again rendered my moccasins wholly inappropriate. It wasn't only the weather that turned ugly. Soon after disembarking the coach, two lads purporting to be members of the Aberdeen Soccer Casuals informed us that Hampden was indeed segregated but not for our benefit; it was the two Glasgow clubs being kept apart, with Aberdeen not being allocated anywhere specific as 'they're all scared of us'. We found this quite amusing until we passed through the turnstiles and climbed to the top of the open enclosure where it became evident that segregation was indeed non-existent. As our small band of by-now bedraggled England fans made our way down to the front of the terrace, we were spat at, jostled and coined by those all around us. I looked to my left and saw similarly exasperated English faces in the next enclosure. This was not how I'd envisaged it.

It soon became an exercise in self-preservation. From trying in vain to hear 'God Save the Queen' above the jeers to our forced ejection at the interval, it was the most scared I've ever felt inside a football ground – The Den included. Acclaimed website That 1980s Sports Blog refers to Stuart Jones' match report for *The Times*, in which he writes, 'The weather was constantly foul, the chants were often obscene, the violence at times was sickening, and the match was for the most part a mess.' If I was scared, there was even more chaos to my left behind the goal where the raising of a Chelsea NF-emblazoned Union Flag at what had been designated as the Celtic end yielded predictable results. All around us there appeared to be sporadic fights breaking out, as what Jones termed 'twisted passion' boiled over. We looked to the police for help but none was forthcoming, at least not until half-time. Then, as both teams trooped off after a goalless first 45 minutes that had largely passed me by, the pen gates were opened and we were led on to the running track where a large police escort formed up. At last, I thought, we're going to be given a designated area.

By now I should've known better. Instead, we were escorted towards the exits where a po-faced police commander ushered us outside with the words, 'Find your coaches and fuck off home.'[172]

Thus, while Richard Gough's 68th-minute looping header eventually secured Scotland's only win in the Rous Cup, we trawled the coach park in search of our getaway vehicle. We found it just before the first gleeful Scots came streaming out, but our adventure wasn't over. As we crawled our way out of Glasgow, it was as part of a large convoy in which Scottish cars and coaches made up the majority of vehicles. Unfortunately for one car-load of jubilant Jocks their taunts and gesticulations were brought to a shuddering halt when an empty whisky bottle was propelled from the rear coach skylight and on to the car's front windscreen.

Perhaps not surprisingly, the Scottish papers showed no sympathy. The *Daily Record* quickly apportioned blame, describing how '300 English football fans were sent packing' and revelling in reports of the opposite end of the ground singing to the police, 'When you're finished with the English send them over here.' It was reported that there were 140 casualties inside the ground, with injuries 'caused mainly by missiles'. Scottish FA secretary Ernie Walker expressed dismay at the trouble, while the paper reported 'confusion over how the English managed to gain tickets in the middle of Scots fans'. In a somewhat futile move I later wrote to Walker blaming his ticketing arrangements. His reply was to apologise if my trip had been 'marred' and to write to the Chief Constable of Strathclyde Police if I wished to pursue my complaint. Walker's English counterpart Ted Croker was quoted as saying that the official 1,500 England tickets 'were for a different area of the ground', in which – according to the police – 'there were no incidents'. I'd love to know where that

172 From That 1980s Sports Blog: The Rous Cup and the demise of the England-Scotland match, 14 June 2017

area was. However, perhaps the most wryly amusing quotes came from Assistant Chief Constable Roddy Ferguson who felt that the switch of venue had 'aggravated the situation' and that his officers had 'decided to take the English fans out of the ground as much for their own safety as anything'. Hmm.

It was gone 11pm when I rolled up at Spiders. My usually pristine-looking flat-top was just flat, I was beginning to develop webbed feet and the day's exertions had left me in desperate need of a shower. For perhaps the only time I felt under-dressed. I was in need of consolation and it came in the form of a *P'tang, Yang, Kipperbang* moment with my Spiders string-puller to 'A Pair of Brown Eyes'. As Shane serenaded us, the days travails melted away and I emerged ready to take on the world again, with the possible exception of Glasgow, of course.

17

Sunglasses After Dark

Gatsby's Bar, Royal Station Hotel:
Thursday, 1 August 1985

I'm on the dance floor. Corky's laying down a non-stop barrage of boppers and jivers, with just the occasional stroller thrown in to cool things down. All the faves are played – 'Mobile Alabama', 'Real Gone Daddy', 'Cat Talk', 'Jitterbop Baby', 'Long Blonde Hair', 'Pink Cadillac', 'Goodbye Goodbye' and we're all up: Lee, Vince, Andy, Reg, Dillon, Mike, Jon and many more. There's about 40 Cats in plus several straights and punks. It's a wonderful, vibrant, sweaty mash-up. I've got work in the morning but I'm not bothered. The beer's flowing, the music's stonking and even 'The Fang' looks good tonight. It may be 1985 outside but in here it's 1958 and the bop just won't stop.

* * *

In the summer of 1985, I was having the sort of party that Paul Hardcastle's n-n-n-n-19-year-olds could only dream of. I was enjoying my work, or rather the social side that came with it and the novelty of being the office 'Hepcat', which always attracted much joviality on nights out. Spiders was by now a weekly fixture, the Adelphi was playing host to some belting gigs and August brought a new regular rock 'n' roll night to town, reviving echoes of the Goodfellowship. Hull was a good place to be for a kid with a quiff again and the bright lights of the big city were proving an irresistible draw.

Helping this new-found lease of nocturnal life was the availability of somewhere to crash out after my exertions, thanks to a chance encounter with Lee, one of the original hepcats I'd come across at the Goodfellowship. Since then I'd only seen him fleetingly at Meteors gigs but when I bumped into him one Friday lunch break it opened up a whole new relationship. A kid with a big heart, Lee soon took pity on me and Carmo (or 'Farmer Dave' as Lee knew him) on account of our taxi ordeal every Saturday and so, in July, he made his Beresford Avenue bedsit available as somewhere to stay after Spiders. It soon became base camp for our increasingly regular forays into town and over the next year or so saved me a fortune in taxi fares. In return, we'd try and help ensure Lee was still able to make it out even when month end was upon him and money was tight.[173]

My first summer there really was 'The Perfect Kiss'. Weekends often became one long session, kicking off with a Friday night party at Spiders and coming to a close on Sunday afternoon. Tickets for the parties were often randomly dished out weeks in advance, with the prevalence of such open invitations reflecting the fact that once your face was known at Spiders you were regarded as one of the family. One such event in July found us decked out in peg suits and dickie-bow ties, creating quite a stir round the 'new town' pubs beforehand. Inside Spiders we took over the upstairs, with my diary noting, 'Corky steals the show in full hipster suit complete with hat; great night but minor disappointment – all jive and stroll, no hot boppers!' The following night Spiders was 'packed

173 Paul Hardcastle's UK number one hit 'Nineteen' was about the average life expectancy age of US soldiers in Vietnam

like never before' with Sunday lunch in Gardeners bringing festivities to a close before I caught the '4.15pm Connor & Graham home'. The latter was one of only two service buses running on a Sunday and would get me home in time to catch some much-needed sleep ahead of the start of another working week.[174]

Alternative ways of getting home were limited, although on one memorable occasion that summer I found myself riding pillion on the motorbike owned by Vince, one of the Hessle Cats. Notwithstanding my aversion to anything on two wheels and ignoring the fact Vince hadn't passed his test (he told his old man that I had a full bike licence!), it soon became obvious that this was also the first time he'd made a journey of such distance. With holdall slung precariously over my leather flying jacket, a borrowed piss-pot helmet and the most impractical pair of peg pants flapping in the breeze, I looked the least convincing pillion passenger of all time. As the sign for Easington finally loomed large, Vince pumped his fist as if meeting the chequered flag at a Moto GP. I'm not surprised. Suffice to say he never offered again and I was back on the bus the following weekend.

Thankfully, Spiders made such adventures worthwhile, as my diary recounts. In August, 'another great turnout' there preceded a 'brilliant all-night party in Hessle'. The following Friday, Jon J, one of the coolest customers I knew at the time, was given a half-hour DJ slot and – briefly but gloriously – the dance floor of one of the country's leading '80s alternative clubs reverberated to sounds of the 1950s. That night was followed by the eagerly anticipated Leeds away game before another sweaty night down Cleveland Street to round things off.

---

174 Title of New Order's 1985 indie chart-topping single and a Spiders floor-filler that summer

The good times just kept coming and they weren't just restricted to Spiders.

8 June 1985
The Guana Batz | The Crazed

The Adelphi Club, De Grey Street; no ticket

The year hadn't actually begun that well on the live gig front. Not only had I missed two belters at Tiffany's on Ferensway in March, according to mates who'd attended Sisters of Mercy and the Pogues (in their Pogue Mahone days), but the one gig I did attend proved a complete flop when the Sting-Rays failed to show at the Trades and Labour on Beverley Road. Support act Frenzied did their best to fill the void but were always on a loser. Thankfully, better news was just around the corner.

It had been over a year since I'd first seen the Guana Batz in the flesh and as such there was a genuine buzz created by news of their upcoming appearance at the Adelphi. Since that night in Nottingham, they'd become my go-to band, mainly on account of their ability to transcend both the Cat and psychobilly camps with what they termed their 'modern rockabilly' sound. Regular John Peel sessions had helped enhance their reputation with the only downside seemingly being a lack of recorded material. This was finally put right with the long awaited release of debut album *Held Down to Vinyl...At Last!* It leapt straight to the top of the indie charts, although in truth it didn't give as good a taste of what to expect at the Adelphi as four tracks that had appeared on the first of the legendary *Stomping at the Klub Foot* live albums the previous year. In particular, the Batz's take on 'Joe 90' was guaranteed to turn the dance floor into a manic mass of limbs.

The line-up of the band at the Adelphi showed one change from that I'd seen at Nottingham, with Sam Sardi on upright bass replacing former Meteor Mick White's electric version. It was described by Craig Brackenridge as 'the first real classic line-up … one which cemented the "Guana Beat" and led to far greater success'. Sardi had previously been a member of The Ricochets, recorders of *Made in the Shade*, another of my favourite early neo-rockabilly offerings. His inclusion gave the Batz a more authentic sound and one I'd been desperate to experience first-hand. I wasn't disappointed. Having by this time become familiar with many among Hull's misfit fraternity, I felt less of an outsider at the gig than at any I'd previously seen. I was on nodding terms with more people; I was in with the in-crowd – almost! This familiarity certainly helped in what was becoming a slightly fractious scene. All families have fall-outs and Hull's rockin' fraternity was no different. In particular, there were signs of a simmering tension between the Cats and psychobillies that was symptomatic of the scene as a whole. Craig Brackenridge explains: 'Generally the rockin' scene comprised of rockabillies with no taste for psycho, psychobillies for whom anything less than non-stop wreckin' was purgatory and a good measure of interested parties on both sides who could appreciate the scene's history and progression.'[175]

I probably fell into the latter category and had a foot in both camps. However, the time was getting nearer where a choice might have to be made. In particular, the prevalence of psychobillies at Spiders (particularly those from out of town) led to a perceived air of superiority among some that irked many in the Cat fraternity. Things came to a head one Friday at Tim 'The New Posey Manager at the Door' Allison's birthday party. A rare outbreak of trouble inside saw Vince and Reggie banned. The atmosphere of mistrust was cranked

175 Brackenridge, Craig, *Hell's Bent on Rockin' – A History of Psychobilly* (London: Cherry Red, 2007) p.49

up between two groups of otherwise very like-minded people. Attending the Adelphi for a Guana Batz gig was one place where things might well boil over again. Thankfully, the fact that the likes of Lee and others were regular Adelphi-goers meant we were on 'home' territory and with Corky asked to spin the records when the Batz were in town, there was no time to engage in any funny business. Even the wreckin' was good-natured.

26 June 1985
Restless | The Ferel Kids | The Housemartins and Others
Hull University Union; no ticket
Two weeks after the Batz flew into Hull, another of the country's top neo-rockabilly bands were in town. Restless, whose early-'80s albums on Nervous Records were among the best in the genre were another outfit that always appeared to be on the cusp of a breakthrough. Indeed, their 1986 ABC album *After Midnight* – described by Craig Brackenridge as 'an unashamedly blatant move by the label to push Restless towards a more mainstream pop audience' – came close to making it for them but at the cost of 'a massive backlash from many psychobillies and rockabillies'. Still, their live reputation was such that getting to see them was another box ticked. It was akin to meeting another of my boyhood heroes.

Lower down the bill were another band of similar persuasion, presumably included due to being housed on campus in Hull. The Ferel Kids hailed from Wigan way and turned out to be bloody good. Simon Brennan (guitar/vocals), Jez Ward (bass) and Darren Foster (drums) yomped their way through a short, punchy set that got the arms flailing. It was enough to prompt me to part with cash for their four-track demo tape. Having imagined beforehand that only one of the eight bands would be of any real interest, their appearance was a surprise bonus as was that of another name on the bill (although I didn't really know it at the time): The Housemartins.

There's plenty of kudos in claiming to have seen a top band when they were first starting out. For example, the number of people who claim to have seen Oasis at the Adelphi far exceeds the venue's capacity, never mind the number owner Paul Jackson actually says were there. Well, anyway, I can genuinely claim to have seen 'the fourth best band in Hull' long before they hit the big time. The fact that I had to be dragged from the bar in order to do so is irrelevant. Almost a year to the day before 'Happy Hour' became a top-three hit single, the fledgling Housemartins took to the stage of the Hull University, the place they'd made their live debut the previous October. In theory I could therefore lay claim to having been one of those who *just knew* they were going to make it from the minute I saw them. Or at least I could if I could remember much about them – well, apart from the fact they just looked like 'nerdy student types'! I do recall some people on the night telling me that they were the next big thing but at the time I saw them as just another distraction from the band I'd really come to see.

When that might be soon became a real cause for debate thanks to the main support act, reggae band Jib Jab. They appeared to have no intention of playing second fiddle to some rockabilly rednecks and there appeared a real reluctance on their part to vacate the stage. Perhaps the sight of so many white kids with shaven heads wound them up, or perhaps they felt that they should be topping the bill? Whatever their reasons, it was way past midnight when the last of countless encores had been played and Restless could finally appear. Unsurprisingly, a truncated set ensued, which pleased nobody, not least the band themselves who looked thoroughly pissed off with the way things had panned out.

* * *

Gigs by a couple of the country's top rockin' bands and a succession of cracking nights at Spiders had already made this summer one to be remembered when, on Thursday, 2 August a new weekly rock 'n' roll night opened in town. The venue was Gatsby's, the small bar below the Royal Station Hotel, and the opening night coincided with Shane's stag do. I'd never met Shane but I was invited along anyway as he was one of Lee's mates. There were a decent number of us, including Vince and Reggie (no longer part of our 'Saturday Night Fish Fry' following their ban from Spiders), Andy, a kid in the Navy called Steve and Lee's downstairs flatmate Mark, the lad who'd made the front page of the *Hull Daily Mail* thanks to the knife wound received at the Donny game the previous season. Mark wasn't one of the rockin' crowd but loved a good night out and was great company. My diary reported an attendance of 'about 40 Katz [note the trendy spelling] plus several straights and punks', making the opening night a success. With Corky at the decks, Gatsby's ticked all the boxes for those of us who'd been yearning for such a night in Hull again. It also introduced me to another fine collection of people: Ian D ('Dillon'), Jon J, Andy L (RIP), Mike S, Jim, Kev and Caroline, Finn, 'Tea Bag' Rich, Nick, Julia and countless others whose names have since escaped me. It even prompted me to get another chart published in the music press, *Sounds* printing a Rockabilly Top 20 accredited to 'Rich (East Coast Katz) from Corky's Rockin' Nite Record Hop, Gatsby Nightclub, Hull'. Oh yes, I'd become a right pretentious twat!

Over the next few weeks, Thursday signalled the start of the weekend and the chance to show off our finery to the townies. We'd agree a collective look beforehand for maximum effect, one that reflected the shifting trends apparent even within the rockin' scene. This Thursday we'd be suited, booted and Slim Jim-tied, the next would see us resembling a dozen Huckleberry Finns straight off the farm. Noel 'Razor' Smith charts the various fads in his *Crazy Man Crazy* memoirs of his time in the Balham Wildkatz. Not surprisingly, he'd experienced them a couple of years earlier – as with most youth cults back then, where London led the provincial towns and cities followed. As well as the clothes, the Hull lads were also undergoing a change of thatch. In attempting to distinguish themselves from the new psychobilly/scooterboy look, many of the Cats had grown their flat-tops out in favour of a more authentic grease-back style. It led to some interesting sights among those still in the transition stage. I somehow managed a sort of halfway house, which about summed up my 'foot in both camps' approach.

Sadly, just as it appeared I'd found the perfect aperitif to Spiders, it disappeared. The end of summer spelled the end of Gatsby's. It didn't get the best of send-offs either, a fractious October night inside ending with an out-of-sorts Lee being involved in an incident outside. But while Gatsby's closing would also signal the end of my active participation at these specialist nights, other venues would spring up for those who remained. Arrows Club on Hessle Road is remembered by some of the lads, along with Fountain Club on Beverley Road, while the Adelphi continued to host its occasional rockabilly, reggae and ska events. Some of the Hull crowd took to heading out of town for their weekend fix, with Doncaster a popular choice, along with rock 'n' roll weekenders at seaside holiday camps like Hemsby, Caister and Brean Sands. It was at the latter where Andy L was tragically killed the following May. His funeral at Hull Crematorium reinforced just how tight-knit Hull's 'alternative' community was – virtually every face I knew from Spiders being in attendance.

A few weeks after the end of Gatsby's, I met up with many of the crowd again at the Adelphi for the latest Guana Batz gig. Five months on from their Hull debut, the band were on the up and would soon be leaving venues like the Adelphi behind them. A sell-out was anticipated and was nearly achieved; my diary recording 'nearly 200 there, mainly psychos with about 20 beleaguered Katz'. Much to my relief there was no trouble. Instead I quite enjoyed the limelight as we took centre stage between sets, dancing to wax spun by Corky as part of the warm-up. After some unknown punk band had opened the bill, main support on the night came from the Ferel Kids. By now well known to most of us (bassist Jez having joined us in Spiders the previous week) they were guaranteed a decent reception and their set was enthusiastically received, setting the stage nicely for another blistering Batz performance. My diary notes, 'Great night, finished off at Spiders.'

* * *

By the year's end I really felt as if I'd completed my graduation into 'town ways'. Due to combining supporting the Tigers with working and playing in the city, Hull was no longer the daunting place it had once seemed. In the same way that I quickly got to know which faces to acknowledge or avoid at the match, I was becoming streetwise enough to do the same around town after dark. As such, some of the pubs I'd previously been wary of going in became firm fixtures on a night out. Soon, the 'new town' pubs visited as part of the Gatsby's warm-up were incorporated into our Saturday night pre-Spiders route.

The starting point was Shire Horse and the list included several other pub names familiar to punters of a certain vintage: Star of the West, Masters Bar, Bass House, Hull Cheese, White Horse, Dram Shop and Trog Bar before last orders in Reflections and/or Queens. Queuing to get in Trog for up to quarter of an hour is something I still can't get my head round – although I seem to recall it was usually worth the wait! On other occasions we'd head down the 'old town', frequenting traditional pubs such as Ye Olde White Harte and The Corn Exchange. There were also the offbeat little venues that would sometimes get a visit: The Kingston and Bonny Boat off Trinity Square or The Sandringham in Paragon Square. Perhaps the quirkiest was The Ship Inn down Hodgson Street, five minutes' walk away from Spiders and a traditional backstreet boozer complete with regular (older) clientele and live turn. Our arrival for last orders soon became a Saturday night fixture and one that appeared to be welcomed by the locals. Many a pub singer found himself suddenly gaining several new backing vocalists to help out with 'Penny Arcade' or 'The Wonder of You'.

After last orders, even though it was always a wrench to not go to Spiders, I soon felt cocky enough to go off and search out previously unexplored pastures, including Hull's more mainstream nightspots. Hence, very occasional Saturday nights would see us queuing to get into either Romeo's on Jameson Street, Waterfront down Dagger Lane or Tiffany's/LA's (Lexington Avenue) on Ferensway. Some of Hull's traditional social clubs were sampled occasionally, the likes of Charleston Club on Walliker Street and Jacksons on the corner of Cott Road and Beverley Road, although this was usually due to a private function invitation. However, even venturing into the unknown had its limits. The joy of 'Tower for an hour' at the bottom of Anlaby Road and the exotic-sounding Bali Hai on George Street remained off-limits as did Henry's on Anlaby Road, a venue we passed as part of our regular walk to Boothferry Park and the source of many a lurid tale involving what went on behind its doors. Perhaps more surprisingly, we never took in the original Silhouette on Spring Bank (my only visit coming just a few weeks before its replacement by its rather less quirky Park Street successor).[176]

Sometimes we'd extend our boundaries beyond the city, with mixed results. On at least two occasions I ended up among the *Hitman and Her* types to be found boarding coaches on Ferensway heading off down the M62 to Rotters and Seventh Heaven in Doncaster or Rooftop Gardens in Wakefield. If these works trips were something of an ordeal, more enjoyable were the future coach excursions to some of the north's cooler clubs: Haçienda in Manchester, the Kool Kat in Nottingham and especially Sheffield's Leadmill towards the end of the decade. By contrast, occasionally we'd opt to stay nearer to home. Sandy Beaches Club at Kilnsea and Teddy's in Withernsea were regularly sampled, along with the odd sortie up the coast to Hornsea's Floral Hall or inland to the short-lived Blitz nightclub in Hedon. I'd be lying if I didn't say I had some enjoyable nights among those listed above but even so, between the spring of '85 and the opening of the new Silhouette Club four years later, I generally regarded any Saturday night away from Spiders as a Saturday night wasted.

14 February 1986
King Kurt
Hull University Union; ticket (lost)

The arrival of 1986 brought another new girlfriend and new aspirations work-wise. Despite gaining an internal promotion at work, I didn't see myself cut out for a lifetime in the Civil Service. A visit to the RAF Recruiting Office offered the

---

176 Romeo and Juliets (formerly Skyline Ballroom/Baileys) above the old Co-op store on Jameson Street

prospect of a drastic change in circumstances and the chance to finally justify what I'd written on the schools careers officers form several years earlier, not to mention putting a smile on Dad's face (I knew he would like nothing better than to see one of his sons maintain the family's forces tradition which had stretched back to his grandad). My medical was set for February, sandwiched between two more belting gigs. My companion to both was that Clan Dew drinking punk from my earliest away trips.

Pozzy was no shrinking violet (as can probably be gathered given his well-aimed punch at Ashton Gate documented in Chapter 14). A kilt-wearing punk with a mohawk haircut and body piercings galore, he was one of the first real characters I came into contact with who combined a love of Hull City with a passion for Spiders. Usually fortified by several bottles of Clan Dew on away trips, his favourite bar tipple was snakebite. He was the most anarchic human being I'd hitherto come across but one you could come to depend on. He was a proper man for the trenches, a fact I discovered not only around the grounds of the Football League but also later on the local football fields of East Riding with Easington where he also rarely took a backward step should the need arise. Therefore, when Pozzy tells you, 'We're not going in there, we wouldn't last five minutes,' you tend to take notice. And so, en route to see latest big hitters King Kurt headlining Hull University's Valentine's Ball, we opted not to have a jar in the Spotted Dog Inn on the North Hull Estate. In fairness it wouldn't have been my first choice of drinking establishment anyway, but fortified by a couple of liveners in Trog Bar earlier and dressed in Hawaiian fancy dress on a night when temperatures were sub-zero, I saw it as a port in a storm before my arms dropped off. Had I not heeded Pozzy's advice I may have had more than my arms to worry about.

Those arms were going to be needed at the uni, if only to perform the *Ooh Wallah Wallah* moves to the pounding rhythms of King Kurt's self-styled 'Zulu Beat'. The band had come to my attention via the music press, which prompted me to buy their debut single. Recorded in 1982 on the indie Thin Sliced label, 'Zulu Beat' was literally a work of art, pressed in jungle camouflage. Signed to Stiff Records, King Kurt maintained the theme with their next single and in October 1983 'Destination Zululand' reached 'the holy grail of 1980s UK pop stardom, a top 40 position'. I remember the song's video appearing on *Saturday Superstore*, the successor to *Swap Shop* as BBC's flagship Saturday morning kids telly programme. Reviewed by host Mike Read, Culture Club's Boy George and, er, Delia Smith it was voted a hit. And so it proved, albeit peaking at 36.

Nonetheless, this was enough to gain the band a live appearance on *Top of the Pops*. Forewarned about their messy reputation, protective sheets were laid across the stage on which the band performed. Evidence that they were pure anathema to those charged with fronting the show came when Tony Blackburn introduced them as 'King Curtis'. Although I'm sure 'saxamophonist' Maggot would have been proud of the comparison, it betrayed total ignorance on the part of someone supposed to be in tune with the nation's musical tastes. The performance itself was the height of non-political correctness with drummer Rory Lyons done up in full Zulu garb, blacked up (apart from his bleached blonde quiff) and using bones for drumsticks. As the song reached its conclusion, he stole out from behind his drums to subject singer Smeg to a spot of tar-and-feathering. Oh how the audience laughed, obviously lapping up their first taste of this strange music – or perhaps simply at what they perceived to be the ridiculousness of it all. It was a never-to-be-repeated appearance. Despite this, King

Kurt's brief dalliance with the singles chart and the publicity created by their debut album *Ooh Wallah Wallah* did cast light on a thriving underground scene.[177]

When Pozzy and I finally arrived at Hull University, to be met by Carmo, his girlfriend and many Spiders regulars, few in the crowd batted an eyelid at our appearance. That wasn't altogether surprising; it could've been worse. Had it been one of the band's infamous 'Kurt Skirt' nights, no bloke would have been admitted wearing shorts or trousers. Other features of Kurt live gigs included the infamous 'Wheel of Misfortune' (in which an unfortunate 'volunteer' from the audience was strapped to a wheel and fed snakebite through a tube before being spun). Free on-stage haircuts were also sometimes an option for those brave enough to step up. And even if we didn't have any of this in Hull, we still expected to go home covered in a combination of flour, eggs and God knows what else; this was a band renowned for getting down dirty. Instead, the Kurts let their music alone whip the audience up into a frenzy.

It was the second Kurt line-up on show in Hull, with new boys 'Whistling' Jim Piper on guitar and Rich 'Dick Crippen' Coppen playing bass. Vocalist Smeg, drummer Rory and of course Maggot completed the quintet. They brought the house down. Although never to revive their *Top of the Pops* appearance, King Kurt lived up to their mantle of 'superstars of the psychobilly underground'. Recording-wise, follow-up singles 'Mack the Knife' and 'Banana Banana' almost matched the success of 'Destination Zululand', peaking just outside the top 50, but the second album *Big Cock* fell victim to the saucy *Carry On* seaside postcard-style humour that went with it. Its suggestive sleeve and appearance in 'throbbing red vinyl'

177 Brackenridge, Craig, *Hell's Bent on Rockin' – A History of Psychobilly* (London: Cherry Red, 2007) p.25

prompted WH Smith to refuse to stock it. The LP proved the band's last release on Stiff Records and despite a promising start with major label Polydor, King Kurt eventually called it a day in 1987.

21 February 1986
The Guana Batz | The Gargoyles
Adelphi Club, De Grey Street; no ticket

Two weeks after the King Kurt gig and the day after my career hopes had been hit by the RAF doctor's need for me to undergo a chest op, I was dossing at Pozzy's house again, this time in order to take in the latest Guana Batz visit followed by a Saturday trip to Brunton Park. As was the norm that February, the second part of the schedule was curtailed by the weather. But that didn't prevent the Adelphi from playing host to another sweaty night. This one had the added bonus of featuring something for the locals in the form of the Gargoyles – one of the three bands in Hull reputed to be better than the Housemartins.

Fronted by the legendary 'Mad' Eddie Smith, the Gargoyles were regarded by Paul Jackson as the local band that had given him most pleasure. They came into being when Smith, Ted Key and Paul Warhurst began writing what they termed 'crazy comedic rockabilly tunes' in 1982. Hugh Whitaker was next to join the band only for him and Key to then jump ship and join the Housemartins, prompting the Gargoyles' initial demise. Reformed in 1986, they enjoyed their most productive period, with the release of the *Mrs Two Dinners* and *Steamflapper* albums and an appearance on the *Tower Compilation* cassette (the first local recording I ever bought). A 12-track collection, it contained several bands with whom I would become vaguely familiar over the next few years. A year later the Gargoyles released the 'Mad Men from the Planet Sex' single on their own Reasonable Records. The title went a long way to summing them up, with the band's real attraction laying in their often-manic live shows. As Jackson said, 'They never came close to making it, simply because on record they couldn't catch the sheer joy that was their live show.'

Smith was the main man, once performing naked at The Tower, on another occasion singing while curled up inside the bass drum case. During a benefit gig for The Warren at Hull City Hall in 1988, he bounced around stage on a spacehopper before climbing up the speaker stacks to run around the balcony. I once read a description of the Gargoyles that termed them 'yet another tenth-rate indie group with left-wing stickers on their anoraks'. They were so much more than that.

While we lapped it up, many of the out-of-town Batz fans inside the Adelphi were perhaps left bemused by the support act and I'm not sure what many of them made of what came next. It was Corky again manning the decks and keeping us all entertained with his usual high-calibre sounds, which concluded with the belting 'Scream' by Ralph Nielsen and the Chancellors, billed as 'the wildest rock 'n' roll song ever' and first heard by me on Peel. It was the sheer excitement of all those rockin' nights condensed into just over two minutes. The Batz then appeared at 10.15pm and reeled off what I noted at the time was a 'very good, usual professional set' that included the new single 'See Through', covers of Gene Vincent's 'Rocky Road Blues' and Johnny Burnette's 'Baby Blue Eyes' as well as 'all the established numbers'. Suitably impressed – and sweaty – we hopped in a taxi to Spiders where a fine end was brought to another enjoyable evening on the Hull live music circuit.

There was even better to come the following month.

30 March 1986
The Cramps | The Sting-Rays

Hull City Hall; ticket £5

Given that nobody could believe it was actually happening, it's safe to say that the Hull visit of US legends the Cramps was easily the biggest musical date in the rocking scene calendar. Coming just two days after a hospital consultation had confirmed the date of my operation I was in need of a pick-me-up. I most certainly got one. The City Hall was a venue I'd last visited four years earlier for that poorly attended Jets show. This time the Cramps were guaranteed to have sweat dripping from the walls.

Although they were formed in Sacramento, California, in 1976 it was five years before I became aware of the band. When I did it was thanks to Al who had their *Songs the Lord Taught Us* album among the collection of tunes we'd listen to on his car cassette, as we cruised around Withernsea on Sunday afternoons trying to impress the townies who flocked to the open market. As Brackenridge rightly says, the Cramps were not a psychobilly band but instead 'belong in their own unique genre'. That said, they were definitely seen as the standard to which subsequent psychobilly bands ought to aspire.

Their Hull show – which in itself was amazing, a band like the Cramps playing a city so many other acts chose to avoid – was part of a tour to promote their third studio LP *A Date with Elvis*, from which came their first UK chart single, 'Can Your Pussy Do the Dog?' Up to this point our only experience of the band 'live' had come via the telly. Having appeared on June 1984's five-hour long *A Midsummer Night's Tube* special, the band performed on the regular show's teatime slot on 7 March 1986 as part of their UK tour, performing 'What's Inside a Girl', 'Hot Pearl Snatch' and the aforementioned hit single. This was the line-up that included temporary bassist Candi Del Mar, which left lead singer Lux Interior flanked by females in a look that played up to the Cramps' themes of sexual double entendres. As an appetiser for their forthcoming Hull City Hall gig it was perfect.[178]

Unfortunately, the pull of the Dram Shop and Trog Bar meant I fell into the usual trap of 'fuck the support band, they'll be shit', only to find out too late that it was the Sting-Rays, the band that had previously failed to turn up twice for dates in Hull. I allowed myself a wry smile at the irony, especially when hearing later that they'd played a blinder of a set. Any slight disappointment at this was soon swept away when the headliners hit the stage. Opening up with a warped cover of the King's 'Heartbreak Hotel', the Cramps romped through a 17-song set that simply blew us away. It was mainly self-penned, 'Chicken', 'How Far Can Too Far Go?', 'Hot Pearl Snatch', 'People Ain't No Good', 'Cornfed Dames', 'What's Inside a Girl?', 'Aloha from Hell', '(Hot Pool of) Womanneed', 'Thee Most Exalted Potentate of Love', 'You Got Good Taste', 'TV Set' and 'Can Your Pussy Do the Dog? There was also a smattering of covers, including Jackie Lee Cochran's 'Georgia Lee Brown', 'Lonesome Town' (the Baker Knight/Ricky Nelson song of *Pulp Fiction*/Pepsi advert fame) and another Elvis track, 'Do the Clam', all coming to a rip-roaring climax with their barnstorming version of the Trashmen's 'Surfin' Bird'.

They were never going to get away without an encore and back they came. The high point, literally, for many came with 'Human Fly', during which Lux – according to one account of the gig – scaled the City Hall organ at the side of the stage and 'hammered on the lid as if he were playing "Phantom of the

178 Brackenridge, Craig, *Hell's Bent on Rockin' – A History of Psychobilly* (London: Cherry Red, 2007) p.16

Opera"' then 'looked back over his shoulder and did the "Baa-B-B-B-Baaaa" opening notes into Beethoven's Fifth'. Simply magnificent. A cover of Dwight Pullen's 'Sunglasses After Dark' and the slightly offbeat choice of Charlie Feathers' 'It's Just That Song' worked us all up into one last sweat-fest and then they were gone. My diary notes didn't really do the gig justice but captured the main points: 'Lux cool, Ivy sensual, nay, orgasmic. What a night!'[179]

As I exited City Hall and swapped the sweaty inside for the cold of a Sunday night in March, little did I think that this marked the start of my leaving the scene behind. In the space of six weeks I'd got to see three of the pioneers of psychobilly. By the time I next saw a band of similar stature in the rocking world – the Stray Cats in Leeds on my 23rd birthday – it would already constitute a nostalgic trip down memory lane. That was March 1989 and I'd long moved on. The combined influence of regular exposure to New Order's *Low-Life* album, an eclectic Spiders playlist and some of Hull's coolest misfit characters was helping shape my musical tastes in a new direction. I was about to go full-on indie.

---

179 Richard Jackson on Hull and East Yorkshire Music Scene, 70s and 80s Facebook page

18

Back in the Big Time

Elland Road: Saturday, 24 August 1985

So here we have it, the first real test of my past versus my present. But it's not really. It's a no-brainer. Over the past few years I've come to feel nothing but an increasing sense of guilt; how could I ever have thought of forsaking my local club for this lot. Looking around me, all I see is arrogance. Arrogance based on a false sense of entitlement and stained by the antics of the Service Crew. Whereas here, in this section of the Lowfields, are lads who've seen their team really do it the hard way, lads who very nearly didn't have a team at all. But here we are now, on the same playing field in the same division as the self-styled 'champions of Europe'. I used to feel disdain for my fellow East Yorkshiremen, the so-called Hull Whites who choose to make this trip every other week in their search to recapture past glories, some real, others imagined. But in reality, I should pity them for they haven't yet grasped that Leeds United are the sepia past; Hull City the technicolor future.

* * *

If supporters thought Hull City's first season back in the Second Division would be one of consolidation then 'they were in for a pleasant surprise', as Mike Peterson writes. It would turn out to be a far better adventure than any of us dared hoped for. Horton's side showed themselves to be very competitive in the higher tier and 'many of the Tigers' opponents got quite a shock'. Among them were the team most City fans couldn't wait to play and thanks to a kind fixture list, they didn't have long to wait. On the second Saturday of the new campaign City made the short trip to Leeds. My old skeleton cupboard was about to be opened.[180]

Making the prospect more adrenaline-fuelled was the climate surrounding the game. As the *Sunday Times* so memorably stated in the wake of the Bradford fire disaster, football in 1985 was 'a slum sport played in slum stadiums increasingly watched by slum people, who deter decent folk from turning up'. Trouble was rife, with headline-grabbing outbreaks of hooliganism culminating at Heysel in May. Just four days after my trip to Hampden Park, my 'ordeal' there was put into perspective by the deaths of 39 spectators, most of them Italian, when a charge by Liverpool fans at the European Cup Final against Juventus led to a wall collapse. Subsequently described as 'the darkest hour in the history of UEFA competitions', it resulted in English clubs being handed an indefinite ban from European football (one that would eventually last for five years for all but Liverpool who served six). Coming hard on the heels of the Millwall riot at Luton, serious disorder at Stamford Bridge after a Chelsea-Sunderland League Cup semi-final and the end-of-season tragedies at Bradford and Birmingham, it was another indelible stain on the image of our national game.

Despite such negative national headlines, there was real anticipation in Hull ahead of City's first season back in the second tier. Not least in the boardroom where The Don was quoted as saying, 'We want to go straight through the Second

180 Peterson, Mike, *A Century of City: The Centenary History of Hull City AFC, 1904–2004* (Middlesex: Yore Publications, 2005) p.77

Division and on to aim towards Europe.' Such comments further energised supporters who, although seeing the club back in what many regarded to be its 'natural home', felt the journey still had miles to run. Having spent the past few years trawling some of the country's football backwaters, the unveiling of the new fixture list was something of a revelation. Where once there was Bury, Mansfield and Newport we now had Blackburn, Manchester City and Norwich. As for local derbies we were really spoilt: Barnsley, Bradford, Grimsby, Huddersfield, Leeds, Middlesbrough and Sheffield United. Bumping into Leeds fans on the way home from the final game of the previous season, one had said to us, 'It's going to be Yorkshire against the world next season,' and although there was little prospect of any such united White Rose front, the prospect of '42 all-Yorkshire games' in the division (according to the *Yorkshire Post*) couldn't fail to whet the appetite.

Squad-wise, Steve McClaren was the highest-profile departure of the summer with his move to Third Division Derby causing some disquiet given he'd made it quite clear he was hankering for a move up the Football League. Coming in was striker Frankie Bunn, signed for £40,000 from Luton Town. Local youngsters Andy Saville and Steve Corkain were also offered professional contracts. Further additions would follow in the shape of Bobby Doyle and, much later, Garry Parker and Pat Heard taking Horton's total spending to £145,000 and supplementing what was already a very good squad, one that Tom Wilson would enthuse about years later in *The Decade*: 'We had a great goalkeeper in Tony Norman. Garry Parker was a Paul Scholes-type player. He never wasted a ball. His vision was second to none. Richard Jobson was like a Rolls-Royce, nothing was too difficult for him and he'd never break sweat. Brian [Horton] would get annoyed with him when he scored because he'd never show any emotion. He played next to Pete Skipper, who was a completely different type of player – totally reliable, not the quickest but just terrific.'[181]

Slightly tempering our pre-season excitement was the news in July that the Kempton, our home for the past four seasons, was to close for necessary repair work. As a result of the Popplewell Inquiry, launched following the Bradford fire disaster, the steps behind the stand were deemed unsafe. In the opening programme of the new season a club statement read, 'We are sorry that standing accommodation at the side of the ground, as distinct from the ends behind the goals, is limited to half of the Well. This is the ruling of the authorities until construction and improvement works are carried out. We want to provide a fine stadium for you, worthy of our team and our status in the league and we shall do so as soon as we can.'[182]

It was a body blow. There was nowhere in the ground as atmospheric as the Kempton, especially when full to bursting. Where else could recreate that level of noise? Certainly not that 'half of the Well' in front of the Best Stand (too small) or even a full Bunkers Hill (too open) but suddenly these were the only areas now accessible to me as season passholder number 748. If this represented the end of an era so did the departure of club legend Chris Chilton, replaced by Dennis Booth in the post of assistant boss. By the season's end there would be another sad farewell when the last shuttle train pulled away from Boothferry Park Halt, shortly after the 2-0 win over Brighton that brought the curtain down (ironically the same scoreline as the game in 1951 that had seen the first train used).

---

181 Gardham, Richard, *The Decade: Ten Years that Transformed Hull City AFC* (Self-published, 2019) p.49

182 Match programme (Hull City v Portsmouth, 17 August 1985)

17 August 1985
Football League Second Division:
Hull City 2 Portsmouth 2
Boothferry Park: South Stand; ticket (no price); programme 50p

Despite being reduced to three sides, Boothferry Park still generated plenty of opening-day excitement, helped by the nature of the opponents: Alan Ball's Portsmouth, one-time champions and FA Cup winners who'd narrowly missed out on promotion the previous season. The Pompey Chimes were back on the up after some lean times. They were very well supported and among their travelling hordes were the infamous 6.57 Crew. Oh yes, City were back in the big time all right, as seen by trouble around the Best Stand before kick-off.

The Tigers' return to the Second Division was greeted by 8,221 spectators. I opted for the South Stand seats, having been tipped off that this would be the new home of the matchday choir. Using my pass to gain entry to the ground, I paid the extra 50p to transfer up above. For the eagerly anticipated first game I found myself back where it had all began ten years earlier: in Row A. My ticket yelled 'SPECIAL ATTRACTION at Boothferry Park' and would be the first of three such offerings before the ticket office finally got its act together and began printing the match details thereon.

On taking up our seats, it was apparent that the bulk of the former East Stand inhabitants had relocated either here or on to Bunkers below. The Grandways terrace housed an excellent away following, along with the end section of the Best Stand seats. If I blocked out the view of an empty stand to my right, the rest of the ground that day looked fantastic and the atmosphere was excellent. The game turned out to be good, too; an entertaining 2-2 draw in which Frankie

Bunn marked his debut with a goal after just ten minutes, quickly cancelled out by Nicky Morgan. Vince Hilaire then gave Pompey the lead on the hour but Big Billy salvaged a point 14 minutes from time. Horton later described it as 'a tremendous advert for football with plenty of skill, good goals and commitment'. To the supporters it was the first sign that we could live with the 'big boys'.[183]

If Portsmouth at home was a taste of the excitement to come over the next nine months, a sobering reminder of what we'd left behind came three days later: Halifax Town away in the League Cup. Having passed through the away entrance of the Shaw Hill Main Stand at The Shay, I was confronted with first-hand evidence of what the new safety regulations meant for football. Just 820 spectators congregated in a ground hit hard by the new legislation. It was a fact referred to by Town manager Mick Jones in his programme notes, in which he criticised 'Mrs Thatcher, [Home Secretary] Leon Brittan and [Sports Minister] Mr McFarlane,' who had 'kicked [football] from pillar to post'. He described that night's match as a reversion to the grassroots days of 'putting coats down for goal posts' and concluded by saying, 'The game is for the good, honest, decent grass roots supporters and for you, I hope the game is a "cracker".' His hope proved forlorn. A drab 1-1 ensued, with David Lamont's *Hull Daily Mail* match report suggesting that City were fortunate to come away still on level terms. 'Cousin' Andy (a late replacement for the injured Whitehurst) cancelled out Adrian Shaw's early goal in a contest that Horton acknowledged was 'a hard-fought game which lacked the quality we are trying to seek at the club'. Most supporters found it a hard watch, especially so given the enforced 'dry' coaches now travelling to football matches

---

183 Match programme (Hull City v Blackburn Rovers, 26 August 1985)

– another post-Popplewell implementation. Thankfully, the prospect of Saturday's trip to Leeds soon consigned a miserable night to memory.[184]

24 August 1985
Football League Second Division: Leeds United 1 Hull City 1

Elland Road: Paddock Centre Stand C; ticket (no price); programme 50p

My age provided my mitigation; I'd been an impressionable youngster, wooed by the best team in the country at a vulnerable stage in my life. To my credit I'd seen the light just in time. Those who persisted in glory hunting the likes of Leeds, Liverpool and Manchester United into adulthood had no such defence. That was my argument and I stuck to it, soon coming to resent the very person I could easily have become: a Hull White. And along with the supporters, the team they followed became collateral damage as I attempted to clear my cupboard of its biggest skeleton. All memories of that afternoon in May 1972, cheering along with Mum as 'Billy Casper' headed past Geoff Barnett were banished to the darkest recesses of my mind – publicly at least. Meanwhile the snazzy Admiral home shirt I'd worn in school PE lessons up until 1979 was banished to the darkest recesses of my wardrobe.

By 1985 there was little glory to be had in supporting Leeds and there was certainly no glory in the antics of some of those who purported to do so. It helped with my estrangement process. In 1982, under Allan Clarke, Leeds were relegated after 18 successive seasons in the First Division. The best finish they'd achieved in three attempts at getting back up was

184 Match programme (Halifax Town v Hull City, 20 August 1985)

seventh. But that was only half the story. As Anthony Clavane writes, 'The further United sank on the pitch the more they tested their superiority off it.' Their notorious Service Crew, formed in the mid-1970s in the wake of the trouble in Paris, were one of the firms featured in Thames TV's 1985 *Hooligans* documentary. Therein members talked openly about their penchant for matchday violence. What Clavane termed their 'xenophobic and sadistic' tendencies ('Elland Road became a recruiting venue for the National Front and the British Movement') made them as reviled among their fellow thugs as the team they supported.[185]

Don't get me wrong, City supporters were no angels and I still shudder at memories of some of our songs and chants of the time. But the element that followed Leeds was a pond-life of its own. The trouble at Birmingham the previous May, following a defeat that dashed any hopes of promotion, was described by Chief Constable Geoffrey Dear as 'possibly the worst crowd disorder ever seen at a football ground in this country'. The riot, which resulted in the death of a 15-year-old supporter attending his first match and saw a snack bar looted and set on fire, happened on the same day as the Valley Parade fire. Almost as if in protest at seeing their actions overshadowed, they would stoop to a new low the following season when setting a chip van alight during their derby with Bradford at Odsal. The title 'Leeds Scum' appeared well-merited. There was certainly no danger of any split loyalties as I boarded the coach at Baker Street.

* * *

For my only previous visit to Elland Road, I'd stood on the Gelderd End, the Spion Kop. If it had felt big then it appeared

---

185 Clavane, Anthony, *Promised Land* (London: Yellow Jersey Press, 2011) p.140

huge today as I looked across to my right from my vantage point in the Lowfields Paddock at the south-east corner of the ground. To our left, in the relatively new South Stand were those we assumed were members of the Service Crew. There were upwards of 2,000 City fans inside Elland Road that day and it was a crackling atmosphere, much of it generated by the visiting support. Disappointingly, the game proved an anti-climax. Barry Foster, writing in the *Yorkshire Post*, described it as the first of what he feared would be a glut of 'stalemates' between the seven Yorkshire teams in the division.

A tight first half saw Tony Norman turn aside John Sheridan's effort before both sides largely cancelled each other out up to half-time, although Foster said City's 'team spirit and will to work gave them the edge for long periods'. Leeds, given a chivvy-up by boss Eddie Gray (there's that boyhood hero link again), started the second half much the stronger. It took two stunning saves from Norman, denying George McCluskey and Ian Baird in quick succession, to preserve parity. Then on 69 minutes, City scored. Richard Jobson beat Denis Irwin to a right-wing cross and flicked the ball past Mervyn Day. Cue pandemonium in the Lowfields. Almost immediately the question was could City hang on? In reality they should have doubled their lead just three minutes later but Frankie Bunn failed to convert a glorious opportunity from a breakaway. His team would pay for his profligacy. From the ninth of ten corners in a 22-minute spell, Baird met Sheridan's cross to equalise, leaving Norman adamant that he'd been impeded by a combination of McCluskey and Tommy Wright. There were just seven minutes remaining. So close. Afterwards, Horton said, 'If we perform like that week in, week out then, yes, we are equipped for this division.' Foster agreed: 'Hull's performance insisted they will not be going straight back down to the Third Division.'

The sixth-highest Football League crowd of the day, 16,689, saw the game. Given this was City's first visit to Leeds in the league for 30 years and there had been genuine potential for disorder, the 'happy crowd' described by Foster will have come as a relief to the Football League secretary Graham Kelly and the FA's adviser on crowd control matters, Sir James Starritt, who were both present. Don Robinson was even quoted as saying, 'It was just like the good old days at football, it was all very encouraging.'

The Leeds game was the first of a Bank Holiday double, with Blackburn Rovers being Monday's visitors to Boothferry. A Rathbone own goal and a Bunn strike contributed City's share of a third successive draw. The wait for that elusive first win finally ended against Halifax in the League Cup second leg but before then came a 3-1 defeat at Oldham in which Bobby Doyle made his less-than-auspicious debut. I watched from the Martins Stand seats, with the reverse side of my ticket encouraging me to 'score at Mother Hubbard's' as part of a fish supper promotion. It may well have been the better option on the day.

7 September 1985
Football League Second Division:
Hull City 0 Middlesbrough 0
Boothferry Park, South Stand; ticket (no price); programme 50p

The aforementioned 32-year-old former Barnsley, Blackpool, Posh and Pompey midfielder Doyle was welcomed to the club by Horton in his programme notes for the visit of Middlesbrough, alongside youngster Nicky Brown who the manager hoped would 'continue his tremendous [reserves] goalscoring record' following promotion to the first-team squad. City's opponents that day arrived in Hull in similarly poor form. One win and three defeats meant Willie Maddren's side sat one place below their hosts in 20th. Regardless of form, this was another game guaranteed to carry an edge. Boro supporters had a fearsome reputation stretching back to the late 1960s. Several lads from the current respective 'firms' were known to each other and there was history between them. Just a couple of years earlier their fans had taken everybody by surprise in a pre-season friendly. This time they'd sought out another method by arriving in transit vans via Beverley Road, resulting in pre-match scuffles in the city centre.

Given such history, it was perhaps a strange choice of fixture for me to again take a female to. But that's what daft young Pisceans do when someone like my Spiders string-puller asks to tag along. Hence, I was more on edge than usual that lunchtime when scanning the comers and goers through Paragon Station, checking for tell-tale signs of impending trouble. Late as always, when my companion finally arrived, dressed for football she most certainly wasn't. This trip to Boothferry Park was just a small part of her hectic weekend social life. I wasn't complaining. It made for more glamorous-looking company than I was accustomed to on matchday (apologies to Carmo and co.) and although the walk to the ground seemed to take forever, the admiring glances received from the regulars as we took our seats did wonders for my self-esteem. The game finished goalless, with City left ruing a Whitehurst penalty miss and me bemoaning the loss of any subsequent celebration.

I was still cursing the big man as we headed away from the ground. Then the real fun began. The familiar manoeuvres down Anlaby Road saw many City 'scarfers' hurried along on their way. Unfortunately, high heels (hers not mine!) meant we were in no position to get a shift on and soon the Boro fans were all around us. I can still recall that knotting of the arse muscles as one of them turned round immediately in front of me. I braced myself for some upcoming dental repair work. Instead, after giving us both the once over and presumably coming to the conclusion that nobody looking as good as her (or with as daft a haircut as me) could have been anywhere near the game, he waved us on. As narrow escapes go it was certainly up there!

* * *

The Yorkshire derbies kept on coming. The following week it was Huddersfield's Leeds Road ground, temporary home to Bradford City. Trevor Cherry's side had completed a double over the Tigers the previous season. In a change of training routine designed in an attempt to buck this trend and improve on the slow start, Horton brought his squad out to the newly opened Patrington Haven leisure camp. It didn't work. The Tigers lost 4-2, a defeat I watched from the away stand seats, having paid an extortionate fiver for the 'privilege'. I felt Horton was speaking for us both in the following week's programme when he wrote, 'To say that I was disappointed … is an understatement.' Back-to-back home games against Millwall and Carlisle gave City a chance to finally kickstart their season. In claiming that his team 'were ahead of our time', Horton employed himself as sweeper, which he said attracted 'accusations from the media on Humberside' that City were a 'defensive team'. The next two results appeared to contradict that view. On the Tuesday, in what the manager described as 'a game we needed to win badly', the Tigers mauled the Lions 3-0 thanks to a Bunn brace and a second Stan McEwan penalty in successive games. Despite the 6,021 attendance being Boothferry's lowest to date, Horton said, 'I thought the crowd were tremendous. They got behind us and

I felt they realised that we had not been far away from getting our first win.'[186]

If that could be described as welcome, Saturday's follow-up success over struggling Carlisle was emphatic. Writing a few years later, the author of an *On Cloud Seven* 'Cloud Pleasers' feature made it clear who he felt deserved the credit. Highlighting Bobby Doyle's 'fearsome drive' that broke the deadlock after a dour half hour, as part of a virtuoso midfield performance', the author concluded, 'At the age of 32 the golden times of Bobby Doyle had seriously begun.'[187]

I celebrated these back-to-back victories with what I noted was an 'average' night at Spiders (diary-speak for 'failed to pull' with any hoped-for 'Boro bounce' having not materialised). Another distinctly average night came the following Tuesday when I watched City succumb 3-0 to First Division QPR in the second round, first leg of the League Cup. It was my first sighting of a plastic pitch. I wasn't impressed. That Loftus Road loss was the first of three successive away games in the space of eight days. The arduous trek to the second of these at Norwich involved a whole new means of away-day transport.

28 September 1985
Football League Second Division:
Norwich City 2 Hull City 0

Carrow Road: Barclay Stand Terrace; no ticket; programme 50p

In his classic account of football hooliganism, *Steaming In*, Colin Ward writes, 'It would be a struggle to find a punch-up in Norwich.' He wasn't there on the day our Dunswell Filling

---

186 Horton, Brian (with Tim Rich), *Two Thousand Games – A Life in Football* (London: Pitch Publishing, 2020) p.97; Match programme (Hull City v Carlisle United, 21 September 1985)

187 *On Cloud Seven* fanzine (Issue 6, May 1990)

Station van rolled into town. We found one fairly easily and sad to say it was a situation all of our own making; the inevitable consequence of a combination of all-day drinking, a 2-0 defeat and a chance meeting with some of City's 'elite' after the game. As a result, at some time past five o'clock, I was one of several lads to be found 'charging' out of the back of a transit van in Norwich city centre, supposedly in order to engage with the local 'firm'. It's not something I'm proud of and, thankfully, aside from a couple of punches thrown by those who were out of the vehicle far quicker than I was, the violence amounted to very little. But how did it even come to this? I blame Heysel.

One of the Government's main policy impositions in the wake of the previous season's escalating football-related violence was to ban alcohol on coaches taking supporters to matches. Thus, the regular mobile bar that had been an out-of-towners coach was no more. This was anathema to the gang of lads who were among its regular passengers. The likes of John B, Metzy, Maysey, Gaz, Stocksy, 'In-Town' Brown, Col 'Theakstons', Glen, Tony, Ginge, Nibs and Pozzy didn't do 'dry'. Alternative plans had to be hatched in order to skirt round the new restrictions, and they came to fruition in the shape of the aforementioned bright blue and yellow Ford Transit van. The looks on our faces as it pulled up at the scheduled pick-up spot, outside the old YEB store on Ferensway, told their own story. Discreet it was not but, with benches down both sides and designated driver Glen at the wheel, it was just the job. Off we set to Carrow Road, home of the reigning League Cup holders and a team recently relegated from the top flight.

Things began well enough, a trip over the Humber Bridge followed by a couple of 'liveners' in a Lincolnshire pub before embarking on the serious drive down to Norfolk. What the van lacked in comfort it compensated for in good banter, with the lads on board taking it in turn to rip the piss out of one another. Given an eclectic mix on board it's no surprise that the van's stereo soundtrack struggled to cater for all tastes, although I recall that The Sweet's 'Ballroom Blitz' became something of a 'van anthem'.

Carrow Road was a three-sided ground at the time of our visit, a situation arising from the need for a rebuild after the old City Stand had burnt down the previous October. The associated scaffolding meant that our view of some of the action was obscured from our position behind the goal. That wasn't necessarily a bad thing. Although I don't remember much about the game – save for City's stylish change kit of white shirts, red shorts and socks – it was another poor performance by Horton's men, as David Lamont reported in the *Hull Daily Mail*. The Tigers had been 'comprehensively outplayed' by a 'stylish' Norwich side set for promotion. The result had given them 'a taste of what is needed to succeed in the Second Division'. The Tigers' misery was compounded by the dismissal of Pete Skipper 12 minutes from time 'for use of a four-letter word'. Lamont commented that the subsequent suspension would at least allow him to rest 'a sore ankle which has troubled him for some weeks'. The reporter also accused referee Malcolm Cotton of doing his best to ruin the game but he couldn't really be held responsible for the result. The Canaries were totally dominant, with Tony Norman hailed as 'superb' on what proved his 'busiest day of the season'. Combined with 'some stout defensive work and a bit of wayward finishing from Norwich' it ensured that the defeat wasn't much heavier as 'Norwich re-enacted the siege of Mafeking'. Robert Rosario's excellent strike and Peter Mendham's 'gift' from Lawrie Pearson consigned City to a second away defeat in a week.

After the obligatory applauding of the players, we boarded our van. The original idea was to get so far home before finding a pub to watch the Barry McGuigan fight, which was being shown live on the BBC. Having our own spot of 'bovver' in the city centre as part of the undercard was not on the agenda. But that's what occurred thanks to a meeting with a couple of City 'elite' minibuses and our agreeing to accompany them off the designated route in search of some 'action'. Thankfully, when we found some, my lack of urgency in disembarking meant our not-so-keen Canaries counterparts had already taken flight by the time I was out. This was possibly a result of Wally from the Kempton wielding a pool cue to good effect (don't ask). Whatever the reason, the contest certainly didn't match up to the main event later that evening. McGuigan retained his WBA world featherweight title with a seventh-round stoppage of American Bernard Taylor in front of an ecstatic crowd at Belfast's Kings Hall.

Three nights later, City bounced back to maintain their fine record against Crystal Palace. The Tigers had lost only three of their 16 meetings with the Londoners in 36 years and they completed a hat-trick of recent wins at Selhurst with a solid 2-0 success. It was achieved courtesy of two cracking goals. Frankie Bunn netted one, with *On Cloud Seven* describing the other as 'a Stan McEwan 35-yard thunderbolt'. There are contradictory factors suggesting whether I was at the game or not. The fact I had just started a new role at work only the previous day, coupled with no diary entry relating to departure times, would suggest I wasn't among the 200 away fans in Croydon that night. On the flip side, I have a suitably creased match programme and seem to remember enjoying the glum faces of the locals as they trudged disconsolately by our coach afterwards. Strange, but when you read what happened on my next two visits to Palace it's perhaps no surprise that my presence at this one remains shrouded in doubt.

19

The Hope that Kills You

Hull 'D' UBO, Market Place, Monday, 10 March 1986

I'm on lunch break. Someone's left a Daily Express *on a nearby table. I flick through it, more in hope than expectation of finding anything about City. But I'm in luck, there's a brief report of Saturday's win at Stoke. What's more it's a very complimentary one. It even tells readers to watch out for a dark horse coming up on the blind side in the Second Division promotion race. That horse is Hull City. I smile. A smile of pride mixed with excitement mixed with trepidation. Tomorrow night I'll be at bottom club Carlisle where City can steal another march on their rivals. I think I already know how this is going to end.*

* * *

Saturday, 5 October 1985 was the date I'd long dreaded. It was the day I'd set aside to have my first driving lesson. It went as badly as expected and was followed by an equally miserable afternoon watching Stoke leave Boothferry with maximum points. 'Twas always so in my experience. At least the day ended on something of a high – the playing of 'Graveyard Stomp' heralded a return of the Meteors to the Spiders playlist. By the state of the dance floor I wasn't the only one glad to see them back! It was carnage. The word could also have been applied to events at Boothferry Park three nights later, where QPR won 5-1 to complete an 8-1 League Cup aggregate win. Hmm, not quite the 'Special Attraction' advertised on my South Stand ticket then! Horton actually felt his side had played 'as well as we had done all season for large periods'. October was proving a testing month.

Defeat by Stoke left City 12th in the table as they headed north to Roker Park for a first meeting with one of the game's ailing giants. At a time when there was much media talk about a proposed new 'Super League', Sunderland were seemingly miles away from any such competition, lying third-bottom of the Second Division following relegation the previous season and two years later would find themselves in the third tier. But they were still seen as a big fish and were under the management of former Southampton boss Lawrie McMenemy. Horton highlighted afterwards, 'The whole setup there is tremendous and our players and supporters (who by the way were tremendous) must have enjoyed the big occasion.' We did. City drew thanks to 'a superb Billy Whitehurst goal' watched by a crowd of 16,180. This figure included 'the largest contingent of visiting fans seen at Roker Park this season' housed in one half of the open Roker End terracing.

The Sunderland result gave City a lift ahead of the visit of Huddersfield, with the absence of any midweek fixture allowing time for the recharging of batteries and the easing of any bumps and bruises. It showed as the Tigers cruised to a 3-1 win courtesy of a Whitehurst brace and one from Neil Williams. Bradford were then thumped 4-1 in the Full Members' Cup before City were thwarted by a goalless draw at Shrewsbury. At the other end of the scale from Roker Park, Gay Meadow retains a place among my favourite away venues. Quaint and homely, what it lacked in size it more than atoned for in the friendliness of the local populace and the excellent riverside pub usually frequented beforehand. A crowd of just 3,587 watched the Shrews hold the Tigers and over half that number turned up at Boothferry Park the following Tuesday, to watch City's reserves in action. It was 'the biggest reserve team gate at Boothferry Park for 20 years', no doubt helped by the fact that the opponents were Manchester United. I was there, sitting in the Best Stand to see Andy Saville's penalty prove the difference. Sixteen-year-old Mark Richardson was one of the City starlets to receive the plaudits afterwards, with Horton saying his performance belied his age. What happened to him then?

2 November 1985
Football League Second Division:
Sheffield United 3 Hull City 1

Bramall Lane: Bramall Lane End, Lower Tier Terrace; no ticket; programme 50p

Attending a reserve team game was the latest first for me in a season full of them. Another came at the start of November when I boarded a 'Football Special' train for the eagerly awaited trip to old foes Sheffield United. I paid £3.50 for the privilege, although whether privilege is the right term is open to debate, as Colin Ward describes: 'British Rail what an institution! Inventor of the "Football Special", in those heady days of the football excursion. Away-day. It meant cheap travel, as much booze as you could consume and as many carriages as you could smash up on the course of the journey. If you vandalised a train really badly they would pull into a station and chuck you on another train.'[188]

---

188 Ward, Colin, *Steaming In: Journal of a Football Fan* (London: Simon and Schuster, 1989) p.9

So by 1985 things were a tad different. The booze was gone for a start. The number of police on board had also been significantly increased from the 'Special' which had taken City fans to the FA Cup tie against Blyth four years earlier. And as far as I'm aware every carriage made it into Sheffield station in one piece. The nearest I recall to anything approaching a disturbance was the sound of one of those god-forsaken 'crow-scarers' being set off some carriages further back. One thing that hadn't changed though was the suitability of station concourses for chanting. This was proved as we spilled off the train before being formed up under police escort for the march to the ground. The noise was fantastic and walking along in such a show of strength it was hard not to feel invincible. Unfortunately, City proved anything but. Hopes of ending their 15-year wait for another win at Bramall Lane were dashed in a 3-1 defeat to a Blades side in which the chief tormentor was Keith Edwards. 'King Edwards rules again' was David Lamont's headline. The former City man completed a hat-trick, with the biggest disappointment coming in the nature of the goals – 'all three coming from defensive lapses' according to Lamont.

The first was the fault of Tony Norman who dropped the ball from a long throw-in, allowing Edwards to head home. It was an awful error from the fans' favourite but still didn't deserve the torrent of abuse it earned from one disgruntled member of the massed Tigers throng, standing just in front of me. 'Fucking 'ell Norman, you useless wanker; you cunt; fuck off; you're shit. FUCK. OFF!' I thought this was a touch uncalled for but I wasn't willing to tell him. Unfortunately, somebody near me didn't quite realise just how vexed this particular individual was. 'Who scored that?' he asked. The man in front of me was on him like a flash: 'NORMAN SCORED THE BASTARD!' It suddenly went very quiet.

It didn't get much easier for Norman, who Lamont thought 'might have been able to stop the second' had he reacted quicker when a pass from Colin Morris dropped between Skipper and McEwan, 'leaving Edwards his second free header from only a few yards'. Edwards duly completed his hat-trick from the penalty spot, his seventh goal in three games after being dropped earlier in the season. Ironically, strike partner Peter Withe had been dealt with well by the City defence and, overall, Horton felt his side had played well 'without getting the right breaks'. That wasn't a view shared among the massed ranks of 'an estimated 3,000-strong army of City fans'. At least my diary reports the day wasn't a complete washout: 'Spiders afterwards with Carmo and Lee – brilliant night!' I must've 'pulled'. As usual I took my consolation where I found it.[189]

* * *

City bounced back from their Bramall Lane setback with two wins in a week. First they dispatched 'a defensive-minded Boro side' 3-1 after extra time in the Full Members' Cup northern semi-finals, before panning Fulham 5-0 at Boothferry the following Saturday. Horton termed his side's finishing in the latter as 'first-class', with McEwan bagging a brace, including one from the spot. But if this was good, the win over another London side next time out was really eye-catching. Charlton Athletic sat second in the table, unbeaten in seven matches at their temporary Selhurst Park home having won six of them. That run was ended thanks to two Frankie Bunn goals in 'a tight end to end very competitive game with chances at a premium'. In the following week's programme Horton wrote, 'Every one of my players gave a never-say-die attitude and in the end gained three deserved points. Our winning goal was

189 Match programme (Hull City v Fulham, 9 November 1985)

an absolute cracker, not just the finish but the build up to it was of the highest quality and one that will be savoured for a long time.'[190]

I've got a feeling it may have been this game and not the Palace one at the same ground that provides those memories of disconsolate home fans trudging past our bus. I was definitely there as my diary records that Carmo and I were back in time for last orders in Trog, then on to Spiders. Another example of how away trips had turned into major logistical operations, with much pre-planning needed in order to arrange meet-ups on our return to town; especially on the longer journeys. The ETA back in Hull was measured in service stations: Watford Gap (two and a half hours), Leicester Forest (two hours) or Hartshead Moor (just over an hour and a half). Phone kiosks were utilised arranging the pub of choice, with the hope then being that we wouldn't hit roadworks, traffic jams or any other unscheduled reason for delay. If all else failed, the message was simple: 'We'll meet you in Spiders.'

The coach ride itself could prove testing. Once the game had been 'all talked out', my main options for killing time were either sleep (often unwise) or listening to sounds on one of the new-fangled Walkman things I'd borrow off Gary or some other passenger. New Order and the Smiths were staple listening material. 'Elegia', 'Well I Wonder' and 'I Want the One I Can't Have' are just three tracks that instantly have me back in my own little world, staring out of a bus window dreaming of what – or rather who – might await me on the return to Hull. A bit like pre-match anticipation, this could often be followed by crushing disappointment.

For home fixtures, the fun began at noon in Trog Bar and ended by the burger van down Cleveland Street some 14

---

190 Match programme (Hull City v Wimbledon, 23 November 1985)

hours or so later. Pre-match drinking was itself a game of two halves; the first in Trog and the second in Hull Cheese, both pubs hosting a lunchtime disco and serving up North Country beer in dimpled glass mugs, with at least a third of your pint often provided by the contents of the spill tray. In terms of sounds and clientele, the pubs couldn't be more different. Trog played to its core biker crowd, Cheese was more akin to a dress rehearsal for the night, with dolled-up punters lapping up the current pop hits. Bon Jovi were one of few acts to be heard in both, while Simple Minds' 'Don't You Forget About Me' instantly has me back in Cheese secretly dreading the 2.45pm arrival of a fleet of Richardson's Cabs white Ladas ready to hurry us along Anlaby Road. Even though the pubs kicked out at three, I usually felt robbed when leaving Cheese early in order to be at Boothferry by kick-off. Reluctance to do so occasionally cost us a cab. One such occasion was December's game against a resurgent Crystal Palace. Having missed our taxi we undertook a forced route-march up Anlaby Road. As we neared the ground several minutes after kick-off, we heard a cheer go up from inside. Questions were asked. 'How loud was that?' 'Was that us or them?' 'It came from this end [North Stand] didn't it?' Then, to the tune of 'Here We Go' came the sound of 'Gow-ing ap, gow-ing ap, gow-ing ap.' Bollocks!

The game itself usually allowed us the chance to sober up before hitting the pubs again at the final whistle. Sometimes, events on the pitch were almost an irrelevance. 'Drew 1-1' constitutes the full extent of my report for November's game against second-placed Wimbledon, probably because the post-match was far more eventful. It involved a 'long, cold, damp walk into town' (due to a bus strike) and 'a crack in the face' while queuing outside Trog Bar after somebody obviously took offence at my acapella rendition of 'Dance the Bop' by the Jodimars. My pals' amusement at my misfortune was to prove short-lived: Mark was denied entry into Spiders and Carmo got ejected from the dance floor for 'wrecking rather too vigorously'. At least Lee had a good night, his successful pursuit of female company relegating Carmo and me to the floor of Mark's downstairs flat!

14 December 1985
Football League Second Division:
Portsmouth 1 Hull City 1

Fratton Park: Milton End Terrace; no ticket (£4); programme 50p

Perhaps bucking the trend at the time, the trip to leaders Portsmouth is remembered solely for the football thanks largely to it being one of City's finest away displays of the season. Pompey were in full chime and during the previous midweek had beaten Spurs in the League Cup. The Tigers had not only lost their last two games but by the time they arrived at Fratton Park they'd also lost Billy Whitehurst to Newcastle for a (then) Magpies record fee of £232,000. Many felt Big Billy's boots were too big to fill. At least the striker had enjoyed a winning send-off, courtesy of victory over Manchester City in the first leg of the Full Members' Cup northern final. Just over 5,000 were inside Boothferry Park to see City upset their First Division opponents in their attempt to reach another inaugural final, following their Associate Members' Cup experience. Frankie Bunn fired them ahead only for David Phillips to level matters but with ten minutes remaining the Tigers won it from the spot, albeit McEwan slotting home the rebound after Eric Nixon had saved his initial penalty kick.

By the Pompey trip, even this crumb of comfort had been snatched away thanks to the cruellest of defeats in the return.

There were 'only' 10,180 people inside Maine Road on a typically miserable Manchester night but, similar to Millwall, they created one of the most intimidating atmospheres I'd hitherto experienced, especially given the disappointingly small Tigers following present. City's overall lead was cancelled out by half-time and I can still see the silhouettes of celebrating Mancs perched atop the crush barriers under the Kippax roof to our immediate right. The prospect of a trip to Wembley clearly excited them. As the second half wore on, City came more into things and Horton claimed with some justification, 'Myself and all the players feel we were finishing the stronger team and had it gone into extra time we would have won the game.' We'll never know. For with virtually the last act, the hosts scored the decisive second thanks to Jim Melrose's rear end. Having been denied Wembley two years earlier, only #TypicalCity could have conjured up such a heartbreaking way to miss out on the Twin Towers this time round.

Expectations therefore weren't great as we boarded the coach for the long drive to the south coast and our mood wasn't improved despite an impressive early arrival in Portsmouth. Excited by the prospect of a jar or two, instead we were told by the local police that this wasn't an option. I imagine I wasn't the only one thinking 'six hours on a coach for this' as we were shown on to the vast open away end, paying an extortionate £4 to stand on a cold, wet terrace, completely sober and with over an hour still to go to kick-off. Thankfully, what promised to be a long afternoon was salvaged by what Horton rightly described as a 'marvellous display'.

City may have been deprived of their talismanic forward but they still boasted a back four of Jobson, Skipper, McEwan and Swann that rivalled the best in the division. They showed it during a first half in which they didn't give their hosts as much as a fleeting glance at goal. With Bunn and Saville doing their utmost at the other end to convince us that there was life after Billy, spirits rose as the game wore on. Indeed, 'Frankie Four Yards' could have had a penalty when turning Noel Blake in the box, while Saville and Neil Williams both passed up decent opportunities. However, ten minutes into the second half Billy Gilbert's deflected shot had the Pompey Chimes ringing out.

For a time the goal appeared to knock the stuffing out of the visitors; that was until Flounders's introduction 15 minutes from the end, which sparked new life into the Tigers. Just eight minutes from time came the moment that made the 12-hour round-trip worth it. We were awarded a free kick in 'Stan the Man' territory, just outside the box. A hush descended on the ground, broken seconds later by the crack of ball hitting net as McEwan's shot found its target, followed by the ecstatic celebrations of the 100 or so away fans behind the goal. We were so busy celebrating we never even saw Garreth Roberts get sent off! City held on for a deserved point and we headed home believing that Whitehurst's departure wasn't the end of the season as we'd feared. Horton described his team's first-half performance as 'the best we have played all season'. He wasn't wrong.

* * *

Christmas 1985 saw Boothferry Park host its first Sunday game. The visitors were Leeds United and, more pertinently, their supporters – allowed to travel again for the first time following the lifting of the ban imposed after Birmingham. In his programme notes, Horton wrote, 'Good morning and a warm welcome to Billy Bremner and everyone connected with Leeds United.' So, not only was the day different but we also had an early kick-off. The rescheduling was probably a condition of the lifting of the ban and it was probably the lifting of the ban that helped swell the gate to what was then a season's best of 11,852. What's more, the majority went home happy as goals from Bunn and Jobson edged City to what at the time appeared a famous 2-1 victory.[191]

The festivities had got off to a great start and they continued the following night when I headed off with the local grebs to the weekly Trog Bar rock night, followed by the monthly Live Wire event at Tiffany's. Rarely had such fun been had on a Monday – especially when Carmo and I brought the dance floor to a complete standstill as we put our own 'chicken dance' moves to use on 'Up Around the Bend' by Hanoi Rocks – but I guess you had to be there. According to my diary, Christmas Eve was 'one of my best nights round town yet' thanks to a combination of work's Christmas party, Trog Bar and a packed Spiders. City's festive period also got better when Grimsby Town were sent scurrying back across the Humber Bridge on Boxing Day. It's a game that appeals to the nerd in me for being the first to have a properly labelled Hull City home match ticket. Finally getting rid of the 'Special Attraction' nonsense, my South Stand ticket No. 2010 has the full match details printed on it. It was the first of four such 'unreserved' tickets that I have in my possession from that season (Oldham, Shrewsbury and Sunderland being the others). Mike Lyons's side were well backed in a crowd of 12,184. The Codheads were up for it, as witnessed when some of their likely lads accosted an old schoolmate of mine outside the ground. 'Where's your boys?' they asked, to which the lad in question boldly replied, 'They don't turn out for shit like you!' Surprisingly, he walked away unscathed. The Mariners didn't. Jobson scored for the second successive game and a Billy Askew goal confirmed the 2-0 win.

---

191 Bremner had replaced the sacked Eddie Gray in October

Back-to-back victories raised expectations ahead of the away game at lowly Millwall two days later. Getting there to back the team was only possible due to the football authorities having lifted another ban, this time on visiting fans at The Den. It was something that could well have been described as a dubious honour, especially given the weather, which had the game in some doubt. Few of us made the trip, just as well given that City simply froze on a frozen pitch and subsided to a five-goal humping. Horton described his team as having been 'murdered'. Thankfully, those of us there to witness it came away unscathed, which was a result in itself, as *Amber Nectar* noted somewhat wryly: 'Let's face it, in the mid-1980s if you got away from Cold Blow Lane with a 5-0 defeat and your nose still in the vicinity of your face, you'd had a decent day out.'

In fact, our self-deprecating rendition of Glenn Miller's 'In the Mood' at three down even earned us applause from the natives nearest to us. We needed something to cheer us up. Only Steve Lowndes's goal separated the teams at the break but a Robert Wilson brace and further goals from Alan Wilson and John Fashanu took the game away from City in the second half. Not one of my best away trips!

1 January 1986
Football League Second Division:
Barnsley 1 Hull City 4

Oakwell: North Stand Terrace; no ticket; programme 50p

Having ended the old year on a low, City began the new one in style by battering Barnsley in their own backyard. The *Hull Daily Mail*'s Malcolm Richardson attributed the win to 'the introduction of Brian Horton as an inspired midfield dynamo and Andy Flounders as an ultra-determined striker'. However, for many of us, it was 'Bobby Doyle Day'. Still struggling to win over a large section of the support, City's new midfield general did just that on this particular snowy afternoon in South Yorkshire.

Ironically, I almost missed it all, having once again over-indulged in the New Year's Eve riches that the east end of Holderness had to offer. Carmo had again come down for the night and, pacing ourselves better this time, we hadn't left the village pubs until 3.30am. The celebrations didn't stop there. Another hour's merrymaking in a local lad's converted loft meant we were both extremely fragile as we stepped on board Simon's bus. Given the weather and that defeat at Millwall, the temptation to miss out must have been great. Things got no better on arrival at a wintry Oakwell where shelter was hard to find on the big open terrace. But City started strongly against their high-flying hosts. Richardson said they were 'driven on by Horton seemingly wielding the whip to his galley slaves'. Pete Skipper headed against the post early on before Jobson converted Askew's corner on 12 minutes. City continued to hold sway until five minutes before the break when 'Gary Swann was adjudged to have pushed Kenny Burns to concede a penalty'. Gordon Owen 'blasted home the spot-kick'.

Suddenly, fears of another Millwall resurfaced. But there would be no need for a rendition of 'In the Mood' this time. Not once Doyle got going – as described brilliantly by Mike Scott in *On Cloud Seven*: 'Time and again he dismissed the challenges of Gwyn Thomas (yes, *that* Gwyn Thomas), removed the ball from Futcher's possession and sprayed delightful balls to City's gleeful frontline. McEwan had converted a penalty for a City lead when Doyle received the ball in the inside right position 45 yards from goal. A body swerve saw off the left-back, a turn of pace removed the centre-half from contention, and as Bobby looked up to see Clive Baker advancing from his goal line, the demi-god from Dumbarton slipped the ball between the keeper's legs and into the net in front of the travelling City hordes.'[192]

In fairness, a footnote to Scott's piece does suggest, '*OC7*'s reputation for scrupulous accuracy may be compromised by this "description", but the circumstances demand superlatives.' And anyway, that's how I also remember Bobby's belter, even if Malcolm Richardson attributes it initially to an awful mistake by Barnsley's Calvin Plummer. Mike Ring capped a superb away-day with a fourth goal. Richardson described how the City players ran 'en masse to their couple of thousand fans behind one goal to give them a round of applause' while Don Robinson 'left his seat in the directors' box to join the players on the Oakwell pitch and congratulated them one by one'. No wonder; the Tigers had mauled the fourth-placed club on their own patch where they'd previously only conceded seven league goals. Horton lauded his players' character whereas his counterpart Allan Clarke (back at Barnsley for a second time) pulled no punches with his group, saying that apart from 'three or four' he'd told the others to come and justify to him why they should pick up their wages.

Setting aside the blip at Millwall, this was a Tigers team that suddenly looked bang in form. The wins continued. A solitary Jobson strike accounted for Bradford before Jobbo and 'Cousin' Andy bagged a brace apiece in the 4-2 win over Oldham. City had climbed to sixth, a feat I celebrated in Withernsea's 'premier nightspot' Teddy's. Horton wrote, 'Hull City are now in the highest position in the league for the last ten years and a good run of results at the present time could make the end of season very interesting indeed. So let us all get together, the supporters, the players and everyone connected

---

192 *On Cloud Seven* fanzine (Issue 6, May 1990)

with the club and see if we can make First Division football a reality in Hull.'[193]

It wasn't only in the league that the Tigers roared. Almost unnoticed, they had also progressed to the fourth round of the FA Cup. What's more they'd done it the hard way, overcoming recent bogey team Plymouth after a replay in Devon. Flounders scored twice in the 2-2 draw at home, before Garreth Roberts's sixth-minute strike rewarded the 50 or so intrepid members of the OSC who'd endured a 330-mile journey for the Tuesday night replay. Braving snowstorms on the way there and back, along with 'torrential rain' on arrival at Home Park, this hardy band were at least moved under cover inside the ground thanks to the hospitality of the local constabulary, which ensured they could celebrate passage into the next round in comparative comfort. How I wish I'd been with them.

There were over 13,000 at Home Park for that replay. It was the sort of attendance that most City fans could only look at with envy. For despite their impressive form on the pitch and two decent crowds over Christmas, getting supporters through the turnstiles was proving a problem, a point picked-up on by Simon Gray in his programme piece: 'Our recent run of four wins out of the last five league games has lifted us up to seventh position and on the fringe of the promotion race. Crowds, however, remain poor. Considering the number of supporters Bradford City brought last Saturday, the attendance of 9,333 was very disappointing even though Hull Kingston Rovers were involved in a cup final and would attract some of the "floating supporters". Next week, therefore, bring a friend and let's have a really big crowd to cheer the team into the fifth round of the cup.'[194]

---

193 Match programme (Hull City v Bradford City, 11 January 1986)

194 Match programme (Hull City v Oldham Athletic, 18 January 1986)

Simon got his wish, well at least as far as the attendance was concerned. A crowd of 12,228 – almost double the season's average – were inside Boothferry Park to watch a belter of a game against Brighton. Unfortunately, most went home disappointed. The Seagulls were soaring early on thanks to two goals in the opening 20 minutes. Justin Fashanu and Terry Connor combined for Dean Saunders to score on 18 minutes and, just two minutes later, former Leeds man Connor doubled the lead. City hit back. First Roberts struck home a tremendous 20-yarder before 'Stan the Man' converted his sixth spot-kick of the season to tie things up. But with 12 minutes left and City looking likely to complete the turnaround, veteran Dennis Mortimer freed Connor to score the Brighton winner. Wembley was cancelled. Again.

In February I made my first trip to Ewood Park since that jaunt with Clarkey and his dad seven years earlier. Glen's white minibus (his toned-down replacement for that conspicuous Filling Station van) was our choice of vehicle and all the usual faces were there: Pozzy, Stocksy, Dutton, John B, Gary, Wally (minus pool cue), Rabid Ray and Col Theakston's. Finding a quiet village outside Blackburn offered the chance for a few pre-match drinks without attracting the attention of the home support or the local police. It meant we were in good spirits as we took up our positions in the Darwen End. City's home crowds may have been disappointing but the level of away support held up well and given a covered terrace could be relied upon to put down a decent barrage of sounds. This was such an occasion and our support was repaid by goals from McEwan and Bunn in a 2-2 draw. It proved the last game to be played for three weeks as the weather closed in, forcing postponement of matches against Huddersfield, Shrewsbury and Carlisle.

The Tigers finally got back into action on Tuesday, 25 February, returning empty-handed from Huddersfield for a second time in the season. After the home game against Norwich had fallen foul of the weather, City appeared to be heading for another loss at home to Shrewsbury. The visitors led 3-2 as the game entered injury time and for the first time since his appointment, I heard Horton's suitability for the job being questioned.

Dissent was in the air. All around me seats were banged shut as the restless natives made an early dart for home. I was almost tempted to join them. But remembering how I'd nearly missed Gary Swann's stunning late cup leveller against Rochdale a few years earlier, I stayed put. My reward came via 'Cousin' Andy's completion of a dramatic hat-trick to clinch a sensational 4-3 win.

The Tigers were back up to eighth and on the Saturday were headed for Stoke, a team level on points with them. With games against relegation-threatened Carlisle and Sunderland following hot on the heels, it was a sequence that could well determine whether Horton's side were genuine promotion challengers or just flattering to deceive. Things began well enough.

Stan McEwan scored the winner from close range directly in front of the 500-strong travelling support on the Stoke End terracing at the old Victoria Ground. If the feeling of elation at that point wasn't enough, the press reaction added to our enthusiasm, courtesy of the aforementioned piece in the *Daily Express*. Tuesday's rearranged trip to Carlisle had suddenly become massive. The hosts sat marooned at the foot of the table, while the Tigers were top six. Another three points on the road would put them right in the mix. We should have known better.

11 March 1986
Football League Second Division:
Carlisle United 2 Hull City 1
Brunton Park: East Stand; no ticket; programme 60p

A midweek trip to Cumbria is always an arduous one. Still, we were upbeat as we bounded off the coach at Brunton Park. Two hours later there was a somewhat darker mood in play. 'Bang goes Tigers' promotion hope' screamed the following night's *Hull Daily Mail* after a defeat that, according to Lamont, 'virtually ended' City's promotion chase. His match report made painful reading, especially given the fact that in his view – and my memory – the Tigers completely dominated the match only to throw it all away. City began poorly and only two minutes had elapsed before Baker smashed the ball past 'an angry Tony Norman'. It could have been worse. In what Lamont termed 'a comedy interlude' Swann came close to slicing into his own net and only a full-length Norman save rescued a 'farcical mix-up worthy of the Keystone Cops'.

Further danger having been averted, 'City got on with the serious business of the evening and, for the next 35 minutes were streets ahead of Carlisle'. Home keeper Scott Endersby kept his team in the game as 'Hull displayed their new slogan – everything but the goal' (cap duly doffed for that one Mr Lamont!). Bunn and Flounders, who between them had 'missed half a dozen chances', finally combined to equalise in the 75th minute, Flounders 'steering the ball through a crowded area' from Bunn's pull-back. Having worked so hard to get back in the game, City now threw it away – literally – when Swann lost possession from a throw-in and Halpin fired in a low cross that Halsall 'rocketed' past Norman. All but a few hundred in the 3,248 crowd celebrated. The Cumbrians had given themselves the faintest whiff of survival and at the same time had effectively snuffed out our hopes of promotion.

Bob Stokoe had monumentally fucked things up for me for the second time in my life.[195]

Horton was understandably angry, telling Lamont, 'I don't know what you've got to do to win but I know what you have to do to lose – we gave it to them.' He added, 'Football's a funny game but no one laughs when you've lost. Little things can cost you the game. We played well for 88 minutes and threw it away in two.' Wimbledon's win at Millwall added to City's misery. The Tigers were now 'running out of games' and Lamont termed their chances of finally achieving that 'unique appearance in the First Division' as 'slim'. Most on our coach would've gone further than that. We knew our time was up; City had missed their big chance.

Unfortunately, defeat wasn't the end of our night's woes. Just outside Penrith there was a smell of smoke and within minutes our fears were confirmed – the coach was on fire! An engine problem was the cause, leading to a three-hour stay in the nearby services while a replacement vehicle could be sourced. Our mood wasn't increased when the Official Supporters' Club refused to get our younger members home, despite having room on board. Gary (our Simon Gray for the night in the organiser's absence) recalls being told it was 'for insurance reasons'. There was nothing to do but sit and wait. When the new coach arrived it came equipped with its own video player and *An American Werewolf in London* was provided for our on-board entertainment. Sadly, even the lovely Jenny Agutter failed to lift this disconsolate Tiger-trekker's spirits, or anything else for that matter. I arrived back in Easington at 4.45am, totally and utterly pissed off.

A disappointing low-key draw at home to the Mackems rounded my birthday week off on a suitably downbeat note.

195 Bob Stokoe was manager of the Sunderland team that beat Leeds in the 1973 FA Cup Final

In fact the only high point was provided away from football, courtesy of the post-match pub crawl round town. In those days, there were very few early opening pubs in the city centre. Star of the West on West Street (near the old *Hull Daily Mail* offices) was one, opening at 5.30pm and coming complete with its own entertainment in the form of several ladies of the night enjoying an early snifter. Their occasional approaches provided quite an eye-opener for us young lads of rustic stock. From there we'd move on to Masters Bar (South Street) at six and then the likes of Dram Shop (George Street) or the Burlington Tavern (Alfred Gelder Street) at half past. It gave us a head start on those arriving for the standard 7pm starting gun. How times have changed.

* * *

If it's the hope that kills you then City ensured our death was a drawn-out one. A 2-1 win at lowly Middlesbrough had Horton claiming, 'We are back in the promotion hunt again.' The cardiograph flickered, briefly. Next up was the visit of Barnsley in front of nearly 8,000, but it was lost 1-0. Flat-lining again. A Tuesday night in Cleethorpes and Flounders's solitary strike sealed a double over the Mariners, again sparking hope. The Tigers were back up to fifth (albeit four points behind third-placed Charlton and having played three games more). Simon wasn't giving up. In his next programme piece he wrote, 'After last Saturday's setback at home to Barnsley, the Tigers stormed back by winning at Grimsby for the first time in 57 years. In front of the Mariners' largest league gate of the season (9,121) and a massive following from the North bank, our dreams of promotion were kept alive.'[196]

---

196 Match programme (Hull City v Sheffield United, 5 April 1986)

They were indeed. But only for one more game. On 5 April, those pesky Blades finally put promotion to bed courtesy of a goalless draw at Boothferry. The game coincided with my mate Big Cam's 21st, which meant it became part of the day's celebrations. Things got off to an adrenaline-fuelled start in Trog Bar where on entry we discovered the usual clientele had been replaced by a large number of 'casually' dressed visitors from the Steel City. Discretion proved the better part of valour and we made an earlier than normal dart to Cheese, from where we could depart for the game as normal. On meeting up again post-match on Ferensway we were thwarted in our attempts to go in Station Bar as it was again occupied by Sheffield football fans. Another reason why 'We only hate Sheff United'! Thankfully, these would be the last disruptions to another good night. This was just as well for the birthday boy who'd only just got over his last live football experience – that trip to Hampden Park the previous year.

The final away game of the season was a trip to newly promoted Wimbledon and involved one of Simon's legendary London all-dayers. The early start allowed for an opening time drop-off in Kilburn, from where we caught the tube south to meet up with members of City's Southern Supporters' Club in the Alexandra Hotel. Copious amounts of beer were consumed prior to the short walk to Plough Lane, with everyone in good spirits. City quashed the mood, serving up a performance totally undeserving of a decent-sized support. The 3-1 defeat left Horton fuming but we didn't let it spoil our day.

Our trawl round the capital's pubs saw us fraternising with all and sundry. These included several groups of Wimbledon fans, a gang of skinheads in traditional West End meeting-place 'Polar Bear, Leicester Square' and the revellers in our final stop, Piccadilly's Glass Blower, where a 50-strong group of us 'entertained' the locals with various ill-informed ditties.

Throw in comical episodes along the way at Pizza Hut and a nearby Ann Summers store and it made for plenty of discussion on the long ride home. Back on the pitch the Tigers rounded things off with back-to-back home wins against champions Norwich ('the best side in the division by miles') and Brighton. Horton wrote, 'I believe we have had a very good season and if we had been more consistent who knows what we might have achieved. We have proved we are as good as anyone in the Second Division and I am pleased we have proven a lot of people wrong who thought we would struggle this season.'[197]

Few among us would disagree. In barely five years the Tigers had gone from fighting for their very survival to come within a whisker of a tilt at a place in the game's top tier. As *On Cloud Seven* later recalled, City had displayed 'style and panache at home, grit and determination away' to ensure that their first season back in the Second Division had given us much to enthuse about. Making the achievement more creditable was that Horton had employed a squad of just 19 players, of whom six first-team regulars had been at City since the Fourth Division days. They had entertained us too, with a goals for tally of 65, albeit the bulk of which had come prior to Big Billy's departure. The final placing of sixth was the club's best since the 1970/71 season. A year later it would have been good enough to get them a shot at promotion via the play-offs. #TypicalCity eh?

197 Match programme (Hull City v Brighton and Hove Albion, 2 May 1986)

20

We Are Family

Boothferry Park: Saturday, 23 August 1986

'Welcome to Hull City AFC – the Family Club'. So reads the cover of the opening match programme of the 1986/87 season, the words draped across a picture showing dozens of youngsters bedecked in black-and-amber (and red). Family club? What's all that about? The theme continues inside, with details of the newly launched Hull City Travel Club, a members-only away match scheme designed to 'curb soccer hooliganism and bring back families to the game we all love'. Brian Horton states his wish is to 'have a trouble-free Boothferry Park and see if we can attract women and children back to our game'. Even the club chaplain, the Rev. Allen Bagshawe, gets in on the act, using the first of his regular pieces to explain the thoughts behind the 'family club' principles. For fuck's sake, the game's gone soft.

* * *

Ten days after the conclusion to City's first season back in the Second Division, I entered Castle Hill Hospital. My operation went to plan and as such my stay proved hugely enjoyable, especially the visits from my work and football mates that created something of a party mood on the ward. Even the immediate post-op days in ICU had their moments of light relief, such as the night the nurses rigged up a portable telly in order for me to watch England's 3-0 win over Mexico in a pre-World Cup friendly. With a newly fitted steel rod in place I was discharged on 27 May. Mexico 86 kicked off four days later. It was perfect timing. Thanks to another England rollercoaster ride there were several occasions over the next few weeks when I feared I may have to be readmitted, none more so than my decision to leap from the settee in celebration of a near-certain Gary Lineker leveller against Argentina, only to see the ball somehow fail to hit the net. I actually thought I'd broken my stitches that night!

After all the positives of the previous season, along with most City supporters I approached the new campaign in optimistic mood. The general consensus was that just a couple of quality additions over the summer really could see our dreams come true. What we didn't realise was that 1985/86 had actually constituted the high point of the next 22 years. Things began to go wrong for Horton early on in an otherwise encouraging pre-season, one that culminated in a draw against First Division Sheffield Wednesday. Unfortunately, it also saw the loss of one of his most influential players during a friendly at Doncaster when Bobby Doyle's leg was broken in a tackle from Dave Cusack. Though not many realised it at the time, the loss of this key component in midfield would ruin what dreams we had of going that extra yard to promotion and the promised land. David Lamont knew it. In his *Hull Daily Mail* season's preview, he described the triumvirate of Askew, Parker and Doyle as 'one of the most feared midfield combinations in the country'. Now, one-third of that combo was gone.

As for supporters' hopes for quality additions, changes were kept to a minimum. The Tigers made just the one summer signing, with Ray Daniel transferring from Luton Town and becoming the first black player in City colours.

It seems strange to highlight such a fact but certain sections of the Tigers' support were not known for their tolerance (remember Bradford and Oxford away). As recently as the previous April, City fans had been involved in ugly incidents involving some of Wimbledon's black players; John Fashanu being handed a banana by one, while Carlton Fairweather retaliated to 'Sieg Heil' chants by offering a mocking Nazi salute in return. Given such incidents, City's new arrival prompted much debate over pre-match pints. By the end of the season, 'Razor' – along with later arrivals Alex Dyer and Charlie Palmer – had become a firm favourite on the terraces. Elsewhere, Tom Wilson was promoted to reserve team coach from his part-time role with the youth team.

Daniel's debut came on the opening day when Ron Saunders' relegated West Brom came to town. For the first time in over a season we were allowed back in the Kempton, though in nothing like the numbers previously. 'Cousin' Andy scored early on and 'the smallest man on the field' Garreth Roberts added a second 'with a brave header' as City began in impressive fashion. The following Tuesday I made my Travel Club debut. One of the new implementations made by the club in order to try and curb hooliganism, for many games the official Travel Club would be the only coaches operating. I only joined in order to be able to access the new members-only East Stand. Still, it also meant that I was one of the 100 or so who celebrated Frankie Bunn's late conversion of a fine Garry Parker pass that brought victory at The Den – and lived to tell the tale.

The Tigers' encouraging start continued on the artificial surface at Oldham where their performance prompted home manager Joe Royle to describe them as 'easily the best' team he'd seen in the Second Division, following a goalless draw. Initially City struggled to adapt to the sand-covered plastic pitch and were thankful to Tony Norman for keeping them on terms at the break against an Oldham side playing what Horton termed 'some unbelievable stuff'. The second half saw the Tigers more dominant and only a late goal line clearance prevented Saville from sending them top. As it was, seven points from a possible nine was an excellent return and helped convince many supporters that another good season lay ahead.

City lost the next three games. Successive home defeats inside a week by Portsmouth and Plymouth were contrasting in style but similar in their effect on fans' morale. The Tigers were totally dominant in the first half against Pompey, producing what skipper Roberts described as the 'best attacking football that Boothferry Park has seen in years'. Failure to convert numerous chances was then punished by two Micky Quinn goals either side of the break. If Horton's team felt aggrieved by this midweek reverse they only had themselves to blame for the following Saturday's 3-0 loss to the Pilgrims. 'A nightmare from start to finish,' said Roberts. Sunderland away was next, a trip that again involved an entertaining excursion aboard Glen's van, which this time included a sun-soaked lunchtime in picturesque Durham. Indeed, the liquid lunch proved so enjoyable we ignored our driver's warnings that we were going to be late to Roker Park. Sure enough, we got in the ground just before 3.30pm with a City side that included on-loan defender Gary Ablett already an early goal down, courtesy of ex-Leeds man Frankie Gray. Despite a greatly improved second-half display, no equaliser was forthcoming. The Tigers had slipped to 13th and that fine start to the campaign suddenly appeared a distant memory.

* * *

Given the dip in form this perhaps wasn't the best time to finally announce a new shirt sponsorship deal that involved the word 'turkeys'. Thankfully, the second part of the Driffield-based company's name was omitted from the shirts, which now had the word 'Twydale' emblazoned across them. It was the club's third shirt sponsorship deal, following on from Hygena and Arrow Air, but was easily the one to attract most ridicule – at least until the word 'Humberside' appeared briefly in 1989. What I deemed to be an awful home shirt continued the Robinson theme of red, but thankfully with a bit more black prevalent courtesy of a horizontal bar across the chest that carried the new sponsor's name. The question now was whether or not the new Twydale-backed Tigers could bounce back from three straight defeats before supporters began drifting away again.

20 September 1986
Football League Second Division:
Hull City 3 Birmingham City 2

Boothferry Park: Bunkers Hill Terrace; no ticket; programme 50p

In a trend continued from the previous season, while City's away support was again excellent, early-season crowds at Boothferry were seen as 'disappointing'. The attendance at the Plymouth game was some 2,000 down on the 8,656 present for the opening-day win over West Brom. It was therefore thanks to a decent following from the Midlands that the attendance for the game against Birmingham was as good as it was (6,851). Unfortunately, by the midway point the majority were already voicing their discontent. A City team with Horton again playing sweeper trailed at home and had Norman to thank for it not being by more. But what happened next is the reason why this match remains memorable.

Having watched the first half from the Kempton – now a somewhat soulless place given the vastly reduced numbers –

we decided to venture to Bunkers during the interval, where we joined some of our mates about halfway up, directly behind Roger Hansbury's goal. Almost as if the season had already bottomed out and we had nothing left to lose, there was a spontaneous outpouring of what can only be termed 'passion' as the second half kicked off. For the first time in many years, Bunkers reverberated to a City support in full voice. 'C-o-o-o-me on you Uuuulll' boomed out and the team responded (okay, so a reported roasting by Horton during the interval might well have played its part too). Roberts soon swept home a cross from Ablett. A minute later Pete Skipper headed City in front. Birmingham replied immediately before an amazing sequence of four goals in five minutes was completed when Roberts raced on to Horton's pass and side-footed the ball past Hansbury for a much-needed winner. At the final whistle there was a mixture of relief and a real sense of pride in playing our part in City's win – something Horton himself acknowledged in his next programme notes. It was another day that simply demanded an alcohol-induced celebration of the Spiders variety. Instead, according to my diary, I went home 'to watch the Housemartins on BBC2'. Well, you can have too much excitement.

If this were a movie, City's stirring comeback against Birmingham would have prompted an unbeaten run that culminated in promotion. But this was Hullywood not Hollywood and after a late Andy Saville goal accounted for Grimsby in the newly sponsored Littlewoods (League) Cup, City's fortunes again took a dive. A week on from the Birmingham win it was Leeds United away. While City had been staging that impressive comeback against the Brummies, Leeds fans were again writing their own much less positive headlines in their 'derby' at Bradford's Odsal Stadium. A year on from the Valley Parade tragedy, those described by manager Billy Bremner as 'the moronic mob that use this club as a convenient vehicle for their wanton acts of hooliganism' sunk to a new low courtesy of a chip van fire at the Bantams' temporary home. On the pitch, defeat saw Leeds slip to fifth in the table and gave City fans hope of leapfrogging them.

We should have known better. The signs were there when Glen's van succumbed to a blown oil seal cap 20 miles from Leeds. Initially this was the signal for an impromptu booze-fuelled party on the hard shoulder, in which we relished the attention of the passing City coaches, including the team bus. But the novelty wore off as the wait for the RAC went on. Eventually we were helped to a nearby garage for a quick fix that we were informed should see us home. But we weren't going home. Ignoring sage advice, we made it to Elland Road just in time for half-time (there's a trend forming here). City, already a goal down, conceded two more. Roberts termed it an 'inept' performance. To compound things we broke down again on the way home and limped into Ferrybridge services to await yet more help. When it came it was not without its drawbacks – the recovery truck driver could only fit five of us in his cab. Pozzy, Stocksy and 'Scunthorpe Gaz' opted to thumb a lift. They beat us back to Hull. There is probably a good reason why my diary entry for the day concludes, 'I've never drunk as much before in Spiders.'

It wouldn't be the season's last incident-packed away trip of the type that helps make away-days so memorable. With Simon's coaches having to conform to strict Travel Club rules, Glen's alternative was a no-brainer and made for great days out spent with a decent set of lads. The new-style 'Family Club' had got themselves a new 'family' following, albeit a different one, committed to enjoying events regardless of result. This was just as well; travelling to City away was a journey full of sharp dips punctuated by the occasional high point. At least such setbacks made the odd away victory an occasion to really savour. The 3-1 win at Huddersfield, in which Saville fired City ahead inside a minute and winger Terry Curran, signed on a short-term deal, was outstanding against his former club, was particularly pleasurable. Meanwhile, the 2-0 victory at bottom club Blackburn included a debut goal from youngster Steve Corkain, a celebratory conga at one end and the burning of a Rovers scarf by home fans at the other!

Glen's van enhanced such isolated successes, as well as helping cushion the more regular disappointments. However, on the rare occasions we were forced to go with Simon, defeat on the pitch could also often mean a long 'dry' day off it too. Brighton has always been a loathsome away trip, mainly for the distance involved and the fact that City usually get a bit of a doing. It's also a trip that Simon had an unfortunate history with. The previous season he'd combined the game with another coach bound for a London weekend. Taking the latter as far as Leicester Forest services, the plan was for us to pick him up as we followed through. Unfortunately our driver was unaware of such plans and took the A1 instead of the M1. Simon was left to get a taxi into Leicester, a train to London and then, after crossing the capital by tube, another to Brighton. He eventually arrived at the Goldstone Ground halfway through the game. Unfortunately, I think I might have been the one who was supposed to tell the driver of the original plan!

Still, I certainly couldn't be blamed for the next entry into what one City fanzine would call Simon's 'magnificent seven' coach cock-ups. That came almost a year later, in November, when more overambitious planning by our organiser meant it wasn't just him who turned up late at the ground. Predicting a small take-up for the football, he decided to double up with a trip to the Motorcycle Show at Earls Court. It was a disaster waiting to happen and from the moment we diverted via Sheffield to pick up the final group of bike enthusiasts we were already running late. Jobbo had given an impressive-looking City a 28th-minute lead before we'd even negotiated our way out of London. We arrived at the game at 4.26pm, just in time to see #TypicalCity slip to defeat before then enduring another mammoth coach ride home. To say we were disgruntled by the day's events would be an understatement.[198]

13 December 1986
Football League Second Division:
Crystal Palace 5 Hull City 1

Selhurst Park: South Stand (Holmesdale Road) Terrace; no ticket; programme 60p

Although episodes like the Brighton ones cast Simon in a poor light, his London jaunts were often the stuff of legend, especially the all-dayers of the type enjoyed at Wimbledon the previous season. It was an option we chose for December's game at Crystal Palace. We left Easington at 6.30am, well before the rest of the organised football traffic. This meant relaxed rules on drinking, which in turn meant that by the time we hit The Pride of Paddington at lunchtime most of our 20-strong crowd were already well oiled. With lubrication comes inspiration and this was the day that City fans first adopted a Housemartins song for use on the terraces. Chart-topper 'Caravan of Love' was the ditty in question: 'Every woman every man, join the transit van from 'Ull. Every living City fan, join the transit van from 'Ull.' I didn't say inspiration always results in perfection!

---

198 *Hull, Hell and Happiness* (Issue 10, Aug–Oct 1990)

Somewhat unusually, we were inside Selhurst Park in time for kick-off, following refuelling stops at The Driver Bar and Travellers Fare in Victoria Station. Standing on an open terracing among a following of around 200 (not bad for pre-Christmas and given City's poor form), our alcohol-induced pre-match optimism didn't last long. The toothless Tigers were thrashed 5-1. What's more, Horton was sent off. In his autobiography he explains how he received an elbow in his face, which split his eye open: 'I ran over to the referee to ask how on earth he missed that.' Having been told by Jeff Radcliffe that he'd have to go off for treatment, Horton flatly refused, saying, 'I'm not finished here,' and subsequently launched himself 'into a reckless tackle' and got himself sent off 'trying to do someone'.[199]

Despite Don Robinson telling him afterwards, 'I rather liked that,' Horton remains ashamed of his actions. In 2021 he said, 'I fined myself a week's wages because that was the rule that I had set. Not only that, I retired myself from first team football and only played in the reserves to help the young players. Sad day.'[200]

The final whistle was only the start of our problems. On leaving the ground it soon became apparent that there was only a token police presence about and the walk to the station would be unescorted. An isolated scuffle down a nearby side street soon turned into something more serious. I'd come out of the ground with Pozzy but the last I saw of him he was landing a telling blow on one particularly aggressive Palace fan. All hell broke loose and self-preservation soon kicked in. Accompanied by Stocksy

199 Horton, Brian (with Tim Rich), *Two Thousand Games – A Life in Football* (London: Pitch Publishing 2020) p.94

200 Horton would play for the first team once more, away at Plymouth. City lost 4-0 in Neil Buckley's debut.

and Tony D (and having lost Pozzy) we reached what I hoped would be the sanctuary of the station. Such hopes were soon dashed. Moments later about a dozen of us were being chased along the platform and on to the tracks by a decent-sized Palace mob who had no intention of joining our 'Caravan of Love'. About half a mile up the line, facing the prospect of being cleaned up by the next train, we clambered up the bank and came out on to a nearby housing estate. Knocking on the first door we came to, the kindly resident – a bloke in his 20s – offered us a brew and a place of refuge while things calmed down. Directed to the next tube station we eventually arrived at pre-designated rendezvous the Polar Bear in Leicester Square.

That wasn't the end of it.

Our delight at being reunited with other bedraggled members of our party – including a laughing Pozzy – was soon tempered by the news that we now had another set of London supporters for company: Millwall. I remember that sudden sinking feeling returning to my heart and nether regions. To our relief, they turned out to be a decent set of lads and they tagged along with us for the rest of the night. Granted they revelled in our having been chased by 'the shit of London' but helped contribute to another excellent night in the capital. A chance encounter with rock god Dante Bonutto from TV's *Music Box Power Hour* topped it off for some of the lads, although I think we'd all have preferred co-host Amanda Redington. Meanwhile, I remain convinced that the lad I mistook for a fellow 1950s aficionado during the evening was actually Paul Denman, mentioned earlier in the story and one of two City fans (along with Stuart Matthewman) in the band Sade. I may have been wrong – I was very, very drunk. Anyway, despite him assuring me that he knew of no 'suitable' pubs or clubs around the area for people like me, much mirth ensued before we departed Embankment at midnight. It was 6.15am when I collapsed into my bed, my mind still racing after easily the most adrenaline-fuelled trip of the season to date.

* * *

Injuries didn't help City's cause over the first part of the season. Back in October Horton had said he had 'never seen anything quite like it', adding that physio Jeff Radcliffe had been kept busy since the summer. That said there were also some genuinely woeful performances; a 4-0 home defeat by Stoke being a particular low point. The 5-1 walloping at Palace dropped City to 15th and there was little festive cheer to follow, with defeats at the hands of Sheffield United and Barnsley. Horton has particular cause to remember the New Year's Day defeat to Barnsley. In his autobiography, he recalls how he found out on the morning of the game that Stan McEwan had been at a party the night before. The defender then compounded matters by being at fault for one of the Tykes' goals. After the game, having got the player to admit his misdemeanour, Horton told him, 'Get your boots and leave the dressing room. You will never play for me again.' McEwan hardly ever did, later joining Wigan.[201]

The weather disrupted January's fixture list but couldn't prevent a 4-0 humping at Plymouth. Jobson's goal in a draw at West Brom extended City's winless run to nine matches and by February they were only three points above relegation. As such, the FA Cup was a more than welcome distraction. That's perhaps why it even had some of us actually dreaming of the Twin Towers.

---

201 Horton, Brian (with Tim Rich), *Two Thousand Games – A Life in Football* (London: Pitch Publishing, 2020) p.95

3 February 1987
FA Cup Fourth Round: Swansea City 0 Hull City 1

Vetch Field: West Terrace; no ticket or programme

Thoughts of Wembley were very distant when the third-round draw sent City to Gay Meadow, a venue at which we'd already lost twice recently. The game was originally scheduled for 10 January but a frozen pitch put paid to it. The following day, my diary records that 'the big freeze' took hold. It would see two further postponements of City's cup tie as well as countless difficulties closer to home. My Monday commute to work became a three-hour trip each way due to heavy snow and the following morning it was confirmed that Easington was physically cut off. Our pipes froze at home and by Thursday our village shop had sold out of just about everything. Dad was even asked if our family estate car could be used as a hearse due to the undertakers being unable to get through for a planned funeral!

The roads were eventually cleared by the Friday but City's home game against Sunderland the following day wasn't so lucky. When the Shrewsbury game was again called off the following Monday, it was rescheduled for the date of the fourth round (31 January). With this being a Saturday and a time when the FA Cup still held pride of place in most fans' calendars, the Tigers were well backed. My diary reads, 'The whole crew's going except Stocksy.' We hit the popular Crown Inn just after 1pm and didn't leave until just before kick-off. Suitably lubricated, we ensured a non-stop barrage of support and celebrated as first-half goals from Bunn and Saville earned a rare away win.

City's reward was an away tie at Fourth Division Swansea and just three days later I was aboard a coach bound for the Vetch. As anyone who ventured to South Wales to follow their team in the 1980s will testify, the welcome awaiting them in the Valleys was not warm in terms of friendship. It was particularly hostile on this occasion. Given the short turnaround since the win at Shrewsbury, it was a much smaller City following that arrived outside the Vetch Field, 'a hardy band of 100' according to David Lamont in the *Hull Daily Mail*. Lack of travelling options meant that our coach contained a rare mix of out-of-towners, half a dozen City Psychos and two complete pissheads (aka Charlie P and Col Theakston's). What a combination! Leaving Hull at lunchtime we arrived late – again – though only by five minutes, which actually made entering the ground easier. Once through the turnstiles the sense of siege was palpable; a feeling that increased after just 20 minutes when City were reduced to ten men with Bunn dismissed for a reckless challenge.

The Swans fancied their chances and the vast majority of the 8,853 inside Vetch Field made a noise befitting a far bigger number. We did our best in response and just nine minutes into the second half we were in ecstasy. City's first worthwhile attack of the game saw 'Neil, Neil, Orange Peel' Williams get down the right and, from his low cross, Jobbo's slightly scuffed strike bounced up past a stranded Mike Hughes and nestled in the net in front of us. This was the cue to 'go Beirut' (as I noted in my diary). It was one of my favourite goal celebrations of the season. For the remaining 36 minutes it became the Tony Norman show as one Welshman defied everything his fellow countrymen threw at him. And when eventually beaten by Sean McCarthy, the linesman's flag came to his rescue. Norman was simply magnificent. So were City. Against the odds, they held on and at the final whistle the players ran over to our end to join in the impromptu party. So what if I wouldn't get home until 5.45am and needed to be up for work an hour later; this was the Football Association Challenge

Cup – the greatest knockout competition in the world. And we were still in it.

The following lunchtime we reconvened in The Empress to relive the previous night's events. Later that day, *Look North* did the same, with the pictures of Jobson's goal and subsequent celebrations including the sight of a luminous green-jacketed Charlie P running up and down the terracing in complete leave of his senses. That's what watching Hull City did to you back then! There's no wonder this trip has gone down as one of those still talked about years later. Four days later City beat promotion-chasing Oldham 1-0 at home thanks to Andy Saville's 'brilliant solo goal'. In 'Brian's Column', Horton thanked the 'many' supporters who had 'travelled nearly 2,000 miles' to take in the four away games since the last match at Boothferry Park. He added, 'Your support has been fabulous throughout our recent lean spell and the lift you gave the lads at Shrewsbury and Swansea was very welcome for us all. Every team has a rough time and it is only when you are having a rough time that you find out who your true friends are. Thankfully things are now starting to go our way. The FA Cup is very special to us and the current buzz around the club at the moment is unbelievable.'[202]

All disappointments of the league campaign were set aside as we prepared for a trip to Springfield Park with a place in the FA Cup quarter-finals at stake. Opponents Wigan, a division below City, were appearing in the last 16 for the first time. We wouldn't get a better chance of making the last eight for the first time since 1971. And once there, who could say what might happen? Even without the suspended Bunn, we were confident; supremely so in some cases.

---

202 Match programme (Hull City v Oldham Athletic, 7 February 1987)

We should have known better and cue another #TypicalCity day. Despite dominating the game, the Tigers crumpled to what David Bond termed 'an ignominious defeat'. Second-half goals from Chris Thompson, Paul Jewell and Bobby Campbell sent the majority of the 11,453 in attendance home happy. City fans were left to rue what was seen as the inexplicable subbing of Billy Askew at 1-0 (a move the manager later acknowledged was a mistake). It prompted boos and howls of derision from the 2,000-strong away following in the seats and on the open mud bank, as well as this wonderful analogy in *On Cloud Seven*: 'Surely Brian Horton's decision to substitute Askew ranks alongside Hitler's decision to advance on Moscow instead of invading Britain, or ITV pulling the plug on Kent Walton and the wrestling as the most calamitous misjudgement of modern history.'[203]

Many among City's support vented their anger in the town after the game, with the trouble serious enough to make the local news headlines for the next few days. Compounding our misery was news of the quarter-final draw: Wigan Athletic versus Leeds United.

The cup exit appeared to ebb all remaining life out of the season, a view reinforced by lack of a singular descriptive piece in my diary for the remaining games. Of course I didn't stop going. Along with around 5,000 others I attended every home match, with the exception of the goalless draw against Huddersfield on 5 March, which I missed due to a short stay back in Castle Hill. Despite sitting in the bottom three throughout March and April, a run of just two defeats in 16 matches eventually lifted the Tigers clear of danger. Not that many of the others were won. The aforementioned Terriers game was one of eight draws in 11 games, five of

---

203 *On Cloud Seven* fanzine (Issue 3, November 1989) p.10

which were goalless and three of which came at home against so-called Yorkshire rivals. Surprisingly, the visit of Leeds didn't warrant a single diary reference, while the Easter Bank Holiday Monday game against the Blades prompted only a slightly bizarre note suggesting that the visitors had 'taken the Kempton'. Surely not!

Andy Saville netted the only goal in the first of the five victories that eventually helped secure safety. Policeman James Bannon's 2014 *Sunday Times* bestseller *Running with the Firm* records the presence of just 21 away fans among the Tuesday night crowd of 5,327 that saw City beat Millwall 2-1 – and that figure included two undercover cops! Brighton and Shrewsbury were also beaten before City ended the season on a high at home to Crystal Palace. 'Crystal Crash' was the bold headline in the *Sunday Mirror* of 10 May 1987. 'Dream is over for sad Coppell' ran the strapline as the report described how his 'brave attempt to bring Palace back to the top flight fell apart when all they needed was a victory'. A win at Boothferry Park would have seen the Eagles sneak into the last play-off place at the expense of Ipswich. Instead they were thumped 3-0. New signing Alex Dyer 'took only 99 seconds to upset the big contingent of Palace fans who had made the long trek north, claiming a simple tap-in after Andy Saville's effort had struck a post'. Another simple finish early in the second half made it two for Dyer before 'Neil Williams put the final nail in the Palace coffin when he raced away, on to a pass from the excellent Peter Skipper. Midfielder Williams outpaced a square defence and claimed a first goal in more than seven months.' The fact that City's win denied Palace a place in the inaugural promotion play-offs was wonderful payback for our harrowing experience at Selhurst Park back in December (and I'm not ashamed to admit that reports of City fans getting the better of exchanges outside the ground prompted a cheeky smile too).

Four nights prior to the Palace finale, we'd also taken great delight in seeing City effectively send Grimsby down thanks to Andy Saville's brace in a 2-2 draw. The striker's second goal in particular was a wonderful effort, completing a turnaround from a goal down. Only Richard Jobson's inadvertent own goal denied City the sweetest of victories. Saville's goals reinforced his reputation as something of a cult hero among our matchday group, not least because it was largely thanks to him that I'd bothered to make as many away trips as I did in that period of post-Wigan despondency. The complimentary seat tickets obtained by Stocksy courtesy of his friendship with Sav encouraged me to take in away games I might otherwise not have bothered with, including Birmingham, Reading, Ipswich, Stoke, Barnsley and Bradford. This friendship also resulted in the surprise arrival of a get well soon card to my bedside at Castle Hill, signed by every member of the City squad. It remains perhaps the most treasured souvenir of a season in which City finished 14th in the Second Division, which if you've been paying attention you'll now know is their accustomed position.

21
London 0 Hull 5

The Adelphi Club: Saturday, 21 November 1987

It's a cold night but that City win has warmed us up. I've just got the beers in and we find a seat. I'm looking forward to this. I've heard this lot were excellent last time. Later on we're heading on to Sugar Shack at the Welly so even though I'm missing Spiders, it's got the makings of a good night. We sit there, chatting and people-watching the mainly student crowd. On the table there's a postcard. It's advertising tonight's support, they're local. The card promises us 'the most musical, leg-shaking cake in the world', with ingredients such as various ounces/tablespoons of 'beat', 'mixed groovy bass', 'sweat and soul', 'funk and guts', 'sweet singing' and, finally, 'every spicy ingredient from Marvin Gaye to Bon Jovi'. The result is described as 'a cake so tasty, fruity, dancy and bouncy, you'd just have to call it THE MIGHTY STRIKE.' I like the sound of it. Tonight may have just got even better.

* * *

The mid-1980s witnessed something of retro fashion resurgence. Encouraged by the hype surrounding the release of Julien Temple's *Absolute Beginners* movie and a clever advertising campaign on the part of Levi jeans, the styles of the '50s and '60s were again back in vogue. After Nick Kamen was filmed walking into a launderette on Boxing Day 1985 and stripping off to Marvin Gaye, it became cool to wear the same jeans as your dad. Hitting on a winning formula, sales of 501s and vintage chinos rocketed over the next two years, accompanied by a host of soul classics. Sam Cooke, Ben E. King and Percy Sledge all enjoyed chart returns on the back of such clever advertising. TV exposure also played its part in *Top of the Pops* returns for Nina Simone, Jackie Wilson and Eddie Cochran, while hip film soundtracks like *The Big Town* simply reinforced the nostalgic feel. Even contemporary teen idols Bros and the aforementioned Kamen got in on the act, sending the retro-look mainstream. Soon, town on a Saturday night was awash with lads sporting Brylcreemed locks and Levi's. The upshot for those of us already immersed in such fashion was that we no longer stood out like sore quiffs; well, not as much as we used to!

It is ironic then that at the same time as the retro Levi's look was courting public favour, my personal musical direction was bringing me bang up to date. Of course I was still buying 'old' stuff – it had become a hard habit to break. The Kent reissue label's 6Ts soul output was a particular obsession at the time; I remember buying Chuck Jackson's *Mr Emotion* LP and thinking it was the finest collection of songs I'd ever heard (especially as I'd just been dumped again).

But I was also getting more and more into the contemporary sounds played by Peel and heard at Spiders. The release of the *NME*'s *C86* compilation got me into a whole new world of jangly guitars. Within a couple of years The Subway Organization had replaced Nervous Records as my label of choice, while by 1987 four cassettes had come to dominate my listening on long away trips: the Smiths' *Meat is Murder*, *Kettle* by the Chesterfields, New Order's *Substance* collection and the majestic *George Best*, debut release from Leeds indie popsters the Wedding Present. There wasn't a slap bass to be heard. Even more sacrilegious perhaps to my rockabilly mates was the fact that it wasn't just the cool nighttime sounds that I was beginning to enjoy. My post-op convalescence in the summer of '86 brought greater exposure to the previously demonised Radio 1 playlist. So-called guilty pleasures like Madonna's 'Papa Don't Preach', 'I Can't Wait' by Nu Shooz and even Wham's 'The Edge of Heaven' will instantly have me remembering the Hand of God and a sizzling week in Great Yarmouth far more than The Bodines' 'Therese' could ever do. I can feel my old Spiders mates disowning me as I type!

* * *

The summer of 1986 was also one in which a band from Hull transcended the gap between pop and pap. After much anticipation, the Housemartins finally hit the big time when their third single 'Happy Hour' became their first top-ten hit, peaking at number three in June. Not only was it the perfect daytime radio tune and a guaranteed nightclub floor-filler, its clever lyrics maintained the band's reputation among serious musos and indie fans alike. Their wonderfully titled debut LP, *London 0 Hull 4*, appealed greatly to the City-supporting fraternity who now had an upwardly mobile local band to latch on to along with their upwardly mobile football team. I'm guessing that Tiffany's, Samples and Rosie O'Grady's in Yarmouth weren't the only places that June to have the deejay fielding requests to 'play the Housemartins for the lads from 'ull'. Despite billing themselves 'the fourth best band' in the city (behind Red Guitars, Everything But The Girl and the Gargoyles) by the year end those 'nerdy student types' whom I'd not paid any real attention to at the previous year's Rag Ball would be celebrating a number one hit, courtesy of their acapella version of 'Caravan of Love'.

But why the Housemartins above all the other laudable bands already mentioned in Chapter 13? Ian Mowforth puts it down to the fact they never appeared 'short of ideas or frightened of hard work, constantly travelling the country in the early years to perform their own brand of pop music' (or 'agitpop' as it was often termed). Charismatic frontman Paul Heaton also gave the band an ability to convert new fans, with Mowforth citing a 1984 gig at the Herne Hill Half Moon as an occasion when it helped 'win over a hostile audience who had only come to see Line Design, London's then-current favourites'. The Housemartins were soon a fixture on telly and daytime radio. They were the city's finest musical export since Bowie's backing band Spiders from Mars and joined an extensive list of 'Hull celebrities' that had hitherto included Tom Courtenay, David Whitfield, Ronnie Hilton, Maureen Lipman, Norman Collier and, er, Roy North who, when he wasn't sticking his hand up a fox, could sometimes be found sporting Hull City pullovers while presenting a kids pop programme on ITV. Although somewhat removed from the band's well-publicised political views and despite the fact their lead singer was a Blade, I and many others couldn't fail to be seduced by their overall likability. I suppose it was the sheer 'Hullness' of it all (despite the non-Hullensian origins of three of the four band members).[204]

Given my admiration for what the Housemartins were doing for the city, it's sad to recall that my first face-to-face encounter with Paul Heaton was something of an embarrassment. It occurred a couple of years later inside the Adelphi, the venue at which the band not only cut their teeth but where they signed their first record deal with Go! Discs. There to see a couple of local bands, I'd moved towards the exit

---

204 *From Hull to Eternity* fanzine (Issue 1, Autumn 1990) p.17

at the end of the gig to begin handing out stickers advertising the new Hull City fanzine I was co-editing. Heaton, who was there as a punter, took particular interest in the bag in which these stickers were stored, on the outside of which was a trade label urging people to 'Buy British: Ensure your country's future'. Within a few moments he'd convinced himself that I was peddling far-right literature. A ridiculous argument ensued, with nothing resolved except the fact that any hopes of an interview for the fanzine had well and truly disappeared.

My next encounter with him came a couple of years later in the salubrious surrounds of LA's toilets on student night and resulted in a far more productive conversation, which revolved around the relative merits of our favourite Serie A teams (Inter Milan and Fiorentina in case you're wondering). Suffice to say he didn't recognise me from our previous tête-à-tête but I chose to take his engagement in friendly dialogue as a form of vindication of my previous stance!

* * *

The confidence emanating from the city's music scene suggested by *London 0 Hull 4* was reflected at the start of 1987 in the release of a new monthly music paper. *First Edition* first hit the streets in March. Edited by Alistair James, it followed in the wake of *Kindred Spirit* and *Swing* and described itself as a 'rash attempt to produce a music paper that covers the Hull scene'. Other media outlets followed suit. Angus Young's weekly 'Ace' column in the *Hull Daily Mail* and Hull-born rock critic Phil Ascough's offerings in the *Yorkshire Post* provided further reading on local bands. On the radio, Jan Bers and Jeremy Hibbard co-presented *On the Rocks*, a Monday night collaboration between local BBC stations Humberside and Leeds that performed a wonderful service in getting local bands welcome exposure.

Hull was happening again – and much of it was happening in the Adelphi Club.

Situated at 89 De Grey Street off Beverley Road, the Adelphi is rightly known as the 'Musical Capital of Hull'. Not only on account of the local bands that have played their first gigs there but also due to the who's who of groups to have visited the venue on their way to the top. A former terraced house built in 1888, it narrowly avoided the Luftwaffe bomb that obliterated three of its neighbours during the Hull Blitz. The resulting gap would become the club's car park. As Dave Haslam writes, 'The Adelphi is unlikely to win design awards or attract a glitzy crowd.' Terms such as 'rough and ready', 'shabby chic', 'ramshackle' and 'idiosyncratic' have been variously used to describe it, while the Guana Batz reportedly once said that there wasn't room to swing a cat in the Adelphi but you might find a few dead ones! That said, it has earned itself a glowing reputation that extends nationwide. Having previously been the Victory Club and Institute, the De Grey Club and the Civil Service Sports and Social Club, it was renamed the New Adelphi Club by new owner Bruce Bramley in the early 1980s. But it was when Paul Jackson bought the venue on 1 October 1984 that the transformation into one of the best-known venues on the gigging circuit began. It soon became the perfect place in which to indulge in my broadening musical horizons.[205]

Initially, the layout consisted of two downstairs rooms, one a front taproom located to the immediate left of the main front entrance, the second a larger concert room at the rear, with a maximum capacity of about 220. The bar was located between front and back rooms, the serving hatch to the front room providing panoramic views of the concert hall.

205 Haslam, Dave, *Life After Dark – A History of British Nightclubs and Music Venues* (London: Simon & Schuster, 2015) p.395

Toilets were to the rear of the building and could only be used by walking through the concert room. The upstairs of the building, accessed through a private door just inside the main entrance, provided living quarters for the club's subsequent owners.[206]

Unlike the time of the *Tube* special, the bands covered in March's *First Edition* were ones I could now get to see live for myself. There were plenty to go at. As the opening editorial said, the Housemartins were 'only the tip of a very big multi-talented iceberg', a fact borne out by reference to around 50 local bands in the self-styled 'mish-mash' debut 20-page issue. Among them were some of city's other big hitters including the Gargoyles (see Chapter 17) who at the time of *First Edition*'s release, were about to launch the video for their latest single, 'Madmen from the Planet Sex'. Typifying their anarchic existence and irreverent approach to life, *First Edition* reported how filming had been carried out in Pearson Park and in a city warehouse 'without permission', where shooting was 'interrupted by an inquisitive park-keeper demanding to know what on earth was going on'! In a later issue, James claimed the video 'would have been a dead cert' for an appearance on *The Tube* but unfortunately the programme had been 'toothless … ever since Jools got canned for being so groovy'. The programme's fifth and final series came to a close on 26 April 1987. The Gargoyles rumbled on for some time longer.

Looking back to that spring of '87 and those early *First Edition* issues, it appeared that Hull had a number of serious contenders seemingly poised to follow in the footsteps of the Housemartins. 3-Action were one set of 'likely lads', having recently clinched a live Radio 1 session for a 'reputedly impressed' Janice Long on the back of their politically

---

206 The New Adelphi website, https://www.theadelphi.com/history/

orientated '(Don't Lose That) Stealin' Feelin'' single. This followed favourable press reviews of debut release 'On the Journey of a Lifetime'. *Record Mirror* compared them to the Jam and the *NME* called them 'serious but not pompous', while *Melody Maker* described another of the band's songs, 'I Can't Help Myself', as 'an attempt to bring the Fall and the Four Tops together'. 3-Action enjoyed high-profile support slots on the road with the Soup Dragons and on the Housemartins' Happy Hour tour.

Another trio, Pink Noise, matched the Housemartins in having an exiled Blades fan for a lead singer in Steve 'Sam' Pickard. They also appeared on the verge of something big. Described in the *NME* as 'unwedded bliss', the 'fast and blatant songsmiths' were about to embark on a national tour, which included well-known London venues the Harlesden Mean Fiddler, Dingwalls in Camden Town and The Sir George Robey in Finsbury Park. In addition, they used the proceeds of a third-place finish at the Scunthorpe Rock Open to record the demo that would eventually result in what Ascough termed the 'mini-classic' single 'Thin End of the Wedge'. Recorded on the Gargoyles' Reasonable Records label, it was distributed by Red Rhino. Guitarist Nick Clay later wrote on his website, 'We got some good press from the *NME*, *Melody Maker* and *Music Week*, and some radio play. We prepared for superstardom.'[207]

Among the others tipped for the top were the Planet Wilson (formed from the ashes of Red Guitars and signed to Virgin), Tough Guys Don't Dance ('one of Hull's best supported bands and (one who) have earned themselves a national following with gigs across the country'), 'ultimate noise purveyors' Death by Milkfloat (soon-to-be-faves of John

---

207 Clay, Nick, www.nickclay.karoo.net/pinknoise.htm

Peel for who the band would record a couple of live sessions), Coyote Trap ('one of Hull's most exciting live bands' featuring former Housemartin Hugh Whitaker), the Velvetones (featuring soon-to-be Housemartin Dave Hemingway) and new kids on the block Looking for Adam.

In addition, a new Hull-based musical agency was established (via the Government's Enterprise Allowance Scheme) to help these bands get noticed. This business, called Modest Music, was keen to promote the 'fistful of terrific bands ready to sign record contracts today and who could easily slide into the charts'. Within a few weeks they had 'well over 20 bands signed up' including 'some from further afield', such as Malcolm's Interview of York and a certain band from Sheffield called Pulp. It all seemed oh so positive. Five years on and I'd be writing the same sort of thing in successive City fanzines – and with the same end result.

* * *

One band only briefly referenced in that debut issue of *First Edition* was the Company. Ian 'Biz' Beharrell (vocals/guitar), Bob Stephenson (bass), Carl Lilley (drums), Gary Andrews (percussion/backing vocals) and Brian Lilley (sax) formed in the summer of 1985. Their live debut followed in October, alongside The Velvetones, 3-Action and Coyote Trap at what Biz termed as 'some left-wingy type benefit'. Despite 3-Action telling them they were 'the best thing seen in Hull for two years', all was not well in the camp and, after just the one outing, Brian Lilley was asked to leave 'for being out of tune as fuck'. A sax-less performance in the main bar at Hull University was followed by regular gigs at the Adelphi where Paul Jackson billed them as 'Hull's answer to the Style Council' or 'A Stylish Hull Council'. In April 1986 Derick Wilson, former trumpeter with fellow Hull soulsters the London Boys joined the band, to be followed by drummer Glenn Smith (also ex-Zoot and the Roots). When Andrews was then replaced by the returning (and 'by now sax god') Lilley the overhaul was complete. It was with this five-piece line-up that the Company formed part of a Hull clean sweep at the prestigious 1986 Scunthorpe Rock Open, finishing ahead of Pink Noise as runners-up to the Gargoyles.

Their reputation was enhanced further via Adelphi gigs with Happy Mondays and the Farm, a well-received stint backing the Jazz Defektors at Hull University's Christmas Ball and a support slot on tour with Zoot and the Roots, which included a sell-out gig at Manchester International. High-profile shows followed with Radio 1's Andy Kershaw at Scunthorpe Baths Hall and legendary soul man Eddie 'Knock on Wood' Floyd in Manchester. A first demo ('Love's Got A Hold'/'Out of the Blue') and a live session for the BBC's regional *On the Rocks* programme ensured 1987 got off to a winning start. By this time Pete Yeadon had replaced Wilson on trumpet and, in September, came a change of name, due to the Company already being in use. Thus the Chevalier Brothers' gig witnessed the official unveiling of the Mighty Strike. Within another two years they would become my musical fix as far as the city of Hull was concerned and – in my opinion – their arrival had pushed the Housemartins down to fifth.

21 November 1987
The Chevalier Bothers | The Mighty Strike
The New Adelphi Club; no ticket

Initially I didn't make the link between the group I'd previously heard good things about and the one appearing on the support bill this particular November night. Ostensibly

I was at the Adelphi to see the Chevalier Brothers. Formed in 1982 and inspired by the jump-jive of Louis Jordan, Slim Gaillard and Louis Prima, their sound was contemporary enough to gain them various TV and radio appearances, among them *The Old Grey Whistle Test*, John Peel and even on Jasper Carrott. I'd got into them during my hepcat days but I'd missed their debut Hull gig earlier in the year and was determined not to repeat my mistake. The venue was in stark contrast to the 'sophisticated' clubs these sharp-suited hipsters were more accustomed to but nonetheless their first show 'drew many new faces to De Grey Street' and had been really well received. I approached the Adelphi in good heart, perhaps more so than Darren and Carmo who still bore the scars of a Back to the '40s show I'd dragged them to at the City Hall the previous week. I'd convinced them that the Chevalier Brothers would succeed where the Herb Miller Orchestra and local Hot Club swingsters Ain't Misbehavin' had failed. I was proved right. The Ronnie Scott's regulars lived up to their *Live and Jumping* reputation and put on a 'Barnyard Boogie' of a set, which prompted many of the audience to try emulating the famous jazz dancers from London's Wag Club. In short, they were excellent. As were their support act.

The Mighty Strike suited a northern crowd. A tight, musical arrangement, topped off by the livewire Beharrell out front who can relate to his audience. In addition to his 'teaspoons of sweet singing', he was a bundle of energy throughout the set. Tracks like 'No Money', 'Making Ends Meet' and the original demo single 'Love's Got a Hold' couldn't fail to get your feet tapping. As described in *First Edition*: 'A danceable, brassy soul number [that] has that certain appeal that almost everyone will enjoy. Musically reminiscent of Dexy's Midnight Runners ... if you like to dance then this is for you, if you can't dance then just listen, you won't be disappointed.' You certainly needed to listen as Biz's stunning vocal range came to the fore on the searing ballad, 'You Strip My Skin', one of the songs featured on the new six-track demo tape that soon found its way into my collection. Although it would be almost six months before I got to pursue my interest, I came away from the Adelphi really believing I'd seen Hull's next big thing and knowing that Billy Askew's goal against West Brom wasn't the only knockout strike I'd seen that day (see Chapter 22).

A ridiculous eight months after their Adelphi gig, I caught TMS (as their distinctive publicity cards promoted them) courtesy of a session on *Great Northern Rock*, a local music programme that was aired across the four Yorkshire BBC radio stations (Humberside, Leeds, Sheffield and York). Preceded by the 'Love's Got a Hold' tape, the band played five live studio tracks – 'I Can't Control It', 'No Money', 'Making Ends Meet', 'Strip My Skin' and 'Hold On a Little Longer'. The songs sounded as good if not better than I'd remembered them the previous November and I recorded the session for posterity on what became the first of six *Humber Rumba* compilation tapes.

I got to see them live again three times in quick succession in August 1988. Two of the gigs were at the Adelphi and the final one an open-air (and consequently very damp) Rocking the Gardens event in Queens Gardens. The first Adelphi gig had been a last-minute affair but the second one, two nights before the Queens Gardens show, was the pick of the three. Helped by a superb support act in the form of York soul band Still Dancin', the Hull boys upped their game accordingly and blew the crowd away. All those Kent compilations I'd acquired were brought to life by a combination of Biz's guitar and vocals, Mike Wilson on bass, Glenn Smith on drums, (the)

Tim Allison on keyboards and the superb brass section of Jim Hague's sax and Pete Yeadon's trumpet. The whole night had me thinking that Jimmy W and those other suedeheads I'd got to know at Spiders really did know their musical onions. This rocking redneck-cum-indie jangler had now discovered his inner soul man.

Unfortunately, despite their undoubted talent and popularity, TMS never achieved the fame many felt was richly deserved. A couple of London gigs even attracted major record company interest but with no end result. Even after the band's eventual split, Biz would always appear to see opportunity knock briefly before it scurried away. An impromptu appearance on stage with the original Temptations at Hull City Hall and a series of productive meetings with Acid Jazz owner Eddie Pillar both offered hope of that life-changing moment that would never be realised. In the event, fame of sorts came via a less likely source – Biz being the bloke on the back of a truck singing the theme song for the soft drink sponsors of Sky Sports's Premier League coverage.

The story of the Mighty Strike is typical of many Hull bands of the time. They were in good company – if you excuse the pun. Far from *London 0 Hull 4* being replicated in the charts, the sounds of the city remained hidden from the population at large. Indeed, if ignoring successors the Beautiful South, it would be the early 1990s before the next band from the city followed the Housemartins into the pop charts. As for the rest, well, perhaps Nick Clay spoke for them when he summed up his own experiences on his blog: 'The best bit ever about being in the band was lying in the bath in 1987 and hearing John Peel play "Thin End of the Wedge". Pretty much everything else was downhill from there on, really. Pink Noise never got on *Top of the Pops* … We never had people write our names on the back of their leather jackets. No one from the national music press ever sought out our opinions on the important matters of the day, and we did not define a generation with our music and stance. But it was a laugh.'[208]

208 Clay, Nick, www.nickclay.karoo.net/pinknoise.htm

22

The Long Goodbye

Elland Road: Saturday, 12 September 1987

Wow! Just wow! What a feeling. What a team. Two-nil. At Leeds! Top four now and unbeaten since the start of the season. What's more we look unbeatable. I smile at Chris D from City Southern Supporters' Club, a man who grabbed Gary so hard immediately after Parker's goal I thought he was going to do him some serious damage! He's still acting like he's possessed now! As for Gary, fully recovered from that bear hug, he's beaming broadly. 'This is it Rich, this is our year!' I know Gary, I know. Promotion to the First Division for the first time ever is surely a mere formality.

* * *

My diary entry for Saturday, 15 August 1987 would suggest that I wasn't exactly bursting with enthusiasm for the new season, which had begun that afternoon. It reads, 'Yes, football's back and I'm bored already.' Perhaps 'frustrated' would have been a better choice of adjective, with City having surrendered a two-goal lead in an opening-day draw against Blackburn Rovers. It would appear I wasn't alone in my apathy given an opening-day Boothferry Park crowd of just 6,426, the lowest since the return to the Second Division. How that mood would change over the course of the next five months as Horton's Hull City again had me and many others daring to dream. Up to second in October and having only suffered four league defeats by the turn of the year, the Tigers looked genuine contenders for at least a play-off spot. Then the wheels came off. Just one win in a wretched 17-match run to the season's end would see them eventually finish 15th and with arguably their most successful manager since Cliff Britton in the mid-1960s having departed the scene.

How the hell did it come to this?

To be fair, my personal lack of enthusiasm in August was very much at odds with the noises coming out of Boothferry Park that summer. The way the previous season had ended created a genuine optimism within the club for the coming campaign. There was a major sponsorship deal with Mansfield Brewery and in his first programme notes Horton wrote, 'I feel a great mood about Boothferry Park.' That was certainly the case when Frankie Bunn and Peter Skipper fired them into a two-goal lead against Blackburn. Still, our frustration at the eventual dropped points was soon forgotten, with the opening game forming part of a ten-match unbeaten start to the season. It was a sequence that brought wins against some of the division's big boys, including Aston Villa, Manchester City and, most satisfyingly of all, Leeds.

The first win of the campaign came at the end of August against a slow-starting Villa but not before hard-earned draws at Stoke and Crystal Palace. The Tuesday night game at the Victoria Ground was the first of several away fixtures that I opted to watch from the seats. Garry Parker gave City the lead in a game that saw Tony Norman set a new club record of 177 consecutive league appearances, a tally stretching back to Rochdale away on 14 May 1983. It was also his 350th game for the club in senior competitions. The following Saturday, Billy Askew marked his 200th senior appearance at Selhurst Park in a game in which England under-21 international Parker was on target again, along with Frankie Bunn, as City scored twice in the first five minutes of a game for the first time since the visit of Blackpool, again in 1982/83. Frustratingly, they failed to hold the lead in either game, with Palace's comeback creating yet another piece of match trivia: Andy Gray became the first player to score two penalties against the Tigers since Malcolm Partridge's brace of spot-kicks for Scunthorpe in that 4-4 draw I'd missed back in October 1981.

Unfortunately, the Palace game wouldn't be remembered for the football. For the second time in south London, the 90 minutes spent on the terraces was perhaps the least memorable part of another eventful London all-dayer. Moments after the final whistle had confirmed a third successive City draw, a more one-sided outcome outside the ground resulted in another chase down those railway lines. This time there was a reception committee awaiting us at Victoria Station, courtesy of the boys in blue, after we'd been picked up by a train whose driver was extremely worried about a group of 'idiots' walking on the tracks. We were lined up on the platform as if on inspection and informed by the police commander as to the precise idiocy of our actions. He didn't seem to want to know about the reasons for our being there (probably because he found it as funny as those Millwall fans had the previous Christmas). We had our details taken, which included the disclosure of any notable scars or birthmarks. When duly disclosing mine the copper's eyes widened. 'Where'd you get that?' he asked.

'Millwall, 1984,' I replied.

'You're joking!'

'Yeah I am. Castle Hill Hospital, 1985.'

He saw the funny side and I was allowed on my way to enjoy another night in the Big Smoke, part of which this time involved gatecrashing a wedding party aboard a boat on the Thames. Luckily the bride and groom didn't see the need to involve the police this time round and we were all accounted for as we hopped on the bus at Embankment just as Big Ben struck midnight.

The Tigers' unbeaten start and a big visiting contingent attracted a crowd of 8,315 to Boothferry the following week for the game against Aston Villa, and those of us who'd been at the three previous matches could finally celebrate a win. It was earned the hard way mind, City rallying after falling behind to a 'ridiculous' penalty to win 2-1. Pat Heard equalised before a wonderful Alex Dyer goal at the Bunkers end clinched matters. Afterwards, two Villa fans were sat in front of me on the bus heading back to town and I admit to revelling in their obvious discomfort. They weren't interested in trouble, hurriedly covering up their claret-and-blue favours as they alighted the bus – earlier than needed – with one telling his mate to watch out for the 'Ull bashers' waiting for them in the station. I smiled, knowing exactly how they must have felt. I didn't hang around to see if their fears were to prove founded as I was headed for a 5.30pm start in Star of the West. City's win was to be enjoyed to the full, something that was helped at Spiders by an introduction to a gorgeous Austrian au pair called Gabi. As my diary records, 'Carmo rated her as "hot stuff" but she wasn't nearly as hot as Alex Dyer!' It was good to see I was getting my priorities in order.

Or was I? I have absolutely no recollection of the long Bank Holiday Monday trip to Swindon which yielded a goalless draw, nor much of what Horton acknowledged as a 'slightly fortunate' 2-1 win over Bournemouth that lifted City up to fourth. Perhaps it was the fact that Gabi had kept in touch? Or perhaps the slap I received inside a nightclub in Scarborough, The Other Place (having decided to celebrate City's lofty position with the wrong choice of female company), had erased them from memory. One thing's for sure; I knew where my priorities lay the following weekend.

12 September 1987
Football League Second Division:
Leeds United 0 Hull City 2
Elland Road: South Stand Terrace; no ticket; programme 60p

As David Goodman writes in *Look Back in Amber*, despite City's unbeaten start and despite the fact that Leeds were struggling, 'It was still a tall order to take Leeds on in front of their own fans.' As such I suspect I wasn't the only one who travelled to Elland Road that day fully expecting our first defeat of the season. How wonderful it was to be proved wrong.

Following the mishaps of the previous season, we played it safe this time and travelled by coach. I was unable to drink, having picked up a virus that required antibiotics, but at least my sobriety meant I could fully appreciate what unfolded before my eyes. Unlike the previous two visits, which had seen us housed in the lower tier of the Lowfields, we were allocated the full South Stand, which not only helped the atmosphere in an 18,205 crowd but also ensured we got a brilliant view of what Goodman rightly terms 'two sublime goals' (check out YouTube if you don't believe me). Firstly Alex Dyer showed typical dexterity to evade several would-be challengers before passing the ball into the net from close range, then Garry Parker thumped home emphatically from just inside the box after 'Diego' Bunn's run had been half-halted, leaving City fans screaming for a penalty for handball. Screams soon turned to delirious cheers. The aforementioned YouTube footage only shows the briefest glimpse of the celebrations behind Mervyn Day's goal but take it from me, it was full-blown Tiger mayhem.[209]

The final whistle signalled only City's second win at Elland Road and their first since 1921. It was thoroughly deserved and wonderful in its execution. No wonder we were getting carried away, so much so that when Gary told me we were going up, of course I believed him. Gary knows his football. To be fair, even Horton appeared genuinely excited. In the following week's programme he wrote, 'The win at Leeds was absolutely magnificent and everyone I spoke to after the game was very complimentary about the side. I said to the lads before the game that the likes of Elland Road are the places to prove to everyone that we are a good side and the players certainly proved that. The atmosphere was tremendous and I must thank our fans for giving us such a fantastic backing and obviously playing their part in a fine victory.'[210]

City sat fourth in the table that evening, just a point behind both leaders Crystal Palace and second-placed Barnsley, with only goal difference placing them behind Bradford. The Leeds game had provided an obvious highlight of a memorable seven-match unbeaten start but things were to get even better. Three successive home games extended the unbeaten run, with the third of them seeing Hull thump a Manchester City side that had been slow finding form after relegation from the top flight. A Tuesday night crowd of 9,650 saw a Bunn brace help the Tigers to a 3-1 win in the teams' first league meeting for 36 years. Parker added the third and Horton's side were up to second spot, just three points off new leaders Bradford. Heady times indeed. All those August doubts looked a million miles away.

---

209 Goodman, David, *Look Back in Amber* (Manchester: Parrs Wood Press, 2005) p.98

210 Match programme (Hull City v Shrewsbury Town, 15 September 1987)

Prior to the win over Manchester City, the Tigers had visited the Blues' more illustrious neighbours in the first round of the League Cup. Coming on the back of the impressive start to the season, it was an optimistic group of lads who gathered in Hull Cheese that particular Wednesday lunchtime before heading off over the Pennines. Despite it being midweek, Cheese was packed and rocking. Loads seemed to be going. Old Trafford hadn't been visited since the mid-1970s and an estimated 5,000 fans made the trip (sources at the ground would later say it was well in excess of that figure, with only Newcastle and Everton reputed to have taken more). Our hosts certainly hadn't anticipated such numbers, with the ensuing chaos prompting this from the Tigers Supporters' Association in their programme piece for the return leg: 'Having commented favourably about Manchester United's reputation and facilities, it is worth mentioning the chaos and disorganisation that greeted many of the thousands who travelled from Hull for the game, arriving before 7pm, only to miss the kick-off. Obviously, the fans were blamed as usual, for not setting off earlier and not having tickets, but as long as supporters are treated with such disregard by clubs, particularly one of such high status, the game of football will continue to have problems. If it had not been for the relative good nature of the queuing Tigers' fans, an ugly situation could have developed.'[211]

I was one of the lucky ones who were inside the ground before kick-off but I can remember being moved along continuously as several extra pens had to be opened behind the goal opposite the Stretford End, with more and more City fans trying to access the ground. The level of noise laid down was impressive. In their programme piece the official

---

211 Match programme (Hull City v Manchester United, 7 October 1987)

Hull City Supporters' Club wrote, 'As some Manchester fans said after the game, it was some of the best support they had seen for a visiting team all season and such teams as Arsenal, Chelsea and Newcastle United have already played at Old Trafford.' Sadly, it went unrewarded in a five-goal drubbing, albeit four of them coming in the last 20 minutes. A week later a shadow United squad completed a 6-0 aggregate win against a City side that included youngsters Andy Payton, Leigh Jenkinson and Les Thompson. The crowd of 13,586 included far too many who I felt had only come to see the visitors. Of course, I remained convinced that this would all change the following season when we'd be mixing it with such teams on a weekly basis.

The resounding League Cup defeat aside, the win over the other Manchester outfit left the Tigers as the only unbeaten team in the Second Division. Indeed, just one more game was required to equal the club's best start to a season and that was at Sheffield United, a team sitting just three places off the foot of the table with only two wins in ten games. It had #TypicalCity stamped all over it and so it proved. Despite Bunn's early headed goal, City lost 2-1. The winner came with nine minutes left and constituted the first time the Tigers had been behind all season. In his next programme notes, Horton wrote, 'To say we were dejected in the dressing room was an understatement.' Those of us who were by now battle-hardened veterans of matches against the Blades probably expected it. After all, there's a reason why 'We only hate Sheff United'.

The Tigers roared back in style. A Les Thompson goal on his debut saw off Ipswich at home in the Second Division's match of the day between second and third. It 'epitomised' what Horton had previously wrote about 'team spirit throughout the camp'. He said, 'The players are working hard for each other, encouraging younger players, but above all, believing in themselves.' This was further reinforced by wins in back-to-back Yorkshire derbies. An injury-hit City team won 3-1 at Barnsley on the Saturday then 2-0 at Huddersfield the following Tuesday to maintain second spot. Ahead of the next home game, Horton wrote, 'You will have seen that the lads are fighting for Hull City and you the supporters. The overall support from the fans, both home and away, speaks for itself. The lads are proud of you, we hope you are proud of them.'[212]

The Tigers had been second for five games but defeat at Plymouth in a game we billed as 'Gary's Birthday Bash' dropped them a place. Three goals inside the first 22 minutes effectively settled the game with Andy Saville's 34th-minute reply providing scant consolation for the 200 or so travelling fans. Our disappointment at the result was compounded when attempts to celebrate our mate's big day with a few sparklers resulted in us exiting the coach sharpish due to fears of a fire on board!

Three nights later, City's biggest crowd for three years – 15,443 – watched what Horton termed a 'first-class display of football by both sides' and a 'great advertisement for the game' in the goalless top-of-the-table clash against Bradford. For a season that had started as 'boring', it was proving anything but.

The big games kept on coming. In November we travelled to Middlesbrough for another second versus third summit. Ayresome Park was at its raucous best with a crowd of 15,709 seeing Stuart Ripley's goal win it for the Boro. It was a day when some of City's 'elite' made the news, courtesy of pre-match trouble and the depositing of cards proclaiming 'Congratulations you've

212 Match programme (Hull City v Leicester City, 24 October 1987)

just met Hull City'. The atmosphere wasn't much friendlier inside the ground. This was the year of the Cleveland child abuse scandal and we were determined to milk it for all it was worth. 'Sex case, sex case, 'ang 'im,' ang 'im, 'ang 'im' was the chosen ditty of most of the City fans aimed almost incessantly at the locals in the South Stand to our left. The content of those chants must have been lost on the City manager who wrote, 'The support at Middlesbrough was tremendous. Almost 2,000 of you travelled up north last weekend and to hear you singing right up to the final whistle was quite emotional. In defeat you were behind the team which made the lads realise that Hull City supporters are very special.'[213]

Monday's *Hull Daily Mail* wasn't quite so complimentary. Its full front-page story was headlined 'Travelling thugs left calling cards'. I also fielded a call from my workmate Mark informing me he wouldn't be in due to having 'a bug' – one that involved an appearance in Teesside Magistrates Court. Despite defeat, City stayed third and in his programme notes for the visit of West Brom, Horton said, 'We are in our current position in the league, not because of sheer luck, but because we have earned the right to be there.' His players responded by preserving their unbeaten home record. A wonderful goal by 'smooth operator' Billy Askew delighted the vast majority of the 7,654 present (including match ball sponsor Paul Denman for all you pop-pickers). As I headed off to a fantastic Saturday night at the Adelphi and Welly Club, there was a real spring in my step. Life couldn't get much better.

By the time Reading visited Hull a fortnight later, City had slipped to fifth courtesy of defeat at Millwall and a few days later Frankie Bunn completed a £90,000 move to Oldham in what Horton termed 'a mutual decision'. The

213 Match programme (Hull City v West Bromwich Albion, 21 November 1987)

manager went on to say, 'Both players and supporters know what is required to gain promotion. Team strengthening is our priority at the moment.' Perhaps crucially he added 'getting the right player at the right price' into the mix. A few days later former England international winger Peter Barnes 'opted out of coming to Hull City at the last minute because he wanted to try his luck in America'. Successive 2-2 draws against Reading (in which the Tigers came from two down) and at lowly Shrewsbury where Horton bemoaned his team's 'luck and a run of the ball' brought further frustration. However, he remained confident, billing December's visit of Crystal Palace as 'a top-of-the-table clash' even though his team were by now eighth in the table, albeit level on points with fifth-placed Manchester City. He was perhaps right to be so bullish. Parker and Dyer were on target in an 'entertaining' 2-1 win over Steve Coppell's side before Dyer again and Pat Heard secured a similar win away at an Oldham side basking in the glory of the previous week's win at Maine Road; 1987 had ended on a real high note.

While City's home form remained impressive, their inconsistency away from Boothferry was proving costly. It did so again as the new year dawned. After the impressive win at Boundary Park, a 5-0 thumping at new leaders Villa (with Withernsea-born Stuart Gray in their starting line-up) saw City slip back to eighth. Things went awry from the moment Heard missed a penalty against his former club at 0-0. Midfielder Andy Gray and substitute Warren Aspinall bagged a brace apiece, with the other goal coming from Scottish striker Alan McInally. A crowd of nearly 20,000 was inside Villa Park, including a big City contingent. I nearly wasn't among them, thanks yet again to New Year's Eve in Easington. I hadn't rolled in until five in the morning and was dead to the world four hours later when Gary (one of several lads crashing over) stuck his head in to say, 'Er, Rich, I don't want to worry you but the bus to Villa goes in half an hour.' With hindsight I'd have been better off rolling over and opting for more kip.

3 January 1988 (morning)
Football League Second Division:
Hull City 3 Leeds United 1
Boothferry Park: South Stand; ticket £4; programme 50p

3 January 1988 (afternoon)
Stones Bitter Championship First Division:
Hull FC 2 Hull KR 11
The Boulevard: Gordon Street Terrace; ticket £3; no programme

Given the hiding at Villa Park there was some trepidation the next day as we did the usual Saturday night pub route and discussed prospects for the Sunday lunchtime meeting with a by this time in-form Leeds. Inside Spiders, which perhaps unusually for the first night after New Year's Eve was packed, the talk was not only restricted to the field of play. Rumours were rife about Leeds fans having been spotted in the 'new town' and large numbers of them having procured tickets for the home ends. Such stories always sat better on a couple of Pan Galactic Gargle Blasters.

Had there been any Leeds fans around us in the South Stand the following day, they would have probably vacated their seats after half an hour. City simply tore their opponents apart in an exhilarating first-half performance. Bunn's replacement Andy Payton set the ball rolling with his first goal in senior football. Jobson and Dyer also scored, while Williams and Roberts both spurned good chances. BBC's *Look North* coverage had Harry Gration describing Billy Bremner as likely being 'apoplectic' about his side's defending. The majority of the 14,694 crowd weren't, we were ecstatic. Even Peter Swan's solitary reply before the break proved mere consolation. Yes, 'mere consolation'. We'd completed a comfortable double over Dirty Leeds. What a start to the day.

If the football had always been on the agenda for this particular Sunday, the second part of my sporting double bill had been more of a late addition, probably following an agreement hatched over a pint or two and one that probably sounded brilliant at the time. It was to reciprocate Darren's rare excursion to a City match. Hence, instead of seeking the sanctuary of home or pub after exiting the South Stand at Boothferry Park that particular cold, wet afternoon, barely an hour later I was to be found on an open terrace at The Boulevard. It was the first of the season's rugby league derbies and the first oval-ball game I'd attended since the 1980 Challenge Cup Final. A lot of things had changed in the meantime, not least my choice of team.

Since that day at Wembley my relationship with rugby league had been a fractious one. For much of the time I'd pitched my tent firmly in the anti-rugby camp. 'We all agree, football is better than rugby' was a ditty that had been given a regular airing on the Boothferry terraces during City's post-receivership renaissance. Gradually, though, my increased time spent in the company of Rovers fans prompted a shift in attitude, especially when coupled with continued anti-City snipes from those mainly of a black-and-white persuasion. Indeed I began to even entertain the idea of attending another game. Another 'derby' appeared the most fitting opportunity, even if this one carried little of the glamour of that unique day in May 1980.

Referring to Wembley, Anthony Clavane suggests that 'although it prompted a revival in both clubs' fortunes, the final itself had the feel of a last hurrah'. By this particular January afternoon, that post-Wembley revival was over. After back-to-back titles in 1984 and 1985, Rovers' fortunes were definitely on the wane. Defeats in the John Player Trophy Final and at Wembley the following season signalled their last flirtation with silverware. The hosts were in a similar situation. Although still involved in the Challenge Cup (wherein they would lose to Halifax in the semi-final), their last trophy win (the Yorkshire Cup in 1984/85) was one that didn't look like being replicated any time soon. This was a meeting of two mid-table teams and one that never looked like attracting the 25,326 attracted to Boothferry Park for the all-Hull John Player Special Trophy Final three years earlier.

Still, a season's best crowd of 8,186 was in attendance at The Boulevard. As at Wembley it proved a game of few scores. Garry Clark's effort in the corner furthest from where we stood proved the decisive one. Mike Fletcher converted and added another two goals, with Wayne Parker dropping a one-pointer. Gary Pearce's penalty constituted Hull's sole reply to leave the home side in the relegation zone. For those like us travelling back across the River Hull, the 11-2 win and Rovers' elevation to seventh capped an excellent day. For me it also marked the tentative beginnings of another sporting love affair, with the team from Craven Park. If only I'd known then that what I'd just witnessed was to prove the highlight of the Robins' achievements for some time to come.

* * *

The new year had brought a new job. With thoughts of a career in the RAF having cooled over the time of my operation and recovery, I'd headed back to my first work experience, the oil and gas industry. I took up a clerical position on the same terminal at which Dad worked. The pros were plentiful: it was on my doorstep, it was better paid and as long as there was enough gas out there it offered the possibility of seeing me through to retirement. In addition there were a few familiar faces around to help me settle in, I had a gaffer who liked to take his team for a lunchtime pint and there was also a very active social side. Indeed, at first glance it appeared that the only drawback was my initial inability to master a temperamental coffee machine.

Along with more money in my pocket, Stocksy's ongoing ticket tie-up with Sav allowed me to take in almost every fixture to the end of the season. That proved something of a mixed blessing as things took a dramatic turn for the worse. City went 13 league games without a win and would be left very thankful for their form over the first half of the season. The run was prompted by a harsh FA Cup exit at the hands of First Division Watford, one that eventually saw the Tigers edged out at the third time of asking, 1-0 back at Vicarage Road. Gates of 12,761 (Vicarage Road), 13,681 (Boothferry) and 15,261 (Vicarage Road part two) again illustrated the appeal of the world's most famous cup competition at the time. The Hornets would go on to reach the quarter-finals, losing to eventual winners Wimbledon. Frustratingly, City had more than held their own in all three meetings. Even a narrow defeat at play-off rivals Blackburn in a game that according to my diary saw 'running fights down the street' wasn't seen as critical. A couple of blank Saturdays to the month's end offered City the chance to regroup and go again. It didn't happen.

A 7.10am start and a six-hour coach journey to Bournemouth in February to see a 6-2 defeat stands out as a particular low point. 'Spiders packed but too sober to enjoy it,' was my diary postscript to the worst result in ages. A goalless draw against Stoke then preceded four straight defeats, the first of which saw Sheffield United complete a double of ending City's unbeaten records away and at home. There's a reason why we only hate Sheff United. Making it worse was the fact it was a real smash and grab, with Horton saying his side should have had the game won by half-time and adding, 'Sheffield only had three chances all game, and scored twice.' Almost pre-empting further disappointment, ahead of the game the manager had written, 'The last few weeks have been frustrating in many ways, this is mainly due to the fact that we haven't been playing league games on a regular basis. This I believe has contributed to our slight stutter in form. Also our lack of luck in the transfer market seems to have given you the impression that we are not having a real go at promotion. I can assure you this is not the case. As I've stated before, if we do not manage to get any new faces, the players we have got will do their utmost to get this club back into the promotion race.'[214]

By the end of March, top scorer Garry Parker had been sold to Nottingham Forest, something that Horton would later regard as 'a fundamental mistake'. Indeed, he says, 'Had he stayed at Hull for another couple of months, our season might have ended better and I might have stayed at Boothferry Park.' City never looked like replacing him, despite unveiling four new arrivals. First through the door were fiery midfielder Ken de Mange (from Leeds) and Peter Barnes – a target back in the autumn – who finally joined from Manchester City. Then just before the deadline, young full-back Wayne Jacobs arrived from Sheffield Wednesday along with the one signing that genuinely excited City fans, 'King Edwards' who re-joined from Scottish club Aberdeen for £60,000. At least this move offered promise of addressing the team's goalscoring

---

214 Match programme (Hull City v Sheffield United, 27 February 1988)

problems and Edwards began well enough on his second debut, at Filbert Street, wheeling round the back of the goal to lap up the cheers of those of us behind it after announcing his return with a typically well-taken finish. Unfortunately, it wasn't enough to prevent an eighth defeat in ten matches.[215]

Since the Stoke game, City's only point in six had come via a home draw against Plymouth. Successive draws at Birmingham and then against Middlesbrough hinted at a possible upturn but not for long. The all-ticket Easter Monday game against promotion-chasing Boro attracted a rare five-figure crowd of 10,752 to Boothferry Park and the usual shenanigans outside. Only the heroics of Tony Norman prevented the visitors completing a double. The Welsh international keeper produced excellent saves to deny Paul Kerr (twice), Bernie Slaven and Trevor Senior. At the other end, Barnes and Edwards came closest for City in an entertaining affair. Two days after the Boro stalemate, City lost 2-0 at Terry Dolan's promotion-chasing Bradford. They were now 15th in the table.

Despite the disappointing run of form, there was no danger of relegation and although there were a few murmurs of dissent among the Boothferry faithful, Horton still appeared to retain the backing of the majority of City supporters. Don Robinson didn't see it that way. Although the manager had publicly stated ahead of the Boro game, 'From now until the end of the season we will experiment with formations and players in an effort to get things back on the right lines again,' when he included several youngsters for the rescheduled visit of Swindon on Tuesday, 12 April it was a gamble that would have massive repercussions. In front of the lowest home gate of the season, 4,853, the Tigers began well and led through a goal

215 Horton, Brian (with Tim Rich), *Two Thousand Games – A Life in Football* (London: Pitch Publishing, 2020) pp.99–100

from youthful winger Jenkinson, in for the stalwart Garreth Roberts. Unfortunately, the visitors levelled before the break and in the second half, as Mike Scott described in a 2007 fanzine piece, 'City capitulated horribly and were spanked 4-1. It seemed that no amount of tinkering could change things.' The defeat extended City's winless run to 13 – a figure that would prove extremely unlucky for Horton, as Scott writes: 'City chairman Don Robinson was reputedly furious with this embarrassing cuffing and flew into a rage after the game, inviting Horton to resign immediately after full time. On learning of this the City players accepted full responsibility and pleaded with Robinson to reverse his rash decision. Don calmed down and sought out Horton, apologised for his haste and offered to reinstate him at the helm. Horton – a proud man – summarily refused and resigned from his job.'[216]

In his autobiography, Horton acknowledges that there had been 'a few rumblings from the crowd' but was still taken aback when Robinson immediately summoned him to his office. 'Suddenly, I knew what was coming,' writes Horton, who then went off to tell Dennis Booth, his wife and parents before his chairman came into the manager's office 'looking upset'. Robinson told him that he had been 'absolutely crucified' by the players, a fact borne out in Richard Gardham's interviews years later in *The Decade*. Therein the likes of Garreth Roberts, Pete Skipper, Richard Jobson and Keith Edwards describe their dismay at the news. Skipper believed it was 'reaction in the stands' to the Swindon defeat that prompted The Don to act in the manner he did. He said, 'The performance of the players was poor. We didn't do our job and let the manager down.' Tom Wilson recalls being 'staggered' at subsequent events, while Jeff Radcliffe simply

216 *Amber Nectar* online fanzine (now defunct)

referred to it as 'a sad night'. It was even sadder for me as it was one of very few games I missed all season. I don't remember the reason why, I don't think there was any female involved so can only put it down to a combination of logistical issues and City's poor form. Having turned the radio off immediately after the final whistle it was Wednesday morning before I heard the news. Like most fellow fans, I was in complete shock. It's fair to say that nobody had seen it coming.[217]

2 May 1988
Football League Second Division:
Hull City 0 Millwall 1
Boothferry Park: East Stand Terrace; no ticket; programme 50p

Dennis Booth and Tom Wilson were entrusted with the job of overseeing things to the season's end. Their first game in charge came 11 days later. The Tigers humped Huddersfield 4-0 to complete their first win since that memorable defeat of Leeds. It simply lent further credence to the view held by many fans that the players had let their previous manager down. There was little else to report as the season drew to its close, with the exception of the May Bank Holiday visit of a Millwall side bound for the First Division. The game attracted national coverage, especially among the tabloids, and had 'potential for disorder' stamped all over it.

The visitors arrived needing a point to clinch a place in the top flight. It was a scenario that caused much unease throughout the country. Back in January, Harry Harris, the *Daily Mirror*'s chief soccer writer, had used the headline 'Please God Don't Let Millwall Win Promotion' after their 10,000-strong following descended on Highbury for the

217 Gardham, Richard, *The Decade: Ten Years that Transformed Hull City AFC* (Self-published, 2019) pp.54–55

first time in 80 years for an FA Cup third-round tie, with predictable results. It wasn't only the domestic game that was on the minds of people like Harris. The rise of Millwall and their notorious following was beginning to threaten the prospect of English clubs being allowed back into European competition after the post-Heysel ban.

In the event it turned out to be quite a low-key affair, although not quite as low-key as Millwall fan James Bannon recounts: 'No one was interested in any trouble. Everyone was behaving themselves.' Such a view goes against other accounts from the day. Still, the lack of large-scale disturbances was just as well given the number the visitors brought. If the big turnout had been anticipated, their choice of pre-match pub most certainly hadn't. Away fans traditionally stayed near the station or up near the ground (although as previously mentioned Sheffield United lads did once venture into Trog). Our meeting point for the day, Dram Shop on George Street, had been selected precisely because it *wasn't* a typical matchday pub. That was my first mistake. In those pre-mobile phone days there was little could be done if the original plan was found to have a flaw. Hence I had no hint of what was to follow as I approached the place just after opening time. Nearing the pub, I could see it looked unusually busy. Fuck me, I thought, City have got some boys out today. That was my second mistake. As I approached the door I was stopped by a couple of bouncers.[218]

'Where you from pal?'

'Hull.'

'Okay, in you go.' And I did, making my third mistake in the process.

'Cheers. I thought it was full of Millwall for a minute.'

218 Bannon, James, *Running with the Firm: My Double Life as a Football Hooligan* (London: Ebury Press, 2014) p.202

'It is.'

Too late. I was already through the door. On getting to the bar I ordered a pint and laid my recently acquired newspaper out on the bar. It was one of the red tops, the ideal prop for the 'I usually come in here for a lunchtime pint' role I was trying to convey. Across the back page was a headline screaming 'Ban them' or something similar, with an accompanying story about calls by some top-flight clubs to block Millwall's anticipated promotion. The bloke to my right immediately picked up on it and beckoned his mates to get in on the act. They gave out exaggerated laughs, which I assumed was purely for the benefit of me and any other poor unsuspecting City fans who'd made the same mistake I had. I laughed along nervously, while flicking round the pub for familiar faces (there were none) and draining my pint in record time. I made a hasty exit, heart racing but underpants still remarkably unsoiled. The bouncers laughed as I brushed past them on the way out. Tossers!

Without a clue what to do next I jumped in a cab and went straight to Three Tuns (the nearest pub to the ground and usually seen as a safe option for home supporters). I'd had enough excitement already for the day and was in the ground well before kick-off. Bannon describes the atmosphere at the game as 'like that of a carnival' helped no doubt by Kevin O'Callaghan's 11th-minute penalty, which proved the only goal of the game. When it went in, pockets of celebrating Londoners were to be seen all around the ground. Thank fuck the Kempton was members only! It was one of those rare occasions when defeat didn't bother me. The final whistle blew and Millwall were now somebody else's problem. As for City, their campaign ended with a goalless draw at Reading that doesn't even warrant a mention in my diary. Attending a Howlin' Wilf and the Veejays gig at the Adelphi and getting 'blown out' by someone called Tracey at Spiders was obviously of far greater importance.

As the dust settled on what really had been a season of two halves, all conversation among City fans harked back to that night in April. Years later, we still debate it. Writing for *Amber Nectar* in 2013, Matthew Rudd described Horton's sacking as having been 'discussed and revisited more than any other dismissal of recent vintage, simply because it came marinated in impetuosity and was followed by a succession of bosses clearly not up to the job'. Described as 'irascible', it's true that he had gained a reputation for being over-strict, especially when imposing fines on younger players for bookings picked up in reserve and junior games and of course what was effectively his 'sacking' of Stan McEwan. Selling Bunn and Parker had also counted against him. Regardless of this there's no doubt that Robinson's decision was made, in Rudd's words, 'through rage rather than reason'.

It was a sad, untimely end of tenure for the man who had taken City back up to the Second Division and had come pretty close to going one better, as well as leaving the club in a far stronger position than he had found it. Although Horton reveals that he'd 'felt things shifting beneath his feet' in the run-up to his sacking the timing still took him aback. He told Richard Gardham, 'The reserves were doing well, the youth team was doing well, and we had money in the bank for a recruitment drive in the summer. The club was in a good state.'[219]

In contemplating life after Brian, it was impossible not to consider what a magnificent ride the past four years had been. Even allowing for the final league position of 15th, the

219 Horton, Brian (with Tim Rich), *Two Thousand Games – A Life in Football* (London: Pitch Publishing, 2020) p.101; Gardham, Richard, *The Decade: Ten Years that Transformed Hull City AFC* (Self-published, 2019) p.54

most recent season had seen some of the best performances I'd watched from a team in black-and-amber. Horton's eye for a bargain in the transfer market had secured some shrewd signings, he'd nurtured some very good youngsters from within and – one of the things that really endeared any manager to me – he was always quick to thank us, the supporters.

I even had first-hand experience of this, following what I felt to be unjust criticism of him and the players by a section of fans. I was moved to share my thoughts in the *Hull Daily Mail* during the early part of 1988. The letter was published and a few days later an official envelope arrived through the door from The Hull City Association Football Club plc. In a hand-written note, Brian Horton thanked me for my 'very constructive letter'. He added, 'I think that people take as much notice when letters like yours are published as my continual articles. I like you feel if people got behind players it would help them far more.' He finished by thanking me for my 'valuable support'.

And to think, back in the summer of 1984 I'd written him off before his team had even kicked a ball. Not to mention my suggesting that he 'do one' after that tonking at Derby. Tell you what – let's store those thoughts in that cupboard with all the other skeletons.

Epilogue

Breaking Up Is Hard to Do

Wembley Stadium: Saturday, 17 May 2014

The minute Leona Lewis breaks into song is the cue for the tears to well again. Almost immediately I'm back with Mum in our front room at 10 Turmarr Villas on that May afternoon in 1972. Back then I just wanted to get to the actual football. Today, I'm soaking up every last drop of the occasion that is the FA Challenge Cup Final. 'Abide with Me' is a major part of that. My thoughts again turn to Mum. She'd have loved seeing City in the final. I also think of those dearest to me for whom – perhaps for one day only – Hull City Association Football Club again looms large in their lives. I look around at the 'sea of black-and-amber' and I wonder if things can get any better than this. Then City go two up.

* * *

The summer of 1988 brought things to a head. From being sat in Tyrolean bars embarrassed at images of England fans rioting at the Euros across the border to spending countless days following another painful year in the history of Yorkshire County Cricket Club, I came to the conclusion that spending my whole life watching underachieving sports teams wasn't all it's cracked up to be, especially when I had what appeared to be an attractive-looking alternative.

In response to much Friday night cajoling down the local I had taken up the option of lacing up the boots. After eight years of watching football on Saturday afternoons, I was going to start playing the game again. So in August 1988, I signed East Riding County League forms for my village team. And as for those inner doubts that tried telling me I was making a big mistake, I assuaged them with the belief that I could still get to see a fair few City games, including all early-season and midweek matches, along with any Saturdays when Easington United were without a fixture. I convinced myself that I wasn't ending my hitherto full-on relationship with the Tigers – it was simply in need of a cooling-off period.

Of course I'd be lying if I try to pretend now that City's poor end to the season hadn't also had a bearing on my decision. Still reeling from Brian Horton's dismissal, I could see nothing but trouble in store for whoever the new man in the hotseat might be. The coming campaign promised to be one of transition at best. What's more, the ongoing problems with the Kempton and an overall decline in numbers turning out suggested that the halcyon days were over. Sadly – and much to my shame – I was about to become the very embodiment of the view expressed by David M. Woods in his notes for the Bank Holiday game at Bristol City three years earlier: 'Unfortunately for the Tigers they have to contend with two famous rugby league clubs in Hull Kingston Rovers and Hull as well as the fickle local public who, while responding to success as witnessed by Hull City's attendances in the late 1940s and middle 1960s, tend to disappear to a greater degree than at most other teams when their side begins to struggle.'[220]

Woods's words had riled me at the time but now I was the living embodiment of them, one of Hull's 'fickle local public'.

220 Match programme v Bristol City (8 April 1985)

Ironically, another meeting with Bristol City 20 years later would further reinforce his opinion.

As the summer progressed, most supporters thought Dennis Booth would be a shoo-in for the manager's job. Not only had he overseen team matters after Horton's sacking, he'd been allowed to spend £100,000 on Watford defender Steve Terry during the summer (a move that would eventually see fans' favourite Pete Skipper depart to Oldham). Don Robinson had other ideas and instead appointed Eddie Gray. Yes, *the* Eddie Gray. The man whose skills I'd done my best to replicate down the left wing for Easington boys was now in charge at Boothferry Park. According to David Goodman, Robinson wanted someone who wasn't 'too close to the club'. It turns out Gray was a hero of his too and although The Don later admitted to having 'done no research on him really' it was the 'name in his head' he went for. Leeds manager at the time of that first visit with City back in 1985, Gray had recently overseen Rochdale's escape from relegation and was keen to take on a bigger challenge. It was an appointment that immediately had me rethinking my Saturday afternoon priorities, as did the arrival of Andy Medcalf at my place of work.[221]

A Withernsea lad, Andy was on internship from Stafford University and within a week or so was floating his idea of introducing a Hull City (and local music) offering into the burgeoning world of football fanzines. It was something he'd been working on at Stafford with fellow exiled City fan Ian Websdale. The result was that in September 1988 I was stood at the works photocopier overseeing the lunchtime production of the first issue of *Hull, Hell & Happiness*, for which I'd also contributed a couple of articles. Over the next four years I

221 Goodman, David, *Look Back in Amber* (Manchester: Parrs Wood Press, 2005) p.102

became a fully fledged 'purveyor of subversive literature'. My fanzine portfolio would include the aforementioned *HH&H* plus *From Hull to Eternity*, *Look Back in Amber* and to a lesser extent, *Tiger Rag*. This involvement brought me into contact with those inside the club, thanks to numerous interviews with players and management, along with a not-so-welcome summons from The Don, after we'd printed something of which he didn't approve.

Fanzine co-editorship also led to appearances in the local press, on local radio and even on the fledgling BBC Radio 5 Live where I spent a wet Wednesday evening in the company of Mark Radcliffe talking Hull music and the Zenith Data Systems Trophy. Most satisfying of all, the fanzines appeared to heighten the credibility of supporting City at a time when, quite frankly, it took a brave man (or woman) to do so. Although fortunes on the pitch rarely lent themselves to enjoyment, some of the stuff we produced via our irreverent publications certainly did. Granted, it wasn't all sweetness and light; I vividly recall one end-of-season encounter at West Brom which served as a sharp reminder that we didn't speak for *all* Hull City fans (not that we ever claimed to). But in the main we came to act as a sounding board for a lot of them at a time when things on and off the pitch weren't at their best.

Having already committed to Easington for the 1988/89 season, I combined my fanzine role with playing on a Saturday while always managing to get to enough City games to keep my hand in. This dual role was helped by Andy asking me to concentrate more on the music side of things, leaving the detailed football discussion to those still attending every Saturday. Thus I became further immersed in the local music scene, trying to take in everything from live bands to specialist club nights. I even got to be a small part of it, courtesy of being in the Chip Shop Boys (one of only three Hull bands at the time 'guaranteed to sell out the Adelphi' – ask Jacko if you don't believe me!) and as one half of Young, Amber and Black who in 1992, along with 'toaster' Leon, recorded the best Hull City anthem never to make it to vinyl. Fact (as I believe youngsters say today). In addition, I enjoyed burgeoning friendships with some of the leading local lights, from Hull dance guru Porky B (the man behind the legendary Pork Recordings) to Cheryl P (one-half of hit pop duo Scarlet). Throw in a list of acquaintances from among the host of bands and individuals desperate to put their city on the musical map and it proved hugely enjoyable – far more so than what was happening at City.

At the time of Brian Horton's departure, nobody could have envisaged just how far-reaching the consequences of his chairman's impetuous decision would prove. The answer came courtesy of another long-running decline in the fortunes of Hull City AFC. A quarter of a century would elapse before there would again be anything to celebrate. In the intervening period supporters would experience recurring disappointment on the pitch, combined with extremely desperate times off it. False dawns and shattered dreams were accompanied by protests and lock-outs. Average attendances fell back to around the 3,000 mark, fewer than the number who'd watched City's previous seasons in the basement. The threat of extinction, first felt by the Tigers of Hull in 1982, loomed large again and again. For some of us, the root of it all could be linked back to that snap decision made by The Don in April 1988.

It would have been much better for my story if the subsequent arrival at Hull City of a former boyhood idol had led to promotion to the top tier of the English game. Instead, Eddie Gray became the first in a succession of managers who tried and failed to exceed or even emulate the feats of Appleton and Horton. Appleton actually got a chance to repeat his earlier success but, along with Gray, Stan Ternent and Terry Dolan, found it difficult to come by. It wasn't just the dugout. At boardroom level, Richard Chetham and Martin Fish learned that following The Don was no picnic either. The result was that the 1990s proved one long downward spiral. Beginning with relegation from the second tier in 1991, the summer of Euro '96 found City again preparing for life in the basement. Their troubles didn't end there. Under the ownership of David Lloyd the club was locked out of Boothferry Park and again faced the possibility of liquidation. On the pitch only an amazing run of form under player-manager Warren Joyce in what was termed the 'The Great Escape' prevented the Tigers from sliding out of the Football League in 1999. The names of Lloyd, Wilby, Hateley, Hinchliffe and Buchanan became synonymous with an ongoing car crash of a club. There's little wonder then that City supporters of my generation would come to regard the post-receivership renaissance as something of a rare high point.

The vast fanzine network of the period helped bring about the type of contact with many like-minded souls from other clubs that would have been unheard of just a decade earlier. Among the first were the lads behind *The City Gent* (Bradford), *Tired & Weary* (Birmingham), *The Leyton Orientear* and Rangers fanzine *Follow Follow*, with whom we eventually recorded and released a compilation cassette of local bands. Another example of such networking also allowed me to make my first sortie into Europe following a British team. This came about thanks to the relationship I struck up with Mike Van Vleck, co-editor of the Manchester Hearts supporters' fanzine *Heartbeat*. From an initial meet-up at City's pre-season friendly against Hibs in July 1989 it would evolve to Hull City/Hearts half-and-half ski hats being worn on the Boothferry Park terraces, as well as groups of Hull lads welcomed by Jambos in places as far afield as Bologna, Madrid, Prague – and Falkirk. It is an association that sees some of us still making the occasional trip to Tynecastle some three decades later.[222]

I actually first met Mike at Craven Park in March 1989 when he came over to support one of his other main sporting loves, Salford's rugby league club. This followed the expansion of my weekend adventures into the oval-ball game, prompted by that new year derby day back in 1988. Within the year I was spending Sundays following Hull KR home and away and, before you jump to conclusions, my belated conversion (excuse the pun) was certainly no case of glory hunting – Rovers were relegated that season. I *was* there when they were shit! A return to the Boothferry Park terraces as passholder 727 in time for the 1990/91 season was also impeccably timed – the Tigers were relegated after six years in the Second Division. #TypicalCity, eh? Thus my weekends regularly involved watching two poor professional teams. Add in local football and a weekly digest of live gigs and nights out, it constituted a hectic social calendar and further copious diary notes. Indeed, there's a book in there if somebody was that way inclined.

It was March 2001 before light finally reappeared at the end of Hull City's tunnel, one that didn't prove to be just another false dawn. With Adam Pearson as chairman, the emotional departure from Boothferry Park (another milestone occasion I was absent from) and subsequent move to a new stadium ushered in promotion celebrations aplenty as the Tigers finally roared again. When Ian Ashbee's super strike clinched a 2-1 win on a rain-soaked afternoon at Yeovil's Huish Park in May 2004, it secured a first promotion in

---

222 *There's Something Stirring in King Billy's Bogs*, a six-track compilation tape featuring The Brontes, Pink Noise, The Gallery, The Penny Candles, The Mighty Strike and Milkfloat

almost 20 years. In *The Guardian*, Jeremy Surcombe wrote, 'Hull City have a stadium fit for the Premiership, the fans to fill it and a chairman whose ambition matches their plush surroundings.' An inexorable climb through the divisions followed until the long-sought-after place in the top flight was finally attained courtesy of that Windass Wembley winner. For those who'd been there every step of the way, there were first-hand memories that will last a lifetime and a feeling of being an integral part of the story – the same sort of feeling I'd experienced 20 years earlier (albeit on a less grandiose scale). As for me, by and large I toasted the Tigers' success from afar. To all intents and purposes, I'd turned into exactly the type of person I resented during my Tiger-trekking days – an 'armchair fan'.[223]

In mitigation, even as something of a bit-part player during this 'bust to boom' era (as *Hull Daily Mail* writer John Fieldhouse termed it in his 2009 book) I clocked up a significant number of games along the way; certainly enough to not feel guilty when securing a Wembley play-off final ticket in May 2008. I pointed to my previous buying history as justification for my involvement in City's biggest-ever day and to reinforce the point I travelled to Wembley on a coach organised by Simon Gray, although I do confess to having a few 'what if' moments before doing so (sorry, Simon!). As things turned out, it seemed only right that our intrepid coach operator should form part of the occasion. And what an occasion it was.

The sight of one half of the national stadium bedecked in black-and-amber was one to very much cherish. It was something I could have only dreamed of for most of my City-supporting life and it reminded me of just how far the club

223 Surcombe, Jeremy, https://www.theguardian.com/football/2004/may/03/match.sport3, *The Guardian*, 3 May 2004

had come. Similarly, when City revisited the stadium for their first FA Cup Final appearance six years later, it was another 'wake me up I'm dreaming' moment. Again I felt no guilt when snapping up a ticket, even though I'd missed the hugely satisfying semi-final victory over our old nemesis from the steel city on account of my eldest daughter's 11th birthday. At the same time as the Tigers were winning an eight-goal epic tie, I was 'enjoying' the delights of Harry Potter World!

* * *

Hence, at teatime on Saturday, 17 May 2014 I took my seat among the 89,345 spectators inside Wembley. I'd guess that just under half were supporting the Tigers against media darlings Arsenal in what was formerly football's showpiece occasion. For 71 minutes it promised to be another wonderful experience. City led 2-1 thanks to early goals from James Chester and Curtis Davies. Indeed, had Kieran Gibbs not cleared Alex Bruce's header off (or maybe from behind?) the line, the Tigers would have been three up inside a quarter of an hour. Even Santi Cazorla's 15th-minute reply didn't prompt an obvious turnaround in fortunes and as the game entered its final third we dared to dream again.

It was all so #TypicalCity. With just under 20 minutes remaining, Laurent Koscielny poked home an equaliser for the Gunners and we knew what was coming next, the only surprise being that it took until the second period of extra time for Aaron Ramsey to score the winner. Even now there was one last glimmer of hope, when Sone Aluko nipped past the committed Fabianski but went for goal from the acutest of angles with at least two City players arriving in the box. Our chance had gone. Arsène Wenger's nine-year trophy drought was ended; City's 110-year-long wait for one went on. But at least the media had the story they wanted.

Despite defeat, European football came to Hull as a result of Arsenal having already secured a Champions League place. City took up the vacancy in the preliminary rounds of the Europa League. Work commitments limited my attendance to the home legs against Slovakian side AS Trenčín and Sporting Lokeren of Belgium. I gambled on manager Steve Bruce taking the competition seriously enough to allow me to make my overseas European debut with the Tigers in the group stages. Sadly, in the eyes of many City fans, the boss prioritised 'a point at Stoke' over progress in Europe. Unbeknown to us then, the high watermark had been reached.

City were relegated the following season and although returning to the Premier League via the play-offs in 2016, the final at Wembley this time around would be remembered as much for the empty spaces in the Tigers' end as for Mo Diamé's wonderful strike that beat Sheffield Wednesday. These were increasingly fractious times, stemming from a proposal in 2013 by the owners to change the club name to Hull Tigers. A bitter dispute ensued with a large section of supporters. In the fine traditions of the Action Group and the Tigers Co-operative (set up during David Lloyd's days) a protest group called City Till We Die was born. They would eventually merge into the Hull City Supporters Trust (successors to the aforementioned Tigers Co-op and an organisation of which I'm now a paid-up life member). As relations between the two sides worsened, the situation wasn't helped by the implementation of a new membership scheme that involved many supporters being moved from their traditional seats, along with the end of child and concession tickets. It proved the final straw for many who now voted with their feet. Eventually, even Bruce grew tired of it all. He resigned just weeks before the start of the Tigers' fifth and hitherto last season in the top flight.

I hadn't lasted as long as the boss. Disillusioned by off-field events in a way that I hadn't felt under any previous regime (as bad as some of them had been), I was one of thousands who succumbed to self-imposed exile. My youngest daughter became collateral damage. She is now lost to football and instead limits her sporting days out with dad to Craven Park and a different-shaped ball. At least she can't be accused of glory hunting. Four years elapsed before I returned. Along the way a pre-booked family holiday in the Canaries spared me the embarrassment of a potentially hypocritical third trip to Wembley in 2016.

In November 2019 I was finally tempted back by the attractive style of football that had lifted new manager Grant McCann's team towards the top end of the Championship. It proved to be another #TypicalCity moment as former Tiger Jake Livermore gave fellow promotion hopefuls West Brom a slightly fortuitous win. There was nothing unfortunate about the next defeat I witnessed, against Nottingham Forest on Boxing Day. The writing was on the wall. Back-to-back wins in the next two games only pre-empted a spectacular slide down the table. The Tigers won one and drew three of their last 20 matches. Relegation duly followed. Thankfully for McCann and the owners, the coronavirus pandemic meant no fans were able to see the administering of the last rites, the nadir which came via an 8-0 defeat at a Wigan side already facing relegation due to a 12-point deduction for going into administration.

* * *

Hull's musical collective never did quite manage to make the same sort of strides as the city's football team. Notwithstanding subsequent acts such as the Beautiful South and Paul Heaton's collaborations with Jacqui Abbott, no Hull band ever has come close to emulating the chart exploits of the Housemartins. Fleeting success did come the way of Kingmaker (born out of Tombstone Graffiti) and Scarlet (ex-Cheap Day Return) in the early 1990s, while the Paddingtons flew the flag for the city into the new millennium and, as I write this, Low Hummer are the latest to attract Radio 1 interest. But even with the added exposure that City of Culture afforded, Hull is yet to boast that one big Premier League hitter.

That said, as I hope I've already shown, chartdom has never been the yardstick by which the Hull music scene gauges success. Testimony to its resilience, vitality and longevity can instead be found annually at the Humber Street Sesh, which pulls in thousands of punters across a weekend in August, with the sounds provided largely by local bands. For the remainder of the year many of those same bands can be found still playing the Adelphi, the Welly and a host of other venues to which the city's music fans owe a debt – the Polar Bear on Spring Bank, Fruit (now The Social) down Humber Street and the countless pubs and clubs in the area willing to put a band on. Meanwhile the opening of the new 3,500-capacity Bonus Arena in August 2018 finally put the city on the map for some of those big national and international acts that hitherto found Hull easy to avoid.

My interest in the local music scene is now largely restricted to Alan Raw's *BBC Introducing* radio show. Regular gig-going has gone the same way as regular pub-going, with weekly trips to town as distant a memory as those packed station-bound Hull Corporation and East Yorkshire buses that used to shed hordes of young hopefuls out on to George Street on a Friday and Saturday night, or the fleet of executive coaches that lined up along Ferensway, waiting to take young clubbers down the M62. This aspect of the 1980s weekend would appear to have gone the same way as many of the pubs and clubs themselves.

That's with one notable exception of course. Prior to the pandemic, Spiders was still offering a warm welcome to those in search of alternative nocturnal pursuits in much the same way as it first did 40 years ago. What's more, in 2017 its enduring appeal and reputation for doing so was celebrated in print. I contributed one of the *Tales from Behind the Web* that formed Andy Roe's history and as part of the celebration I stepped inside the place for the first time in two decades. Apart from the shock of hearing Wham! (apparently, upstairs is now 'cheesy '80s') it was all so wonderfully familiar. Moreover, the presence of us oldies among the hip young crowd went virtually unnoticed – and the drinks were still cheap. An alternative way to recapture the essence of those nights without the prospect of bumping into your offspring is Cleveland Classics, the monthly event hosted by former Spiders DJ Chris Von Trapp. If shaking our ageing hips to the sounds of weekends past or simply reminiscing over a pint or two in between floor-fillers, it's an escape back in time to when Saturday was 'City Day'.

* * *

As I put the finishing touches to the story, Hull City are back in the second tier of English football, where it all started for me in 1975. Redemption of sorts for Grant McCann came via promotion from League One at the first attempt, accompanied by the club's first divisional title since the year I was born. The euphoric scenes witnessed outside the ground even lent themselves to suggestion of a possible thaw in the relationship between owners and supporters, offering hope of brighter times ahead. Meanwhile, winning promotion in a year in which fans were not allowed to actually attend matches and clinching the title on a weekend on which most sports club held a social media boycott was perhaps the most #TypicalCity thing ever.

While delighted to see the club enjoy success, there's a part of me that shudders at our return to the higher tier. Recent events have shown that football at elite level continues to loosen any claims it once had to be the working man's game. A gradual process that began with the advent of the Premier League nearly 30 years ago shows no sign of letting up. City fans have already had a taste of this during their time spent dining at the top table. In addition to the huge financial factors, eyes were opened to the arrogance, the sneering attitudes and the sense of entitlement that pervade among many of those associated with the so-called 'big clubs'. When you add in the media's often patronising coverage, it soon becomes apparent that just because your name's on the list, you're not necessarily welcomed in.

The recently rejected plan for a proposed new European Super League, which would have seen six top-flight English clubs take this exclusivity to another level, was further sign of the direction in which football is headed. It once again illustrated how low the paying punter who actually attends games has sunk in the list of priorities. Even though a club like Hull City need have no fears (yet!?) about such matters, recent experience of the upper echelons (including the Championship) showed that getting bums on seats inside the stadium is not the financial necessity it once was. Far more lucrative revenue streams are to be found elsewhere, leading to fears that watching your club on pay-per-view TV, as happened during lockdown, could soon be part of the dreaded post-pandemic 'new normal' we're all expected to embrace.

My yearning for the gentler attractions of lower-league football is perhaps a touch contradictory given the theme of the book, not to mention inconceivable to those supporters desperate to have another crack at the big boys. After spending the best part of a century waiting to fine dine, why would anyone now opt to go back to the greasy spoon? Perhaps the Jarrow-born playwright (and City supporter) Alan Plater explained it best in 1991. Following relegation and just prior to the birth of the Premier League, he penned a wonderful piece for the *Sunday Times* under the headline 'It's great to be back in the Third Division'. Therein he wrote that 'the wonder of life in the nether regions is that hardly anybody lusts for success'. Those who do were given directions to Leeds or Manchester, said Plater before adding, 'We have greater possibilities.' Recounting the details of City's 3-1 win at Rochdale in the Fourth Division in May 1983, he described how the 'true glory' of the day came via a half-time PA announcement: 'In a pure and lovely Rochdale accent the man said, "For the benefit of the Hull City supporters who came on buses, your buses have now been moved. Now, I could tell you where they've been moved to, but you'll only forget. So your best plan's to ask a policeman."'

Plater went on to describe how the announcer then sought support for a sponsored walk to Wigan in aid of club funds, before concluding his article by saying, 'I wouldn't trade the culture of the lower divisions for all the executive boxes in north London.' Neither would I, Alan. Neither would I.[224]

* * *

So there you have it, my very own 'Confessions of a City supporter' (to quote Alan Plater's 2004 stage production). I do hope you've enjoyed it. To those of you with no previous knowledge of – or even interest in – the subject matter, I hope it has given you a feel for what it was like to be an unfashionable young man following an unfashionable football

224 Plater, Alan, Article 'It's great to be back in the Third Division', *Sunday Times* (11 August 1991)

team from an unloved city in a much-derided era. As for my fellow City fans, if you were around at the same time and I've helped revive your own wonderful memories, that's a bonus. However, the people I hope will benefit most from this book are those who contributed to it by their deeds at the time – that team of battlers who brought so much pleasure to me and several thousand others. If this account of what I regard as a criminally ignored period in the history of the city and its football club can somehow compensate for the lack of recognition afforded them, it will have served its purpose. The strides the club eventually made in the wake of those dramatic days of 1982 has left me feeling even more privileged to have been there at the start of it. They say you have to experience the worst of times before you can truly enjoy the best. Well, I reckon I did. Perhaps that's why I really cried at Wembley. Twice.

Bibliography

Books

Bannon, James, *Running with the Firm: My Double Life as a Football Hooligan* (London: Ebury Press, 2014)

Bond, David, *'Meet Me on Bunker's Hill' – A Revealing and Personal Look at the Hull City Story* (Hull: Tykesport, 2006)

Bond, David, *The Hull City Saga: The Seesaw Tale of the Tigers* (Derby: Breedon Books, 1999)

Brackenridge, Craig, *Hell's Bent on Rockin' – A History of Psychobilly* (London: Cherry Red, 2007)

Brackenridge, Craig, *Let's Wreck – Psychobilly Flashbacks from the Eighties and Beyond* (Retford: Stormscreen, 2nd Edition 2005)

Burford, Brian, *Kelly Moran: A Hell of a Life* (Stroud: History Press, 2014)

Chaplin, John, *Ivan Mauger: The Man Behind the Myth* (Stroud: History Press, 2012)

Clark, Gary, *From Boothferry to Wembley* (Hull: Riverhead, 2008)

Clavane, Anthony, *Promised Land* (London: Yellow Jersey Press, 2011)

Clavane, Anthony, *Moving the Goalposts – A Yorkshire Tragedy* (London: Riverrun, 2017)

Décharné, Max, *A Rocket in My Pocket – The Hipster's Guide to Rockabilly Music* (London: Serpent's Tail, 2010)

Edwards, Keith (with Pack, Andy), *Edwards … One-Nil!: The Keith Edwards Story* (Vertical Editions, 2014)

Elton, Chris, Hull City: *A Complete Record 1904–1989* (Derby: Breedon Books, 1989)

Gardham, Richard, *The Decade: Ten Years that Transformed Hull City AFC* (Self-published, 2019)

Goodman, David, *Look Back in Amber* (Manchester: Parrs Wood Press, 2005)

Groak, Vince, *Last One Out … When Hull Invaded Wembley* (Leeds: Scratching Shed, 2017)

Haslam, Dave, *Life After Dark – A History of British Nightclubs & Music Venues* (London: Simon & Schuster, 2015)

Hornby, Nick, *Fever Pitch* (London: Victor Gollancz, 1992)

Horton, Brian, *Two Thousand Games – A Life in Football* (Worthing: Pitch Publishing, 2020)

Hulbert, Roger, *Hull Speedway 1930–1981* (Stroud: Tempus, 2004)

Jordan, Gary, *Out of the Shadows: The Story of the 1982 England World Cup Team* (Worthing: Pitch Publishing, 2017)

Peterson, Mike, *A Century of City: The Centenary History of Hull City AFC, 1904–2004* (Middlesex: Yore Publications, 2005)

Peterson, Mike, *Farewell to Boothferry Park* (Hull: Arenasport, 2002)

Rayner, Stuart, *The War of the White Roses: Yorkshire Cricket's Civil War 1968–1986* (Worthing: Pitch Publishing, 2016)

Roe, Andy, *Spiders: Tales from Behind the Web* (Self-published, 1st Edition 2017)

Sandbrook, Dominic, *Who Dares Wins – Britain, 1979–1982* (London: Allen Lane, 2019)

Sandbrook, Dominic, *State of Emergency – The Way We Were: Britain 1970-1974* (London: Allen Lane, 2010)

Simper, Paul, *Pop Stars in My Pantry* (London: Unbound 2017)

Smith, Noel 'Razor', *Crazy Man Crazy: Teds vs Punks and Other Gang Wars* (London: Rocket 88, 2016)

Stewart, Graham, *Bang! A History of Britain in the 1980s* (London: Atlantic, 2013)

Swanton, E.W., *Barclay's World of Cricket: The Game from A–Z (2nd Edition)* (London: Collins, 1980)

Tordoff, Shaun, *City Psychos: From the Monte Carlo Mob to the Silver Cod Squad* (London: Milo, 2002)

Turner, Alwyn M., *Crisis? What Crisis? Britain in the 1970s* (London: Aurum Press, 2008)

Turner, Alwyn W., *Rejoice! Rejoice! – Britain in the 1980s* (London: Aurum, 2010) p.60

Turner, Nicholas, *Hull City – The Boothferry Park Years* (Thatcham: Dolman Scott, 2018)

Ward, Colin, *Steaming In: Journal of a Football Fan* (London: Simon & Schuster, 1989)

Articles

Adams, Owen: 'Was 1979 the last great year for pop?' – *The Guardian* (24 July 2009)

BBC News (Humberside), 'City of Culture 2017 Hull takes its rightful place', bbc.co.uk/news (20 November 2013)

BBC News (Entertainments and Arts) 'Hull to be UK City of Culture 2017', bbc.co.uk/news, (20 November 2013)

Buckingham, Phil, 'Out of cash and up for sale: The story of how Hull City almost went to the wall' – *Hull Live* (hulldailymail.co.uk) (31 March 2020)

Buckingham, Philip, 'The inside story of how Hull City's chart-topping song eclipsed Duran Duran' – *Hull Live* (hulldailymail.co.uk) (8 April 2020)

Clay, Nick, 'Pink Noise and other crap Hull bands from the 80's' (karoo.net)

English, Charlie, 'To Hull and back: the rebirth of Britain's poorest city' *The Guardian*, (11 September 2014)

Irwin, Colin, Buried Treasure | Nyam Nyam (wordpress.com) (originally *Melody Maker*, 1985)

Marco on the Bass 'Exclusive: Interview with Nik Akrylyk About His Days Playing in Hull's Very Own 2-Tone Era Ska Band The Akrylykz', www.marcoonthebass.blogspot.com (5 January 2009)

McNulty, Bernadette: 'Why Orange Juice still sound fresh after all these years' – *Daily Telegraph* (5 February 2014)

Moore, Rowan, 'City of Culture 2017: Will Hull have the last laugh?' *The Guardian*, (14 February 2016)

The Newsroom, 'The Welly goes back to rock roots to celebrate 100th year' | *Yorkshire Post* (22 August 2013)

The Newsroom, 'What the FA Cup Final really means to Hull fans.' | *Yorkshire Post* (15 May 2014)

Nyam Nyam, 'Mrs Wilson and other personalities' (wordpress.com)

Plater, Alan, Article 'It's great to be back in the Third Division', *Sunday Times* (11 August 1991)

Rudd, Matthew, 'Great Football League Teams 45: Hull City 1982/83' *The Two Unfortunates* website (11 Sep 2013)

Shelton, Robert, 'Cat clothes and the Curtis cut', *History of Rock*, Volume 1 Part 6, p.116, Orbis (1981–1984)

Simper, Paul, 'My residency on Sade's sofa', *Shapers of the 80s* website

Surcombe, Jeremy, *The Guardian* (Yeovil Town 1-2 Hull City, Match Report, 3 May 2004)

Trinder, Richard, 'Hull Is City Of Culture!' (yorkshiretimes.co.uk) (20 November 2013)

Unknown, 'Welcome to the theatre of hate', *Yorkshire Post* (29 September 2001)

Wagg, Michael, 'Old music: The Housemartins – Sheep', *The Guardian* (26 January 2012)

Irish, Oliver, 'Do you remember when Yorkshire last won the county championship?' *The Observer* (2 September 2001)

Yorkshire CCC, 'Throwback Thursday: Hull', Yorkshire CCC website (16 April 2020)

Fissler, Neil, Where are they now? Yorkshire – Sunday League winners 1983', www.thecricketpaper.com (6 October 2015)

The Vets | ReverbNation

That 1980s Sports Blog: The Rous Cup and the demise of the England-Scotland match (14 June 2017)

Other publications

Hull City AFC match programmes

Hull Vikings match programmes

The *Hull Daily Mail* newspaper

Hull, Hell & Happiness fanzine

On Cloud Seven fanzine

From Hull to Eternity fanzine

Look Back in Amber fanzine

Shoot! magazine

Tiger Rag fanzine

Blogs and Websites

Amber Nectar (now defunct)

Bored Teenagers (boredteenagers.co.uk)

Hull Music Archive (& Facebook page)

Hull & East Yorkshire Music Scene, 70s & 80s Facebook page (@Hull.Beat)

John Rowley's Page (redguitars.co.uk)

Kindred Spirit – The Story of a 1980's Hull Fanzine (kindredspiritfanzine.blogspot.com)

Marco on the Bass (marcoonthebass.blogspot.com)

Punk Girl Diaries (punkgirldiaries.com)

The Millwall History Files (millwall-history.org.uk)

The New Adelphi website (theadelphi.com)

Picture credits:

Alamy

Ali Caldwell

Hull Daily Mail

Ian Beharrell

Jules Brown

Sue Cracknell

David Featherstone

Roger Hill

Gary Jones

Ian Lees

Keith Middleton (via Richard Catton)

Matthew Nicholson

Karl Skirrow

Andy Roe

Lindsay Walters